EXEMPLARY INSTRUCTION IN THE MIDDLE GRADES

Exemplary Instruction
in the Middle Grades

Teaching That Supports Engagement
and Rigorous Learning

EDITED BY

Diane Lapp
Barbara Moss

THE GUILFORD PRESS
New York   London

© 2012 The Guilford Press
A Division of Guilford Publications, Inc.
72 Spring Street, New York, NY 10012
www.guilford.com

Printed in the United States of America

This book is printed on acid-free paper.

Last digit is print number: 9   8   7   6   5   4   3   2   1

Library of Congress Cataloging-in-Publication Data

Exemplary instruction in the middle grades : teaching that supports engagement
and rigorous learning / edited by Diane Lapp, Barbara Moss.
   p. cm.
   Includes bibliographical references and index.
   ISBN 978-1-4625-0281-3 (pbk.)–ISBN 978-1-4625-0293-6 (hardcover)
   1. Reading (Middle school)   2. Content area reading.   3. Middle school
teaching—United States.   I. Lapp, Diane.   II. Moss, Barbara, 1950–
   LB1632.E94 2012
   428.4071—dc23

                                                            2011023880

About the Editors

Diane Lapp, EdD, is Distinguished Professor of Education at San Diego State University. She has taught elementary and middle school and is currently a high school English/literacy teacher. Her research and instruction focus on issues related to struggling readers and writers who live in economically deprived settings, their families, and their teachers. Dr. Lapp has published numerous journal articles, columns, chapters, books, and children's materials. She has received honors including the Outstanding Teacher Educator of the Year Award and the Manning Public School Service Award from the International Reading Association, and is a member of both the California and the International Reading Halls of Fame.

Barbara Moss, PhD, is Professor of Literacy Education at San Diego State University, where she teaches courses in literacy, children's literature, and language arts at the credential and master's levels. She has been an English language arts teacher at the secondary level, a literacy teacher at the elementary level, and a reading supervisor. Dr. Moss has published numerous articles in journals including the *Journal of Literacy Research, The Reading Teacher,* and *Reading Research and Instruction,* and has authored or edited several books. She currently works as a literacy coach in an urban high school in San Diego.

Contributors

Peggy Albers, PhD, Department of Middle and Secondary Education and Instructional Technologies, College of Education, Georgia State University, Atlanta, Georgia

Christianna Alger, PhD, School of Teacher Education, San Diego State University, San Diego, California

Cynthia H. Brock, PhD, Department of Educational Specialties, University of Nevada, Reno, Reno, Nevada

Heather Casey, PhD, Department of Education, Rider University, Lawrenceville, New Jersey

Jill Castek, PhD, Graduate School of Education, University of California, Berkeley, Berkeley, California

Douglas Fisher, PhD, School of Teacher Education, San Diego State University, San Diego, California

Nancy Frey, PhD, School of Teacher Education, San Diego State University, San Diego, California

Kathy Ganske, PhD, Department of Teaching and Learning, Vanderbilt University, Nashville, Tennessee

Maria Grant, PhD, College of Education, California State University, Fullerton, Fullerton, California

Dana L. Grisham, PhD, Department of Teacher Education, National University, San Diego, San Diego, California

Jane Hansen, PhD, Central Virginia Writing Project and Department of Curriculum Instruction and Special Education, Curry School of Education, University of Virginia, Charlottesville, Virginia

Jennifer I. Hathaway, PhD, Department of Reading and Elementary Education, University of North Carolina at Charlotte, Charlotte, North Carolina

Rebecca Jesson, PhD, School of Arts, Languages and Literacies, Faculty of Education, University of Auckland, Auckland, New Zealand

Kelly Johnson, PhD, Health Sciences High and Middle College and College of Education, San Diego State University, San Diego, California

Joan Kindig, EdD, Department of Reading Education, College of Education, James Madison University, Harrisonburg, Virginia

Diane Lapp, PhD, School of Teacher Education, San Diego State University, San Diego, California

Virginia S. Loh, PhD, Department of Education, San Diego State University, San Diego, California

Barbara Moss, PhD, School of Teacher Education, San Diego State University, San Diego, California

Jennifer D. Morrison, MS, Department of Educational Specialties, University of Nevada, Reno, Reno, Nevada

Judy M. Parr, PhD, School of Arts, Languages and Literacies, Faculty of Education, University of Auckland, Auckland, New Zealand

Julie L. Pennington, PhD, Department of Educational Specialties, University of Nevada, Reno, Reno, Nevada

Melissa Provost, MSEd, Portsmouth School District, Portsmouth, New Hampshire

Stephanie Schmier, EdD, Rossier School of Education, University of Southern California, Los Angeles, California

Timothy Shea, PhD, Department of English, Millersville University, Millersville, Pennsylvania

Marjorie Siegel, EdD, Department of Curriculum and Instruction, Teachers College, Columbia University, New York, New York

Lina B. Soares, PhD, Department of Teaching and Learning, Georgia Southern University, Statesboro, Georgia

Dianna Townsend, EdD, Department of Educational Specialties, College of Education, University of Nevada, Reno, Reno, Nevada

Susan Troutman, MA, School Mathematics Project, Rice University, Houston, Texas

Robin A. Ward, PhD, School Mathematics Project, Rice University, Houston, Texas

Thomas DeVere Wolsey, EdD, Richard W. Riley College of Education and Leadership, Walden University, Minneapolis, Minnesota

Karen D. Wood, PhD, Department of Reading and Elementary Education, College of Education, University of North Carolina at Charlotte, Charlotte, North Carolina

Preface

Think about classes you've taken where you really felt that you had a powerful learning experience. What factors caused this to occur? An abundance of research suggests that the degree of students' learning is significantly correlated with the teacher's knowledge and instructional practice (McCutchen, Green, Abbott, & Sanders, 2009; Spear-Swerling & Brucker, 2004). More specifically, Pressley (2006) noted that effective teachers possess the following qualities:

1. A strong subject knowledge base.
2. An understanding of how to integrate literacy within their subject area.
3. The ability to fluidly allocate instructional time across the whole group and small groups.
4. The actuality of differentiating instruction regardless of group size.
5. The ability to utilize ongoing performance assessment to determine student need and then to provide scaffolded learning experiences that support acquiring the knowledge and language needed to succeed.
6. "Over-the-top motivation" that is both personal and continuous.

What this means in actuality is that the teacher has such a good understanding of the content that he or she is able to adapt both the information and the instruction to accommodate a range of student levels of knowledge. To do so requires the teacher to use student assessment data as information sources to design motivating learning tasks that are implemented through a variety of grouping patterns.

Although this may be a fairly common professional-development conversation, have you ever wondered why some teachers continue to implement instruction that doesn't seem to support their students' learning to the degree that they probably intended? As we wondered about this common mismatch between instructional intent and learning outcomes, we talked with some well-intentioned teachers who embody this very situation. It was interesting that upon reflection several said that their primary reason for continuing to implement questionable instructional practice was that this was how they were taught, not in their teacher preparation courses or during their professional development sessions, but rather during their own K–12 experiences (Vaca, Lapp, & Fisher, 2011). The practices they used were therefore very familiar and within their personal zone of comfort. They continued to return to these practices even when they realized that they were not achieving the student learning outcomes that they desired. A second reason often identified for abandoning responsive instruction for comfortable instruction is that teachers continue to use practices that are familiar—ones that don't take too much time to plan and that, as one teacher put it, "work for the majority of students."

Yes, most strategies work for those students who are very similar to those of us who became teachers. These are students who are growing up in what Gee (1996, 1999) calls mainstream homes. These are students who, because of their lived experiences at home, are able to share the same language and social and academic beliefs and practices as those required at school. But what about all of the other students, those who are not succeeding at school? They are often children of economic poverty and also those who are learning English as an additional language. They deserve instruction from teachers with the knowledge to guide their learning by first assessing their needs and then selecting instructional strategies and materials that support their acquisition of the intended information. Students need teachers who understand how to support their learning as they move from whole-class to small-group instruction so that the appropriate responsive instruction can be shared. They need teachers who have a thorough understanding of research-supported practice.

This volume has been designed, with the understanding that teachers definitely have the power to affect the lives of their students through their teaching (Darling-Hammond, 2007), as a resource for teachers of all content areas, at grades 6–8, who are wondering how to share responsive, engaging instruction with their middle grade students. It has been expressly designed to assist teachers as they support and expand learning for *all* of their students. To achieve this goal, we have identified those familiar practices often used in middle schools that are ineffective and not research supported and offered examples of alternative, easy-to-implement research-supported instruction that promotes learning for all students, especially those who need in-depth responsive instruction.

The goals of this text are to help teachers strengthen their instructional knowledge bases by reflecting on alternatives to common pedagogical practices that are not well supported by research. The examples provided illustrate how to implement content-area literacy practices by making connections that promote thinking, conversing, evaluating, analyzing, and questioning the information and motives conveyed through informational texts. The exemplary teachers depicted in these chapters illustrate that teaching students to engage critically with text involves bringing new multimodal and multifaceted literacy experiences into the world of the classroom. We propose that the result will be motivated students who are challenged to persistently develop the content-related literacy skills requisite to sustain their continuous 21st-century learning and production.

ORGANIZATION OF THE BOOK

Exemplary Instruction in the Middle Grades contains three sections and 20 chapters. Part I, *Teaching Content Literacy*, contains examples of how to support students' learning to read myriad text types throughout the content areas, ideas illustrating how to remix known and new literacies, and lessons that support the development of motivated readers who are also critically literate. Part II, *Developing Spoken and Written Language*, defines differences between academic and content-based language, offers practical suggestions for teaching and assessing collaborative oral language and writing across the curriculum, and shares powerful examples of well-integrated vocabulary instruction and rubrics that support writing instruction and assessment. Part III, *Establishing Effective Learning Routines*, provides chapters exemplifying the power of book clubs, question asking, note taking, Foldables™, homework, technology, and media as ways to support middle school learning.

Each chapter, which begins by identifying the *key points to be shared*, is designed as a case study of a teacher who is using strategies that he or she is questioning because they don't seem to be effecting the type of student growth anticipated. Following a *bird's-eye view of the targeted classroom practice*, the authors offer a brief *description of the research base* to help readers understand why the instruction that is occurring is not accomplishing the instructional intentions of the teacher. The next and major segment of each chapter provides *multiple instructional alternatives* that better support the teacher in accomplishing the instructional intent. Because we are attempting to address all middle school grades, content areas, and new literacies, each lesson concludes with additional *online lesson examples and resources*.

We hope that you find the included lesson examples supportive as you plan, implement, and reflect on instruction that you determine to be responsive to the needs of your students. Our daily task as middle school teachers is enormous as we attempt to accommodate students moving into their adolescent years and out of self-contained classrooms. These students are also encountering more complex and difficult content-area materials than ever before, and in many cases this is occurring while they are working to master a second language. We can accomplish the goal of providing responsive instruction if we never lose sight of the fact that we are preparing each student to become a productive and valued citizen in the world of the future. We cannot afford to lose a single child as a consequence of ineffective instruction, and we hope that these lesson examples motivate you to continuously energize your instruction so that it remains both rigorous and responsive.

> The task of the excellent teacher is to stimulate "apparently ordinary" people to unusual effort. The tough problem is not in identifying the winners: it is in making winners out of ordinary people.
> —K. PATRICIA CROSS

We'd love to hear your ideas and responses regarding other topics or chapters you wish we had included. Thanks so much.

DIANE LAPP
lapp@mail.sdsu.edu

BARBARA MOSS
bmoss@mail.sdsu.edu

REFERENCES

Darling-Hammond, L. (2007). Third annual Brown Lecture in Educational Research—The flat earth and education: How America's commitment to equity will determine its future. *Educational Researcher, 36*(6), 318–334.

Gee, J. P. (1996). *Social linguistics and literacies: Ideology in discourses* (2nd ed.). London: Taylor & Francis.

Gee, J. P. (1999). *An introduction to discourse analysis: Theory and method.* New York: Routledge.

Pressley, M. (2006). *Reading instruction that works: The case for balanced teaching* (3rd ed.) New York: Guilford Press.

McCutchen, D., Green, L., Abbott, R. D., & Sanders, E. A. (2009). Further evidence for teacher knowledge: Supporting struggling readers in grades three through five. *Reading and Writing: An Interdisciplinary Journal, 22,* 401–423.

Spear-Swerling, L., & Brucker, P. (2004). Preparing novice teachers to develop basic reading and spelling skills in children. *Annals of Dyslexia, 54,* 332–364.

Vaca, J., Lapp, D., & Fisher, D. (2011). Designing and assessing productive group work in secondary schools. *Journal of Adult and Adolescent Literacy, 54*(5), 372–375.

Contents

PART II. DEVELOPING SPOKEN AND WRITTEN LANGUAGE

PART III. ESTABLISHING EFFECTIVE LEARNING ROUTINES

PART
I

Teaching Content Literacy

CHAPTER 1

If They Can't Read Their Science Books— Teach Them How

Maria Grant

Key Points for This Chapter

- The practice of volunteer reading targets only those readers who want to read and neglects those who are uncertain about their reading skills and/or hesitant to read aloud.
- Volunteer reading does not enhance content comprehension because readers are frequently focused on their public execution of the reading.
- To comprehend challenging content texts, students need background knowledge, concrete experiences, and academic and content vocabulary knowledge.
- Read-alouds, think-alouds, reciprocal teaching, discussion webs, GIST, directed reading–thinking activities, vocabulary self-awareness charts, and semantic feature analysis charts are strategies that support comprehension of challenging science texts.

A BIRD'S-EYE VIEW OF CLASSROOM PRACTICE

Mr. Isaacs has been teaching eighth-grade physical science for 10 years. Year after year he struggles to find ways to coax his science students to read and think about the textbook. He knows that the book has relevant information that supports his instruction, yet he finds his students are resistant to reading. They tell him that the words are too big and are unfamiliar. They also claim that there's too much information on each page, and they repeatedly lament that the book is too heavy. Although Mr. Isaacs would certainly agree that most textbooks adopted by school districts today might seem a bit overwhelming, he knows that they hold valuable information that students should access. Additionally, he knows that students who may eventually go on to college need to know how to read a science textbook. Because of this, Mr. Isaacs never sways from issuing a text to each eager incoming eighth grader. He diligently has volunteer students read aloud as the rest of the class listens—usually a half a chapter at a time. He pauses after the class has listened to about five to eight pages of reading and then summarizes the content for the students. He knows that they don't "get it all," but concedes that, "some science understanding is better than no science."

Despite years of instituting this practice, Mr. Isaacs has grown increasingly concerned about the blank, wearied faces he sees when he glances across his classroom—usually after only 5 minutes of whole-class reading. He's become more aware of how frequently the volunteer readers stumble over terms as they read, and correspondingly, how little students seem to know after a reading session. Most of his students can't even respond to a postreading question regarding the main ideas of the reading. This is why Mr. Isaacs summarizes the readings.

Although overall, Mr. Isaacs is comfortable with his usual volunteer reading practice, he's begun to think about the growing number of newcomers from Vietnam and Somalia populating his class. They never volunteer to read. They never have an opportunity to talk about the reading. More and more, he's entertained thoughts of foregoing science text reading in favor of straight lecture accompanied by note taking. Despite these nagging feelings, Mr. Isaacs really doesn't want to relinquish his now dim, 10-year-old dream of having all his eighth graders move on to high school equipped with the tools needed to read a science text. Mr. Isaacs is clearly at an educational crossroad—a place where it's time to make an instructional decision.

DEFINING THE TARGETED PRACTICE

The practice of volunteer reading targets only those readers who want to read. A student typically raises his or her hand and is called upon to read a section of the text, as indicated by the teacher. This practice comes out of the desire of educators to avoid embarrassing struggling readers, shy students, and/or English learners, all of whom are never called on to read aloud, unless they volunteer.

WHAT DOES THE RESEARCH SAY
ABOUT READING SCIENCE BOOKS?

The latest research in the area of science reading looks at the creation of coherent mental representations that integrate both textual information and background knowledge (van den Broek, 2010). There are two components to integrating information from science texts: *comprehension*, which is dependent on the reader's background knowledge, and then the ultimate goal, *learning*. How well a reader can draw on background knowledge is dependent on motivation and on specific skills, such as reasoning and reading fluency (van den Broek, 2010). The recollection of background knowledge is central to reading comprehension. A recent study suggested that using particular questioning strategies can help guide students to draw on background knowledge as they read challenging texts (Smith, Holliday, & Austin, 2010). One such strategy, called *reciprocal teaching* (Palincsar & Brown, 1984), is a method in which students learn to (1) predict the meaning of the content by using headings, pictures, and other cues on a page of text; (2) question the text for main ideas and details; (3) clarify difficult ideas, new words, or confusing phrases; and (4) summarize key ideas. Contrastingly, Mr. Isaacs's style of volunteer reading includes no time for questions or discussion of the text. The focus is solely on public reading, with no check-in to assess the appropriate discipline-specific background knowledge held by students prior to the reading.

While the research indicates the need for foundational content knowledge as a basis for science reading, there is also strong evidence that having a working knowledge of common science text structures is key to reading in this content area (Fisher & Frey, 2004; Grant & Fisher, 2010; Olson & Mokhtari, 2010). For example, the "if . . . then" structure usually indicates a cause and effect event—a very common feature of science texts. Unfortunately, Mr. Isaacs, who himself is highly proficient when it comes to reading a text that utilizes this and other common science text structures, is not cognizant of the value of his students having such knowledge. He therefore does not teach students to recognize common science text structures when reading. Additionally, there is evidence that students develop a better understanding of abstract ideas, such as those offered in science texts, when they have had concrete laboratory experiences (Olson & Mokhtari, 2010). Conversely, Mr. Isaacs uses the textbook to introduce new ideas; only later does he move to laboratory activities. Most of his middle school colleagues do the same.

Finally, it should be noted that since Mr. Isaacs uses the text to introduce new concepts, he rarely concerns himself with whether or not students are acquainted with any of the science vocabulary prior to reading. As a matter of fact, Mr. Isaacs is content with his belief that the text will help

teach any unfamiliar words that students may encounter. He sees vocabulary instruction as the task of the English teachers, and if students do find
a word that is unclear, Mr. Isaac simply directs students to the textbook
glossary. In contrast, Rupley and Slough (2010) state that science word
recognition goes hand in hand with reading comprehension. Simply stated,
students need to have vocabulary knowledge in order to comprehend what
they are reading in science. Knowing that science is a vocabulary-rich content area, strewn with technical and academic words that are typically
unfamiliar to the novice reader, teachers like Mr. Isaacs must incorporate a
variety of word-learning activities/tools into their instructional practices.

Given the documented need for background knowledge, concrete
experiences, and vocabulary knowledge, there are clearly ways that Mr.
Isaacs can better support his students to be able to accomplish the goal he
has set forth for them but has yet to fully accomplish: that of reading and
comprehending the science text book.

WHAT ARE SOME ALTERNATIVES?

Conduct a Read-Aloud to Build Word Knowledge and Background Knowledge

Mr. Isaacs might begin with the need to build foundational science background knowledge and word knowledge. In order to bridge the gap between
the more technical textbook and the lack of background knowledge, Mr.
Isaacs could strategically select appropriate trade books. For instance,
when he's teaching his unit on geology, he might employ the book *Over the
Coasts: An Ariel View of Geology* (Collier, 2009), which looks at coastal
landforms and how human structures impact them. When preparing to
discuss forces, tension, and stress, Mr. Isaacs could select *Secret Subway*
(Sandler, 2009), a book about the construction of the first subway in New
York City. It's not enough just to select a content-related trade book to read
out loud to students; a teacher has to prepare and implement a read-aloud
in a way that extracts and showcases the features of the text that are key
to building both background knowledge and vocabulary. How can this
be done? There are several key steps that a teacher can follow in order to
ensure that a trade book's effectiveness is maximized (Albright & Ariail,
2005; Fisher & Frey, 2004; Lapp & Flood, 2005):

1. In order to model fluent, proficient reading, practice the reading.
   Be sure to think about inflection, tone, mood, word pronunciation,
   and places that are best suited for pausing for student reflection.
2. Establish the purpose for reading. Make connections between the

text and the course content clear, and be sure that students under-stand why you are reading the particular book.

3. Articulate your thoughts as you read, so that you can model how you ask questions, identify and clarify confusing parts or terms, focus on key vocabulary, draw on background knowledge, and summarize what you've read.

4. Build in time for students to make connections to the text. Model how you do this by articulating how you link previously learned content to new concepts.

5. Ask students to re-present text information in another format. Consider having groups or partners make posters, write summaries, or create graphic organizers. This kind of activity will foster content conversations and guide students to create a usable record of the read-aloud content.

Model Proficient Textbook Reading

Most people don't know how to tackle a science textbook. Even Mr. Isaacs recognizes that his students don't know how to read, think, and comprehend the physical science text. Mr. Isaacs could begin to remedy this problem by modeling how he thinks about the text as he reads. He could consider noting particular text structure—that which is commonly found in science texts—or he might ponder a challenging vocabulary term as a way to share how he questions, considers, and reflects on the text as he reads science content. Let's consider a piece of text, dealing with the topic of momentum, from a physical science textbook. For this *think-aloud*, Mr. Isaacs could model in this manner:

> (*Mr. Isaacs reads aloud from the book.*) "As a sled rolls down a hill and increases it's speed, it becomes harder to stop."
>
> (*Then he pauses to articulate his thoughts.*) "Well, I've never been sledding, but I've seen the luge and bobsled events in the Olympics. I know that the farther the sleds go down the hill, the faster they go. That must be what they are talking about in this text." [Here Mr. Isaacs is modeling how to draw on prior knowledge.]
>
> (*Mr. Isaacs continues to read the text.*) "Increasing the speed or velocity of an object makes it harder to stop. Similarly, increasing the mass of an object makes it harder to stop."
>
> (*He pauses again to think aloud.*) "I understand how going faster makes it harder to stop an object, but I need to think about what it means to stop an object that has a greater mass than another object. I see that there's a picture of two cars in the

margin—a big one and a little one." [Here, Mr. Isaacs models that it's important to pay attention to charts, graphs, and pictures.] "I guess a truck would be harder to stop than a little Volkswagen Bug, if they were moving at the same speed. I'm going to keep reading."

(*Mr. Issacs resumes reading.*) "The *momentum* of an object is a measure of how hard it is to stop a moving object. Momentum depends on an object's mass and velocity, and is symbolized by *p*."

(*Thinking aloud again, Mr. Isaacs says:*) "I know what it means for the basketball team to have momentum—the team is doing well. But what does the momentum of an object mean? It looks like it might be something you can calculate because the book says it depends on mass and velocity, and I know that those are values that we can measure." [Mr. Isaacs shows that you can draw on what you have previously learned by connecting his knowledge of velocity and mass to what the text states about momentum.]

Mr. Isaacs would show students how he thinks about a text while he reads. He can demonstrate that it's important to pause and think about what he has learned or experienced previously. He can share how he makes connections and summarizes main ideas. In essence, he would articulate what goes on in the mind of a skilled science reader, and his students would see that perseverance, questioning, and clarifying are all part of the skill set for science reading.

Provide Opportunities for Students to Practice Metacognitive Skills

Although it's important for a teacher to model how he or she thinks about a science text, it is not enough to merely show students how to do it. The students must be given opportunities to practice using the metacognitive skills that are required for thinking about a text that presents a high volume of technical terms, charts, and graphs that hold complex theories and data for interpretation. Reciprocal teaching, a tool for fostering student conversation about text, is an excellent way to guide students to act in the investigative, inquiry-based manner that scientists in the field have adopted as a protocol themselves. When scientists meet at conferences to discuss papers or the latest research, they use their common technical vocabulary to predict ideas, to ask questions, to clarify ideas for each other, and to summarize key points. These are the characteristics of the dialogue they use. Because of the complex nature of science writing, the interpretation of science text is well suited to a collegial, collaborative setting. Additionally, science is a content area in which one idea often leads to another, with the hope that the result will be a greater, more cohesive body of knowledge. By allowing students to develop comprehension and build knowledge together with their peers, a teacher is modeling the process by which science practitioners collaborate to generate new theories. Reciprocal teaching prompts students to predict, clarify, question, and summarize. The following might be used as a guide when teaching students how to implement this tool for reading and discussing science text (Grant & Fisher, 2010):

1. *Predicting.* Using cues from both words and features (e.g., bold print, headings, and figures), students anticipate and forecast what will happen next.
2. *Clarifying.* When students encounter a word or phrase that is confusing or unclear, they use context clues, knowledge of root words and word parts, and help from others in the group to decipher meaning. In some cases, they simply acknowledge the need for further clarification and must persist with the reading until future opportunities to clarify are presented.
3. *Questioning.* Students read a chunk of text, then create a question or two that correlates with the reading. They answer their own questions as they read, or they may develop questions that could be answered through further reading or research.
4. *Summarizing.* Students summarize content as they read by noting key ideas and themes.

To implement reciprocal teaching, Mr. Isaacs would first model how to *predict, clarify, question,* and *summarize.* In particular, he would articulate how he negotiates the following as he reads: (1) the use of data charts, graphs, and tables, which often accompany science text, to predict meaning and to address questions that arise as he reads; (2) the deciphering of text meaning, given the preponderance of technical and academic vocabulary; and (3) the connection of background knowledge to novel ideas presented in the text as a way to interpret and build meaning. Mr. Isaacs could use the think-aloud approach to share how each aspect of reciprocal teaching is conducted. Following this, he might consider a "fishbowl" approach for guided practice. This would entail having a group of four students interpret text aloud for the rest of the class, using the four components of reciprocal teaching. Mr. Isaacs would guide the group by offering prompts and cues, as each student takes on a role: predictor, clarifier, questioner, and summarizer. While it helps to have students start with an individual role, the intent is to eventually allow all to practice each component of reciprocal teaching for the purpose of gaining proficiency in all areas. The ultimate goal is for students to be able to read a text and then discuss with peers by fluidly predicting, clarifying, questioning, and summarizing when appropriate and when needed. In essence, the formulaic way in which reciprocal teaching is first presented should eventually yield to a vibrant conversation about science text in which all students are using the metacognitive skills needed to address what they encounter as they read. Moving students from the rigid aspect of having a role (predictor, clarifier, questioner, and summarizer) to the dynamic place of reading and interpreting with colleagues takes a great deal of planning, effort, and formative assessment on the part of the teacher. To make this transition happen, Mr. Isaacs would have to (1) monitor group discussions while providing relevant feedback, (2) allow all students to experience all roles, and (3) choose texts that encourage students to draw on background knowledge, interpret data, and wrestle with new concepts. The potential outcome for students would be well worth the effort on the teacher's part.

Provide Opportunities for Students to Collaborate as They Evaluate a Topic Using Multiple Texts

Scientists often build their own background knowledge by reading several texts that relate to a topic. Having a store of prior understanding clearly helps the scientist to think, talk, and write about an issue. Having the experience of considering and discussing ideas from multiple texts dealing with the same topic builds vocabulary along with the capacity for practicing metacognitive skills. These skills are the same foundational skills needed to read a science textbook. Consider the current hot topic *acidification of the oceans*. How might Mr. Isaacs support his students as they tackle several different readings on this topic? One option might be to implement a discussion web (Alvermann, 1991). Using this tool, students read several texts related to the given topic. Mr. Isaacs could provide the *Scientific American* articles "How Acidification Threatens Oceans from the Inside Out" (Hardt & Safina, 2010) and "Making Carbon Markets Work" (extended version; Victor & Cullenward, 2007), both of which students would be required to read and review within a group of three or four. Students might even use the guidelines of reciprocal teaching to do this reading task. Next, group members are asked to weigh in on an issue related to the readings. For example, Mr. Isaacs might pose this issue for student consideration: *The United Nations should mandate increased restrictions on the burning of fossil fuels due to the rise in ocean acidification.* After considering the content of the articles read, students indicate the aspects of each article that support and oppose the issue—in this case, either in support or in opposition to the implementation of emissions restrictions to prevent ocean acidification (see Figure 1.1). After documenting, with supporting evidence, the position(s) of each article, the group has a discussion in which participants

Taking it step by step

share their individual views, given their prior knowledge and/or the new knowledge acquired through reading. Students use the skills of debate, persuasion, and consensus building to try to come to a group position, which they record in the discussion web template depicted in Figure 1.1. Using this method of collaborative practice, students receive the support of peers when trying to negotiate and integrate complex ideas from several texts. Although this activity sounds like its success rests on the shoulders of individual students participating in the group, Mr. Isaacs's role is integral and could even be transformational for certain students. Mr. Isaacs's task would be to move around the room so that he could monitor progress, assess students' abilities, and provide scaffolds whenever needed. If a student is having trouble understanding how increased CO_2 produces acidic ocean water, Mr. Isaacs might refer him or her to an equation showing the chemical reactions that occur in the production of carbonic acid. He might also provide academic language templates so that students are better able to converse in a scientific manner. For example, if Mr. Isaacs wants to help students with the language needed to disagree respectfully, he might offer these templates:

teacher involvement equals success

★ teaching social skills!

I understand your position, but have you considered this evidence: _____.

When considering _____, I've come to the conclusion that _____.

I see your position, but after reviewing the evidence, I think _____.

Position of article/text Evidence in support		Statement/question	Position of article/text Evidence in opposition	
Text 1		The United Nations should mandate increased restrictions on the burning of fossil fuels due to the rise in ocean acidification.	Text 1	
Text 2			Text 2	
My opinion				
My group's opinion				

FIGURE 1.1. Discussion web for ocean acidification conversation.

These are all scholarly and considerate ways for students to speak to each other. Frey, Fisher, and Everlove (2009) state that when students engage in face-to-face, peer-led interactions, they deepen their own understandings of concepts through the more prevalent use of metacognitive statements and questions. The discussion web format has built-in accountability for both individual students and groups. This type of accountability is essential for the success of any collaborative task.

Foster the Ability to Synthesize Ideas

When reading a science textbook, students need to know when it's time to pause after reading a chunk of text, think about what they've read, and then synthesize the ideas into key points. One way to foster this ability is to have students use a method of writing called *generating interactions between schemas and text* (Cunningham, 1982). This method of writing, better known as *GIST*, is actually a 20-word written summary of what the student has just read. When a reader is conveying the *gist* of a text, he or she is determining and stating the essential elements of the reading. To do this, the reader must engage in all of the following: reading, thinking, rereading, metacognitive questioning (asking *who, what, where, when, why,* and *how*), and determining the key points. This series of activities helps students to internalize and integrate main ideas into existing knowledge banks.

To take this approach one step further, a teacher, such as Mr. Isaacs, could have students work with a partner to create the GIST. The partner element would encourage conversation, decision making, and the collaborative honing of ideas to get to the "heart" of what was read. Additionally, it would likely foster a more accurate determination of essential ideas. To help students process their own ideas in preparation for talking with a partner about the GIST, Mr. Isaacs could use a template that guides students to ask *who, what, where, when, why,* and *how* (see Figure 1.2). Then students would be required to jot down their own GIST thoughts, as a precursor to working with a partner to write a collaborative GIST. As students become more and more proficient at writing GISTs, Mr. Isaacs could help them progress to creating *mental* GISTs as they read sections of the textbook. For example, at certain points in a shared reading, Mr. Isaacs might pause and ask students to individually think about a GIST they might write. Each student then thinks, in his or her head, about the *who, what, where, when, why,* and *how* of the segment of text just read. With practice, this skill becomes increasingly intuitive and automatic—exactly what Mr. Isaacs would want, because this is what proficient science readers do when they read critically for information and knowledge integration.

Such a task is foundational to science textbook reading. After a proficient science reader reads a few paragraphs of text, especially if it is

Text title: **Author:**	
Describe **who** the text is about.	
Determine **what** the text is about.	
Determine **where** the ideas/concepts occur or were developed.	
Determine **why** the ideas are presented or **why** they were studied.	
Determine **how** the ideas are presented or came about.	
My ideas for a GIST (20-word summary; use the ideas above to help you write this).	
GIST written with my partner.	

FIGURE 1.2. GIST template for science partner writing.

particularly dense in terms of content and vocabulary, he or she will want to pause to synthesize and consolidate ideas. While this is usually done either in written note form or mental note form, practicing this skill with a partner in a formal, teacher-mediated manner will help build the habit and capacity to summarize main ideas throughout a sustained session of textbook reading.

Ask Students to Make Predictions as They Read and to Check Their Thinking

When proficient science readers tackle a new text, they make predictions using cues provided within the text. Then they read to check their predications. This type of reading is compatible with the inquiry nature of science. Mr. Isaacs could employ a directed reading and thinking activity (DR-TA; Stauffer, 1969) to help students practice this reading skill. DR-TA employs three questions, which students continually ask themselves as they read:

1. "What do I think about this section of the reading?"
2. "Why do I think this?"
3. "How can I prove it?"

DR-TA

Clearly these questions prompt students to monitor, evaluate, and revise their thinking, DR-TA is best used for chunks of text. Fisher and Frey (2004) suggest that instructors guide students to tap into background knowledge throughout the reading. To do this, a student begins by scanning the first segment of the text to make a prediction about the content, using text clues and prior knowledge. Next, the student reads to confirm or revise his or her predication. At this point, the student begins to ask the DR-TA questions. Mr. Isaacs could scaffold this activity by providing a DR-TA reading guide (see Figure 1.3). For each section of text, students predict upcoming content and then ask themselves the three metacognitive DR-TA questions listed in the guide. Eventually, Mr. Isaacs could remove this scaffold and simply ask students to pause to mentally ask themselves these questions. This process could occur frequently, throughout the reading. Because science text

Prediction: What will this section be about?		
Reading Section 1	What do I think about this section of the reading?	
	Why do I think this?	
	How can I prove it?	
Prediction: What will this section be about?		
Reading Section 2	What do I think about this section of the reading?	
	Why do I think this?	
	How can I prove it?	
Prediction: What will this section be about?		
Reading Section 3	What do I think about this section of the reading?	
	Why do I think this?	
	How can I prove it?	

FIGURE 1.3. DR-TA reading guide.

is typically dense, with technical terms, chunking the text and pausing to consider content is essential. DR-TA is a means by which to guide students to employ these habits of reading.

Teach the Science Vocabulary Needed to Understand the Text

As mentioned at the start of this chapter, science vocabulary is key to understanding science textbooks. Although read-alouds, shared readings, and wide readings of various science texts are the best ways for students to build vocabulary knowledge, direct vocabulary instruction is also important, especially for terms that are critical to understanding. Mr. Isaacs would do well to post key vocabulary terms, in a word wall form, for each textbook chapter he plans to read. He can then easily refer to the terms that he's posted by simply walking over and pointing to a word—for example, *momentum*—when discussing the impact of a crash test car on a wall during collision. In fact, Mr. Isaacs might even have students predict the meaning of this term, along with an example that illustrates its applications, by having them complete a vocabulary self-awareness chart (see Figure 1.4). At the start of a unit, the teacher provides a list of content-related terms. Students are asked to indicate if they can provide a definition and/or example for each word. If a student is not able to do either, he or she simply indicates this on the chart. The teacher notes the learning needs based on the students' charts and proceeds with appropriate instruction. After content instruction is completed, which could be at the end of the unit of study, students are asked to revisit and revise their vocabulary self-awareness charts. The intent is for them to add the information that was lacking prior to focused instruction. Vocabulary self-awareness helps students focus on upcoming content, provides a mechanism for tapping

Vocabulary term	Know definition	Know example	Don't know either	Definition	Example
velocity	✓	✓		The speed and direction of an object	My sister drove at 60 miles per hour, going west on the freeway.
momentum	✓				The product of mass and velocity.
collision		✓			When objects hit each other.

FIGURE 1.4. Vocabulary self-awareness chart for a unit on momentum.

Layers of the atmosphere	Key features					
	Increasing temperature with increasing altitude	Decreasing temperature with increasing altitude	Thins with increasing altitude	Weather occurs here	Absorbs ultraviolet radiation	Meteorites often burn up in this layer
troposphere		+	+	+		
stratosphere	+		+		+	
mesosphere		+	+			+
thermosphere	+		+			

FIGURE 1.5. Semantic feature analysis chart for layers of the atmosphere.

into prior knowledge, and helps students note what they have learned at the close of a unit.

Another method of vocabulary instruction that is particularly well suited to science is the semantic feature analysis chart. In science, there are many categories of related words that have similarities and differences that should be noted by the learner. Consider the layers of the atmosphere: the troposphere, stratosphere, mesosphere, and thermosphere. These layers have features that are easily comparable. When students create a semantic feature analysis chart (see Figure 1.5), they go beyond simple, superficial definitions as they explore the characteristics that give words deeper meaning. For example, by definition the *troposphere* is the lowest layer of the atmosphere. This definition indicates only relative location. It doesn't mention density, temperature, weather occurrence, or any other features that help a learner to develop a working knowledge of the term. Students completing a semantic feature analysis chart for layers of the atmosphere would indicate which layers have certain designated features and which don't. Vocabulary in science is far more than a glossary representation. For students to fully and fluidly be capable of using a term, they must have a deep understanding of the meaning of the word. Semantic feature analysis charts help facilitate such deeper understandings.

CONCLUSION: SET UP STUDENTS FOR SUCCESS

If Mr. Isaacs wants to meet his annual goal of sending students on to the next grade with an increased ability to greet the challenge of reading the science textbook, he will have to alter his mode of instruction. His current preference for volunteer reading must yield to an array of instructional tools vocab predicting, questioning, clarifying, summarizing

that will promote increased vocabulary knowledge alongside the fostering of metacognitive reading skills, such as predicting, questioning, clarifying, and summarizing. Additionally, Mr. Isaacs will need to model the processing of comprehending science concepts by articulating how he thinks when reading science texts, and he will need to provide opportunities for students to practice reading skills with peers. If Mr. Isaacs makes these modifications to his instructional plans, his students will surely grow in their ability to tackle a challenging text and will gain the confidence needed to persevere when encountering complex science ideas.

ADDITIONAL LESSON EXAMPLES

The following lesson examples from the International Reading Association's ReadWriteThink support science reading and comprehension, and provide an alternative to volunteer reading.

Finding the Science Behind Science Fiction through Paired Reading

www.readwritethink.org/classroom-resources/lesson-plans/finding-science-behind-science-927.html

Textmasters: Shaking Up Textbook Reading in Science Classrooms

www.readwritethink.org/classroom-resources/lesson-plans/textmasters-shaking-textbook-reading-1180.html

Critical Literacy in Action: Multimodal Texts on Global Warming

www.readwritethink.org/classroom-resources/lesson-plans/critical-literacy-action-multimodal-1139.html

TRADE BOOKS CITED IN TEXT

Collier, M. (2009). *Over the coasts: An aeriel view of geology.* New York: Mikaya Press.
Sandler, M. W. (2009). *Secret subway.* Washington, DC: National Geographic Children's Books.

REFERENCES

Albright, L., & Ariail, M. (2005). Tapping the potential of teacher read-alouds in middle schools. *Journal of Adolescent and Adult Literacy, 48*, 582–591.
Alvermann, D. E. (1991). The discussion web: A graphic aid for learning across the curriculum. *The Reading Teacher, 45*, 92–99.
Cunningham, J. (1982). Generating interactions between schemata and text. In J.

A. Niles & L. A. Harris (Eds.), *New inquiries in reading research and instruction* (pp. 42–47). Washington, DC: National Reading Conference.

Fisher, D., & Frey, N. (2004). *Improving adolescent literacy: Strategies at work.* Upper Saddle River, NJ: Pearson Education.

Frey, N., Fisher, D., & Everlove, S. (2009). *Productive group work.* Alexandria, VA: Association for Supervision and Curriculum Development.

Grant, M., & Fisher, D. (2010). *Reading and writing in science: Tools to develop disciplinary literacy.* Thousand Oaks, CA: Corwin Press.

Hardt, M. J., & Safina, C. (2010, August 9). How acidification threatens oceans from the inside out. *Scientific American.* Retrieved from *www.scientificamerican.com/article.cfm?id=threatening-ocean-life.*

Lapp, D., & Flood, J. (2005). Exemplary reading instruction in urban elementary schools: How reading develops, how students learn, and teachers teach. In J. Flood & P. Anders (Eds.), *The literacy development of students in urban schools: Research and policy* (pp. 153–179). Newark, DE: International Reading Association.

Olson, J., & Mokhtari, K. (2010). Making science real. *Educational Leadership, 67*(6), 45–62.

Palincsar, A. S., & Brown, A. L. (1984). Reciprocal teaching of comprehension fostering and comprehension-monitoring activities. *Cognition and Instruction, 1,* 117–175.

Rupley, W., & Slough, S. (2010). Building prior knowledge and vocabulary in science in the intermediate grades: Creating hooks for learning. *Literacy Research and Instruction, 49*(2), 99–112.

Smith, B. L., Holliday, W. G., & Austin, H. W. (2010). Students' comprehension of science textbooks using a question-based reading strategy. *Journal of Research in Science Teaching, 47*(4), 363–379.

Stauffer, R. G. (1969). *Teaching reading as a thinking process.* New York: HarperCollins.

van den Broek, P. (2010). Using texts in science education: Cognitive processes and knowledge representation. *Science, 328,* 453–456.

Victor, D. G., & Cullenward, D. (2007, September 24). Making carbon markets work (extended version). *Scientific American.* Retrieved from *www.scientificamerican.com/article.cfm?id=making-carbon-markets-work.*

CHAPTER 2

If They Can't Read Their Social Studies Books— Support Their Learning with Guided Instruction

Karen D. Wood
Jennifer I. Hathaway
Lina B. Soares

Key Points for This Chapter

- Discussion and peer interaction can be fostered through the use of discussion and interactive reading guides.
- Understanding new words can be supported through vocabulary overview guides.
- Comprehension can be supported with strategy guides.
- Writing in the content areas can be developed by using quick writes and admit–exit slips.

A BIRD'S-EYE VIEW OF CLASSROOM PRACTICE

Ms. Dixon has been teaching sixth-grade social studies for many years and has adhered to the same practices week after week. On Monday, she announces to the class the topic for the week and then reads aloud the preview section in the teacher's manual to give the students an idea of what is to follow. Then she writes 8–10 words on the board and tells the students to look them up in the glossary or dictionary. She heard at a workshop that preteaching vocabulary ahead of reading the selection is beneficial for helping students remember the words later. The students typically divide the list with a friend, with each taking turns writing down the first or the shortest definition, whether it fits with the context of the selection or not. On Tuesday, she tells the class to open their books and begin reading. Most of the time she tells them to read silently, but sometimes she varies the lesson by having students read aloud. In that case, she calls on them to read sections of the text, one after the other, using the round-robin reading approach, until each student gets a turn to read. They are not allowed to discuss the chapter content and must remain in their straight rows and assigned seats, she says, "to maintain order" in the classroom and to make sure that the class doesn't get "out of control."

Depending on the length of the chapter, Wednesday looks the same. Then, typically on Thursdays, the students are finished with the chapter reading and are required to answer the end-of-chapter questions. They are instructed to first "write the question from the chapter" on their papers and then "write their answers below the question." Ms. Dixon does this to keep the students engaged and to incorporate more writing with social studies, which helps the students get ready for the state writing assessment.

Fridays are either test days or video days. On video days, Ms. Dixon turns off the lights and directs the students' attention to the classroom TV, where she plays a video related to the topic discussed that week. Some students put their heads on their desks and others pass notes to one another or whisper about their plans for the weekend. Ms. Dixon sees this time as an opportunity to "catch up on grading" while "extending students' learning beyond the textbook," as suggested in a recent staff development session.

DEFINING THE TARGETED PRACTICE

Ms. Dixon has engaged in many ineffective practices and has misinterpreted staff development messages to incorporate writing and use multiple sources of content to deepen students' knowledge and experiences. Among the ineffective practices she employs are the following: reading a preview instead of eliciting and building students' background knowledge; merely listing words on the board; calling on students to read aloud; preventing discussion and peer interaction with the topic; assigning end-of-chapter questions; and using a single textbook and video as the sole sources of content.

WHAT DOES THE RESEARCH SAY
ABOUT READING SOCIAL STUDIES BOOKS?

The research is explicitly clear that meaningful social studies learning is an active social construction process (Reynolds, Sinatra, & Jetton, 1996) that begins when teachers link new information to students' prior knowledge. Conversely, when teachers limit the introduction of new information by simply reading a short preview without tapping into students' background knowledge, the process may act as a stumbling block to understanding because students have not been given an adequate context for interpretation. The deliberate use of prior knowledge in the presentation of new information permits students to create a network of experiences, ideas, and relationships, known as schemas, that have been termed the "building blocks of cognition" (Rumelhart, 1982). Presenting new material in its relationship to the old not only helps students learn the new information before reading, but also strengthens the old information during and after reading (Byrnes, 1995; Pearson & Spiro, 1982). New knowledge does not replace prior knowledge; rather, new knowledge reengages prior knowledge.

Lack of vocabulary development and knowledge are common problems that teachers face in social studies classrooms; however, experts in the field (Nagy, 1988; Stahl, 1986; Wood, Harmon, Kissel, & Hedrick, 2011) maintain that merely listing words on the board is insufficient in producing students who have a deep and lasting understanding of vocabulary. Identifying and pronouncing words listed on the board from a dictionary is not an indicator of vocabulary knowledge, but rather signifies listening and decoding skills. Additionally, learning words by rote does not prepare students to encounter those same words in context and construct meaning for those words, based on conceptual understanding and prior background experiences (Beck, McKeown, & Omanson, 1987). Rasinski and Padak (2001) posit that mindless repetition and defining of words and failure to provide connections to students' lives, interests, and to other familiar words and concepts are insufficient methods to use for vocabulary instruction. Instead we want to see meaningful, "robust" vocabulary instruction that leads to comprehension and engages the learners in the task (Beck, McKeown, & Kucan, 2002).

Meaningful vocabulary development is also achieved when teachers provide students with direct instruction (Bromley, 2007; Nagy, 1988), offer multiple opportunities to use words (Vacca, Vacca, & Mraz, 2010), and utilize instruction that teaches students how words are used in their natural context (Harmon, Hedrick, Wood, & Gress, 2005). Calling on students to read aloud is an age-old method and may have more disadvantages than merits; yet, teachers continue to call on students one at a time to read a passage aloud to members of the class. Johnson and Lapp (Chapter 16, this volume) address the practice of round-robin reading and provide many viable alternatives.

Research into best instructional practices for middle grade learners has continuously endorsed a program that fosters peer discussion and interaction (Brown & Knowles, 2007). Recognizing the social needs of young adolescents, researchers emphasize that teachers should create collaborative learning experiences for their middle grade students (Brown, 2002; Slavin, 2000; Wolfe & Brandt, 1998) as a way to enhance students' social and academic development. Based on the premise that engaged students are socially interactive, many variations on collaborative learning are possible in a social studies classroom and include peer interaction, small-group discussions and investigations, and learning circles.

Today, the typical classroom approach to foster students' comprehension of content material is all too often the read–question–respond format (Alvermann, Swafford, & Montero, 2004). Research does not support this approach. According to Wiggins and McTighe (1998), good teachers teach like coaches. They show students how to read using specific comprehension strategies (Vacca & Vacca, 2005). They model how to think aloud and help students learn to ask questions of the content before, during, and after the reading. This means they focus more on the process and how to read challenging content material. In an area such as social studies, where the content is demanding and the vocabulary can be technical, the teacher's ability to skillfully support students' reading comprehension is vital to academic success.

According to research, textbooks should not be used as the sole source of information in a social studies classroom. Textbooks have been criticized for failing to focus on building concepts (Sinatra, Beck, & McKeown, 1992) and for placing too much emphasis on facts. Immense technical concepts found in social studies textbooks have little or no meaning for students unless specific vocabulary or concept development instruction is first taught. At times, teachers use textbooks that are old, outdated, and contain errors because the content does not reflect the changing times in the real world (Hunter, 2006). Most importantly, the traditional notion of using one textbook limits students' understanding of diverse perspectives that multiple sources of information can provide. Guillaume (1998) proposes that social studies teachers compliment textbooks with a variety of resources, including trade books, historical fiction, magazines, newspapers, videos, and websites.

WHAT ARE SOME ALTERNATIVES?

Ms. Dixon engaged in some of these practices for the same reason many teachers do; we often "teach as we were taught," especially when we lack a repertoire of alternative practices. She has relied on the teacher's guide to help her introduce the lesson rather than engaging the class in an interactive discussion that elicits their participation. This practice is an aberration of a read-aloud, includes an overreliance on the guide book, and involves merely "telling" rather than enlisting active student involvement in the lesson. With this "telling, mentioning, assigning" approach (Durkin, 1978–1979; Pressley, 2000) students will have no more knowledge of the topic to be discussed than they would if she did nothing during this phase of the lesson.

Ms. Dixon knows that vocabulary development is important and that preteaching vocabulary in advance of a lesson can be a beneficial means of providing multiple exposures to key vocabulary terms. However, the approach she chose is a passive one that involves minimal effort on her part and only superficial involvement on the part of the students. Because the definitions chosen by the students may not match their usage in the text, the students will likely have difficulty understanding how the target words are used when encountered in context.

Rather than chance losing control of her class of adolescents, Ms. Dixon chooses an extreme alternative involving no talking, no movement, and, consequently, no learning. Collaborative learning is one of the most powerful means of ensuring understanding. Students learn from their interaction with other students and, as we show later, discussion is how we recall, remember, and comprehend.

Answering end-of-chapter textbook questions has been a mainstay in classrooms for decades upon decades, despite the fact that it has long been identified as an ineffective practice. Ms. Dixon not only assigns that task each week, but she also asks students to write the question stem as well. This misguided practice is not an opportunity to "integrate writing across the curriculum," as Ms. Dixon maintains. On the contrary, it is a classic example of "busy work" that once again does not allow for peer discussion and requires little or no thinking beyond the literal level of the text.

There are alternatives to these practices that are engaging, motivating, and certain to help students understand content at a deeper, more meaningful level. We share a few of them here, focusing on peer discussion, comprehension and thoughtful literacy, meaningful vocabulary development, and writing across the curriculum.

Discussion and Peer Interaction

In order "to maintain order" in the classroom, Ms. Dixon required her sixth-grade students to read a chapter in their social studies textbook and to answer the questions at the end of the chapter. However, this assignment prevented her students from interacting and discussing the text. Mercer (1993) asserts that learning requires talk; learning is enhanced when students have opportunities to talk about their own ideas and to respond to the ideas of others. This premise is supported by a variety of researchers who have asserted that high-quality discussion and exchange of ideas are central to improved reading comprehension, higher-level thinking skills, and increased motivation (Alvermann et al., 1996; Eeds & Wells, 1989; Gambrell & Almasi, 1996; Guthrie, Schafer, Wang, & Afflerbach, 1995). Correspondingly, Kucan and Beck (2003) posit that group discussion supports intellectual engagement with texts and offer that if students are going to learn to think at higher levels about text, then they need opportunities to participate in conversation with others.

Learning through Discussion

Ms. Dixon could have used Hill's (1977) *learning through discussion* (LTD) approach as a means to facilitate her students' understanding of the social studies material. LTD is a reading strategy that involves active peer learning in the acquisition of knowledge. The task guides readers through a series of cognitive activities to discover significant concepts, principles, and key ideas in content material and to help learners acquire reasoning skills with which to analyze new information. The strategy further requires students to tap into information from outside the textbook, relate the information to their textbook reading, and then apply the information to their own lives, the text, and real-world contexts.

The following steps can modified in varied ways to accommodate the goals of a particular lesson. In this instance, the first four tasks would be individually completed by students as they prepare for discussion. The remaining steps in the LTD would be completed as a group during group discussion time.

- *Step 1: Definition of terms.* Select the terms you consider important and necessary.
- *Step 2: Major themes, concepts, and key points.* Identify what you believe to be the major themes, concepts, and/or key points.
- *Step 3: Statement of the author's message.* State in your own words a general description of the author's message in the text.
- *Step 4: Integration of information with other knowledge.* Use the knowledge you have learned in class to integrate with the knowledge from the discussion reading.
  - How useful is the group discussion text for understanding our study?
  - How is your understanding improved, challenged, or expanded?
- *Step 5: Application of the assignment.* Apply the knowledge you have learned from our classroom discussion and the discussion reading.
  - Apply this knowledge to your own life.
  - Apply this knowledge to other texts.
  - Apply this knowledge to real-world events.
- *Step 6: Evaluation of the reading.* Write your reactions and evaluations to group reading.
  - What do you think is the most significant event, idea, or person in the reading?

o What do you think is the most interesting or controversial point in the reading?

o How would you change events in the reading and why?

- *Step 7: Questions.* Write two questions about this assignment that you would like to discuss in class.
- *Step 8: Additional sources of information.* Consult other sources of information. State the source of information and how it contributes to your understanding.

Interactive Reading Guide

To capitalize on the social aspect of learning, Ms. Dixon could have utilized interactive reading guides (Wood, 1988). Unlike typical reading guides that students complete independently with little teacher support, interactive reading guides elicit responses from individual, pairs, and small groups of students during reading. The teacher takes an active role in the reading process by guiding students through the reading, monitoring student understanding throughout the process, and supporting productive group interactions (Wood, Lapp, Flood, & Taylor, 2008). Interactive reading guides are particularly helpful when used with texts that may be too difficult for many students to read independently (Buehl, 2009). Because students work in pairs and small groups during part of the reading, teachers can design student groupings to support students who may struggle with the reading task due to limited background knowledge or other difficulties with reading.

like the textbook

As students complete each section of the interactive reading guide, the teacher leads discussions to ensure understanding of the content. It is important to note that it may take several days for students to complete an interactive reading guide. However, once completed, the guide provides a summary of the content that students can study and review (Wood et al., 2008). Figure 2.1 is an interactive reading guide developed by a teacher, Faith Dibble, on the topic of North Carolina's natural resources. Notice how this example provides opportunities for students to combine traditional text reading with online resources. Notice, too, the many opportunities for group interaction and discussion of the content as well as the higher-order thinking abilities used as students respond to questioning and research prompts.

Meaningful Vocabulary Development

Ms. Dixon knew that building students' vocabulary was essential for their understanding. However, her efforts at teaching vocabulary before reading, by having students define words from their chapter using the glossary, were less than effective. Often, words studied in such isolated ways are quickly forgotten by students. In order for students to develop rich,

In your group, preview (look at the pictures) pages 38–43. With your group members, write down your ideas of what kinds of resources can be found in North Carolina.

Read about North Carolina's soil resources and record at least five things that are grown in North Carolina. Share with your preassigned partner. Discuss why these resources are found in particular regions of the state.

Read to remember "North Carolina's Mineral Resources." Think about what we do with mineral resources. Be ready to discuss this information with the rest of the class.

a. Whisper read with a partner the section called "North Carolina's Vegetation." Together locate at least three national or state forests in North Carolina on a map.

b. Write down why you think it is important to have forests as a natural resource and share your thinking with your partner.

Using online references in combination with your textbook, with your partner, write your ideas about animal habitats. Discuss the importance of these habitats for the animals found in North Carolina.

With your group, discuss the differences between a natural resource and a product. Record your thinking and findings in chart format.

With your group, choose a natural resource in North Carolina. Locate additional information online about the selected resource and its uses. Then make a PowerPoint presentation for your classmates.

FIGURE 2.1. Interactive reading guide: North Carolina resources. Contributed by Faith Dibble, Gaston County Schools, North Carolina.

lasting understandings of new vocabulary, they need to encounter new words multiple times and in a variety of meaningful contexts (Blachowicz & Fisher, 2010). Because of this, considering new vocabulary words as they are encountered in texts is a valuable practice (Buehl, 2009).

Vocabulary Overview Guides

Vocabulary overview guides are one approach that can help teachers scaffold their students' learning of new vocabulary while reading, especially in content areas such as social studies. These guides (Carr, 1985) are graphic organizers that help students monitor their own understanding of new vocabulary as they read. Not only does this approach help students develop deeper understandings of new words, it also supports the development of individual word-learning skills that can be applied to any reading. Although overview guides can be completed by students individually or in small groups, the teacher should first model the process, helping students to develop independence with the approach.

In general, Carr (1985) describes three stages in using a vocabulary overview guide approach: identifying and defining words to study, completing the overview guide, and studying the new words. First, students use the context to identify and define new words. After surveying the reading material (e.g., the chapter in Ms. Dixon's classroom example) to develop a general idea of what it is about, students skim the text to identify unknown words and then stop and read the surrounding sentences to see if they can determine the meaning of the words from the context. After checking the accuracy of their initial definitions using the glossary or through discussion with other students or the teacher, students record these definitions to use as they read. After this initial interaction with new vocabulary, students read the text for understanding, using the recorded definitions to support their comprehension.

After reading, students complete the vocabulary overview guide, as shown in Figure 2.2. The guide includes spaces for recording the title of the passage, the topics described by the vocabulary words, the identified vocabulary words, the definition or explanation of the words, and clues for connecting the new words to students' prior knowledge. Space can also be added for students to record how the word is used in the reading (Buehl, 2009).

The final step is to have students study the new vocabulary identified during their reading. The review begins with students reading the title and labels used to describe the topics addressed in the reading. This step helps to reactivate students' background knowledge about the text. Students then review the meaning of each word in the guide. They can cover the information in the guide and try to explain the word from memory. If they cannot,

natural resource	
My clue:	*soil*
Definition:	*a material from the Earth that is useful*

renewable	
My clue:	*trees—more can be planted when others are cut down*
Definition:	*can be replaced as it is used up*

nonrenewable	
My clue:	*oil—"When it's gone, it's gone."*
Definition:	*once something is used up, it can't be replaced*

FIGURE 2.2. Vocabulary overview guide: Earth's natural resources. Based on Carr (1985).

then they can uncover the personal clues included in the guide to jog their memory. Finally, if needed, they can uncover the definition or explanation of the word. As students encounter the words in new readings, they can modify their personal clues, refine their definitions, or add additional synonyms to support their understanding of the identified vocabulary words.

Comprehension and Thoughtful Literacy

Ms. Dixon instructed her students to answer the questions at the end of the social studies chapter they had just read. Her intentions were to engage her students and to utilize more writing in her classroom. However, this assignment ignored what Allington (2001; Dennis, Lefsky, & Allington, 2009) has referred to as *thoughtful literacy*. In other words, reading is a highly metacognitive activity wherein the reader not only thinks about the material he or she is reading, but also monitors that thinking. To achieve thoughtful readers, teachers model how to think aloud and help students learn to ask questions of the content before, during, and after the reading.

Critical Profiler Guide

To build her students' comprehension, Ms. Dixon could have used the critical profiler guide (Soares, 2008), a comprehension tool that scaffolds students' reading experiences, moving them through prereading activities to during-reading activities to the actual guide itself. This combination of prereading, during-reading, and the critical profiler guide activities for after reading provides opportunities for students to think about, question, and discuss the textual content, then organize and synthesize information from the text in order to evaluate the author's purpose and interests in writing. The ultimate goal is to teach students to become discerning, thoughtful readers who gain new knowledge from texts while learning to assess texts from multiple perspectives and to read from a critical stance.

Prereading activities should lay the foundation for students to develop a critical stance. For example, before reading *Across Five Aprils* (Hunt, 1964), the story of a farm family in southern Illinois that struggles to survive the upheaval of the Civil War years, students could be prompted to read firsthand accounts of participation in the war and diaries of both slave owners and slaves to analyze the different perspectives.

To support students' abilities to analyze perspectives and build critical awareness during reading, the teacher models how to think critically by analyzing and evaluating the textual content and by deliberately questioning the author's perspectives. The teacher might scaffold the students' reading of *Across Five Aprils* from a critical stance, using questions such as these:

What do Bill's words and actions reveal about him?
Does this character seem true to life?
Why might the author have chosen a family member from a Southern
    state to visit the Creightons at this time?
What opinions do the different family members have about the war?
How does the author support their viewpoints?

With these types of questions, students do more than just respond to what is asked; they must position themselves and decide how they will respond. As they consciously engage in the lives of the literary characters and explore the nature of the events in which those characters live, students in turn confront their own beliefs, values, and attitudes and begin to develop alternate ways of perceiving. The critical profiler guide, such as shown in Figure 2.3, is then used to extend students' learning as they complete one or more of the listed activities.

Integrating Writing

Reading and writing are reciprocal processes, so practice in one area helps build performance in the other (Graves, Juel, & Graves, 2010). Students need opportunities to write every day, in every class period. The writing experience does not need to be formal, essay-like writing graded by the teacher and handed back to the students days later. Neither should it be merely copying down the content written by others, as was the case in Ms. Dixon's classroom. Having students informally write within different

After-reading critical stance questions	Student responses after reading	Student follow-up alternative view
• Whose viewpoint is expressed in the novel? • What does the author want you to believe about the reasons for going to war? • How might alternative viewpoints be represented? • How does the author elicit empathy for Bill?		• Write a speech that you would deliver to President Lincoln. Take a stand on his decision to restore order in the South. • Write an editorial for a newspaper expressing your views on the formation of the Confederate States. • Create a slide presentation that shows multiple scenes and views of the war.

FIGURE 2.3. Critical profiler guide: *Across Five Aprils.*

content areas allows them to express their thoughts, emotions, and opinions as they respond to and examine ideas they encounter in their reading (Vacca, 2002). Writing can be spontaneous; it can also be collaborative, as in the case of "communal writing," wherein four or five heterogeneously grouped students are asked to put their heads together in the composition of a single product (Wood, 2002); and it can be integrated into all subject areas, as we have seen in the examples shown previously, such as the interactive reading, vocabulary overview, and critical profiler guides. Two more strategies are described next.

Quick Writes

Quick writes (Buehl, 2009; Tompkins, 2009) are informal writings that allow students to explore or form a personal response to a topic by synthesizing information. When participating in a quick write, students write for a short period of time (typically 5–10 minutes) to capture their ideas about the content, connections between ideas, and reflections on new understandings (Tompkins, 2009). The teacher may provide a prompt for the writing, or students can select their own focus for writing. Because quick writes are an informal type of writing, the focus is on capturing students' thinking and reflections rather than creating a polished piece of writing. Thus, it is important that students write for the entire time period and that they not spend time reviewing and revising their writing (Buehl, 2009). Students can share their quick writes with their classmates, or teachers may collect them to read (Buehl, 2009).

Admit–Exit Slips

Admit–exit slips are described by Buehl (2009) as an extension of the quick-write format. Before beginning a lesson, students complete admit slips that allow them to be "admitted" to the day's discussion (Robb, 2003). On these slips students record at least one important idea they remember from the previous day's discussion or reading. At the end of a lesson, students complete exit slips in which they record new facts or concepts learned as well as lingering confusions. Teachers can offer prompts for the admit–exit slips or allow students to select their own format for response. In addition to providing students the opportunity to synthesize their own understanding, admit–exit slips also help the teacher identify common misconceptions and misunderstandings, to be addressed in future lessons (Buehl, 2009).

CONCLUSION

We have outlined some of the problems associated with Ms. Dixon's teaching practices and have provided numerous alternatives for assisting with the implementation of research-based best practices. We have focused on meaningful vocabulary development in place of the "look-the-words-up-in-the-dictionary" assignments that prevail in Ms. Dixon's classroom. We also illustrated ways to foster discussion, higher-order thinking, and group interaction—rather than the straight rows, assigned seating arrangement, and teacher-dominated practices described earlier. And, we emphasized the need to get students to write in all forms and in all subject areas as a means of improving both their reading and writing abilities.

ADDITIONAL RESOURCES

Just Read Now!

www.justreadnow.com

This website offers strategies for promoting productive student discussion, active involvement with text, vocabulary learning, and comprehension, including numerous graphic organizers that can be used in content-area reading.

PBS Teachers

www.pbs.org/teachers/classroom/6-8/

Middle school teachers can find lesson ideas, interactive tools, and audio and video sources for all content areas at this website.

Scholastic Teachers

www2.scholastic.com/browse/home.jsp

Scholastic's website offers a variety of teaching resources, including lesson ideas and online and interactive learning tools.

Social Studies Central

www.socialstudiescentral.com

This site offers links to help teachers locate primary source documents to support their social studies teaching. Social Studies Central also offers ideas to help teachers plan for this type of instruction.

TRADE BOOK CITED IN TEXT

Hunt, I. (1964). *Across five Aprils*. Chicago: Follett.

REFERENCES

Allington, R. L. (2001). *What really matters for struggling readers*. New York: Addison-Wesley Longman.

Alvermann, D. E., Swafford, J., & Montero, K. M. (2004). *Content area literacy instruction for the elementary grades*. Boston: Allyn & Bacon.

Alvermann, D. E., Young, J. P., Weaver, D., Hinchman, K. A., Moore, D. W., Phelps, S. F., et al. (1996). Middle and high school students' perceptions of how they experience text-based discussions: A multicase study. *Reading Research Quarterly, 31*(3), 244–267.

Ariail, V., & Albright, I. K. (2006). A survey of teacher read-aloud practices in middle grade schools. *Reading Research and Instruction, 45*(2), 69–89.

Beck, I. L., McKeown, M. G., & Kucan, L. (2002). *Bringing words to life: Robust vocabulary instruction*. New York: Guilford Press.

Beck, I. L., McKeown, M. G., & Omanson, R. C. (1987). The effects and uses of diverse vocabulary instructional techniques. In M. G. McKeown & M. E. Curtis (Eds.), *The nature of vocabulary acquisition* (pp. 147–163). Hillsdale, NJ: Erlbaum.

Blachowicz, C., & Fisher, P. J. (2010). *Teaching vocabulary in all classrooms* (4th ed.). Boston: Allyn & Bacon.

Bromley, K. (2007). Nine things every teacher should know about words and vocabulary instruction. *Journal of Adolescent and Adult Literacy, 50*(7), 528–537.

Brown, D. F. (2002). Self-directed learning in an 8th grade classroom. *Educational Leadership, 60*(1), 54–58.

Brown, D. F., & Knowles, T. (2007). *What every middle school teacher should know*. Portsmouth, NH: Heinemann.

Buehl, D. (2009). *Classroom strategies for interactive learning* (3rd ed.). Newark, DE: International Reading Association.

Byrnes, J. P. (1995). Domain specificity and the logic of using general ability as an independent variable or covariable. *Merrill–Palmer Quarterly, 41*, 1–24.

Carr, E. M. (1985). The vocabulary overview guide: A metacognitive strategy to improve vocabulary. *Journal of Reading, 28*, 684–689.

Durkin, D. (1978–1979). What classroom observations reveal about reading comprehension instruction. *Reading Research Quarterly, 14*, 481–533.

Eeds, M., & Wells, D. (1989). Grand conversations: An exploration of meaning construction in literature study groups. *Research in the Teaching of English, 23*(1), 4–29.

Gambrell, L. B., & Almasi, J. F. (Eds.). (1996). *Lively discussions! Fostering engaged reading.* Newark, DE: International Reading Association.

Graves, M. F., Juel, C., & Graves, B. B. (2010). *Teaching reading in the 21st century: Motivating all learners.* New York: Allyn & Bacon.

Guillaume, A. M. (1998). Learning with text in the primary grades. *The Reading Teacher, 51*(6), 476–486.

Guthrie, J. T., Schafer, W., Wang, Y. Y., & Afflerbach, P. (1995). Relationships of instruction to amount of reading: An exploration of social, cognitive, and instructional connections. *Reading Research Quarterly, 3*(1), 8–25.

Harmon, J. M., Hedrick, W. B., Wood, K. D., & Gress, M. (2005). Vocabulary self-selection: A study of middle-school students' word selection from expository texts. *Reading and Writing Quarterly, 26*, 313–333.

Hill, W. F. (1977). *Learning through discussion: A guide for leaders and members of discussion groups.* Beverly Hills, CA: Sage.

Hunter, K. (2006). The textbook case. *T.H.E. Journal, 33*(15), 48–50.

Kucan, L., & Beck, I. L. (2003). Inviting students to talk about expository texts: A comparison of two discourse environments and their effects on comprehension. *Reading Research and Instruction, 42*, 1–29.

Mercer, N. (1993). Culture, context, and the construction of knowledge in the classroom. In P. Light & G. Butterworth (Eds.), *Context and cognition* (pp. 26–46). Hillsdale, NJ: Erlbaum.

Nagy, W. E. (1988). *Teaching vocabulary to improve reading comprehension.* Newark, DE: International Reading Association.

Pearson, P. D., & Spiro, R. (1982). The new buzz word in reading is schema. *Instructor, 89*, 46–48.

Pressley, M. L. (2000). What should comprehension instruction be the instruction of? In M. L. Kamil, P. B. Mosenthal, P. D. Pearson, & R. Barr (Eds.), *Handbook of reading research* (Vol. III, pp. 545–561). Mahwah, NJ: Erlbaum.

Rasinski, T., & Padak, N. (2001). *From phonics to fluency.* New York: Longman.

Reynolds, R. E., Sinatra, G. M., & Jetton, J. L. (1996). Views of knowledge acquisition and representation: A continuum from experience centered to mind centered. *Educational Psychologist, 21*, 93–104.

Robb, L. (2003). *Teaching reading in social studies, science, and math: Practical ways to weave comprehension into your content area teaching.* New York: Scholastic.

Rumelhart, D. E. (1982). Schemata: The building blocks of cognition. In J. Guthrie (Ed.), *Comprehension and teaching: Research reviews* (pp. 3–26). Newark, DE: International Reading Association.

Sinatra, G. M., Beck, I. L., & McKeown, M. G. (1992). A longitudinal characterization of young students' knowledge of their country's government. *American Educational Research Journal, 29,* 633–662.

Slavin, R. E. (2000). *Educational psychology: Theory and practice.* Boston: Allyn & Bacon.

Soares, L. B. (2008). Critical profiler guide. In K. D. Wood, D. Lapp, J. Flood, & B. Taylor, *Guiding readers through text: Strategy guides for new times* (2nd ed., pp. 53–59). Newark, DE: International Reading Association.

Stahl, S. (1986). Three principles of vocabulary instruction. *Journal of Reading, 29*(1), 662–668.

Tompkins, G. E. (2009). *50 literacy strategies: Step by step* (3rd ed.). Boston: Allyn & Bacon.

Vacca, R. T. (2002). Making a difference in adolescents' school lives: Visible and invisible aspects of content area reading. In A. E. Farstrup & S. J. Samuels (Eds.), *What research has to say about reading instruction* (3rd ed., pp. 184–204). Newark, DE: International Reading Association.

Vacca, R. T., & Vacca, J. A. (2005). *Content area reading: Literacy and learning across the curriculum* (8th ed.). Boston: Pearson.

Vacca, J. T., Vacca, J. L., & Mraz, M. (2010). *Content area reading: Literacy and learning across the curriculum* (10th ed.). Boston: Pearson.

Wiggins, G., & McTighe, J. (1998). *Understanding by design.* Alexandria, VA: Association for Supervision and Curriculum Development.

Wolfe, P., & Brandt, R. (1998). What do we know from brain-based research? *Educational Leadership, 56*(3), 8–13.

Wood, K. D. (1988). Guiding students through informational text. *The Reading Teacher, 41*(9), 912–920.

Wood, K. D. (2002). Including diverse learners in the classroom community: Focus on comprehension. In C. C. Block & M. Pressley (Eds.), *Comprehension instruction* (pp. 155–180). New York: Guilford Press.

Wood, K. D., Harmon, J. H., Kissel, B., & Hedrick, W. (2011). Research-based vocabulary instruction: Recommendations for struggling readers. In J. Paratore & R. McCormack (Eds.), *After early intervention, then what?* (2nd ed., pp. 66–89). Neward, DE: International Reading Association.

Wood, K. D., Lapp, D., Flood, J., & Taylor, D. B. (2008). *Guiding readers through text: Strategy guides for new times* (2nd ed.). Newark, DE: International Reading Association.

CHAPTER 3

If You Want to Motivate the Learning of Mathematics— Use the Visual Arts as a Lens to Learning

Robin A. Ward
Susan Troutman

Key Points for This Chapter

- Passive learning environments that support "chalk talk" and teacher-telling are not effective.
- An integrated curriculum nurtures students' motivation to learn and provides connections between real life and students' classroom learning experiences.
- Teaching mathematics using the lens of the visual arts can deepen students' understanding of and appreciation for mathematics.

A BIRD'S-EYE VIEW OF CLASSROOM PRACTICE

Mr. Kamau shows his sixth-grade class a coordinate grid with several labeled points on it. He attempts to help students understand how to identify points; that is, ordered pairs, on a coordinate grid by making an analogous connection to plotting points on a number line. He explains: "To find the coordinates for the point labeled A, start at the origin, move 2 points to the right on the x-axis, and then up 1 point vertically in the direction of the *y*-axis. You are now at point *A* and the coordinates for this point are (2, 1)." He continues on, explaining step-by-step how to identify the (*x*, *y*) coordinates of 2 more points. The students are then asked to identify and record the ordered pairs for the other 7 points on the worksheet. Mr. Kamau circulates about the room, assisting students when needed. After several minutes, he calls on individual students to identify the coordinates of each point. Pleased that the majority of the students correctly identified the coordinates of the points, Mr. Kamau assigns several similar problems for homework and begins covering the next topic.

DEFINING THE TARGETED PRACTICE

The instructional practice employed by Mr. Kamau is called *direct instruction*, a mode of pedagogy attributed by some to Flanders (1970), whereas others credit Rosenshine (1979); it is designed to help students master a skill or set of skills and acquire factual knowledge.

WHAT DOES THE RESEARCH SAY ABOUT DIRECT INSTRUCTION?

Typically, a teacher uses direct instruction when skills need to be taught in a step-by-step fashion. The teacher first prepares students for learning (through an anticipatory set or by recalling prior knowledge), explains and/or demonstrates the steps, provides guided practice, and then allows for more time to practice after supplying feedback (Howley & Kelley, 2004). A critical instructional goal of direct instruction is to teach skills in a manner that facilitates retention over time. Thus, providing sufficient practice for initial mastery and an adequate review for retention are essential aspects of this instructional model (Stein, Kinder, Silbert, & Carnine, 2006).

Curriculum reformists criticize the direct instruction model because it is a very teacher-centered approach and therefore a more passive form of learning. Kuhn (2007) asserts that this model is based on "wrong" behavioral theories and tends to be overused in many classrooms. However, in a well-designed lesson, direct instruction can encourage active participation on the part of students, and thus it is a "valuable approach to teaching and one that should be in every teacher's repertoire" (Arends & Kilcher, 2010, p. 190). Although direction instruction can be used across the curriculum and works best when teaching topics that can broken down into specific steps, teachers need to consider what might be the most appropriate learning environment for students and find ways to provide students with rich opportunities for practice (Arends & Kilcher, 2010).

WHAT ARE SOME ALTERNATIVES?

Mr. Kamau's direct instruction approach to teaching coordinate graphing by using a contrived worksheet with no context did not promote student thinking, encourage collaboration, or challenge students mathematically. Furthermore, he did not provide students with rich opportunities for practice consistent with the recommendations of reform movement organizations (National Council of Teachers of Mathematics [NCTM], 1989, 1991, 2000; National Research Council [NRC], 1989, 2001). For example, the NCTM (2000) advocates that middle-grade geometry teachers help students use visualization to solve problems and engage in investigations that connect to other school subjects, such as art and the sciences, as a means to encourage students to appreciate and understand the beauty and utility of geometry. Students in Mr. Kamau's class were denied this type of a learning opportunity.

Teaching Using an Integrated Curriculum

Gaining momentum is the movement by PreK–8 teachers to integrate their teaching across content areas, with the goal of building connections between and among the various subject matters taught in school. A growing body of literature continues to document the effectiveness of an integrated curriculum on student achievement (Arhar, 1997; Cornett, 2003; Drake & Burns, 2004; National Association for Core Curriculum, 2000; Vars, 1997; Vars & Beane, 2000) and its ability to increase student motivation, elicit higher-order thinking, and build stronger interpersonal skills (Vars, 1997). An integrated curriculum engages teachers, stimulates students, and energizes classroom learning environments (Meinbach, Fredericks, & Rothlein, 2000). It also enables teachers and students to make connections between real life and their classroom learning experiences (Bailey, 2000; Caskey, 2001).

Additionally, a growing body of evidence documents that learning in the arts involves principles shared with other academic disciplines (Bransford et al., 2004; Deasy, 2002; Fiske, 1999). In particular, teaching mathematics using the lens of the visual arts can nurture students' motivation to learn by emphasizing active engagement, disciplined and sustained attention, persistence, and risk taking (Ruppert, 2006). NCTM (2000) asserts that students can improve their sense of shape, symmetry, and similarity through the study of art and thus build connections between and among mathematics, the visual arts, and their world. Furthermore, integrating the visual arts into the teaching of mathematics can deepen students' understanding of mathematical concepts by making these concepts less abstract and, instead, more concrete, visual, and tangible (Ward, in press).

Let's see how another teacher, Ms. Shipper, teaches coordinate graphing, but in a more effective, engaging manner (as compared to Mr. Kamau), by using an integrated approach to teaching this concept.

A Sunday Afternoon on the Island of La Grande Jatte (1884–1886) is perhaps one of Georges Seurat's most famous pointillist works. Measuring nearly 7 feet by 10 feet in size, the work features a variety of objects as well as animals and people, relaxing and playing on an island in the Seine. Ms. Shipper displays an image of Seurat's work on the whiteboard and shares a few biographical facts about this French postimpressionist painter who is best known for his painting technique, *pointillism.*

Ms. Shipper places her students in pairs and hands each pair a hardcopy of Seurat's masterpiece. She also distributes to each pair a premade transparency with an image of centimeter grid paper on it. Using an overhead pen, she guides students in creating a Cartesian coordinate system by drawing a scaled x- and y-axis on the grid and marking the origin $(0, 0)$. She instructs students to center the origin of their transparency grid on top of the face of the girl wearing the white dress, situated in the center of the painting.

Ms. Shipper models while explaining how to find the coordinates of a few objects featured in the artwork. Then she asks students to work collaboratively to identify the coordinates of several objects appearing in Seurat's artwork, such as the cloud in the sky, the top of the man's cane, and the four coordinates that would outline a square about the monkey and the sailboat. She calls on various students to share their answers, encouraging them to articulate how they moved along the x-axis first, followed by the y-axis, to obtain the point in question.

Students gain further practice with plotting and identifying points on the Cartesian coordinate system by engaging in a friendly version of the game *Battleship*, whereby students call out and keep track of (x, y) coordinates—that is, hits and misses—in hopes of sinking one of the three hidden objects appearing in Seurat's work, preselected by Ms. Shipper.

For homework, students are challenged to find another piece of artwork to bring to class the following day. In pairs, students superimpose a Cartesian coordinate system on the artwork and challenge one another to locate the coordinates of various items appearing in it.

Like Mr. Kamau, Ms. Shipper employed direct instruction as she led students step by step through the procedure of identifying points on a coordinate grid; however, Ms. Shipper's integrated approach engaged students far more by providing a richer and more meaningful context in which students could view and apply the Cartesian coordinate system. Furthermore, students in Ms. Shipper's class worked collaboratively and were encouraged to explain their reasoning while engaged in the art-based investigation. Additionally, Ms. Shipper's students were given the opportunity to appreciate and understand the beauty and utility of geometry, which is exactly what the NCTM (1989, 1991, 2000) and MENC (1994) advocate.

ADDITIONAL RESOURCES

The following are useful resources should a teacher choose to integrate the pointillist work of Georges Seurat into the teaching of the Cartesian coordinate system.

Interactive Coordinate Game

www.shodor.org/interactivate/activities/GeneralCoordinates

Virtual Manipulatives—Point Plotter

nlvm.usu.edu/en/nav/frames_asid_331_g_3_t_2.html?from=category_g_3_t_2. html

Pointillism Practice Page

www.epcomm.com/center/point/point.htm

Seurat and La Grande Jatte: Connecting the Dots by Robert Burleigh (Abrams, 2004)
Learn about the life of the artist and the story behind one of his most famous works.

Profiles in Mathematics: Rene Descartes by Steven Gimbel (Morgan Reynolds, 2008)
Discover the life of Rene Descartes and how his coordinate system bridged algebra and geometry.

A BIRD'S-EYE VIEW OF CLASSROOM PRACTICE: SEVENTH GRADE

Miss Bonner begins teaching a lesson on scale factors to her seventh-grade students. She distributes a worksheet to students while telling them that they will need to rely on and apply their multiplication facts to solve the problems. As she points to its definition, which is written on the board, Miss Bonner recites what a scale factor is and tells students to record its definition in their notebooks. She then models how to compute the scale factor by referring to and completing the first few problems on the work-sheet.

Miss Bonner tells students that, to find the scale factor, you must take the ratio of two corresponding lengths in two similar figures. "So in the first problem," she says, "the sides measuring 24 inches and 12 inches are corresponding sides. So take 24 over 12, creating a ratio of 2 to 1. Thus, the scale factor is 2." She continues: "Notice that the perimeter of the larger shape is two times larger as compared to the smaller shape, but the area of the larger shape is four times bigger than the smaller shape, because each side was increased by a scale factor of 2."

While completing the second problem, Miss Bonner tells the class: "The two corresponding sides in these two similar figures measure 10 centimeters (cm) and 30 cm. So place 10 over 30, which gives us a scale factor of one-third." She tells students: "Notice that the perimeter of the smaller shape as compared to the larger shape is one-third times smaller, but the area of the smaller shape is one-ninth of the larger shape, since each side of the figure decreased by a scale factor of one-third."

Satisfied that students seem to understand the procedure for finding a scale factor and determining its effect on the area and perimeter of a shape, Miss Bonner directs students to finish the remaining problems on the worksheet, encouraging them to work with a neighboring student. For each problem, she calls on a student to state the scale factor as well as its impact on area and perimeter, correcting students when they provide an incorrect response. She then assigns a similar worksheet for homework.

DEFINING THE TARGETED PRACTICE

Miss Bonner demonstrates the widespread practice of "teaching mathematics by telling," where *telling* means that teachers demonstrate the proper sequence of steps in a mathematical procedure (Borko et al., 1992; Putnam, 1992; Stodolsky, 1985). Given that students do not know the procedures to be taught, they must derive their knowledge from their teachers. Thus, students are required to listen carefully and practice diligently due to their teachers' reliance on a step-by-step procedural display (Smith, 1996).

WHAT DOES THE RESEARCH SAY
ABOUT TELLING AS TEACHING?

Teachers who teach by telling do so due to their "apprenticeship of observation" as students (Lortie, 1975, p. 61), whereby they themselves have been listening students of mathematics for 12–16 years, and have therefore participated in the practice of teaching by telling (Smith, 1996). Because teaching mathematics by telling has strong and deep roots in experience, it consequently provides a basis on which teachers can build a sense of efficacy: Teachers can provide clear prescriptions for what they must do with the content to affect student learning (Smith, 1996). Additionally, teaching mathematics by telling allows teachers to display their mastery of the content to their students and to themselves, further reinforcing teachers' self-efficacy, as this pedagogical approach serves as a reminder that they are competent to teach (Holt-Reynolds, 1992).

However, in the current age of the mathematics reform movement, teaching by telling is no longer acceptable, as students should not learn mathematics as passive listeners. Instead, teachers should plan and implement innovative lessons that foster active learning and meaningful discourse. In particular, middle school students studying mathematics should engage in thoughtful activities that pique their curiosity, invite speculation, promote reasoning, and give them the opportunity to predict, infer, generalize, construct mathematical arguments, and communicate their mathematical thinking clearly to peers, teachers, and others (NCTM, 1989, 1991, 2000). In order to make sense of mathematics, students must take mathematical action in the form of conjecturing, building models, and collaborating (NCTM, 1989, 1991, 2000; NRC, 1989, 2001). Although teachers who teach by telling feel effective in their knowledge of the content, how to explain it, and what to say in response to students' questions (Borko et al., 1992; Prawat, 1992; Thompson, 1984; Wilson, 1994), this model does not accommodate the type of learning defined by reform movement organizations.

WHAT ARE SOME ALTERNATIVES?

Miss Bonner's approach to teaching her students the concept of scale factor by telling them what to do in a systematic, controlled way reduced learning to a very sterile and passive activity, which lacked any discovery or exploration. Furthermore, she provided no connections to how scale factors are abundant in real-world applications.

Teaching Using an Integrated Curriculum

The benefits of an integrated curriculum have been noted by several educational philosophers, curriculum theorists, as well as others (Beane, 1993; Bruner, 1977; Dewey, 1924; Drake & Burns, 2004; Gelineau, 2003; Jacobs, 1989; Kim, Andrews, & Carr, 2004; McDonald & Fisher, 2006; Schwartz & Pollishuke, 2005). When implementing an integrated curriculum, a teacher can focus on the problems and interests of young adolescent learners, which can serve as a valuable lens for understanding student thinking (Perkins, 1989). The National Middle School Association (NMSA; 1995) argues that the school curriculum needs to be integrative in order to help young adolescents make sense out of their life experiences and connect school experiences to their daily lives outside of the classroom.

The arts (visual art, music, movement, and drama) present an ideal and unique forum through which students can express their ideas, thoughts, and emotions. In particular, the visual arts, which range from "drawing, painting, sculpture, and design, to architecture, film, video, and folk arts" (MENC, 1994, p. 33), embody mathematics, and students can explore such interrelated concepts as patterns, line, shape, and form via this venue. While learning the characteristics of and mathematics embedded in the visual arts, students can collaboratively engage in communicating, reasoning, and investigating, activities that both the NCTM (1989, 2000) and the MENC (1994) strongly advocate. Thus, it is not surprising that efforts to integrate the arts with other content areas are growing (Efland, 2002; McDonald & Fisher, 2006; Phillips & Bickley-Green, 1998; Walling, 2005; Ward, 2008; Ward & Muller, 2006).

Let's consider a more pedagogically sound and mathematically effective approach to teaching the concept of scale factor by using an integrated approach that makes rich connections between mathematics and the visual arts.

As students enter Ms. White's room, they banter back and forth as to why their algebra teacher has asked them, for homework, to bring a live or silk flower to class. They quickly discover why, as Ms. White announces that they are going to use the artwork of the American painter Georgia O'Keeffe to explore the mathematical concept of scale factor.

Students are handed a sheet of centimeter grid paper and are asked to sketch their flowers in the center, trying to draw them true to size and shape, as best they can. Once drawn, Ms. White asks her students to determine the area and perimeter of their flowers. This initiates an interesting discussion among students, as some are unsure how to compute either measurement, since their flowers do not bear familiar polygonal shapes.

Ms. White encourages her students to share their thoughts and reasoning, listening as they argue whether they can or cannot compute the area and perimeter of a shape that is not what they consider a traditional polygon. She encourages them to reflect on the definition of area and perimeter, even asking one student to define area and perimeter in her own words, and to determine if these definitions could apply to their free-form flower sketches. After a few students present strong enough arguments affirming that one can compute the areas and perimeters of shapes that are not necessarily polygons, all the students move forward with the task and use their sketches to count the grid blocks in order to obtain the two measurements.

Next, Ms. White introduces the concept of scale factor to students by having them view several images of Georgia O'Keeffe's boldly colored flower artwork on the classroom's whiteboard. Because O'Keeffe painted her flowers as if magnified, students visually grasp the concept of scale factor almost immediately. Using this real-life example of scaling, Ms. White next directs her students to sketch their same flower again on another piece of centimeter grid paper, but this time *scaling* it several times larger, enough to fill the grid, as if they themselves were Georgia O'Keeffe at the easel.

As students sketch their newly scaled flowers, Ms. White engages them in a line of questioning that enables them to recognize that all parts of the flower (stem, leaves, petals, etc.) have to be made equally longer and larger in size. Thus, in experimenting with the concept of scale, students draw upon their prior mathematics knowledge and discover for themselves that figures drawn to scale are similar, but not congruent.

After their scaled sketches are complete, Ms. White asks students to make visual predictions about the relationships between the area and perimeter of their new sketches as compared to those of their original sketches. She calls on a few students to share their thinking and reasoning. She then directs the students to compute the areas and perimeters of their scaled sketches to test their predictions. Students discover for themselves that the perimeter of a shape increases (or decreases) by a factor equal to the scale factor, but that the area increases (or decreases) by the scale factor squared. They confirm this by sharing their sketches and measurements in small groups.

Although the students in Ms. Bonner's and Ms. White's classes gained an understanding of the concept of scale factor, how to compute it, and its effect on area and perimeter, the integrated approach to teaching employed by Ms. White allowed students to engage in decision making, reasoning, and problem solving. Furthermore, students were allowed to self-discover and investigate scale, not by completing a rote worksheet, but through the rich connections offered by the visual arts.

ADDITIONAL RESOURCES

The following are useful resources should a teacher choose to integrate the larger-than-life artwork of Georgia O'Keeffe into the teaching of scale.

Georgia O'Keeffe Museum
www.okeeffemuseum.org

Virtual Manipulatives—Dilations
nlvm.usu.edu/en/nav/frames_asid_295_g_3_t_3.html?open=activities&from=grade_g_3.html

Georgia Rises: A Day in the Life of Georgia O'Keeffe by Kathryn Lasky (Farrar, Straus & Giroux, 2009)
Inspired by Georgia O'Keeffe's own letters, enjoy a day in the life of the artist. Text written in prose.

A BIRD'S-EYE VIEW OF CLASSROOM PRACTICE: EIGHTH GRADE

Mr. Godinez's eighth-grade class is studying how to solve algebraic equations. He models for his students how to use inverse operations, or the "undoing" method, to solve for the unknown variable. He writes the equation $3n + 6 = 24$ on the board and gives the following explanation: "I need to solve for n. The opposite of adding 6 is to subtract 6. So 24 minus 6 is 18. Then the opposite of multiplying by 3 is dividing by 3. So 18 divided by 3 is equal to 6. The answer is 6."

Mr. Godinez continues with his lesson by solving a few more problems on the board in the same fashion. He then distributes to students a worksheet of similar problems and asks his students to work in small groups to solve them using the undoing technique that he just modeled.

DEFINING THE TARGETED PRACTICE

Mr. Godinez chose the method of using inverse operations, also known as undoing or working backward, to teach students how to solve algebraic equations. Although the undoing approach is a legitimate method for solving algebraic equations and is often used as an introductory approach to equation solving (Bernard & Cohen, 1988), many students in middle school are not successful when using this technique, especially when they are taught this strategy as a rote manipulation of numbers and symbols.

WHAT DOES THE RESEARCH SAY ABOUT UNDOING WHEN SOLVING ALGEBRAIC EQUATIONS?

Algebra for many middle school students means learning how to untangle numbers, operation signs, and letters to get solutions to cumbersome equations that lack any context or meaning. When studying algebra, solving equations involves understanding mathematical operations and relationships and representing them through the use of variables and the equal sign. Many beginning algebra students view the equal sign as a "do-something signal" (Behr, Erlwanger, & Nichols, 1976; Kieran, 1981), rather than a symbol of the equivalence between the left and right sides of the equation. Consequently, students demonstrate reluctance to accept such statements as $5 + 3 = 7 + 1$ or $4 = 4$. Instead, students believe that the right side of the equation should indicate the answer—that is, $5 + 3 = 8$. When studying algebra, students must come to respect the true meaning of an equation as a statement in which a balance exists between the two sides.

When carrying out the undoing method, a student begins with the numerical result on the right side of the equal sign and then, proceeding from right to left, the student undoes each operation by replacing it with the operation's inverse. Using this approach, a student could operate exclusively with numbers and thereby avoid dealing with the equivalence structure so fundamental in an algebraic equation (Kieran, 1992). Also problematic are the findings of a study by Kieran (1988) in which students erroneously generalized this method to equations involving multiple operations and simply undid each operation as they came upon it. Furthermore, students whose preference for solving an algebraic equation was the undoing method were, in general, unable to make sense of the important formal equation-solving procedure of performing the same operation on both sides (Kieran, 1988). This is problematic because the procedure of performing the same operation on both sides emphasizes the symmetry of an algebraic equation.

WHAT ARE SOME ALTERNATIVES?

To gain an understanding of how to solve algebraic equations, students need extensive experience in interpreting relationships among quantities in a variety of problem contexts. Furthermore, students need experiences with developing meaning for themselves (Foster, 2007).

Teaching Using a Context-Based Approach

Tabach and Friedlander (2008) assert that, when they are in the initial stages of learning algebra, and, in particular, discovering the equivalence of algebraic expressions, students should be taught using a context-based approach that provides "points of references that students can review at a more advanced stage of learning" (p. 478). That is, real-life situations can constitute "the starting point and the main process for understanding concepts and the performance of operations" (Tabach & Friedlander, 2008, p. 223). Furthermore, teaching mathematics in context enables students to learn algebraic procedures in meaningful ways, and it raises their motivation and willingness to become engaged in the learning activity (Tabach & Friedlander, 2009). Additionally, a context-based approach can enhance students' facility with symbol manipulation (NCTM, 2000) and facilitate learning processes by providing real or concrete meanings for an otherwise abstract concept or algorithm (Heid, Choate, Sheets, & Zbiek, 1995).

Let's consider a more pedagogically sound and mathematically effective approach to teaching the concept and skills of solving algebraic equations to middle school students by using a context-based approach featuring the visual arts. As a means of connecting the notion of balance in algebra to the notion of balance in art, Mr. Parr begins class with a Pow-erPoint presentation showcasing several images of the colorful and curi-ously balanced mobiles created by 20th-century American artist Alexan-der Calder. Mr. Parr encourages his eighth-grade students to describe what they see, and he guides their comments to focus on how seemingly unbal-anced, yet balanced, Calder's mobiles appear. Next, he tells students that they are going to discover the algebraic balancing magic behind Calder's mobiles.

Mr. Parr engages his class in a penny balancing activity whereby stu-dents, using a Popsicle stick placed perpendicularly on a pencil, create a lever onto which they try to balance an unequal number of pennies on each end of the stick. As they experiment with their levers, placing pennies on either end of the stick, students quickly notice that the weight of the pennies on both sides of the lever affects the balance and, further, that the distance of the pennies on both sides of the stick from the fulcrum (also known as the balancing point) affects the balance.

Mr. Parr likens the movement of each pair of students' levers to a see-saw. He poses questions to the class, inquiring as to what happens when there is no weight (i.e., no pennies) on a seesaw, an equal weight (i.e., the same number of pennies) on both ends of a seesaw, unequal weights (i.e., a different number of pennies) on both ends of a seesaw, and how shifting the weight (i.e., the pennies) affects the balance of the seesaw. In creating this visual and verbal metaphor for his students, in conjunction with the concrete manipulatives of the pennies and their levers, students develop an understanding of balance as an equality—in particular, an equality affected by weight and distance to the fulcrum. With his assistance, students assign variables to represent the components affecting balance: namely, the weight on the left-hand (W_L) and on the right-hand (W_R) sides of the lever, and the distance of the weights from the fulcrum on both the left-hand and right-hand sides of the lever, respectively (D_L and D_R).

Working in pairs, students perform a series of trials, adding a different number of pennies to both sides of their Popsicle stick, obtaining balance, and then recording the weights of the pennies and their distances from the fulcrum on a spreadsheet. Students then derive the law of levers, which states: $W_L \times D_L = W_R \times D_R$. Discovered and proven by Archimedes, the law of levers states that the weight of the objects suspended, multiplied by their distance from the fulcrum on the left side of a lever, must equal the product of the weight of the objects suspended and their distance from the fulcrum on the right side of a lever.

Mr. Parr challenges students to numerically and algebraically under-stand the law of levers by assigning specific values to the variables that com-prise the equation and then asking them to determine the missing variable.

For example, if the weight of the pennies is 3 grams on the left side of the lever and 4 grams on the right side, and if the distances of the pennies from the fulcrum on the right side of the lever are 6 centimeters, what must the distance be from the fulcrum on the left side of the lever? If the two distances of the weights on the left and right sides of the lever are 10 inches and 6 inches, respectively, what might the two weights be?

The class then revisits the previously shown images of Calder's mobiles, and Mr. Parr informs them that Calder, who worked as an engineer prior to his career as an artist and sculptor, applied the law of levers to create his mobiles. As students view the images of each mobile, Mr. Parr asks his students to discern the location of the fulcrum. Students then apply the law of levers visually by observing that a heavy weight situated just a short distance from the fulcrum on the left side of a Calder mobile was balanced by a lighter weight placed at a greater distance from the fulcrum on the right side of the mobile. Students then test their predictions by creating similar scenarios using their Popsicle sticks and pennies.

The activity continues with students working collaboratively to make a Calder-inspired, three-tiered mobile using string, dowel rods, and foam stickers and washers for weights. In creating their mobiles, students are required to record all measurements (distances and weights) and to verify the law of levers as each tier is constructed. When finished, students hang their mobiles around the classroom and discuss how each achieves balance.

By using a context-based approach with a focus on the visual arts—namely, the mobiles of Alexander Calder—Mr. Parr brought the teaching and learning of balancing and solving algebraic equations to life. Students learned abstract algebraic concepts and procedures in meaningful ways by investigating a real-life application of variables and equivalence. Furthermore, this context-based activity, which not only bridged mathematics with the visual arts, also connected both subject areas to the sciences, specifically, to physics. Unlike the students in Mr. Godinez's classes, Mr. Parr's students were given the opportunity to develop a deep understanding of the notion of equivalence in an algebraic equation by physically manipulating a lever and then deriving the algebraic equation that models its movement—that is, the law of levers. Furthermore, in experimenting with the placements and amounts of varying weights (pennies) on their levers and then creating their own balanced Calder-inspired mobiles, these beginning algebra students could visually and physically see and understand how variables change in value. Thus, while engaged in this cross-curricular investigation, students were given rich and multiple opportunities to analyze, reason, judge, and communicate activities advocated by the NCTM (1989, 1991, 2000).

ADDITIONAL RESOURCES

The following are useful resources should a teacher choose to integrate the mobile-making art of Alexander Calder into the teaching of beginning algebra concepts and skills.

Alexander Calder Foundation
www.calder.org

National Gallery of Art NGAKids Mobile
www.nga.gov/kids/zone/mobile.htm

Virtual Manipulatives—Algebra Balance Scales
nlvm.usu.edu/en/nav/frames_asid_201_g_3_t_2.html?open=instructions&from =grade_g_3.html

Alexander Calder and His Magical Mobiles by Jean Lipman (Hudson Hills Press, 1981)
Biography detailing Alexander Calder's life and career.

Additionally, see Muller and Ward (2007) and Ward and Muller (2006) for a more detailed articulation of this context-based, algebra–visual arts activity.

CONCLUSION

Middle school students should not learn mathematics in passive "chalk talk" environments, by "teacher-telling" and simply watching and repeating prescribed steps. Instead, they should have frequent encounters with interesting and challenging problems, so that they acquire an appreciation for, and develop an understanding of, mathematical ideas (NCTM, 2000). By implementing an integrated, context-based approach to the teaching of mathematics—in particular, one that focuses on the use of the visual arts—teachers can challenge students to use and apply their reasoning abilities, spatial skills, and visual perception skills while engaging in problem-solving situations that underscore mathematics not as a secular, unconnected subject, but as a content area rich with interconnections to other subject areas.

REFERENCES

Arends, R., & Kilcher, A. (2010). *Teaching for student learning: Becoming an accomplished teacher.* New York: Routledge.

Arhar, J. (1997). The effects of interdisciplinary teaming on students and teachers. In J. L. Irvin (Ed.), *What current research says to the middle level practitioner* (pp. 49–56). Columbus, OH: National Middle School Association.

Bailey, L. (2000). Integrated curriculum: What parents tell us about their children's experience. *Educational Forum, 64*(3), 236–242.

Beane, J. (1993). *The middle school curriculum: From rhetoric to reality* (2nd ed.). Columbus, OH: National Middle School Association.

Behr, M., Erlwanger, S., & Nichols, E. (1976). *How children view equality sentences* (PMDC Technical Report No. 3). Tallahassee: Florida State University. (ERIC Document Reproduction Service No. ED 144802)

Bernard, J., & Cohen, M. (1988). An integration of equation solving methods into a developmental learning sequence. In A. Coxford & A. Shulte (Eds.), *The ideas of algebra, K–12* (pp. 97–111). Reston, VA: National Council of Teachers of Mathematics.

Borko, H., Eisenhart, M., Brown, C., Underhill, R., Jones, D., & Agard, P. (1992). Learning to teach hard mathematics: Do novice teachers and their instructors give up too easily? *Journal for Research in Mathematics Education, 23,* 194–222.

Bransford, J., Catterall, J., Deasy, R., Goren, P., Harman, A., Herbert, D., et al. (2004). *The arts and education: New opportunities for research.* Washington, DC: Arts Education Partnership.

Bruner, J. (1977). *The process of education.* Cambridge, MA: Harvard University Press.

Caskey, M. (2001). A lingering question for middle school: What is the fate of integrated curriculum? *Childhood Education, 78*(2), 97–99.

Cornett, C. (2003). *Creating meaning through literature and the arts.* Upper Saddle River, NJ: Merrill Prentice-Hall.

Deasy, R. J. (Ed.). (2002). *Critical links: Learning in the arts and student academic and social development.* Washington, DC: Arts Education Partnership.

Dewey, J. (1924). *Democracy and education: An introduction to the philosophy of education.* New York: Macmillan.

Drake, S., & Burns, R. (2004). *Meeting standards through integrated curriculum.* Alexandria, VA: Association for Supervision and Curriculum Development.

Efland, A. (2002). *Art and cognition: Integrating the visual arts in the curriculum.* New York: Teachers College Press.

Fiske, E. B. (Ed.). (1999). *Champions of change: The impact of the arts on learning.* Washington, DC: Arts Education Partnership.

Flanders, N. A. (1970). *Analyzing teaching behavior.* Reading, MA: Addison-Wesley.

Foster, D. (2007). Making meaning in algebra: Examining students' understandings and misconceptions. In A. H. Schoenfeld (Ed.), *Assessing mathematical proficiency* (pp. 163–175). New York: Cambridge University Press.

Gelineau, R. (2003). *Integrating arts across the elementary school curriculum.* Belmont, CA: Thomson Wadsworth.

Heid, K., Choate, J., Sheets, C., & Zbiek, R. (1995). *Algebra in a technological world.* Reston, VA: National Council of Teachers of Mathematics.

Holt-Reynolds, D. (1992). Personal history-based beliefs as relevant prior knowledge in course work. *American Educational Research Journal, 29,* 325–349.

Howley, J., & Kelley, D. (2004). Teachers helping teachers: A process that honors and supports teacher development. In E. Joiner, M. Ben-Avie, & J. Comer (Eds.), *Dynamic instructional leadership to support student learning and development: The field guide to Comer schools in action* (pp. 157–175). Thousands Oaks, CA: Corwin Press.

Jacobs, H. (1989). The interdisciplinary concept model: A step-by-step approach for developing integrated units of study. In H. H. Jacobs (Ed.), *Interdisciplinary curriculum: Design and implementation* (pp. 53–65). Alexandria, VA: Association for Supervision and Curriculum Development.

Kieran, C. (1981). Concepts associated with the equality symbol. *Educational Studies in Mathematics, 12,* 317–326.

Kieran, C. (1988). Two different approaches among algebra learners. In A. F. Coxford (Ed.), *The ideas of algebra, K–12: 1988 Yearbook of the National Council of Teachers of Mathematics* (pp. 91–96). Reston, VA: National Council of Teachers of Mathematics.

Kieran, C. (1992). The learning and teaching of school algebra. In D. A. Grouws (Ed.), *Handbook of research on mathematics teaching and learning* (pp. 390–419). New York: Macmillan.

Kim, M., Andrews, R., & Carr, D. (2004). Traditional versus integrated preservice teacher education curriculum. *Journal of Teacher Education, 55*(4), 341–356.

Kuhn, D. (2007). Is direct instruction the answer to the right question? *Educational Psychologist, 42,* 109–113.

Lortie, D. (1975). *Schoolteacher: A sociological analysis.* Chicago: University of Chicago Press.

McDonald, N. L., & Fisher, D. (2006). *Teaching literacy through the arts.* New York: Guilford Press.

Meinbach, A., Fredericks, A., & Rothlein, L. (2000). *The complete guide to thematic units: Creating the integrated curriculum.* Norwood, MA: Christopher Gordon.

MENC: The National Association for Music Education. (1994). *National standards for arts education.* Reston, VA: Author.

Muller, D., & Ward, R. (2007). Art and algebra?: Middle school students discover algebra in Calder mobiles. *Mathematics in School, 36*(3), 15–21.

National Association for Core Curriculum. (2000). *A bibliography of research on the effectiveness of block-time, core, and interdisciplinary team teaching programs.* Kent, OH: Author.

National Council of Teachers of Mathematics. (1989). *Curriculum and evaluation standards for school mathematics.* Reston, VA: Author.

National Council of Teachers of Mathematics. (1991). *Professional standards for teaching mathematics.* Reston, VA: Author.

National Council of Teachers of Mathematics. (2000). *Principles and standards for school mathematics.* Reston, VA: Author.

National Middle School Association. (1995). *This we believe: Developmentally responsive middle level schools.* Columbus, OH: Author.

National Research Council. (1989). *Everybody counts: A report to the nation on the future of mathematics education.* Washington, DC: National Academies Press.

National Research Council. (2001). *Adding it up: Helping children learn mathematics.* Washington, DC: National Academies Press.

Perkins, D. (1989). Selecting fertile themes for integrated learning. In H. H. Jacobs (Ed.), *Interdisciplinary curriculum: Design and implementation* (pp. 67–76). Alexandria, VA: Association for Supervision and Curriculum Development.

Phillips, P., & Bickley-Green, C. (1998). Integrating art and mathematics. *Principal, 77*(4), 46–49.

Prawat, R. (1992). Are changes in views about mathematics teaching sufficient?: The case of a fifth-grade teacher. *Elementary School Journal, 93,* 195–211.

Putnam, R. (1992). Teaching the "hows" of mathematics for everyday life: A case study of a fifth-grade teacher. *Elementary School Journal, 93,* 163–177.

Rosenshine, B. (1979). Content, time, and direct instruction. In P. Peterson & H. Walberg (Eds.), *Research on teaching: Concepts, findings, and implications* (pp. 28–56). Berkeley, CA: McCutchan.

Ruppert, S. (2006). *Critical evidence: How the arts benefit student achievement.* Washington, DC: National Assembly of State Arts Agencies.

Schwartz, S., & Pollishuke, M. (2005). Planning an integrated curriculum. In K. Revington (Ed.), *Creating the dynamic classroom: A handbook for teachers* (pp. 44–69). Toronto: Pearson Education Canada.

Smith, J. P., III. (1996). Efficacy and teaching mathematics by telling: A challenge for reform. *Journal for Research in Mathematics Education, 27*(4), 387–402.

Stein, M., Kinder, D., Silbert, J., & Carnine, D. (2006). *Designing effective mathematics instruction: A direct instruction approach* (3rd ed.). Upper Saddle River, NJ: Prentice Hall.

Stodolsky, S. (1985). Telling math: Origins of math aversion and anxiety. *Educational Psychologist, 20,* 125–133.

Tabach, M., & Friedlander, A. (2008). The role of context in learning beginning algebra. In C. Greenes & R. Rubenstein (Eds.), *Algebra and algebraic thinking in school mathematics: 2008 yearbook of the National Council of Teachers of Mathematics* (pp. 223–232). Reston, VA: National Council of Teachers of Mathematics.

Tabach, M., & Friedlander, A. (2009). The money context. *Mathematics Teaching in the Middle School, 14*(8), 474–479.

Thompson, A. (1984). The relationship of teachers' conceptions of mathematics teaching to instructional practice. *Educational Studies in Mathematics, 15,* 105–127.

Vars, G. (1997). Effects of integrative curriculum and instruction. In J. E. Irvin (Ed.), *What current research says to the middle level practitioner* (pp. 179–186). Columbus, OH: National Middle School Association.

Vars, G., & Beane, J. (2000). *Integrative curriculum in a standards-based world.* ERIC Digest. (ERIC Document Reproduction Service No. ED 441618). Available at *www.ed.gov/databases/ERIC_Digests/ ed441618.html.*

Walling, D. (2005). *Visual knowing: Connecting art and ideas across the curriculum.* Thousand Oaks, CA: Corwin Press.

Ward, R. (2008). Integrating mathematics and the visual arts. *Charter Schools Resource Journal.* Retrieved October 26, 2010, from *www.ehhs.cmich. edu/~tcsrj/Ward3.pdf.*

Ward, R. (in press). *Math + art = fun: Activities for discovering mathematical magic in modern art.* Houston, TX: Bright Sky Press.

Ward, R., & Muller, D. (2006). Algebra and art. *Mathematics Teaching, 198,* 22–26.

Wilson, M. (1994). One preservice secondary teacher's understanding of function: The impact of a course integrating mathematical content and pedagogy. *Journal for Research in Mathematics Education, 25,* 346–370.

CHAPTER 4

If You Want to Move Beyond the Textbook— Add Young Adult Literature to Content-Area Classes

Virginia S. Loh

Key Points for This Chapter

- Using adolescent novels can effectively enhance and supplement standards-based content area instruction and textbooks.
- Using adolescent novels can increase student expertise and knowledge in specific content-area topics and increase student motivation and interest, thereby encouraging students to read more in the content areas.
- Using adolescent novels can help teachers differentiate instruction for students at different levels.

A BIRD'S-EYE VIEW OF CLASSROOM PRACTICE

Mrs. Gill, an eighth-grade science and math teacher, feels that the textbook is extremely important to her instruction. She notes: "The textbook lays out exactly what we are supposed to teach in order to align with state standards and testing expectations. The district spends a lot of money on these textbooks, so I want to use them. I feel good knowing that my students are being exposed to topics that will be covered on the test, but I'm not sure they really get the importance of science. At times, I do feel limited in what and how I can teach." In her science instruction Mrs. Gill has students read the textbook chapters, gives chapter tests on the reading, and asks students to perform simple lab experiments that are explained in the textbook. She knows that her students have knowledge about scientific topics and procedures as evidenced by their performance on tests and lab reports. But she is not confident in their knowledge of how science relates to their lives, and she worries that her students are not as engaged in science class as they might be.

Expressing similar sentiments, Mr. Zubrod, a seventh/eighth-grade history teacher, states: "With all of the content standards I need to cover, it is hard to make time for experiences that allow students to engage with history through materials other than the textbook. As it is, most students never get past World War I because there's no time to get through the entire textbook before the school year ends." Mr. Zubrod's history courses consist mainly of lectures based on the textbook readings, chapter and unit tests, and four short papers. Throughout the year, he likes to have the students work on group projects and debates; he admits that he isn't able to implement such activities as much as he would like. He also likes to use primary documents and speeches to supplement the textbook; he states, "I want to show students that history is real and is created by real people, different people. I also want to show them that they are making history right now. I want them to see that history is more than names and dates. I'm not sure they are connecting to the topics or the big ideas."

Lastly, Ms. Moaveni, a sixth-grade language arts teacher, states: "I use the core literature books approved by the district, the grammar textbook, and the textbook anthology because these readings are easily available. At least I know I'm covering state standards and my department's expectations." As all the teachers mentioned, the textbook provides a standards-based guide for coverage. Ms. Moaveni adds: "I know it's not enough. The grammar textbook is especially boring. I would love to be able to teach grammar using real books and to introduce my students to the books I love and to different viewpoints and authors, but I'm not sure how to make this happen." In using school-sanctioned materials, Ms. Moaveni does the best she knows how to make it comprehensible and interesting.

It is obvious that the teachers described in these scenarios want their students to be successful in their respective content areas. They make sure that their students have the knowledge to perform well on both class and state tests. However, all three teachers lament the fact that their students lack a real understanding and appreciation of their discipline. The teachers struggle with how to make their content area come to life; they want their students to understand the value and relevance of their respective content areas. They recognize the need to go beyond the textbook but lack certainty about how to make that happen.

DEFINING THE TARGETED PRACTICE

As these scenarios indicate, textbooks are the main teaching tool in many content-centered classrooms. Textbooks have a significant place in the classroom. Typically, they are distributed directly to school districts and are useful for ensuring that teachers provide students with standards-based content. The ability to learn from textbooks is essential for students' academic success, since textbooks represent an essential tool for learning at virtually every grade level from first grade through college.

Past research has indicated that teachers use textbooks 75–90% of the time (Miller, 1987; Palmer & Stewart, 1997). Vacca, Vacca, and Mraz (2010) argue that textbook-driven curriculums often promote teacher lecturing to the exclusion of student-centered practices. Beck and McKeown (1991) noted over 20 years ago that textbook-centered content-area reading and lecture may not be substantial enough to support deep content understanding for all students.

One means of expanding reading materials in content classrooms is to supplement the basal text with young adult literature—that is, with trade books that are published for general distribution and sold via booksellers. Young adult literature (YAL) includes adolescent novels, which are fictional chapter books, and books from other genres such as poetry, folklore, fantasy, and nonfiction. YAL also includes books with unique visual formats such as picture books and graphic novels. These books address a wide range of topics across virtually all content areas. Young adult books typically feature teenage characters or subjects and are usually written from the viewpoint of this population (George & Stix, 2000); as such, they are more likely to be read and enjoyed by teenagers, who feel connected to the young people featured in the book. Such literary works can be great enhancements and complements to what is being learned from textbooks (Bean, 2003).

As the three teachers depicted in the scenarios illustrate, many teachers are unsure of how to effectively supplement textbooks with young adult books. Many teachers are unfamiliar with the many outstanding books available, are not sure how to gain this knowledge, and therefore do not feel comfortable recommending titles or using these books in their classrooms (Loh, 2008). However, learning about available titles is easier today than in times past, given simple Internet searches from which lists and annotated reviews can be generated. Taking the time to learn about trade books for various subjects is worth the effort in terms of student achievement and engagement (Hiebert, 2009). There are definitely benefits to using both textbooks and young adult books in the classroom; by doing so, teachers can provide opportunities for building and enhancing content knowledge, for increasing student motivation to read and to further study the content area, and for differentiating instruction based on reading strengths and topical background knowledge.

WHAT DOES RESEARCH SAY ABOUT RELYING ON TEXTBOOKS?

The teachers mentioned in the beginning of this chapter recognize that teaching exclusively with textbooks has both strengths and limitations. They want their students to gain deeper understandings of their content-area topics, understandings that can be achieved only by supplementing textbook content with other resources, including topically related YAL. Scholars in the past have criticized textbooks for their lack of stimulating content, their encyclopedic formats, and their inaccuracies (American Association for the Advancement of Science, 2002; Fradd, Lee, Sutman, & Saxton, 2001; Kesido & Roseman, 2002). Today's textbooks are dramatically different from, and much improved over, the ones of the past. In fact, many of today's textbooks include actual young adult book titles or excerpts; in addition, they often provide lists of appropriate trade books that can complement the textbook.

Despite these improvements, one key limitation of textbooks is that they are still designed to give a lot of information in a small space, which may lead to surface and literal understandings, since much information is excluded (Vacca et al., 2010). Young adult books can often provide opportunities for students to acquire a deeper understanding of content-area topics. Research suggests that experiences with YAL may contribute to increased reading achievement; for example, the Center for the Improvement of Early Reading Achievement School Change Study (Taylor, Pearson, Peterson, & Rodriguez, 2003) found that achievement in reading increases if teachers emphasize deep understandings (the how and the why) rather than literal knowledge (the what, when, and where). Furthermore, Guthrie, Wigfield, and Perencevich (2004) found that focusing on conceptual goals increases reading interest and enjoyment; students find it motivating to develop "expertise," which is the knowing of content, the ability to connect it to other learning, and the ability to explain it. Siefert and O'Keefe (2001) found that students prefer conceptual themes that foster the meaningful building of learning strategies over the factual knowledge of distinct topics that is more typical of textbooks. Specifically, adolescent readers read to get something out of the text; they want to dig deeper, and they need texts that allow them to do so (McGill-Franzen & Botzakis, 2009). George and Stix (2000) conclude that the use of these books in the content area leads to more interesting classroom discussions and increased understandings, more meaningful student involvement and interest, and more motivation to learn and make connections; it also allows students to apply content and conceptual learning (Bean, 2003). Teachers who used trade books in addition to the textbook made significant achievements with their students on the National Assessment of Educational Progress (NAEP), when compared to teachers who relied on the textbook as the core of their curriculum (McGill-Franzen & Botzakis, 2009).

This research seems to suggest that textbooks need to be accompanied by effective instruction and supplemented by additional materials such as YAL in order to build necessary background and content knowledge and to add depth and emotion to the subject matter. Furthermore, in doing so, teachers not only supplement content learning, but they can also accommodate varying reading and knowledge levels and motivate student participation and engagement. Furthermore, by creating bridges to school-assigned texts, teachers can provide the necessary supports to make these school-sanctioned texts more interesting and more accessible.

WHAT ARE SOME ALTERNATIVES?

Rationale for Using Adolescent Literature

By using YAL to supplement textbook learning, the content-area classroom can become an ideal place for teachers to extend, enhance, and enrich their curricula as students are supported in making deeper meanings and connections and identifying relevance. Adolescent literature, which includes both narrative- and expository-type texts, can provide students with access to a range of reading materials, thereby promoting multiple perspectives, reading for pleasure at an appropriate reading level, and digging deeper into content-related concepts. According to Bean (2003), reading in a content area increases literacy by building background knowledge, by motivating students to read widely and subsequently more, and by being able to accommodate different reading and learning abilities. With these supports, which enable the development of topical language, background knowledge, and concepts, students will be better able to read the class textbook.

Building Background and Content Knowledge

Adolescent novels can provide a rich context for learning across the content areas, even in mathematics classes, by contextualizing vocabulary, connecting abstract concepts, and showcasing ways that math can cross disciplines (Austin, Thompson, & Beckman 2005; Wallace & Clark, 2008; Whitin & Wilde, 1992). Wallace and Clark (2008) found that middle school math concepts and standards are, in fact, represented in adolescent novels; however, the efficacy of these novels is not necessarily in the math concepts but the real-life questions raised: Why is math important to the story? What function does math play in the story? In considering such questions, students may make connections to mathematics in the real world as well as in their own lives. Thus, reading fiction allows students to internalize content in ways that are meaningful to them (Bean, 2000); in doing so, content-area knowledge expands as students add personal accounts, question texts, and make connections (Harvey & Goudvis, 2000).

Furthermore, Norris, Guilbert, Smith, Hakimelahi, and Phillips (2005) describe the "narrative effect" in which reading fiction in a science class increases student interest, retention of information, and understanding of content. Worthy, Moorman, and Turner (1999) reported that because adolescent readers are familiar with the narrative format, using adolescent novels can be a scaffold, further aiding comprehension. For example, if Mrs. Gill wants to use a fictional text to explain a scientific concept, the students will be faced with only one unfamiliar domain—meaning, they will be able to spend most of their time and energy focusing on the content rather than the text structure.

Students should be encouraged to read books on the same topic from diverse viewpoints; by reading these multiple texts, students have the opportunity not only to develop multiple viewpoints about a particular time, place, or events but also to scaffold their understanding by focusing on an area of interest or by utilizing their previous knowledge to allow them to focus primarily on the new content material. For example, reading a variety of trade books about a topic such as the Great Depression from the perspectives of African Americans, Japanese Americans, and other groups exposes students to the experiences of a culturally diverse society and provides a variety of viewpoints for students to synthesize. Such an opportunity strengthens content knowledge, literacy, and critical literacy insights. Students need books that reflect and represent the contemporary realities of diverse cultures and perspectives, realities that may not be included in textbooks; by reading diverse adolescent novels widely, students may increase their self-awareness and cultural understandings (Loh, 2006). Through these experiences students can compare and contrast different titles and examine more deeply the themes and concepts addressed in multiple books. In this way they can acquire a body of disciplinary knowledge from wide reading that is a powerful resource in supporting reading comprehension and developing in-depth knowledge (Jetton & Alexander, 2001).

By employing multiple texts, teachers can deepen students' understanding of a concept. For example, in order to enhance his unit on American slavery, Mr. Zubrod might assign the following adolescent novels: *Chains* (Anderson, 2010), *Day of Tears* (Lester, 2007), *Many Thousand Gone* (Hamilton, 2002), and *Numbering All the Bones* (Rinaldi, 2002). Using the guided reading and summarizing procedure (GRASP) strategy (Vacca et al., 2010), as outlined below, Mr. Zubrod could have students write a summary of the slave experience:

1. Have students recall and record all the important elements/details about American slavery.
2. Have students delete unimportant information from their lists.
3. Have students organize the information into categories.
4. Have students use the categories as a basis for their summary writing.

Instead of having the class read all the novels, Mr. Zubrod could also divide students into small groups and assign each group to read one of the novels. Students could read these novels and then compare what they learned about slavery from each text. To do this, he could create a matrix that compared various aspects of slavery addressed in each title. He could then have each group be responsible for completing their section of the matrix. The students could then use this matrix to complete the GRASP activity.

Motivating Learning and Reading

Adolescent literature has the potential to motivate students because they become more personally and emotionally involved with the character, setting, plot, and subject than is typically the case with a textbook; as such, students are more likely to see the relevance of the concepts in their personal lives and are more able to think about the larger questions of the world (Jones, Howe, & Rua, 2000; Salvner, 2001). Students may also be affected in such a way as to positively alter their attitudes toward the subject; for example, research (Ford, 2005; Ford, Brickhouse, Lottero-Perdue, & Kittleson, 2006) found that including fiction reading in science warmed girls to the idea of studying the content.

The ability to engage motivation is one of the most compelling reasons to use adolescent novels in the content-area classroom. Middle and secondary students are far less likely to read on their own than younger students; as such, content-area teachers need to promote reading whenever possible (McGill-Franzen & Botzakis, 2009). When students are given opportunities to interact with adolescent novels that deepen and strengthen textbook content, they have a better chance of making meaning and of becoming lifelong readers. Studies show that reading "real" books for "real" purposes increases reading engagement in addition to comprehension (Knapp, 1995; Purcell-Gates, Duke, & Martineau, 2007); adolescent novels are a perfect way to coach and coax students into reading more, or rather, into reading for *pleasure* (Lamping, Mack, & Johnson, 2007). According to Atwell (2007), pleasure reading is a critical factor in high student performance on standardized tests; thus, a major predictor of academic success is the amount of time a student spends reading; her research suggests that the top 5% of U.S. students read up to 144 times more than the kids in the bottom 5%.

Middle school students' interests are impressionable in that they are wide and varied, which means that content-area teachers are in a position to recommend more and diverse reading to students. Furthermore, recommendations from teachers and friends play a huge role in the reading habits of teens (Loh, 2008; Worthy et al., 1999). It is important for teachers to conduct book pitches and book talks and to offer recommendations about excellent titles with relevance to content-area topics. Stallworth (2006) featured a 10th-grade teacher who found student-led book talks to be effective at motivating reading; this teacher would have her students share books they had read with their peers. She found that even reluctant readers wanted to share, jumping at the chance to take ownership of a book that was meaningful to them. The greater benefit of this is that students may be inspired to read *more* books. Wide reading in a content area increases literacy (Bean, 2003).

In order to increase her students' scientific literacy (Norris & Phillips, 2003) and promote independent reading, Mrs. Gill could consider employing Gambrell's (2008) "three-a-day" strategy; this can also be strategically done during the last month of the school year to promote summer reading. Such an approach introduces students to numerous options and opportunities for reading. In each session, teachers share at least three books with the same theme, each book representing different genres. For example, in order to support a unit on global warming, she could share the following books via book pitches or book trailers: *The Carbon Diaries 2015* (Lloyd, 2010), which is a science fiction novel; *The Twilight Zone: The Midnight Sun* (Serling, Kneece, & Spay, 2009), which is a graphic novel; and *An Inconvenient Truth: The Crisis of Global Warming, Adapted for a New Generation* (Gore, 2007), which is a nonfiction text. In this way Mrs. Gill is able to introduce students to current scientific ideas while supporting literacy practices in science (Ebbers, 2002). This is especially urgent for Ms. Gill because according to Worthy and colleagues (1999), most middle school students do not choose to read books that could develop their scientific literacy; they need to be exposed to such books and encouraged to read them. If the teacher shows an interest in the books, then students are more likely to take an interest.

Especially for adolescents, making reading more social can be motivating. Middle school students are social creatures; collaborative and cooperative strategies are preferred by many students, since they offer opportunities for working together and communicating about a shared or common topic (George & Stix, 2000; Kucer, 2009; Wentzel, 2005). Reading for adolescents is contextualized in that they are motivated to read in order to learn something and/or to participate in a social event; for example, adolescents will read a book, on their own, with the goal of being able to talk about it with a friend (Stairs & Stairs, 2007). For adolescents, it would seem that reading is most valuable when there is a personal or social connection involved (Smith & Wilhelm, 2002). Considering this, content-area teachers should create opportunities for students to be social readers by facilitating Socratic seminars and/or book discussion groups (Lamping et al., 2007). In literature circles (Burns, 1998; Daniels, 1994; Peterson & Belizaire, 2006), students form small groups and are assigned roles; in book clubs (Raphael, Florio-Ruane, & George, 2004; Raphael & McMahon, 1994), students participate in a variety of groupings to respond to text. Designed specifically to meet the needs of adolescent readers, strategies that promote a community of practice hold students accountable while promoting collaboration and providing a social experience (Wilfong, 2009).

Middle schoolers are very social online as well; teachers should also consider using teen literacies such as social media, promoting a 21st-century learning environment wherein learning happens outside of traditional classrooms via collaborating, questioning, and discussing. For example, Mrs. Gill could create an online discussion for her math class (Larson, 2009) using a variety of social networking sites, including Facebook. She could set up a page for her class and have students post their individual e-responses to the reading on the class wall. These are immediate and quick responses, similar to quick writes. In teaching algebra, she could use the following books: *An Abundance of Katherines* (Green, 2006), *Do the Math: Secrets, Lies, and Algebra* (Lichtman, 2007), *The Number Devil: A Mathematical Adventure* (Enzensberger, 2000), and/or *A Gebra Named Al: A Novel* (Isdell, 1993). She could also have the students read available e-books. During and after the reading, she could lead critical online discussions in the discussion forum page about how math is used in these texts, about the accuracy of the math, and about how the math can be applied to their own lives. These are more formal responses, similar to book club discussions, and they require e-facilitation. The following are some resources for e-book reading and online responding (Larson, 2009):

Free e-Books
www.getfreeebooks.com
Public library websites (library card is often required)

E-Books for Purchase
www.ebooks.com
www.fictionwise.com

Online Literature Responding

www.moodle.org
www.epals.com
www.pbwiki.com

By creating e-communities of practice, teachers could increase the conceptual understanding of standards in content areas such as algebra; in Mrs. Gill's case, students may be able to more effectively apply algebraic skills and concepts to the real world. In addition, by employing technology and creating social incentives, teachers may increase students' interest and accountability in learning in the content area.

Differentiating and Scaffolding Instruction

Middle school teachers often find it challenging to address all levels of readers. Using YAL makes it possible for teachers to effectively differentiate instruction through the use of multiple trade books. Providing middle grade students with opportunities to read multileveled texts allows teachers to match students with books at their independent reading levels, in addition to giving them a choice in book selection—practices that have been associated with gains in achievement and an increase in student motivation to read (George & Stix, 2000). By the time they reach middle school, many students spend most of their school day attempting to read texts that are far beyond their instructional levels. By providing the opportunity to read topically related books at appropriate levels, students become more engaged in what they read and more motivated to continue reading. For example, Mr. Zubrod could scaffold his unit on the Great Depression by assigning *A Jar of Dreams* (Uchida, 1993), which is at a fifth-grade reading level, to English language learners (ELLs) who have prior knowledge about being a cultural minority and who can relate to those issues; he thereby gives these students an opportunity to read comfortably at their level and to make textual connections while increasing their content knowledge about the Great Depression. By acting strategically regarding his reading assignments, Mr. Zubrod will be able to engage these students in the topic by addressing their reading levels and their knowledge bases.

A creative way Ms. Moaveni could differentiate reading levels in her English class is by allowing her students to choose from a menu of book options, followed by a "dinner party" activity (Vogt, 2000). One of the novels on her required reading list is Homer's *Odyssey*; this book selection also aligns with sixth-grade social studies standards. In order to support this text, Ms. Moaveni could offer her students choice in terms of selecting some of the following titles as reading options: *The Sea of Monsters* (Riordan,

2006), which is leveled at grade 4.7; *Time Warp Trio: It's All Greek to Me* (Scieszka, 2004), leveled at grade 4.1; *Penelopiad* (Atwood, 2005), leveled for high schoolers; *Waiting for Odysseus: A Novel* (McLaren, 2000), leveled at grade 6.2; or *The One-Eyed Giants* (Osborne, 2003), leveled at 4.6. Students, with the teacher's help, could choose a book at their reading level; they would also choose a character to represent. After reading, they would participate in a "dinner party" wherein they would role-play various characters from the stories and respond to questions as that character; because these books all convey similar content knowledge, there will be common ground for the dinner conversations. Ms. Moaveni could create a "menu" of questions for each small group (see Figure 4.1). Ms. Moaveni could also have the students come up with discussion prompts. To further scaffold, she could provide scripts, guided notes, and character sketches. Students are expected to have deeper knowledge of their character and of the historical context; they are also expected to articulate clearly and appropriately. As such, students are mastering core standards in the English language arts and the social sciences.

Bridging to School-Sanctioned Texts

Blasingame (2007) argues that using contemporary, popular adolescent novels as a bridge to the classics and/or other school-approved texts is not contrary to standards-based instruction, nor does it shortchange students

---

APPETIZERS
What happened in the beginning of the story?
How would you describe yourself? Your strengths and weaknesses?
Do you have any adversaries? Allies?
What do you think of the current state of our society?

MAIN COURSE
What happened in the middle of the story?
What is the climax?
What is the problem and/or conflict?
What are some of the obstacles you have had to endure?

DESSERT
What happened at the end of the story?
How was the problem resolved?
How have you changed?
How is our society affected by your actions?

FIGURE 4.1. "Menu" of small-group questions.

in that common themes and literary elements are evident in both canonical and contemporary texts. In fact, by using these popular books, teachers will not only meet grade-level expectations but they will also enhance students' engagement with, and understanding of, the texts. By using literature that reflects students' lives, teachers will be in a better position to introduce them to more complex material. This practice is most easily applicable to the English classroom; for example, Ms. Moaveni could use Gordan Korman's *Jake, Reinvented* (2005) as a great bridge to F. Scott Fitzgerald's *The Great Gatsby* (1925).

CONCLUSION

Content-area teachers have an awesome responsibility. Not only are they charged with teaching the subject matter of their discipline, but they are also accountable for the literacy (reading, writing, and speaking demands) in their content area; in other words, content-area teachers need to make sure that their students are able to articulate in a sophisticated manner about the discipline. Students need to be able to think, act, and behave like a practitioner: historian, scientist, humanitarian, mathematician, writer, and so on. The best way for content-area teachers to deepen understandings and promote lifelong reading habits is to go beyond the textbook and employ YAL, which tends to be more interesting, relevant, and broader in scope than school textbooks. As such, students may want to read more, thus increasing their knowledge and reading skills.

Let's revisit the three teachers mentioned in the beginning of the chapter. Imagine how much more language and content knowledge would occur, not to mention the enjoyment, if students in Mrs. Gill's science class also had the opportunity to read *The House of Scorpion* (Farmer, 2002) as part of a unit on genetics; they would be able to emotionally respond to the ethical issues of cloning. In Mr. Zubrod's history class, they could read *The Boy in the Striped Pajamas* (Boyne, 2006) as a way to dig deeper into the human issue of the Holocaust. Lastly, in Ms. Moaveni's English class, they could read *The Hunger Games* (Collins, 2008) as a bridge to *1984* (Orwell, 1949) to make better connections across time. In all three cases, adolescent novels would make the content come to life; as a result, they could be used to motivate students to read about, and to further study, the concepts. Content-area disciplines are filled with good stories; as teachers, we need to get these stories into our students' hands.

To close, consider the comment made by a student participant in Kornfield and Prothro's (2005) study, in which students were asked to assume the role of teachers and design their model history class: "In this class, we do not only teach the students the regular history as known in other schools, we also make the students think of ideas to change the world. Instead of just learning useless facts, we want them to extend their knowledge and think out of the box and into the real world" (p. 236). This model can be achieved by going beyond the textbook and incorporating YAL.

ADDITIONAL RESOURCES

Many Internet sources can be used to easily identify book titles, among them the following.

The ALAN Review
scholar.lib.vt.edu/ejournals/ALAN

Amazon.com: Teens
www.amazon.com/exec/obidos/tg/browse/-/28/103-6565692-4644611

American Library Association
www.ala.org

Book Links
www.ala.org/ala/aboutala/offices/publishing/booklinks/index.cfm

Booklist
www.booklistonline.com

Book lists for young adults on the Web
www.seemore.mi.org/booklists

Carol Hurst
www.carolhurst.com

Center for Children's Books
ccb.lis.illinois.edu

Children's literature Web guide
people.ucalgary.ca/~dkbrown

Cyberteens Connect
www.cyberteens.com/cl/books.html

Cynthia Leitich Smith
www.cynthialeitichsmith.com

Follett library resources
titlewave.com

Horn Book Magazine
www.hbook.com/magazine/default.asp

Kirkus Reviews
www.kirkusreviews.com/book-reviews/childrens-books

Rhode Island Teen Book Award Committee
www.yourlibrary.ws/ya_webpage/ritba/ritbaindex.htm

School Library Journal
www.schoollibraryjournal.com

Teachers at Random
www.randomhouse.com/teachers/index.html

Teen Reads
www.teenreads.com

Vandergrift's young adult literature
comminfo.rutgers.edu/professional-development/childlit/YoungAdult/index.html

Young Adult Library Services Association
www.ala.org/yalsa

ADDITIONAL LESSON EXAMPLES

The following lesson examples from the International Reading Association's ReadWriteThink support using adolescent novels to increase content-area learning.

Becoming History Detectives Using *Shakespeare's Secret*
www.readwritethink.org/classroom-resources/lesson-plans/becoming-history-detectives-using-1037.html

Finding the Science Behind Science Fiction through Paired Readings
www.readwritethink.org/classroom-resources/lesson-plans/finding-science-behind-science-927.html

Exploring Free Speech and Persuasion with *Nothing but the Truth*
www.readwritethink.org/classroom-resources/lesson-plans/exploring-free-speech-persuasion-394.html

Traveling the Road to Freedom through Research and Historical Fiction
www.readwritethink.org/classroom-resources/lesson-plans/traveling-road-freedom-through-864.html

Young Adult Literature about the Middle East: A Cultural Response Perspective
www.readwritethink.org/classroom-resources/lesson-plans/young-adult-literature-about-1136.html

TRADE BOOKS CITED IN TEXT

Anderson, L. H. (2010). *Chains*. New York: Atheneum.

Atwood, M. (2005). *The penelopiad*. Toronto: Knopf.

Boyne, J. (2006). *The boy in the striped pajamas*. New York: David Fickling Books.

Collins, S. (2008). *Hunger games*. New York: Scholastic Press.

Enzensberger, H. M. (2000). *The number devil: A mathematical adventure*. New York: Holt.

Farmer, N. (2002). *The house of the scorpion*. New York: Atheneum.

Fitzgerald, F. S. (1925). *The great Gatsby*. New York: Charles Scribner's Sons.

Gore, A. (2007). *An inconvenient truth: The crisis of global warming, adapted for a new generation*. New York: Viking Juvenile.

Green, J. (2006). *An abundance of Katherines*. New York: Dutton.

Hamilton, V. (2002). *Many thousand gone: African Americans from slavery to freedom*. New York: Knopf Books for Young Readers.

Isdell, W. (1993). *A gebra named Al: A novel*. New York: Free Spirit.

Korman, G. (2005). *Jake, reinvented*. New York: Hyperion.

Lester, J. (20017). *Day of tears*. New York: Hyperion.

Lichtman, W. (2007). *Do the math: Secrets, lies, and algebra*. New York: Greenwillow Books.

Lloyd, S. (2010). *The carbon diaries 2015*. New York: Holiday House.

McLaren, C. (2000). *Waiting for Odysseus: A novel*. New York: Atheneum.

Orwell, G. (1949). *1984*. New York: Plume.

Osborne, M. P. (2003). *The one-eyed giants*. New York: Hyperion.

Rinaldi, A. (2007). *Numbering all the bones*. New York: Hyperion.

Riordan, R. (2006). *The sea of monsters*. New York: Miramax Books.

Scieszka, J. (2004). *Time warp trio: It's all Greek to me*. New York: Puffin.

Serling, R., Kneece, M., & Spay, A. (2009). *The twilight zone: The midnight sun*. New York: Walker Books for Young Readers.

Uchida, Y. (1993). *A jar of dreams*. New York: Aladdin.

REFERENCES

American Association for the Advancement of Science. (2002). AAAS Project 2061—middle grades science textbooks: A benchmarks-based evaluation. Retrieved October 28, 2010, from *www.project2061.org/tools/textbook/ mgsci/mgbooks.htm.*

Atwell, N. (2007). *The reading zone.* New York: Scholastic.

Austin, R. A., Thompson, D. R., & Beckman, C. E. (2005). Mathematics teaching in the middle school. *Mathematics Teaching in the Middle School, 10*(5), 218–224.

Bean, T. W. (2000). Reading in the content areas: Social constructivist dimensions. In M. L. Kamil, P. B. Mosenthal, P. D. Pearson, & R. Barr (Eds.), *Handbook of reading research* (Vol. III, pp. 629–644). Mahwah, NJ: Erlbaum.

Bean, T. W. (2003). *Using young adult literature to enhance comprehension in the content areas.* Naperville, IL: Learning Points Associates.

Beck, I. L., & McKeown, M. G. (1991). Social studies texts are hard to understand: Mediating some of the difficulties (research directions). *Language Arts, 68*(6), 482–90.

Blasingame, J. (2007). *Books that don't bore 'em: Young adult books that speak to this generation, grades 5 and up.* New York: Scholastic.

Burns, B. (1998). Changing the classroom climate with literature circles. *Journal of Adolescent and Adult Literacy, 42*(2), 124–129.

Daniels, H. (1994). *Literature circles: Voice and choice in the student-centered classroom.* York, ME: Stenhouse.

Ebbers, M. (2002). Science text sets: Using various genres to promote literacy and inquiry. *Language Arts, 80*(1), 40–50.

Ford, D. (2005). Representations of science within children's trade books. *Journal of Research in Science Teaching, 43*(2), 214–235.

Ford, D., Brickhouse, N. W., Lottero-Perdue, P., & Kittleson, J. (2006). Elementary girls' science reading at home and school. *Science Education, 90*, 270–288.

Fradd, S. H., Lee, O., Sutman, F. X., & Saxton, M. K. (2001). Promoting science literacy with English language learners through instructional materials development: A case study. *Bilingual Research Journal, 25*, 417–439.

Gambrell, L. B. (2008). Closing the summer reading gap: You can make a difference. *Reading Today, 25*, 18.

George, M. A., & Stix, A. (2000). Using multilevel young adult literature in middle school American studies. *Social Studies, 91*, 25–31.

Guthrie, J. T., Wigfield, A., & Perencevich, K. C. (Eds.). (2004). Scaffolding for motivation and engagement in reading. In J. T. Guthrie, A. Wigfield, & K. C. Perencevich (Eds.), *Motivating reading comprehension: Concept-oriented reading instruction* (pp. 55–86). Mahwah, NJ: Erlbaum.

Harvey, S., & Goudvis, A. (2000). *Strategies that work: Teaching comprehension to enhance understanding.* New York: Stenhouse.

Hiebert, E. H. (Ed.). (2009). *Reading more, reading better.* New York: Guilford Press.

Jetton, T. L., & Alexander, P. A. (2001, July/August). Learning from text: A multidimensional and developmental perspective. *Reading Online, 5*(1). Available at *www.readingonline.org/articles/art_index.asp?HREF=/articles/handbook/jetton/index.html.*

Jones, M. G., Howe, A., & Rua, M. J. (2000). Gender differences in students' experiences, interests, and attitude toward science and scientists. *Science Education, 84,* 180–192.

Kesido, S., & Roseman, J. E. (2002). How well do middle school science programs measure up?: Findings from Project 2061's curriculum review. *Journal of Research in Science Teaching, 39,* 522–549.

Knapp, M. S. (1995). *Teaching for meaning in high-poverty classrooms.* New York: Teachers College Press.

Kornfield, J., & Prothro, L. (2005). Envisioning possibility: Schooling and student agency in children's and young adult literature. *Children's Literature in Education, 36*(3), 217–239.

Kucer, S. (2009). *Dimensions of literacy: A conceptual base for teaching reading and writing in school settings.* New York: Routledge.

Lamping, S., Mack, N., & Johnson, A. B. (2007). Promoting engagement: Young adult literature, picture books, and traditional themes for secondary students. *Ohio Journal of English Language Arts, 47*(2), 38–47.

Larson, L. C. (2009). Reader response meets new literacies: Empowering readers in online learning communities. *The Reading Teacher, 62*(8), 638–648.

Loh, V. (2006). Quantity and quality: The need for culturally authentic trade books in Asian American young adult literature. *ALAN Review, 34*(1), 36–53.

Loh, V. (2008). *Asian-American children's literature: A qualitative study of cultural authenticity.* Unpublished doctoral dissertation, San Diego State University–University of San Diego.

McGill-Franzen, A., & Botzakis, S. (2009). Series books, graphic novels, comics, and magazine. In E. H. Hiebert (Ed.), *Reading more, reading better* (pp. 101–117). New York: Guilford Press.

Miller, D. E. (1987). The reader, the text, and the social studies teacher. *Social Studies Review, 26*(1), 52–58.

Norris, S. P., Guilbert, S. M., Smith, M. L., Hakimelahi, S., & Phillips, L. M. (2005). A theoretical framework for narrative explanation in science. *Science Education, 89,* 535–556.

Norris, S. P., & Phillips, L. M. (2003). How literacy in its fundamental sense is central to scientific literacy. *Science Education, 87,* 224–240.

Palmer, R. G., & Stewart, R. A. (1997). Nonfiction trade books in content area instruction: Realities and potential. *Journal of Adolescent and Adult Literacy, 40,* 630–641.

Peterson, S., & Belizaire, M. (2006). Another look at roles in literature circles. *Middle School Journal, 37*(4), 37–43.

Purcell-Gates, V., Duke, N. K., & Martineau, J. A. (2007). Learning to read and write genre specific text: Roles of authentic experience and explicit teaching. *Reading Research Quarterly, 42*(1), 8–45.

Raphael, T. E., Florio-Ruane, S., & George, M. (2004). Book club plus: Organising your literacy curriculum to bring students to high levels of literacy. *Australian Journal of Language and Literacy, 27*(3), 198–216.

Raphael, T. E., & McMahon, S. I. (1994). Book club: An alternative framework for reading instruction. *The Reading Teacher, 48*(2), 102–116.

Salvner, G. (2001). Lessons and lives: Why young adult literature matters. *ALAN Review, 28*(3), 9–13.

Siefert, T. L., & O'Keefe, B. A. (2001). The relationship of work avoidance and learning goals to perceived competence, externality and meaning. *British Journal of Educational Psychology, 71*, 81–92.

Smith, M. W., & Wilhelm, J. D. (2002). *"Reading don't fix no Chevys": Literacy in the lives of young men.* Portsmouth, NH: Heinemann.

Stairs, A. J., & Stairs, S. A. (2007). Recommended reading for young adults from young adults. *SIGNAL Journal, 30*(2), 17–22.

Stallworth, B. J. (2006). The relevance of young adult literature: Inviting young adult books into the canon helps adolescents connect to literature and confront weighty life problems. *Educational Leadership, 63*, 59–63.

Taylor, B. M., Pearson, P. D., Peterson, D. S., & Rodriguez, M. C. (2003). Reading growth in high-poverty classrooms: The influence of teacher practices that encourage cognitive engagement in literacy learning. *Elementary School Journal, 104*, 3–28.

Vacca, R. T., Vacca, J. L., & Mraz, M. (2010). *Content area reading: Literacy and learning across the curriculum* (10th ed.). Boston: Pearson Education.

Vogt, M. (2000). Active learning: Dramatic play in the content areas. In M. McLaughlin & M. Vogt (Eds.), *Creativity and innovation in content area teaching* (pp. 73–90). Norwood, MA: Christopher Gordon.

Wallace, F. H., & Clark, K. (2008). Young adult literature in middle grades mathematics classrooms. *Journal of Content Area Reading, 7*(1), 29–53.

Wentzel, K. R. (2005). Peer relationships, motivation, and academic performance at school. In A. J. Elliot & C. S. Dweck (Eds.), *Handbook of competence and motivation* (pp. 279–296). New York: Guilford Press.

Whitin, D., & Wilde, J. (1992). *Read any good math lately?: Children's books for mathematical learning K–6.* Portsmouth, NH: Heinemann.

Wilfong, L. G. (2009). Textmasters: Bringing literature circles to textbook reading across the curriculum. *Journal of Adolescent and Adult Literacy, 53*(2), 184–171.

Worthy, J., Moorman, M., & Turner, M. (1999). What Johnny likes to read is hard to find in school. *Reading Research Quarterly, 34*(1), 12–27.

CHAPTER 5

If You Want Students to Read— Motivate Them

Joan Kindig

Key Points for This Chapter

- Motivating readers requires honoring their current reading level.
- Motivating readers requires offering choice in what they read.
- Motivating readers requires finding titles that are relevant to today's middle school students.

A BIRD'S-EYE VIEW OF CLASSROOM PRACTICE

On every desk is a copy of *A Tale of Two Cities* (Dickens, 1859/2003b) as a class of middle schoolers flood through the doorway. There's lots of chatter as the kids pour in until the bell rings and they dutifully take their seats. Engaged in talk, these social creatures are busy catching up on everything from Taylor Swift's recent concert to the latest movie they saw. When the bell rings, they settle down and their attention falls to their desks.

"What's this?" they want to know, eyeing *A Tale of Two Cities* suspiciously. "I'm glad you're interested," says Mrs. Rawlings, and she launches into the importance of the book sitting before them. The kids hear "Dickens," "the late 1800s," "French Revolution," and the word *classic*. Silence *huge reasons!*

falls over the room. Here, once again, is a book with which they have absolutely no connection, no interest in, and for many of them, no possibility of actually being able to read. Once size fits all is clearly the teacher's belief because even the weakest readers in the class are expected to read the book before them.

Let's face it, Dickens did produce some incredible books. Some, like *A Christmas Carol* (Dickens, 1843/2008), are part of our very culture. And in a perfect world, everyone would be able to read his work and see a book such as *Oliver Twist* (Dickens, 1837/2003a) for the great social commentary it is and as a snapshot of the Victorian era, warts and all. It's this desire that drives Mrs. Rawlings to give students these classic but archaic books year after year after year—that, and a mistaken belief that she is required to teach only the classics to her students. When asked if the kids liked the book, Mrs. Rawlings sighed and said sadly, "Not as much as I do."

DEFINING THE TARGETED PRACTICE

Mrs. Rawlings is teaching students with a one-size-fits-all approach with no thought to making reading relevant to them, honoring their instructional reading levels, and providing them choice in what they read. Mrs. Rawlings is not alone in her thinking that teaching the "classics" is the only option for her classroom. All of the other English teachers in her middle school are teaching the same canon, and she has mistakenly assumed that the state standards demand it. If asked, Mrs. Rawlings would admit that she knows that her students are all on different reading levels, but she clearly does not take that into account when selecting the books for them to read. This mismatch between the students' reading levels and what they are required to read in school is a common occurrence in American classrooms (Ivey, 2002). Even if Mrs. Rawlings's enthusiasm for *A Tale of Two Cities* did manage to pique their interest, most of her students could not read it. They are left with a one-size-fits-all task that, despite employing all the skills they have as readers, they cannot read. Although differentiation in the classroom is common practice in elementary classrooms, middle school teachers adhere to the "stand and deliver" model wherein teachers lecture and students listen (Lenski & Lanier, 2008). Similarly, they select books with no thought to their students' actual reading levels, and the kids are expected to read and understand them. Differentiating by reading levels represents a huge shift in the pedagogy with which middle school teachers are most comfortable (Ivey & Broaddus, 2000). Nevertheless, if their goal is to motivate students to read widely, then they must make changes in regard not only to reading level but to other motivational concerns such as relevance and choice.

WHAT DOES THE RESEARCH SAY
ABOUT MOTIVATING ADOLESCENT READERS?

The research on motivation is plentiful, and it does not support the instructional practices of the well-intentioned teacher whose class is mentioned above. It does, however, mention repeatedly the particular aspects of reading that do motivate middle schoolers to read. These are relevance, honoring instructional reading level, and providing choice in their reading.

Relevance

As mentioned above, *A Tale of Two Cities* is a wonderful book, but it is not to the liking of adolescent readers and for good reason. Many middle schoolers think ancient history is the Beatles and the civil rights movement, after all. They have always had eBay, DVDs, and since they could walk and talk, iPods. Most are not going to pick up a book written in Victorian times, with its accompanying archaic style, and relish it. The story describes the political and social climates in London and Paris that led to the American and French Revolutions and begins with this famous quote:

> It was the best of times, it was the worst of times, it was the age of wisdom, it was the age of foolishness, it was the epoch of belief, it was the epoch of incredulity, it was the season of Light, it was the season of Darkness, it was the spring of hope, it was the winter of despair, we had everything before us, we had nothing before us, we were all going direct to Heaven, we were all going direct the other way—in short, the period was so far like the present period, that some of its noisiest authorities insisted on its being received, for good or for evil, in the superlative degree of comparison only.

Not only do adolescents care little about what happened in what they consider the Dark Ages, but they would also have a great deal of trouble reading the language that Dickens uses. It is so different from their normal language that even the best readers would have to work their way through it carefully. Why they would put that kind of effort into something that is boring to them is a good question to ask. The answer is that most won't. Since the story is not relevant to their lives, they have no reason to work that hard. What about average and/or struggling readers then? They will have very little success with it, if they even bother to try.

Fisher and Ivey (2007) hit the nail on the head in their article "A Farewell to a Farewell to Arms," when they related an incident on a nighttime bus ride returning from a National Honor Society field trip: "Nearly a third of the students clustered at the back of the bus with the Cliffs Notes for *The Scarlet Letter*, not because they needed to read it by the following morning but because they had to read it and write a critical analysis of it by the following morning!" These were National Honor Society members who turned to Cliffs Notes. What were the lowest readers in that same school doing when assigned the same book? Nancie Atwell, in a video response to a *New York Times* article criticizing the issue of choice in classrooms, offered seven myths about the reading workshop approach to teaching that relies heavily on choice (Atwell, 2010). Myth #4 was that "students actually read the classics their English teachers assign." She goes on to say, "The dirty little secret of high school English is how many students fake their reading." Middle school readers are much the same. Cliffs Notes and SparksNotes are big sellers in bookstores because so many kids avoid their assigned reading—they couldn't care less about its subject matter, and/or they simply cannot read it. Keep in mind that Dickens wrote for adults, and his characters are adults dealing with adult concerns. *A Tale of Two Cities* was never intended for an adolescent audience. Teachers can continue assigning *The Scarlet Letter* and *A Tale of Two Cities*, but they should not be surprised when the books go unread. If they are going unread, what exactly is the point of the whole exercise? It is counterproductive at best.

Middle schoolers do not necessarily hate reading. Middle schoolers *do* hate being assigned books they find boring and irrelevant. Research has shown that students who found books that interested them developed an internal desire to read (Moss & Hendershot, 2002). If our goal as teachers is to motivate kids to read, then providing them with a variety of books from which to choose makes a great deal of sense. The more they are drawn to reading, the better they will become as readers and more and more books will become accessible to them. If we get kids reading and show them what awaits them in the world of books, one day they might find Dickens and enjoy and appreciate him—or not. If they don't find Dickens to their liking, the prognosis is that they will still go on to lead productive and happy lives.

Honoring Instructional Reading Level

Yudowitch, Henry, and Guthrie (2008) talk about the low self-efficacy of struggling readers when they approach text that is too hard for them. They are doubtful about their aptitude to begin with, and as they find themselves in over their heads, they disengage with the text. Even though they might actually be able to struggle through, they assume they cannot—because reading is not their long suit and they stop trying. The downward spiral starts. Negotiating the text is pivotal to their overall success in the classroom, and if they don't read the book, they cannot participate in discussions, answer questions on a test, or write anything about it that would get them a passing grade. This failure feeds future failures as the student begins to avoid all reading and disconnects from the learning that is going on in the classroom.

When children enter a sixth-grade classroom, they are issued texts that are purportedly written on a sixth-grade level. Although that is fine and dandy for those kids who are actually reading on a sixth-grade level, it sets up those students who are not proficient readers for failure. Why bother trying when you have been given reading material that you cannot read? In good conscience, how can we expect them to? It's akin to asking kids to play football without helmets, shoulder pads, or a football. *Reading level must be considered every time a book is put on a desk for a child to read.* The stark reality of schools today (and likely always) is that there are no homogeneous classes wherein all kids are reading on grade level. There are also no classes where all the kids are eager to read; readers need to be cultivated and shown that books are accessible if chosen carefully and that what is in them is worth reading.

Ivey and Fisher (2006) say that it is difficult to find a struggling reader who went on to become a competent and motivated reader who has not spent a great deal of time engaged in text. The notion that the more students read, the better they get at it is simple logic. Equally important, it should be noted, is that they must be reading on their instructional reading level. Such readers do not improve in reading unless they are reading books that they can read. If they can read the majority of the words correctly, they are fast going to become fluent readers. Fluency is defined as "the ability to read quickly, effortlessly, and efficiently with appropriate, meaningful expression or prosody" (Rasinski, 2003, p. 26). As the definition implies, fluency doesn't come when the text is too difficult and the reader is stumbling over words. Continued exposure to, and practice with, text are what make a reader fluent. Practice makes an enormous difference. If a child is avoiding reading, becoming fluent is not going to happen for him or her, so attending to the child's instructional level becomes even more crucial. Becoming fluent has the added benefit of helping the child comprehend what he or she is reading (LaBerge & Samuels, 1974). If readers have to agonize over each word they encounter, they will have little cognitive energy to devote to understanding what they read (Duke, Pressley, & Hilden, 2004). More reading equals fluency, which, in turn, makes comprehension more likely. Putting books in front of students that are motivating to them and also on their instructional reading level means putting away *A Tale of Two Cities* for some and bringing out *Diary of a Wimpy Kid* (Kinney, 2007) for most students.

Providing Choice

If students are avoiding their reading assignments because they find them irrelevant or too difficult, providing choice for them is the obvious strategy. Nancie Atwell's seminal book, *In the Middle*, was first published in 1987, and it changed how teachers taught reading in many schools across the country. Although it was intended for middle school teachers, her notion of the reading workshop filtered down to the elementary level, oddly enough, where teachers found that choice made a huge difference in getting students to read. My son had a fantastic fifth-grade year with a wonderful teacher who provided loads of books and the opportunity to choose which book to read, when. Nick was a typical 10-year-old boy who, when someone called "Baseball!", would be out the front door. Nick read over 50 books that year, and I often look back at the list he kept of the books he read and smile at what a great year he had.

 Choice is a powerful factor in motivating engagement in students (Guthrie & Humenick, 2004; Lapp & Fisher, 2009). When students are allowed to select the texts they want to read, their level of engagement is high and sustained (Allington, 2007). If choice makes for more motivated readers, they are going to read more and, as a consequence, become the fluent readers we want. Allington does specify that choice does not mean that the classroom becomes a free-for-all where kids can read absolutely anything. He refers to it as "managed choice" whereby students select from a library that has been carefully chosen by effective teachers.

Choice meets the developmental needs of adolescents to a tee. Adolescents are beginning to see themselves as being somewhat autonomous. In truth they really aren't, but as they mature they want to control things more and more. In middle school language arts classrooms, *control* is the operative word. What the kids read is entirely determined by the teacher and, in many cases, the books are irrelevant or inaccessible to the kids who are reading them. In two studies on reading motivation in high school students, it was found that students (1) rarely read anything other than the textbook for instruction, (2) seldom collaborated with other students to interpret books, and (3) only infrequently had the opportunity to choose a book on their own (Grigg, Daane, Jin, & Campbell, 2003; Levine, Rathburn, Selden, & Davis, 1998). We know that motivation for reading declines as social motivation rises (Otis, Grouzet, & Pelletier, 2005). With that knowledge in hand, we need to grab onto what is becoming all encompassing to kids at this point in their lives—their need to connect with others—and use it. Reading can be something shared with others in a variety of ways, not the least of which is providing time to talk about the books they're reading and collaborating on literacy projects. Changing the balance of power in our classrooms by allowing students to take the lead in choosing what they read gives them the sense of autonomy they desire while handily achieving literacy goals.

WHAT ARE SOME ALTERNATIVES?

Relevance

There is evidence to suggest that when students get to middle school the amount of reading they do decreases. A relatively recent National Endowment of the Arts (2007) study reports that less than one-third of 13-year-olds are daily readers. In school, the books they are asked to read are most often teacher-selected, culturally irrelevant to them, or too far above their reading levels. No wonder they aren't reading. What to do? Middle school teachers have to be willing to take a chance and move away from the "classics" with which they are so enamored and choose books that will grab the interest and attention of their students. To insist upon reading the canon means that there will be no change in the reading habits of their students. Conversely, books that are relevant to students will have a positive effect, and reading will become an activity in which they are keen to engage. More reading makes for fluent readers with stronger comprehension skills.

Where does a teacher begin who wants to offer his or her students relevant books? What books are relevant to middle school audiences? On *Barnes and Noble.com* the following middle school books were listed on their top 100 books (in no particular order):

> *The Ugly Truth* (Diary of a Wimpy Kid Series #5) by Jeff Kinney (Abrams, 2010)
> *The Lost Hero* (Heroes of Olympus Series #1) by Rick Riordan (Hyperion, 2010a)
> *The Red Pyramid* by Rick Riordan (Hyperion, 2010b)
> *Hunger Games* by Suzanne Collins (Scholastic, 2008)
> *Catching Fire* by Suzanne Collins (Scholastic, 2009)
> *Mockingjay* by Suzanne Collins (Scholastic, 2010)
> *Big Nate* by Lincoln Pierce (Harper, 2010)
> *Harry Potter and the Sorcerer's Stone* by J. K. Rowling (Scholastic, 1997)

What do these titles tell us about what is relevant to middle schoolers? The *Diary of a Wimpy Kid* series is tailor-made for the middle school crowd. It follows the trials and tribulations of a middle schooler named Greg who is the quintessential wimpy kid. Alongside the narrative are comic-like illustrations that are funny in their dorky simplicity. It resonates with kids because it mirrors exactly the ups and downs, the hits and misses, that middle schoolers deal with every day. It has the ring of truth, but it is hilarious in the telling. *The Lost Hero* and *The Red Pyramid* are two new series from the creator of the *Percy Jackson and the Olympians* series. The *Percy Jackson* series was immensely popular because Riordan brought to life the adventures of the Greek gods through his character, a middle school student named Percy Jackson. Riordan was a middle school teacher for 15 years and clearly understood what a middle school audience is looking for. The *Hunger Games* series (including *Catching Fire* and *Mockingjay*) also is as adventure-packed as they come. The three futuristic stories feature a female protagonist named Katniss in a world where teenagers from each "district" in their country must go to the Capitol for the Hunger Games. It is there that the 24 contenders fight to the death as TV viewers watch this reality TV-like fight. *Big Nate* is similar to the *Wimpy Kid* series in that it has comic-like illustrations, which are hilarious to read, and gives the reader a taste of what a graphic novel is like. Again, Nate is a middle schooler negotiating all the pitfalls he faces every day in school, at home, and socially. Middle schoolers clearly like adventure, so it is not surprising that *Harry Potter* is still atop the bestseller lists. *Harry Potter* also satisfies their longing for fantasy stories. Adventure, humor, alternative formats, fantasy, and seeing themselves in the characters make for good reading for middle school students. Knowing what appeals to them as readers makes it even clearer that Dickens is not appropriate for kids at this age and stage.

Honoring Instructional Reading Level

Not only do we want students to read habitually, we want them to do it on their independent or instructional level where all the reading gains can be made. If a book is on a children's instructional level, they will be able to read with relative ease, stopping for help only now and then from their teacher or peer, making the experience a positive one. On their independent level, they will breeze through the book effortlessly with no external help. This makes it more likely that they will pick up another book and keep the positive cycle going.

When teachers are beginning to choose books for their classrooms, they need to be aware of the reading levels of their students and the reading levels of the books they choose. A typical sixth-grade classroom has kids reading anywhere from a second-grade level up to high school and beyond. So how do you accommodate all of those reading levels? A general rule of thumb is to find books that fall into three broad categories. These books are meant to be used during daily free reading time and also in small groups to help the students utilize discussion as a comprehension tool.

In this example, the first category would address the students reading on the second- to fourth-grade levels. There are two series from Orca Book

Publishers that are written on lower levels and are thematically intended for middle school students. They are Orca Soundings and Orca Currents, and they look just like the books the other kids are reading. Graphic novels can be helpful for this group of students as well. Lapp, Fisher, Wolsey, and Frey (in press) recently found that low-performing students who are initially motivated by graphic novels often lose interest when they find the actual reading level is out of their reach. Reading level matters whether we are choosing graphic novels or a mainstream work of fiction for students. Some graphic novels will be too difficult for students reading on a second- to fourth-grade level. However, some are less challenging textually. Take, for example, *Yummy* by G. Neri (Lee & Low, 2010), which is accessible for readers on a third- to fourth-grade reading level. A series put out by Classical Comics actually offers some Shakespearean plays in graphic novel format. They offer the plays in the original text, plain text (the original script is translated into modern English), and the quick text version. In the quick text version, the story remains the same, but the readability is much easier. The *Bone* series by Jeff Smith (Scholastic, 2005) would also be in this first category, as would *The Invention of Hugo Cabret* by Brian Selznick (Scholastic, 2007). With the help of a librarian or a bookseller, you can find more graphic novels that accommodate your lower readers. Some of my lowest readers in middle school have been reading and passing around the *Lunch Lady* series by Jarrett J. Krosoczka (written on about a second-grade level; Random House, 2009). These humorous books about a cafeteria lady who is actually a super spy agent transcend the reading level in these readers' eyes.

The second category would address the fifth- and sixth-grade readers and would feature many of the books mentioned above in the relevance section. The final category would be age-appropriate books that are written for teen readers. In all categories, nonfiction should be represented. It is nonfiction that gives a teacher a little wiggle room. The extraordinary nonfiction that is being published today suits low readers with the gorgeous photography offered and the captions that go along with it. Stronger readers like those features too, and they can access the text as well. A great example of nonfiction for this age group is *Phineas Gage: A Gruesome but True Story about Brain Science* by John Fleischman (Houghton Mifflin, 2002) tells the story of Gage who, in 1848, experienced a horrific accident in which a 13-pound iron rod went through his head. Gage lived to tell about it despite the threat of infection and hemorrhaging. What did occur, though, was damage to the frontal lobe, and his personality changed forever. *Dr. Jenner and the Speckled Monster: The Search for the Smallpox Vaccine* by Albert Marrin (Penguin, 2002) is another one that kids gravitate toward. The book chronicles the identification of the source of smallpox. Found only in cows up until that time, it was the milkmaids who led Dr.

Jenner to the vaccine. A recent book, *They Called Themselves the KKK: The Birth of an American Terrorist Group* by Susan Campbell Bartoletti (Houghton Mifflin Harcourt, 2010) offers the history of a hate group that still exists today in our nation. A sure-fire hit with middle school students is Jon Scieszka's autobiography, *Knucklehead: Tall Tales and Almost True Stories of Growing Up Scieszka* (Viking, 2008). Filled with one hilarious story after another from his childhood, this slightly irreverent autobiography makes teen boys see that there are books out there that they really do want to read.

The third category are your readers who can read anything they care to read. They are not restricted by their reading level; in fact, their reading is at an adult level. Finding books for them can be a challenge, but the challenge is in the appropriateness of the theme rather than the reading level.

Providing Choice

I have been consulting in a middle school in a rural area of Virginia for the past year, assisting the teachers in moving away from anthologies as their only resource for instruction to a readers workshop model. It started with one teacher who read *The Book Whisperer: Awakening the Inner Reader in Every Child* by Donalyn Miller (Wiley, 2009) and felt that she had hit on a way that she could better engage her kids in reading. Her students' reading scores had not been increasing, and she knew that the books she was asking them to read were not grabbing them in the slightest. What if she gave them books they actually *wanted* to read? She went on to read everything she could find on the readers workshop approach and became more and more excited about trying it out. Her enthusiasm spread and, before long, the rest of the language arts faculty was on board. With the support of the principal, language arts instruction changed dramatically over the year. Classrooms were stocked with as many books as the budget would allow, on a variety of reading levels, and kids were allowed to choose what they wanted to read. The teachers are following the state guidelines in terms of the genres they need to address, and they are incorporating mini-lessons for those pieces of the English curriculum that also need attention (e.g., grammar, punctuation, vocabulary, word study). Each teacher was given *Teaching Reading in Middle School* (Robb, 2010) to have concrete examples of how to implement the reading workshop approach in his or her classroom. Choice has made all the difference. Kids are reading daily in class and at the before-school program (which they never did before), and they are talking to each other about the books they are reading. They are reading widely across genres and are actively engaged in the books they choose.

The teachers at this middle school shifted to providing choice by learning as much as they could about how choice makes a difference in the amount of reading students do. They invited in a book person who could suggest titles that were tried and true with young adults. They began reading the books themselves and found that they really liked what they were reading. They "book-talked" the books they liked with their students, and the students responded to their enthusiasm.

For those teachers who still want to cover the themes that arise in the "classics," there are teen books with those very themes. Some are obvious in their titles, such as *Hamlet* by John Marsden (Candlewick, 2009); *Ophelia* (Bloomsbury, 2006) and *Lady Macbeth's Daughter* (Bloomsbury, 2009) by Lisa Klein; *The Third Witch* by Rebecca Reisert (Washington Square, 2002); and *Saving Juliet* by Suzanne Selfors (Walker, 2008). Others, like the 2010 Printz Award winner, *Going Bovine* by Libba Bray (Delacorte, 2009), are less obvious. *Going Bovine* is a quest fantasy based on the Don Quixote story. Similarly, National Book Award finalist, *The Story of a Girl* by Sara Zarr (Little, Brown, 2007), addresses the same themes found in *A Scarlet Letter*, but it is contemporary realistic fiction—one of the genres that middle schoolers like best. The protagonist has a sexual experience as a young teen and ever since then has had a reputation in school as being "easy." Deanna never repeated that mistake, but the reputation lingers throughout her high school years. Like Hester Prynne, she is persecuted by her peers and has to find a way to redeem herself and move beyond the past. Given the similar themes of these two books and the fact that the language mirrors middle schoolers' own, this book can be a wonderful alternative to Hawthorne's novel. In a choice classroom, some students will opt for these books and won't even know that they are reading a story based on a Shakespearean play unless you tell them.

Some tips for becoming a young adult literature expert are included below to provide a sense of what it takes to become well versed in the books you will be using. It also will offer comfort that, like in any other field, it takes time to become an expert.

How to Become a Young Adult Literature Expert in 14 Easy Steps

1. Read! Read! Read!
2. One of the most reliable sources for recommendations is your librarian. Introduce yourself to the local librarian and befriend your school librarian. Ask them to recommend some children's books that would be of interest to the students whom you teach.
3. Find out what the kids themselves are reading. *Harry Potter and the Sorcerer's Stone* didn't become a bestseller because teachers recommended it. *Kids* discovered it, fell in love with it, and they told their friends about it.
4. Visit bookstores and browse the children's and young adult

departments. Ask a knowledgeable bookseller for some books that he or she feels you shouldn't miss (this is more productive in an independent bookstore). Remember, it's not always the ones being displayed up front.

5. Talk to your librarian and ask him or her to book-talk five or six books once a month at a faculty meeting. In a few short book talks, your librarian can identify a great poetry book, a great non-fiction book, a great chapter book, a great transitional chapter book, a great beginning reader, and a great picture book. You will find that it will pique faculty interest in books, and it will send a strong message that the faculty cares enough about literacy to encourage such sharing in faculty meetings. Not to mention that it will likely be the highlight of the faculty meeting!

6. Notice where the "Best of" lists in journals are published and when. For instance, *School Library Journal* has a best-of-the-year list in their December issue. *The Reading Teacher* features their "Children's Choices" list in October. The *Bulletin for the Center of Children's Books* (*bccb.lis.illinois.edu*) showcases their Bulletin Blue Ribbons list in the January issue. Your librarian should be able to let you know when each of these appear and, perhaps, would be willing to photocopy a copy of each and put them in your mailbox.

7. Use the Internet to browse at different sites for book recommendations. Some suggestions are the websites for Capitol Choices, American Library Association, State Award sites, the International Reading Association, and Guys Read. Their URLs are listed in the Websites sections at the end of this chapter.

8. Seek out your state reading association's list. Plan on using it in your classroom and, if possible, schoolwide. These lists are generally put together to turn kids on to books they might have otherwise missed. The selections tend to be ones that students enjoy and might motivate them to read more and more. A website that contains links to all of the state awards can be found at Cynthia Leitich-Smith's website in the Websites section.

9. Ask your librarian to create a book cart of young adult titles that he or she thinks would be worthwhile summer reading for your faculty. An honor system checkout is all that is needed—and you have some great books to read at the pool all summer. The added benefit is that the school already owns these books, so you can recommend them to students knowing that they will be readily available to them.

10. Take advantage of the book clubs and book fairs from Scholastic and local national and independent booksellers. The book clubs

are a great source for inexpensive books for your classroom. Check with your librarian for the strong titles and stock up.

11. Go to regional, state, and national conferences where authors are featured. Bring your signed books back to share with your students and tell them what you learned about the author. This brings the authors alive to them and makes them want to read that author's work.

12. Check out the American Library Association's website, which features complete lists of Newbery, Caldecott, Coretta Scott King, and Printz awards, among others. Do keep in mind, however, that some of the Newbery titles can be a bit dated. Remember, in 1952 *Secret of the Andes* by Ann Nolan Clark won the Newbery. While certainly a strong book, it is the Honor book we all remember from that year: *Charlotte's Web* by E. B. White.

13. Start a young adult book discussion group in your school for faculty or parents. Reading a book a month as a faculty is a wonderful way to commit yourself to reading. The discussion that follows will help you to decide whether this book is one that you would want to use with your students. Furthermore, it sharpens your discussion skills as well as book selection skills. Parents are often eager to be part of their child's schooling, and reading good books together is a positive way to make the home–school connection.

14. Linda Sue Park, author of the 2002 Newbery Award winner *A Single Shard*, said in her Newbery acceptance speech that her father regularly took her and her siblings to the library when she was a child. A Korean immigrant and unable to speak English very well, he made it his business to find out what American children were reading so that his children might have the same advantages. Years later, she asked him where he had gotten his ideas, and he showed her an accordion file of book lists he had clipped from newspapers or found in libraries so that he had ideas at the ready. In the days of the Internet, lists such as these are at your fingertips. In Park's case, those lists helped form a Newbery Award winner. What can it do for your students?

CONCLUSION

Our educational system is seemingly set up to throw hurdles in the way of students becoming successful readers. By forcing a one-size-fits-all paradigm in the classroom via the textbooks provided, many students are unable to participate in their own learning. These students, unable to read the texts, find themselves doubting their own abilities as learners—which becomes a self-fulfilling prophecy. The chances of their ever becoming strong readers is slim while this paradigm is in place. We have the chance to make it right and get all students reading on their instructional level by choosing books that are relevant to them, making sure that the books are written on their instructional level, and by providing a wide array of titles from which students can choose. With these provisos, every child has the chance to participate fully in his or her learning and to grow as a reader and learner. Reading widely in self-selected books can potentially turn the most reluctant readers into avid readers over time. All we have to do is motivate them.

ADDITIONAL RESOURCES

Books

Beers, K., Probst, R. E., & Reif, L. (Eds.). (2007). *Adolescent literacy: Turning promise into practice*. Portsmouth, NH: Heinemann.

Guthrie, J. T. (Ed.). (2008). *Engaging adolescents in reading*. Thousand Oaks, CA: Corwin Press.

Krashen, S. (1993). *The power of reading: Insights from the research*. Englewood, CO: Libraries Unlimited.

Lapp, D., Fisher, D., Wolsey, T. D., & Frey, N. (2011). *Graphic novels: What teachers think about their instructional value*. Manuscript under review.

Lenski, S., & Lewis, J. (Ed.). (2008). *Reading success for struggling adolescent learners*. New York: Guilford Press.

Lesesne, T. (2003). *Making the match: The right book for the right reader at the right time, grades 4–12*. Portland, ME: Stenhouse.

Lesesne, T. (2006). *Naked reading: Uncovering what tweens need to become lifelong readers*. Portland, ME: Stenhouse.

Miller, D. (2009). *The book whisperer: Awakening the inner reader in every child*. San Francisco: Wiley.

Robb, L. (2010). *Teaching reading in the middle school (2nd ed.): A strategic approach to teaching reading that improves comprehension and thinking*. New York: Scholastic.

Websites

American Library Association
www.ala.org

Capitol Choices
www.capitolchoices.org

Children's Literature Web Guide
www.acs.ucalgary.ca/~dkbrown/index.html

Cynthia Leitich-Smith (state awards information)
www.cynthialeitichsmith.com

Guys Read
www.guysread.com

International Reading Association
www.reading.org

National Book Awards
www.nationalbook.org

New York Public Library Best Books for Children
kids.nypl.org/reading/recommended.cfm

Orca Book Publishers
www.orcabook.com

Printz Award winners
www.ala.org/ala/mgrps/divs/yalsa/booklistsawards/printzaward/Printz.cfm

TRADE BOOKS CITED IN TEXT

Bartoletti, S. C. (2010). *They called themselves the KKK: The birth of an American terrorist group.* New York: Houghton Mifflin.

Bray, L. (2009). *Going bovine.* New York: Delacorte Press.

Clark, A. N. (1952). *Secret of the Andes.* New York: Viking.

Collins, S. (2008). *Hunger games.* New York: Scholastic.

Collins, S. (2009). *Catching fire.* New York: Scholastic.

Collins, S. (2010). *Mockingjay.* New York: Scholastic.

Dickens, C. (2003a). *Oliver Twist.* New York: Penguin Books. (Original work published 1837)

Dickens, C. (2003b). *A tale of two cities.* New York: Penguin Books. (Original work published 1859)

Dickens, C. (2008). *A Christmas carol.* New York: Penguin Books. (Original work published 1843)

Fleischman, J. (2002). *Phineas Gage: A gruesome but true story about brain science.* New York: Houghton Mifflin Harcourt.

Hawthorne, N. (1981). *The scarlet letter.* New York: Random House.

Kinney, J. (2007). *Diary of a wimpy kid.* New York: Abrams.

Kinney, J. (2010). *The ugly truth.* New York: Abrams.

Klein, L. (2009). *Lady Macbeth's daughter.* New York: Bloomsbury.

Klein, L. (2006). *Ophelia.* New York: Bloomsbury.

Krosoczka, J. J. (2009). *Lunch lady* series. New York: Random House.
Marrin, A. (2002). *Dr. Jenner and the speckled monster: The search for the small-pox vaccine.* New York: Penguin.
Marsden, J. (2009). *Hamlet.* Boston: Candlewick Press.
Neri, G. (2010). *Yummy.* New York: Lee & Low.
Park, L. S. (2001). *A single shard.* New York: Clarion Books.
Pierce, L. (2010). *Big Nate.* New York: Harper.
Reisert, R. (2002). *The third witch.* New York: Washington Square Press.
Riordan, R. (2005). *The lightning thief.* New York: Disney/Hyperion Books for Children.
Riordan, R. (2010a). *The lost hero.* New York: Disney/Hyperion Books for Children.
Riordan, R. (2010b). *The red pyramid.* New York: Disney/Hyperion Books for Children.
Rowling, J. K. (1997). *Harry Potter and the sorcerer's stone.* New York: Scholastic.
Scieszka, J. (2008). *Knucklehead: Tall tales and almost true stories of growing up Scieszka.* New York: Viking.
Selfors, S. (2008). *Saving Juliet.* New York: Walker Books.
Selznick, B. (2007). *The invention of Hugo Cabret.* New York: Scholastic.
Smith, J. (2005). *Bone* series. New York: Scholastic.
White, E. B. (1952). *Charlotte's web.* New York: HarperCollins.
Zarr, S. (2007). *The story of a girl.* New York: Little, Brown.

REFERENCES

Allington, R. L. (2007). Effective teachers, effective instruction. In K. Beers, R. E. Probst, & L. Reif (Eds.), *Adolescent literacy: Turning promise into practice* (pp. 273–288). Portsmouth, NH: Heinemann.
Atwell, N. (1998). *In the middle: New understanding about writing, reading, and learning.* Portsmouth, NH: Heinemann.
Atwell, N. (2010). Response to the *NY Times* article on the place of student choice in reading. Available at *www.heinemann.com.*
Duke, N. K., Pressley, M., & Hilden, K. (2004). Difficulties with reading comprehension. In C. A. Stone, E. R. Silliman, B. J. Ehren, & K. Apel (Eds.), *Handbook of language and literacy: Development and disorders* (pp. 501-520). New York: Guilford Press.
Fisher, D., & Ivey, G. (2007). Farewell to *a farewell to arms*: Deemphasizing the whole-class novel. *Phi Delta Kappan, 88,* 494–497.
Grigg, W. S., Daane, M. C., Jin, Y., & Campbell, J. R. (2003). *The nation's report card: Reading 2002* (Publication No. NCES 2003-521). Washington, DC: U.S. Government Printing Office.
Guthrie, J. T., & Humenick, N. M. (2004). Motivating students to read: Evidence for classroom practices that increase motivation and achievement. In P. McCardle & V. Chhabra (Eds.), *The voice of evidence in reading research* (pp. 329–324). Baltimore: Paul Brookes.

Ivey, G. (2002). Getting started: Manageable literacy practices. *Educational Leadership, 60*(3), 20–23.

Ivey, G., & Broaddus, K. (2000). Tailoring the fit: Reading instruction and middle school readers. *Reading Teacher, 54*(1), 68–78.

Ivey, G., & Fisher, D. (2006). *Creating literacy-rich schools for adolescents.* Alexandria, VA: Association for Supervision and Curriculum Development.

LaBerge, D., & Samuels, S. A. (1974). Toward a theory of automatic information processing in reading. *Cognitive Psychology, 6,* 293–323.

Lapp, D., & Fisher, D. (2009). It's all about the book: Motivating teens to read. *Journal of Adolescent and Adult Literacy, 52*(7), 556–561.

Lenski, S., & Lanier, E. (2008). Making time for independent reading. In S. Lenski & E. Lanier (Eds.), *Reading success for struggling adolescent readers* (pp. 133–152). New York: Guilford Press.

Levine, R., Rathburn, A., Selden, R., & Davis, A. (1998). *NAEP's constituents: What do they want?* Report of the National Assessment of Educational Progress constituents' survey and focus groups (Publication No. NCES 98521). Washington, DC: U.S. Government Printing Office.

Miller, D. (2009). *The book whisperer: Awakening the inner reader in every child.* San Francisco: Jossey-Bass.

Moss, B., & Hendershot, J. (2002). Exploring sixth graders' selection of non-fiction trade books. *The Reading Teacher, 56,* 6–17.

National Endowment of the Arts. (2007). To read or not to read: A question of national consequence (Research Report #47). Retrieved from *www.nea.gov/research/toread.pdf.*

Otis, N., Grouzet, F. M., & Pelletier, L. G. (2005). Latent motivational change in an academic setting: A 3-year longitudinal study. *Journal of Educational Psychology, 97,* 170–183.

Rasinski, T. V. (2003). *The fluent reader: Oral reading strategies for building word recognition, fluency, and comprehension.* New York: Scholastic.

Rich, M. (2010, August 30). A new assignment: Pick books you like. *New York Times,* p. A1.

Robb, L. (2010). *Teaching reading in middle school: A strategic approach to teaching reading that improves comprehension and thinking* (2nd ed.). New York: Scholastic.

Yudowitch, S., Henry, L. M., & Guthrie, J. T. (2008). Self-efficacy: Building confident readers. In J. T. Guthrie (Ed.), *Engaging adolescents in reading* (pp. 65–82). Thousand Oaks, CA: Corwin Press.

CHAPTER 6

If You Want Students to Use New Literacies— Give Them the Opportunity

Stephanie Schmier
Marjorie Siegel

Key Points for This Chapter

- Using computers to complete school reading and writing assignments does not necessarily give students opportunities to experience new literacies.
- *New literacies* means using digital technologies to design multimodal texts that invite the collaboration and participation of audiences beyond the classroom.
- Digital tools for creating podcasts, designing comics, and engaging in online conversations about media provide opportunities for students to use new literacies.

A BIRD'S-EYE VIEW OF CLASSROOM PRACTICE

Room 210 at East Side Middle School is the type of computer lab that is common in many middle schools, where teachers reserve 45-minute blocks of time for their students to use the computers to support a classroom project. Mr. Stern, an eighth-grade English teacher at the school, brings his class into the lab to write responses to the literature they have been reading—a practice designed to prepare them for the district's periodic assessment they must complete each quarter. He leads his class through the writing process in the lab, having them use Inspiration[1] software as a tool for prewriting to organize their thoughts into an outline they can use to guide their writing. Students then type their essays using a word-processing program, which they appreciate, especially because the software allows them to revise their pieces much more quickly after they receive feedback from Mr. Stern. Their final essays are printed out and handed in for Mr. Stern to read and evaluate.

Next door to the computer lab that Mr. Stern uses is Mr. Cardenas's classroom, where he teaches a journalism and digital media studies class during sixth period. Mr. Cardenas's digital media studies students use many of the same tools (e.g., Inspiration software, a word-processing program) as Mr. Stern's class when writing copy for their online school newspaper. However, unlike in Mr. Stern's class, the assignment does not end with a written piece turned in to the teacher. This difference is largely due to the fact that Mr. Cardenas's class is an elective and is therefore not focused on the district assessments that anchor the curriculum in students' core content classes. As a result of the curricular freedom Mr. Cardenas has in designing his elective class, he is able to extend the writing assignment into a podcast project in which students design a downloadable audio or video version of their newspaper articles. This process requires students to consider the differences in audience and mode that written, audio, and video formats offer and to adapt their pieces accordingly. For example, one student, Marie, transformed her written profile of a new teacher through a process that included editing her recorded interview, writing and recording an introduction and conclusion, and adding music. Another student, Vincent, developed and produced a video podcast review of the Wii video game system that incorporated anime images from video games and fast-paced background music with a narrated argument to convince his student audience that the gaming system was worth buying, despite its high price tag. The podcasts are published as part of the online school newspaper, which provides a forum for members of the school community, including students, teachers, and parents, to comment and provide feedback to the designers. As a result, these expanded, downloadable versions of the students' original newspaper articles allow their writing to achieve a "digital afterlife" (Soep, 2010) beyond the classroom, and even beyond the online newspaper.

---

[1] Inspiration (*www.inspiration.com*) is a software program that allows students to visualize their thinking by creating concept webs that can be quickly converted to outlines for writing.

DEFINING THE TARGETED PRACTICE

As the descriptions of the two classrooms above illustrate, teachers at East Side Middle School use technology with their students in a variety of ways. Although Mr. Stern does make use of the technology tools in the computer lab in ways that support student writing, the process of outlining, drafting, revising based on teacher feedback, and printing a final copy for the teacher to evaluate represents a traditional form of literacy and not the *new literacies* that characterize learning in Mr. Cardenas's class. Specifically, Mr. Cardenas's students have the opportunity to use digital technologies to design multimodal texts that are highly collaborative and participatory, engaging readers beyond the classroom to comment and contribute to each of their pieces (Lankshear & Knobel, 2006). In this chapter, we share ways in which teachers can give their students opportunities to use new literacies, using the tools they have available in their classrooms.

WHAT DOES THE RESEARCH SAY ABOUT NEW LITERACIES?

We are living in a time of extraordinary social, economic, and technological change, and nowhere is this change more apparent than in daily communication. On any given day, we might check e-mail, send a text from our phones, participate in an online conversation, listen to a podcast while on the go, watch and rate the latest viral video on YouTube, play video games with a guild of players, collaborate with colleagues on a wiki, read and comment on a favorite blog, and so on. As this list suggests, the rise of the Internet has produced a shift "from page to screen" (Snyder, 1998) that has led to new forms of communication that challenge our long-held ideas about literacy. In the not-so-distant past, literacy was defined as reading, writing, listening, and speaking about print-based texts, but today literacy includes interpreting and designing multimodal texts with moving images, sounds, and hyperlinks working together to convey complex meanings (Kress, 2003). Beyond new texts, cultural media theorist Henry Jenkins (2009) identifies collaboration as a defining characteristic of new literacies. According to Jenkins, "new literacies almost all involve collaboration and networking" (p. 29). From this perspective, students need to have opportunities to collaborate when designing texts as well as spaces to share and receive feedback both within and beyond the classroom.

The term *new literacies* is often used in reference to the new forms of texts and practices made possible through digital technologies such as online social networking (e.g., Facebook, Twitter), text messaging, and blogging. However, as the earlier example of Mr. Stern's classroom illustrates, simply using computers and cell phones to create texts does not mean that one is using new literacies (Leu, Kinzer, Coiro, & Cammack, 2004). However, these new technologies are an essential component to new literacies, as they enable students to design new types of texts in ways that, in the past, required expensive equipment and extensive time (Lankshear & Knobel, 2007b). It is now possible, for example, to capture video on a mobile phone and edit it quickly and easily using software that is either inexpensive or sometimes even free.

Lankshear and Knobel (2007a) define new literacies as requiring both new "technical stuff" (p. 7) and new "ethos stuff" (p. 9). As mentioned above, new *technical stuff* means the availability of simple techniques—such as keying, clicking, cropping, and dragging—that make it easy to create a variety of digital texts. The phrase *new ethos* points to a number of significant changes in our globalized and networked world, including the shift from an individualistic to a distributed view of intelligence, expertise, authority, and knowledge, as well as a shift from two-way to networked communication. The rise of Wikipedia and We Media (Bowman & Willis, 2003) can capture the new ethos that distinguishes the first generation of Internet use (Web 1.0) from the second (Web 2.0). Web 1.0 was heralded as the information highway to which users had easy access, like an electronic encyclopedia or newspaper. Visiting the Encyclopedia Britannica or CNN websites offered people a storehouse of information but no opportunity to comment on or contribute to the information—as if they were using a telephone that limited them to listening, not speaking (Rushkoff, 2011). Web 2.0 changed that, providing users with a portal to participation in making knowledge and paving the way for collective intelligence and authority as citizen journalists or Wikipedia contributors.

Leu and colleagues (2007) identify four components that are essential to a new literacies perspective. First, new skills, strategies, and dispositions are required in order to effectively leverage the potential of the Internet and new mobile technologies. For example, students need strategies for evaluating information on the Internet, as the author and source of content online is not as readily apparent as in printed texts. Second, new literacies are deictic, ever changing as new technologies emerge. Third, new literacies are central to providing students with opportunities to fully engage as citizens in our increasingly globalized workplaces and social spaces. The New London Group's (1996) concept of "multiliteracies pedagogy" addresses ways in which students can learn to become active participants in our culturally, linguistically, and technologically diverse communities. Specifically, multiliteracies pedagogy encourages teachers to incorporate the unique cultural practices and "funds of knowledge" (Moll, Amanti, Neff, & Gonzalez, 1992) their students bring to school into the learning process, while at the same time building students' abilities to communicate effectively with others from diverse backgrounds across multiple contexts in their lives. Finally, new literacies are multiple, multimodal, and multifaceted. As the New London Group articulated, multiliterate students can consume and design texts in multiple modes (e.g., able to read and design images, video, hyperlinked texts), for multiple purposes, and to communicate with diverse cultural and linguistic audiences.

For today's middle school students, the new literacies landscape is "no big deal," having grown up as " 'digital natives' . . . 'native speakers' of the digital language of computers, video games and the Internet" (Prensky, 2001, p. 1). As a result, technology has become such an ordinary part of their everyday lives that, to them, it is nearly invisible (Lewis & Fabbos, 2005). Young people are less likely to describe their engagement with digital media as "using technology" than as "hanging out, messing around, and geeking out" (Ito et al., 2008, pp. 1–2). In a 3-year ethnographic study of youth across multiple sites, researchers in the MacArthur Foundation's Digital Youth Project (Ito et al., 2008) documented the ways young people engage with digital media to learn, play, socialize, and participate in civic life. They found that youth use online networks to extend their friendships (e.g., using instant messaging; Lewis & Fabbos, 2005) and interests (e.g., writing online fan fiction; Thomas, 2007), and in both contexts peers engaged in self-directed, peer-based learning (Ito et al., 2008). Finally, in a recent review of research on youth participation in the new literacies across a range of contexts, Mills (2010) called attention to three commonalities of new literacies: They (1) blend and combine literacy practices to create new texts not anticipated by those who designed the digital technologies; (2) produce, not just consume, new media; and (3) allow collaboration among members of online communities (pp. 256–267).

Taken together, research on new literacies has shown that a new ethos as well as new technologies has become an integral part of our social, economic, and civic lives. The question educators must consider is whether the kind of literacy education students encounter in schools today is adequate preparation for their participation in designing new social futures we cannot yet imagine (New London Group, 1996). Many literacy education researchers believe that this question has already been answered; they propose that school literacy be redesigned so that students can develop the broad repertoire of literacy skills and knowledge they will need to successfully participate as citizens of local and global communities that are characterized by constant change and increasing diversity (Anstey & Bull, 2006). Adopting a new literacies perspective can assist literacy educators in considering how best to prepare their students to navigate our emerging literacy landscape.

Yet, for teachers who did not grow up with digital media, technology can challenge their sense of expertise as well as their ideas about what literacy means and how to teach it. The literature on new literacies conveys an urgency to redesign school literacy for the 21st century that is not observed in classroom practice (Rowsell & Casey, 2009; Stolle, 2008; Tierney, 2009). Why is it, then, that literacy seems to be changing everywhere but in schools? We need only to consider the current policy climate—which puts intense pressure on teachers and students to produce high achievement on high-stakes tests—to understand why teachers' supposed lack of "tech-savviness" cannot be the reason there is little space for new literacies in school.

WHAT ARE SOME ALTERNATIVES?

There are many ways in which teachers we have observed have incorporated a new literacies perspective into their literacy instruction. In what follows we share some examples that teachers can try out in their own classrooms. First, we describe how Mr. Cardenas extended a writing assignment into a multimodal and interactive podcasting project. Next, we explore how teachers have used VoiceThread, a social media tool that allows students to take up multiple identities to participate in a conversation about texts of various kinds (images, videos, diagrams, presentations) by commenting through different media, including phone, webcam, microphone, written text, and file upload. Last, we examine the way a fifth-grade teacher, Ms. Aaron, stretched the meaning of literacy in her classroom by inviting students to design comics as part of writer's workshop.

Podcasting

Podcasts have been described as "homebrewed radio shows" (Newitz, 2005) that combine the ethos of blogging with the portability of mobile technologies. Specifically, a podcast is a downloadable audio or video file recorded as a broadcast that can be accessed from any personal computer (PC) or MP3 player. Podcasts are powerful because they allow for those outside of mainstream media to broadcast their viewpoints to a global audience.

Creating a podcast requires students to engage with all of the components of the new literacies perspective described above. First, creating a podcast requires students to learn new skills and strategies. That is, students need to learn how to use the software to create and distribute the podcast as well as the genre. Next, podcasts address the deictic nature of a new literacies perspective because students can incorporate new technologies as they emerge into subsequent episodes of their podcasts. Podcasts also provide students with unique opportunities to participate as global citizens because they can design broadcasts addressing issues important in their local and global communities, to be shared with audiences far and wide, as the example that follows illustrates. Furthermore, the platform is multimodal and multifaceted, allowing students to integrate spoken language, music, still images, and video to convey their messages in complex ways. Finally, podcasts provide for the types of collaboration and networking that Jenkins (2009) articulated, as audience members can subscribe to podcasts and leave feedback in the form of written comments. In this way, podcasting allows students to engage a broad audience in conversation around topics that are of particular interest in their lives.

Creating podcasts in the classroom does not require the purchase of any expensive equipment or software. Some of the most popular software programs used to create podcasts are inexpensive or even come free with many computers and include iMovie and GarageBand for Macintosh computers and Windows Movie Maker for PCs. These software applications are designed to provide users with the ability to create "professional-looking" audio and video podcasts in a simple and user-friendly way. Furthermore, students can use the built-in computer microphones and gather images from the Internet, as described in the following example.

Mr. Cardenas, who was introduced at the beginning of this chapter, invites his eighth-grade students to design video podcasts as part of the school's online newspaper. To do so, students engage in the following activities. First, students research their chosen topic. This includes interviewing school and community members, visiting locations around the community, and conducting Internet research. They also gather images from the Web and are encouraged to take pictures in the community when relevant to their topic. Students document the information they gather in their writer's notebooks and save the images to folders on the classroom computers. Furthermore, as they conduct their research, students are taught to evaluate the information they gather from the Web by considering (1) the source of the content, (2) the purpose of the site, and (3) the authenticity of the information gathered.

After they have finished conducting their initial research, students are taught to use the timeline feature of the software to sequence the images they have saved (see Figure 6.1). They simultaneously use a word-processing program (or their writer's notebooks, if they choose) to write the narration for their podcasts. After completing the scripts, students record their narratives by speaking into the built-in computer microphone.

After students record their podcasts and sequence their images, they go into "postproduction." Mr. Cardenas regularly has his students view different video texts and note how music, sound effects, title slides, and transitions are used to tell the story. Thus, after recording their narratives, students add text, title slides, transitions, and music to their own pieces. Finally, students work in pairs or groups to view each others' podcasts and

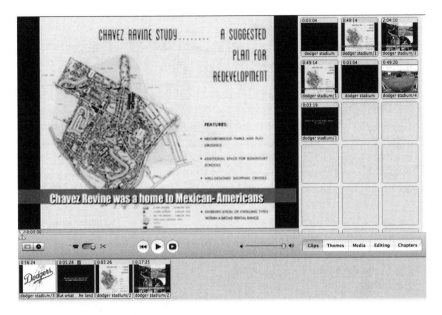

FIGURE 6.1. Using the timeline feature of iMovie.

provide critical feedback. After receiving feedback, students utilize the software, which allows for the easy manipulation of images and rerecording of narratives, in order to redesign their texts by incorporating the feedback they received from their classmates and teacher.

Through this process all students learn how to successfully design podcasts. If they choose, they also have the opportunity to upload their podcast to the Web, where they can track the number of times their podcast is viewed as well as interact with their audience, most of whom are from their school community, through written comments. Figure 6.2 shows an excerpt from the video podcast created by Vincent, which we described in the introduction to this chapter. Vincent had interviewed several students at the school who were interested in learning more about all of the new video gaming systems that were being released at the time. By engaging in the activities described above, Vincent, who was learning English as an additional language, created a podcast that met the specific needs of his audience, as the example below illustrates. He signs off at the end of the podcast, "That's it for today's video game podcast. See you next time." In so doing, Vincent lets his audience know that he is committed to providing them with the latest information on video gaming in an easily accessible format.

Hello people this is Vincent from the East Side Middle School Tribune. Today I will Be talking about the Nintendo Wii. Let's begin

The Nintendo Wii is a new kind of system that uses a sensor bar which makes you get out of your seat and move around with your controller.

You can use the Wii shop channel to buy old video games from systems like Nintendo 64 so you could play them on the Wii.

If you don't know whether to get the Xbox 360, the PS3, or the Nintendo Wii I would recommend you to get the Nintendo Wii because it's a lot cheaper. Also its unique control system makes it a lot easier to use and it's fun for the whole family.

FIGURE 6.2. Vincent's video game podcast Wii episode.

VoiceThread

VoiceThread is a free digital tool that allows students to have conversations around media, in essence, inviting them to experience the new ethos of the new literacies perspective across the curriculum. Participation, distributed intelligence and expertise, and collaboration are all possible using the affordances of this digital tool. Teachers have experimented with several different ways to design VoiceThread experiences that keep one eye on the curriculum and an ear to the new ethos they hope to support. The first option, designed to generate discussion among the participants, often involves juxtaposing two texts so as to promote critical, generative readings and reflections. The artifact (e.g., text, video, presentation) to be discussed is selected, digitized, and uploaded to VoiceThread. Students, who must register in order to comment on the artifact, may then either phone, write, audiotape, videotape, or upload their contribution. An intriguing feature of VoiceThread is the opportunity for participants to register more than one identity, which makes it possible for students to participate using different identities as well as to switch between them. One teacher tried out VoiceThread as part of a study of character archetypes, juxtaposing images of Miss Piggy the Muppet with Narcissus. Students typed or used audio recording to comment on how they thought Miss Piggy and Narcissus were alike and different (see Figure 6.3).

Another teacher posted two paintings of the "first" Thanksgiving and found that her students' observations and questions offered a productive starting point for their inquiry into the historical meaning of Thanksgiving.

FIGURE 6.3. VoiceThread on character archetypes (Miss Piggy/Narcissus).

Listening to her students voice their thoughts led her to provide more space for knowledge and expertise other than her own than she typically allowed. This teacher's reflections on using VoiceThread suggest that teachers and students may find it productive to play with a new literacies perspective rather than assume it is an "all-or-nothing" undertaking. Designing Voice-Threads in which students' drawings, writing, or digital stories are uploaded for peer response is another way this tool can be used across the curriculum. One teacher uploaded maps students had created as part of a study of map making in social studies, and another uploaded digital stories students had produced by using Animoto (an online video slideshow tool) to remix their written and drawn texts with music they had selected. Finally, Voice-Thread offers an avenue for collaborative composing that takes advantage of its multimodal affordances.

Designing Comics

Ms. Aaron, a fifth-grade teacher, introduced her students to Comic Life, an inexpensive software program that makes it easy to create comics, so they could design a multimodal text as part of a unit of study on narrative writing. The Comic Life interface offers comic creators a full palette of options from which to select when designing a comic (see Figure 6.4). On the right side of the screen, students can select from many different

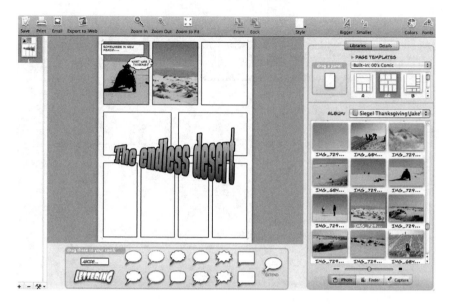

FIGURE 6.4. Comic Life interface.

templates; the fact that these templates are organized by year (e.g., 1940s) or type (e.g., Manga, conceptual) indicates that choosing a particular template represents a design choice that, together with the choice of moment, frame, image, word, and flow (McCloud, 2006), produces the possibilities for meaning making. Below the panel of templates, the user can access her or his iPhoto library (consisting of photos students have either taken or collected) to include in their comic. To make a comic, the student selects a template and drags it to the left side of the screen, where it clicks into place. The same drag-and-drop move is then used to select the images and words (speech/thought balloons, settings, and sound effects). The choice of "moment" involves deciding which moments of a narrative to include or exclude; the choice of "frame" requires that the comic maker choose the distance and angle from which to view the moment; and the choice of "flow" serves to guide the viewer through the comic frames, thus producing a potential viewing path.

Ms. Aaron had multiple reasons for incorporating Comic Life into the personal narrative unit of study. On the one hand, she was eager to tap her students' knowledge of and interest in comics while also expanding their understanding of how texts work. She introduced the Comic Life project after students had already published a personal narrative, and she offered them two choices: They could (1) take up a "revision lens," reread their narrative, sketch the narrative "graphic novel" style, gather images, create a comic, and revise their original narrative based on images and words selected; or (2) they could choose the "brainstorming/planning lens," following the same plan as in the first option but starting with selecting an entry from their writer's notebook rather than a published piece. Prior to the start of these projects, Ms. Aaron immersed the students in comics, tapping their textual histories as comic readers, before teaching brief minilessons. Her dual purpose was for students to explore how comics worked as multimodal texts as well as to develop a shared language for talking about the modal resources that comics employed.

Bryan chose the revision lens option and reread a narrative he had published about a time his dad had driven through a big puddle without remembering to roll up the car windows. His sketch for his comic showed four panels, each one representing a key moment in the narrative. What was interesting, however, was that his sketched comic included stick figures with speech balloons, whereas the comic he designed using Comic Life (see Figure 6.5) did not include any people. Instead, he constructed the narrative of his comic life through the choice of images, moments, and frames (a lone car driving on a rainy night put the emphasis on the moments of the story he wanted to include) and words (the speech/thought balloons and the sound-effect words highlighted the thoughts and feelings to intensify both the drama and humor of the event). After revising his original narrative, Bryan responded to Ms. Aaron's request for a written reflection on the project, and here is what he wrote:

> When doing this project for my personal narrative I experienced a whole new way of writing and learned how to use a new program on the computer. I think when I did this project it made my writing piece more interesting and it showed more than it told. I was able to add dialogue and actually get to use pictures to show people what I really experienced. Also I used a lot more sound effects to make it seem like readers were actually in the story. It helped me show thought bubbles in my story and speech bubbles.
>
> When I do my next writing pieces I think it will affect the way I write because when I did this project I was able to put more dialogue and what I was thinking. Because of this it made me a better writer.

CONCLUSION: REMIXING NEW LITERACIES IN MIDDLE SCHOOL CLASSROOMS

We began this chapter by contrasting the way in which two middle school teachers, Mr. Stern and Mr. Cardenas, incorporated technologies into their English and journalism classes, respectively. From the new literacies perspective we have outlined, it seems clear that Mr. Stern made room for

FIGURE 6.5. Bryan's comic.

new technologies but not for the new ethos of participation, collaboration, and expanded expertise. In other words, he used new technologies to teach traditional school literacy, whereas Mr. Cardenas embraced both new technologies and a new ethos. However clear and easy it might be to create this dichotomy between "old" and "new" literacies in action, we think it produces more problems than it solves. First, it treats new literacies as an either–or practice, as if reading and writing printed texts had no value in the changing communicative landscape. As Jenkins (2009) notes, the "new" literacies build upon a foundation of traditional literacies, although students can take different roads to achieve those literacies. Second, the old–new dichotomy not only oversimplifies contemporary literacy practice, but reinforces the dichotomy, treating it as if it were real rather than a heuristic for thinking through the question of what we mean by literacy and how it should be taught. Finally, we believe that this dichotomy may unintentionally undermine teachers' sense of efficacy by suggesting that they lack what it takes to give students opportunities to engage with new literacies. More than ever before, teachers have come under fire as overpaid public service employees who are responsible for the achievement gap and our diminished national standing. Thus, maintaining the old–new dichotomy does not leave many pathways open to teachers who may want to experiment with new technologies and the new ethos, but find themselves restricted by federal, state, and local mandates for literacy curriculum and assessment or by access to the resources they need to get started.

Ms. Aaron's use of Comic Life is a good example of how a teacher stretched the meaning of literacy in her classroom without displacing the mandated school literacy curriculum. Her reflections are instructive on this point. She wrote:

> When first thinking about this [unit of] study, I felt the need to connect it to more formal writing. However, what I've realized throughout the process is that even without the formal writing, my students were engaged in important literacy practices. The conversations they had with me and one another through this process reflected high-level thinking and revealed insight into their literacy that I would never have seen without this exploration. In one particular instance, a boy who really struggles with reading and writing created a comic in which he showed discrepancy between what he was saying and what he was thinking. This humor that he possesses rarely transfers to paper, but through his comic it did! The pride he felt in having his voice validated was priceless. It made me very aware of the need for me to expand my definition of what it means to be literate and what counts as "real" literacy.

Why not embrace the practice of remix and hybridity that Mills (2010) identified as a practice cutting across various new literacies, and treat it as a stance toward teaching and learning for both teachers and students? The recent interest in eWorkshops (i.e., electronic reading and writing workshops) in which students blog in response to the books they read, and give and receive comments on the drafts of their writing they post on a class wiki (Larson, 2008), is just one example of a hybrid literacy curriculum. We encourage teachers to take up the spirit of new literacies and remix their literacy curriculum by blending and combining literacy practices to create new opportunities for students not anticipated by those who conceptualized the new literacies perspective.

ACKNOWLEDGMENTS

We gratefully acknowledge the inspired and innovative teaching of all the teachers whose practice we describe in this chapter. We thank them for allowing us to study their teaching and learning and to share both with the broader community of educators. Further thanks to the Carnegie Corporation of New York and the National Academy of Education for their generous support of this research.

ADDITIONAL RESOURCES

American Library Association
www.ala.org/ala/mgrps/divs/acrl/publications/crlnews/2005/feb/comicbooks.cfm
Comic books and graphic novels.

Comics in Education
www.humblecomics.com/comicsedu

Comics in the Classroom
www.comicsintheclassroom.net

Comic Life
Free 30-day trial
plasq.com/products/comiclife/mac
(also available for Windows)

Comic Life Education Community
plasq.com/forum/edu

National Association of Comics Art Educators
www.teachingcomics.org

National Council of Teachers of English

http://www.ncte.org

Search for comics and graphic novels.

Read Write Think comic ideas

www.readwritethink.org/student_mat/student_material.asp?id=21

VoiceThread

voicethread.com

Free tool.

- Link to a VoiceThread wiki with helpful resources:
  digitallyspeaking.pbworks.com/w/page/17791585/Voicethread
- An example of a VoiceThread that compares Johann Sebastian Bach and
  Paul McCartney:
  voicethread.com/share/563090
- New York Public Library VoiceThread demo:
  nypl.voicethread.com/share/498440

REFERENCES

Anstey, M., & Bull, G. (2006). *Teaching and learning multiliteracies: Changing times, changing literacies.* Newark, DE: International Reading Association.

Bowman, S., & Willis, C. (2003). *We media: How audiences are shaping the future of news and information.* Reston, VA: Media Center at the American Press Institute.

Ito, M., Horst, H., Bittanti, M., Boyd, D., Herr-Stephenson, B., Lange, P. G., et al. (2008). *Living and learning with new media: Summary of findings from the Digital Youth Project.* Chicago: MacArthur Foundation.

Jenkins, H. (2009). *Confronting the challenges of participatory culture: Media education for the 21st century.* Cambridge, MA: MIT Press.

Kress, G. (2003). *Literacy in the new media age.* New York: Routledge.

Lankshear, C., & Knobel, M. (2006). *New literacies: Everyday practices and classroom learning* (2nd ed.). New York: Open University Press.

Lankshear, C., & Knobel, M. (2007a). Researching new literacies: Web 2.0 practices and insider perspectives. *E-Learning, 4*(3), 224–240.

Lankshear, C., & Knobel, M. (2007b). Sampling "the new" in new literacies. In M. Knobel & C. Lankshear (Eds.), *The new literacy sampler* (pp. 1–24). New York: Peter Lang.

Leu, D. J., Kinzer, C. K., Coiro, J. L., & Cammack, D. W. (2004). Toward a theory of new literacies emerging from the Internet and other information and communication technologies. In R. B. Ruddell & N. J. Unrau (Eds.), *Theoretical models and processes of reading* (5th ed., pp. 1570–1613). Newark, DE: International Reading Association.

Leu, D. J., Zawilinski, L., Castek, J., Banerjee, M., Housand, B. C., Liu, Y., et al. (2007). What is new about the new literacies of online reading comprehension? In L. Rush, A. J. Eakle, & A. Berger (Eds.), *Secondary school literacy: What research reveals for classroom practice* (pp. 37–68). Urbana, IL: National Council of Teachers of English.

Lewis, C., & Fabbos, B. (2005). Instant messaging, literacies, and social identities. *Reading Research Quarterly, 40*(4), 470–501.

McCloud, S. (2006). *Making comics: Storytelling secrets of comics, manga, and graphic novels.* New York: HarperCollins.

Mills, K. A. (2010). A review of the "digital turn" in the new literacy studies. *Review of Educational Research, 80*(2), 246–271.

Moll, L., Amanti, C., Neff, D., & Gonzalez, N. (1992). Funds of knowledge for teaching: Using a qualitative approach to connect homes and classrooms. *Theory into Practice, 31(2), 132–141.*

New London Group. (1996). A pedagogy of multiliteracies: Designing social futures. *Harvard Educational Review, 66*(1), 60–92.

Newitz, A. (2005). Adam Curry wants to make you an iPod radio star. *Wired, 13*(3), 111–113.

Prensky, M. (2001). Digital natives, digital immigrants. *On the Horizon, 9*(5), 1–6.

Rowsell, J., & Casey, H. K. (2009). Shifting frames: Inside the pathways and obstacles of two teachers' literacy instruction. *Linguistics and Education, 20,* 311–327.

Rushkoff, D. (2011, April). *Teaching and learning from digital natives.* Keynote address to the Teachers College Reading Writing Project Calendar Day on Digital Kids: Media, Literacy, and the New Generation, New York.

Snyder, I. (Ed.). (1998). *Page to screen: Taking literacy into the electronic era.* New York: Routledge.

Soep, E. (2010). *Drop that knowledge: Youth Radio stories.* Berkeley: University of California Press.

Stolle, E. P. (2008). Teachers, literacy, and technology: Tensions, complexities, conceptualizations, and practice. In Y. Kim, V. J. Risko, D. Compton, D. Dickinson, M. Hundley, R. Jimenez, et al. (Eds.), *57th Yearbook of the National Reading Conference* (pp. 56–69). Oak Creek, WI: National Reading Conference.

Thomas, A. (2007). Blurring and breaking through the boundaries of narrative, literacy, and identity in adolescent fan fiction. In M. Knobel & C. Lankshear (Eds.), *The new literacy sampler* (pp. 137–165). New York: Peter Lang.

Tierney, R. J. (2009). Shaping new literacies research: Extrapolations from a review of the *Handbook of research on new literacies. Reading Research Quarterly, 44*(3), 332–339.

CHAPTER 7

If You Want Students to Evaluate Online Resources and Other New Media— Teach Them How

Jill Castek

Key Points for This Chapter

- Restricted Web exploration does not aid students in developing strategies for critically evaluating online information.
- Engaging students in online inquiry provides an opportunity and an authentic reason to critically evaluate online information.
- Teaching how to evaluate the content of websites and other new media on the Internet will enhance students' ability to make sense of online information.
- Providing students with supported opportunities to locate online resources as they complete assignments will aid them in making critical evaluation a routine part of reading online.

A BIRD'S-EYE VIEW OF CLASSROOM PRACTICE

Students in Mr. Murphy's sixth-grade science class are examining the effects of climate change on Earth's systems. Mr. Murphy recognizes that the Internet has up-to-date information about climate change that could benefit students' conceptual understanding of this complex topic. He is also interested in exposing students to the online citizen science campaigns that promote society's conservation of natural resources locally and globally. He has designed an assignment in which students will explore several Web resources to learn what they can do to lessen the effects of climate change in their community.

Mr. Murphy understands that climate change is a controversial topic among global scientists and that some assert that global warming is nothing but a myth. In reflecting on the content as he prepared the lesson, he came to a conclusion: Students should not encounter websites that doubt the existence of climate change because they will confuse students' emerging understanding of the topic.

Mr. Murphy opts to create an assignment-specific webpage students can get to from his classroom website. Here he has grouped, labeled, and annotated links to a variety of Web resources and new media that he pre-screened as suitable for his students. He spent a good deal of his time examining each of the recommended Web resources carefully to ensure that they are well matched to the project's goals. Those he included came from reputable sources, were easy to navigate, and did not introduce alternative or potentially biased opinions.

Mr. Murphy takes his students to the computer lab to facilitate Web exploration. As a component of the assignment, he requires them to explore only the resources he selected to complete the project. To maximize individual involvement, he encourages students to each log in to one of the computers and to work individually on the assignment. When asked about his choices, he explained that the Internet tends to overstimulate and confuse students because it is easy to be led astray and to misinterpret information in an online context. He asserted that structuring students' experiences with the Internet and vetting quality websites in advance ensures their success in using the Internet in ways that support content learning.

DEFINING THE TARGETED PRACTICE

The practice that Mr. Murphy is using is known as *restricted Web exploration*. To apply this practice, the teacher takes responsibility for (1) designing an assignment, activity, or project; (2) locating a bank of online information that is suitable for students to use to complete their work; (3) examining the resources to determine that the information they contain is accurate, reliable, and comes from reputable sources; and (4) ensuring that the resources are a good match to students' information needs. Although engaging in the practice of prescreening resources in this way may seem instructionally beneficial, it takes away valuable opportunities for students to conduct their own online inquiries and critically evaluate the diversity of online resources they are likely to find on the Web. When this practice recurs, students learn to rely on the teacher as a broker to online information and as a result, they do not acquire the essential critical thinking skills needed to distinguish useful information from less reliable sources.

WHAT DOES THE RESEARCH SAY
ABOUT RESTRICTED WEB EXPLORATION?

There is very little research that supports the practice of restricted Web exploration. Many beneficial instructional approaches involve a predictable sequence of guided instruction, reinforcement, and assessment, but structuring Web exploration in an overly guided manner has not proven to be beneficial (Castek, in press; Jonassen, 1996). Even so, teachers opt for restricted Web exploration because school-based curricula are not often organized to support the skills of inquiry. Experience with inquiry, teachers' comfort with releasing control to students, and the age and experience of learners are all factors that affect how teachers choose to structure Web exploration. However, it is important to recognize that restricting Web exploration may curtail the development of foundational knowledge for critical evaluation, squelch intellectual curiosity, and suppress the formulation of meaningful questions that drive the learning process (Bransford, Brown, & Cocking, 2000). Moreover, Hirsh (1999) found that inviting students to search for information to complete a school assignment netted higher motivational levels than having students perform more structured task with questions posed by an external researcher. This finding suggests the need to shift away from prescriptive learning situations toward engaging learners in open-ended learning that involves self-guided inquiry and free exploration (Kuiper & Volman, 2008).

In contrast to restricted Web exploration, online inquiry appears to be a promising context for students to develop critical evaluation skills. Online inquiry encourages critical thinking, promotes collaboration, and builds students' capacity for higher-level thinking and learning. New technologies are particularly well suited to enable students to work with greater autonomy, collaborate with peers, and gain access to information related to their own interests. Exploring online information in this way has the potential to increase students' investment in their own learning processes, which may create an authentic desire to evaluate resources for quality, reliability, and accuracy.

Deep, engaged learning occurs when students explore self-selected, open-ended questions about which they are genuinely interested. The self-direction that inquiry learning promotes involves students in reading widely. Because inquiry-based teaching approaches encourage, guide, and support learning attempts, students often approach inquiry tasks with more engagement and motivation to learn (Bransford et al., 2000). Inquiry teaching recognizes the importance of student ownership of knowledge. In fact, Frechette (2002) argued that inquiry activities should form the basis of curricular approaches that integrate the Internet because they provide a meaningful context for learning. When used as a vehicle for self-driven inquiry, searching for information online does not become an end in and of itself, but instead is part of a useful process for answering broader questions and solving problems.

Blumenfeld and colleagues (1991) suggest that the Internet offers new opportunities to support inquiry learning. They identified several ways that networked technologies enhance inquiry learning. These enhancements include sparking student interest and motivation; improving access to a wide range of information; allowing active, changing representations; managing complexity; and aiding in the production of ideas. Free exploration and open inquiry allow students to build on and expand their own natural problem-solving abilities (Bransford et al., 2000), and thereby support students in making stronger connections between classroom activities and their own lives and interests. Approaches that support open access to online information are structured around challenging learning goals that help students explore ideas and that encourage critical thinking (Bloom & White, 1993).

WHAT ARE SOME ALTERNATIVES?

To begin identifying alternatives, let's consider the reasons Mr. Murphy has restricted Internet exploration and prescreened online resources for his students. First, he recognized that his students might not have the prerequisite background knowledge to search for their own resources effectively online. Second, he understood that students lacked experience with interpreting the diversity of information they would be likely to find if they conducted their own Internet searches. Finally, he was aware that students would come across differing viewpoints in their Internet exploration and that they would be unable to fully reconcile conflicting ideas, given the content they explored in class. Because he had not yet invested time in teaching students to evaluate online content to determine source reliability, he felt it would be quicker and easier to make decisions about what students should read for them, knowing full well that selecting the best information from the abundance of links search engines make available requires new interpretive reading strategies that go above and beyond skimming or scanning.

Though Mr. Murphy had good reasons behind the design of his instruction, he overlooked the basic reality that critical evaluation of online resources is one of the most essential strategies involved in online reading. Instruction in online reading should emphasize the important role of healthy skepticism toward the information encountered online. Middle school teachers should begin to help students develop both the skepticism and the critical evaluation skills needed to successfully negotiate the range of information that appears online (Leu et al., 2008). The first step in teaching critical evaluation involves guiding students to search effectively and sift through search results to find the resources that best meet their needs. Students often lack sufficient strategies to distinguish between relevant and irrelevant information online because we are too helpful as teachers. Once a student successfully locates online resources and information related to an assignment, a self-generated question, or a problem, critical evaluation of the resources located is of primary importance (Coiro, 2003).

In contrast to providing students with prevetted Web resources from which to gather information, this chapter advocates for teaching students strategies for critically evaluating the resources they themselves locate when conducting online research. Evaluating Internet resources and other online media involves three levels of critical thinking (Coiro, 2009b):

1. Questioning, analyzing, and comparing resources
2. Judging quality of information in terms of various characteristics
3. Defending opinions with evidence from multiple sources and prior knowledge

These critical thinking abilities are situated in a broader definition of online reading, which involves problem-based inquiry skills, strategies, dispositions, and social practices that take place as students use the Internet to answer questions or solve problems (Leu, O'Byrne, Zawilinski, McVerry, & Everett-Cocapardo, 2009).

Why Teach Students to Critically Evaluate Online Resources?

Gathering information online has become a popular method of researching for middle school students (Roberts, Foehr, & Rideout, 2005). Because students are reliant on the Internet to find information, it is even more paramount to their success as online readers to be able to evaluate the validity and reliability of Web resources (Leu et al., 2008). However, the Internet demands new forms of critical literacy, critical thinking, and analysis, especially around locating reliable information resources (Bråten, Strømsø, & Britt, 2009). Because open networks such as the Internet provide a platform for anyone to publish anything without scrutiny, new dimensions of critical literacy are needed to determine what information is most reliable (Iding, Crosby, Auernheimer, & Klemm, 2002). For example, in order make use of online information in ways that best support learning, students must come to understand that not everything they find online is accurate and unbiased. As reliance on Web-based information increases, the importance of critical evaluation skills becomes central to teaching and learning at the middle school level.

The ability to take a critical stance toward information is an important part of the middle school curriculum. However, studies of middle and high school students' online reading have shown that critical evaluation skills are underdeveloped (Graham & Metaxas, 2003). In a study focused on the Internet reading skills of proficient online readers in seventh grade, only 4 out of 50 students were able to determine that a website offering information about a fictitious animal known as the Pacific Northwest Tree Octopus was a hoax (New Literacies Research Team and Internet Reading Group, 2007). These proficient readers seldom enacted strategies for critically evaluating information encountered online, even though, when surveyed, all of these students indicated that the information they found online was not always true. This finding suggests a discrepancy between what students know and how they act on what they know. It also suggests that teachers not only need to teach critical evaluation but also to guide students to use these critical thinking strategies as they read online.

Students need extensive practice in determining not only whether resources are a good match to their purpose for learning, but also whether those sources are reliable and trustworthy (Clemmitt, 2008). Because online resources are less frequently regulated for quality and accuracy (Harris, 2008), many students have a difficult time determining what criteria to use in determining reliability (New Literacies Research Team & Internet Research Group, 2007). Although it is every reader's job to be critical of online information, to determine whether it comes from a reliable source, and to evaluate whether the information suits the purpose of the inquiry (Harris, 2008), it is our responsibility as educators to support students in developing this multifaceted proficiency. If we expect students to think critically about the information they read online, then providing multiple opportunities to engage in these practices with the support of their peers and teachers is fundamental to the achievement of that expectation.

Evaluation of online resources is one of the most essential strategies involved in online activity (Iding et al., 2002). Online information can be found in multiple formats, such as text, video, or audio, and includes a combination of diverse facts, opinions, and/or interpretations. In many cases, these messages are intended to inform, to persuade, to sell, to present a viewpoint, and/or to create or change an attitude or belief. Online resources are less frequently regulated for quality and accuracy than offline materials. Sorting through online information leads to clicking on links and following them to other websites. Thus the reading experience we each construct online is continuously being created, revised, and refined (Leu et al., 2008). Each resource, therefore, requires readers to integrate and apply different types of critical evaluation skills and strategies.

One form of critical evaluation may be especially important to consider during online reading: the determination of how reliable information from a particular website is. But, all too frequently, students do not spend enough time on a site to warrant examining its reliability. Wallace, Kupperman, Krajcik, and Soloway (2000) reported that students scrolled through sites too quickly to read them and rarely followed links to investigate any sites in depth. This study concluded that students rarely spend time working toward understanding or evaluating the information they retrieve online, but instead focus on quick answers and make shallow interpretations of information. Fidel and colleagues (1999) and Hirsh (1999) found that students often used surface-level strategies, such as critiquing the quality of the graphics, to determine reliability. Thus, across these studies of critical evaluation, it is clear that students have difficulty determining the reliability of websites.

Find Out What Students Know about Critical Evaluation

As is the case when teaching any new skill or strategy, tapping into the knowledge students already have and using it as a bridge to new understandings is an important and useful construct. McVerry and O'Byrne (2011) have developed an online assessment that may be useful as a starting point (see Critical Evaluation: *sites.google.com/site/criticalevaluation-instrument/home*). These 20 multiple-choice questions tap into four constructs of critical evaluation:

1. Identify the author, evaluate level of expertise, and understand how the author's perspective influences what he or she writes.
2. Identify sources, such as the use of primary and secondary sources in a document, and evaluate the reliability of these sources based on information given.
3. Identify the publishers and evaluate the credibility of the company, brand, or entity.
4. Identify bias by locating instances of online text involving strong words or images intended to influence readers' perspective.

This online assessment can be completed as a pretest to evaluate how closely students reflect on the material they read online, and again after instruction, as a posttest, to determine how proficient they are with the skills and strategies you have taught for evaluating online information. The ultimate test, however, is whether students utilize these strategies as they read and navigate the Web on a daily basis. A combination of careful observation coupled with timely teacher feedback and reflection prompts can support students' widespread use of critical evaluation strategies.

Challenge Students to Gather Information from a Spoof Site

Although students are often aware that not all information found on the Internet is reliable, trustworthy, or useful (Scott & O'Sullivan, 2000), many have a difficult time determining what criteria to use in determining reliability (New Literacies Research Team & Internet Research Group, 2007). Students who are less experienced online readers often focus on the URL and decide whether the site is reliable by whether its extension is *.com* or *.edu*—rather than by engaging in a more intricate examination of the author and content (Hoffman, Wu, Krajcik, & Soloway, 2003). Even though many students are able to state otherwise (Lorenzen, 2001), when it comes to online reading in daily practice, most believe that nearly all the information on the Internet is reliable (Hirsh, 1999; Large & Beheshti, 2000; Schacter, Chung, & Dorr, 1998). Students can, however, learn to become more skeptical of information found on websites. For example, a class of sixth-grade students initially assumed that all the information they found online was true, but with instruction, they learned to become more critical of online information, and they became skilled at discerning fact from opinion by verifying facts on other sites (Kafai & Bates, 1997).

It can be difficult to begin the conversation about critical evaluation with middle school students who have spent most of their lives emersed in using new technologies and navigating online resources. Many consider themselves experts with new media and may resist engaging in strategies that slow down their processing. One way to encourage students to evaluate online media is to explore a range of spoof sites that appear trustworthy on the surface. Having students examine a few of these sites (e.g., All about Explorers [*allaboutexplorers.com*]; the RYT Hospital [*www.rythospital.com/2011*], which features the first human male pregnancy [*www.malepregnancy.com*], or the Ova Prima Foundation [*www.ovaprima.org*]) without alerting them to the fact that they are spoofs, will allow students to experience just how easy it is to be fooled by false information on websites that look professionally designed and information rich. Instead of using this discussion as a means of teaching students about credibility, first listen to students' ideas. This will help you develop a baseline understanding of their critical thinking processes. Having an open conversation will aid you in determining where to target instruction.

Once students have experienced several spoof sites and you have discussed what characteristics to look for when critically evaluating information, challenge students to use critical evaluation in an everyday context without a reminder to do so. For example, pose an open-ended question such as, "Would you send your dog on a journey to explore The Dog Island (*www.thedogisland.com*)? Why or Why not?"

Asking students to explore websites that are hoaxes without alerting them to the fact that they contain misleading and untrue information might cause them some discomfort. However, this is precisely the reason for teaching critical evaluation skills—so that students will become aware that unreliable information is abundant online. Assure them that each such reminder will help them become better able to spot less credible websites from those that are more reliable as they read online independently.

Following exploration of The Dog Island, invite students to comment on the website and share their opinions. Ask volunteers to demonstrate in small groups and in front of the class the strategies they used to identify the author, determine the author's motives, and verify reliability. You may find it helpful to pose the questions that follow in a turn-and-talk format to encourage critical thinking and a useful exchange of ideas.

- What information is The Dog Island website trying to convey?
  - Ask students to address how they know (being as specific as they can and referring in a detailed way to the areas of the website they explored).
- Is Dog Island a real place? Why or why not?
  - Have students tell the reasons why it might be a real place. Then, invite them to discuss the reasons why it might not be real.
  - Ask students to address how they know (being as specific as they can and referring in a detailed way to the areas of the website they explored).
- What information did you examine to verify the reliability of information on the site?
  - Which of these strategies could be used to evaluate other websites?
  - What resources beyond the website itself could be used to check the veracity of the information The Dog Island contains?

Once you have begun to challenge the manner in which students critique online information, introduce a video resource entitled *Discovering the Internet: Credibility* (*www.watchknow.org/Video.aspx?VideoID=2078*). This video does an excellent job of explaining why critical evaluation is so vital when reading online and interacting with all forms of digital media. Questions such as "Why should I believe the source?" and "How does this source know the information?" are introduced as well as strategies for addressing them.

Create a Customized Search Engine to Support Online Inquiry

Given the sheer volume of information on the Internet, teaching students to search, locate, and evaluate resources that are specific to their goals may seem like a time-consuming and somewhat daunting task. However, new tools are available for educators that can make things easier. For example, Google provides a free service that lets users create and customize their own search engines (see The Google Customized Search Engine at *www.google.com/educators/p_cse.html*). The customized search engine has the same look and feel as a standard Google search, but the websites listed in customized search results are limited to those the search engine creator has indexed in advance. Since this tool allows a teacher to preselect the sites he or she wants students to examine, he or she can guarantee that students' searches will yield a limited number of highly relevant search results. Narrowing search results to a more targeted and manageable size ensures that students gain valuable practice searching for information using key words, sifting through results, and evaluating resources in a timely manner. The additional support customized search offers helps students build skills and makes the time they spend online more efficient and purposeful. As students become more proficient, this scaffold can be faded out and skills gained can be applied directly to unscaffolded searching.

To set up a customized search engine, simply establish a Google account. Then, navigate to custom search (*www.google.com/cse/?hl=en*) and click on "create a custom search engine." Next, name the site (e.g., Combating Climate Change) and add a description of the search engine (e.g., a sampling of websites that will help Mr. Murphy's class complete their climate change design challenge). Finally, enter the URLs of the websites and resources you would like students to access. Figure 7.1 shows an example customized search engine for sixth graders who are studying ways to lessen the effects of climate change (Combating Climate Change, *www.google.com/cse/home?cx=014465768746147993326:rncbgcerhjk&hl=en*).

Teach the Five W's of Website Evaluation

Once students have located resources, walk them through evaluating information using the five W's of website evaluation. The five W's are guidelines students can follow to conduct a simple evaluation of any website (see Figure 7.2). Guide students through a few websites that have different

Google custom search

Combating Climate Change

[Google™ Custom Search]   (Search)

Search engine details

A sampling of websites that will help 6th grade students complete
their design challenge. The challenge will be evaluated on the
following goals: 1) keeps the Earth from warming up too much, 2)
keeps greenhouses gasses out of the air, and 3) lessen the
effects of climate change (make the effects less harmful).

searches sites including: http://www.epa.gov/climatechang...,
http://www.epa.gov/climatechang..., http://tiki.oneworld.net
/global..., http://www.nature.org/initiativ...,
http://www.sofreshandsogreen.co...

Last updated: March 8, 2011

Add this search engine to your Google homepage: [Google]
Add this search engine to your blog or webpage »

Create your own Custom Search Engine »

FIGURE 7.1. Google customized search engine designed for sixth graders (*www.
google.com/cse/home?cx=01446576874614799332:rncbgcerhjk&hl=en*).

purposes, such as commercial, educational, and persuasive. Then prompt
them to ask: (1) Who wrote this information (is he or she an expert)?; (2)
what is the purpose of the site?; (3) when was the site created?; (4) where
does the information come from?; and (5) why is it useful for my purpose?
Then provide time for students to examine a range of Web resources and
new media, including those that would be considered noncredible. Encourage students to question what they are reading, viewing, and exploring.
Work with students to create a list of indicators that lead to high degrees
of credibility. Finally, reinforce the five W guidelines until they become a
habit.

The five W's will guide students to conduct a simple evaluation of any website:

- **Who** is the author(s)? Is he or she an expert in the field?
- **What** is the purpose of the website? Is it designed to be informational,
  commercial, persuasive, or other?
- **When** was the site created, updated, or last worked on?
- **Where** does the information come from? Does the author include
  citations and/or links to known sources?
- **Why** is the information useful for your purpose?

FIGURE 7.2. The five W's of website evaluation. Adapted from Kathy Schrock's original resource (*kathyschrock.net/abceval/5ws.pdf*).

Model Critical Evaluation Strategies

In a recent study, Sanchez, Wiley, and Goldman (2006) developed a curriculum unit in which students were taught to consider the source, evidence, explanation, and evaluate the information given in terms of their prior knowledge (SEEK). This unit included a set of activities designed to help learners adopt a critical stance while doing research online and with multiple sources. The procedure encouraged students to (1) think about the reliability of sources, (2) evaluate the evidence and explanations provided, and (3) relate new information to prior knowledge. Thus, this training encouraged students to consider not only information about the source itself, but also the nature of the information presented by each source. The SEEK procedure introduces yet another structure for teaching critical evaluation skills.

When modeling critical evaluation strategies, demonstrate what readers should do when they first arrive at any unfamiliar website: look for a link to source information. A good online reader evaluates the source before reading any information. If a link to the source is not available, greater skepticism is needed since the creator may be trying to conceal his or her identity and why he or she is providing this information. When source information is unavailable or difficult to locate, show students how to use online resources and tools to uncover who the author is, his or her level of expertise, and what others think about this information. Model a procedure for going back to search engine results and examining them to look for indications that the author is untrustworthy. Over time, introduce additional strategies, such as searching for the author (or the topic of the information) on Wikipedia. Model for students how to review the discussion links within Wikipedia, especially if there is some controversy about the topic or the Wikipedia entry. Though this may be a useful initial source for developing background knowledge, it should not be used as the sole source.

Another strategy would involve conducting a search on Facebook or Twitter to see what others are saying and writing about the topic or a particular website. This approach can often provide information quickly about opinions and discussions that have happened recently. It may also be helpful to review discussion boards for such information. To locate relevant discussion threads, show students how to search for the topic (or a particular website) using a search engine. Adding "discussion" to the key words will surface related discussions. Scanning the search results will give readers an indication of what others are thinking about the information, the author, and/or the website. Finally, Snopes.com (*www.snopes.com*), an online source for fact-checking urban legends, folklore, myths, rumors, and misinformation, can be a useful resource. The Snopes entry for The Dog Island states that "this site was created as a hoax by students as a project for a

Contagious Media class." The entry goes on to discuss that though The Dog Island is a real place located off the northern panhandle of Florida, it is not operated as a sanctuary for dogs.

Encourage Peer Support for Critical Evaluation

Johnson and Johnson (1999) described five elements that are common to successful collaborative learning activities. These elements include positive interdependence, individual accountability, face-to-face interaction, social skills, and group processing. When students collaborate in constructing meaning from text, they create what Kucan and Beck (1997) referred to as "multiple resources at the reading construction site" (p. 289). This means that readers not only draw on their own knowledge but also the knowledge of others within the group (Lapp, Fisher, & Wolsey, 2009; Putney, Green, Dixon, Durán, & Yeager, 2000). The process of constructing meaning could later transfer to an internalization of the strategic processes and independent application of strategies by individuals. Barron (2003) has found that collaborative groups engage in "huddling," wherein group members provide and receive explanations from peers, exchange alternative points of view, examine their own knowledge and beliefs, and pool collective prior knowledge sources.

A promising instructional model, Internet reciprocal teaching (Leu et al., 2008), draws on the aforementioned collaborative models of instruction and the proven intervention, reciprocal teaching (Palincsar & Brown, 1984), to teach strategies for online reading and critical evaluation. Adaptations to reciprocal teaching include:

- Modeling and scaffolding strategies collaboratively toward increasing online reading comprehension (including critical evaluation of online resources).
- Facilitating collaborative dialogue among students to develop useful skills and awarenesses of how to transfer those skills to new online reading contexts.
- Building in time for discussing the evaluation of online content.
- Enacting student-centered approaches for critically evaluating information in ways that transform the classroom culture by creating a healthy skepticism about online resources.

Palincsar and Brown (1984) have shown that student-to-student scaffolding has also been effective in learning new skills. These dynamic, situation-specific supports provided by peers can substantially facilitate the learning process (Brush & Saye, 2000). Inviting students to work together to demonstrate strategies they have learned for evaluating Web content aids students' application of critical evaluation strategies when reading online independently (Castek, 2008).

CONCLUSION

The Internet is becoming an increasingly important source of information for middle school students (Lenhart, Madden, & Hitlin, 2005). As teachers, we know that being skilled and strategic with its use is a critical component of academic and economic success. To use online resources and new media responsibly, students need to think critically to assess and evaluate the messages they contain. For example, students need to learn the skills to determine the validity of a website, understand the point of view and potential bias within YouTube videos, read blogs and understand how or why certain images are embedded, and listen to podcasts and determine the features of the presentation that affect its tone and message. If we do not provide opportunities to teach such skills, we will not be facilitating the growth of responsible citizens. To prepare all students to succeed in a world where these skills are so important, we need to create opportunities for students to use the Internet for learning. Providing opportunities for online inquiry and teaching strategies for thinking critically about online resources will aid students in developing a healthy skepticism toward online information and the skills to critically evaluate what they read online. These skills are exceptionally valuable as online texts, tools, and reading/writing contexts continue to change (Leu, Kinzer, Coiro, & Cammack, 2004). However, the importance of teaching students to skillfully evaluate online information will always remain constant (International Reading Association & National Council of Teachers, 2010).

ADDITIONAL RESOURCES

Middle school students need many opportunities to practice their emerging critical evaluation skills. Several online resources can be used or modified for this purpose. For example, Coiro (2009a) has assembled a set of seven student challenges that address the essential components of successful evaluation: relevancy, accuracy, reliability, bias, and an overall healthy skepticism (*www.lite.iwarp.com/CoiroCritEval.html*). The downloadable activity sheets can be customized to suit your curriculum goals.

To engage students in working collaboratively as they critically evaluate online information, Castek (2006) designed an Internet reciprocal teaching lesson focused on evaluating information from spoof sites (*ctell1.uconn.edu/somers/quag.htm*). This activity was designed to encourage peer support for critical evaluation. For example, students are asked to brainstorm all strategies they could use to determine if a website is valid and reliable. Then students are challenged to work with a partner to put the strategies they listed into action as they work through four steps:

1. *Predict*: Do you think the website is a reliable source of information?
2. *Question*: How do you know the website has accurate information?
3. *Clarify*: How do you go about checking on the validity of websites?
4. *Summarize*: Which strategies were most useful? Which were not?

This module was designed to help students become more sensitive to the misinformation that is prevalent on the Internet and to encourage students to apply strategies for evaluating information whenever they read online. Resources that serve similar aims are included below. These sites can be easily accessed from *http:// tinyurl.com/696eqh*.

Critical Evaluation Assessment Tool (developed by J. Greg McVerry & Ian O'Byrne)
sites.google.com/site/criticalevaluationinstrument/home

Critical Evaluation for Information Resources (University of Oregon Libraries)
libweb.uoregon.edu/guides/findarticles/credibility.html

Discovering the Internet: Credibility (video by Nortel Learn & Discover IT)
www.watchknow.org/Video.aspx?VideoID=2078

Evaluating Internet Resources (developed by Larry Johnson and Annette Lamb)
eduscapes.com/tap/topic32.htm

Evaluating Online Resources (developed by Common Sense Media)
cybersmartcurriculum.org/researchinfo/lessons/9-12/evaluating_online_ resources

Identifying High Quality Sites (developed by Common Sense Media)
cybersmartcurriculum.org/researchinfo/lessons/6-8/identifying_high_quality_ sites

Instructional Strategies for Critically Evaluating Online Information (developed by Julie Coiro)
www.lite.iwarp.com/CoiroCritEval.html

Internet Reciprocal Teaching Strategies for Critically Evaluating Websites (developed by Jill Castek)
ctell1.uconn.edu/somers/quag.htm

Kathy Schrock's Guide for Educators: Critical Evaluation Information
school.discoveryeducation.com/schrockguide/eval.html

Knowing What's What and What's Not: The 5Ws and 1H of Cyberspace
(developed by the Media Awareness Network)
*www.media-awareness.ca/english/resources/special_initiatives/wa_resources/
wa_shared/tipsheets/5Ws_of_cyberspace.cfm*

Lessons and Resources for Evaluating Website Content
exworthy.tripod.com/teachreswebeval.htm

Practice Evaluating Online Resources (developed by Tammy Payton)
www.tammypayton.net/courses/print/evalweb.shtml

Website Evaluation Activity (developed by Mark Bobrosky, Walter Reed Middle
School Library, Los Angeles Unified School District)
*www.reedmstech.com/library/index.php?option=com_content&task=view&id=
12&Itemid=52*

REFERENCES

Barron, B. (2003). When smart groups fail. *Journal of the Learning Sciences, 12,*
307–359.

Bloom, L. Z., & White, E. M. (Eds.). (1993). *Inquiry: A cross-curricular reader.*
Englewood Cliffs, NJ: Prentice-Hall.

Blumenfeld, P. C., Soloway, E., Marx, R. W., Krajcik, J. S., Guzdial, M., & Palincsar, A. (1991). Motivating project-based learning: Sustaining the doing,
supporting the learning. *Educational Psychologist, 26,* 369–398.

Bransford, J. D., Brown, A. L., & Cocking, R. R. (Eds.). (2000). *How people learn:
Brain, mind, experience, and school.* Washington, DC: National Academies
Press.

Bråten, I., Strømsø, H. I., & Britt, M. (2009). Trust matters: Examining the role
of source evaluation in students' construction of meaning within and across
multiple texts. *Reading Research Quarterly, 44,* 6–28.

Brush, T., & Saye, J. (2000). Design, implementation, and evaluation of student-
centered learning: A case study. *Educational Technology Research and Development, 48,* 79–100.

Castek, J. (2006, April). Adapting reciprocal teaching to the Internet using tele-
collaborative projects. In D. J. Leu, Jr. (Chair), *Developing Internet reading
comprehension strategies among adolescents at risk to become dropouts.* A
structured poster session presented the American Education Research Association, San Francisco.

Castek, J. (2008). *How do 4th and 5th grade students acquire the new literacies of
online reading comprehension? Exploring the contexts that facilitate learning.* Unpublished doctoral dissertation, University of Connecticut, Storrs,
CT.

Castek, J. (in press). New technologies: Have computers and other new technologies enhanced classroom instruction? In J. Eakle (Ed.), *Debating issues in American education*. Thousand Oaks, CA: Sage.

Clemmitt, M. (2008). Internet accuracy: Is information on the Web reliable? *CQ Researcher, 18*(27), 625–648. Retrieved from *www.cqpress.com/docs/CQ_Researcher_V18-27_Internet_Accuracy.pdf*.

Coiro, J. (2003). Reading comprehension on the Internet: Expanding our understanding of reading comprehension to encompass new literacies. *The Reading Teacher, 56*, 458–464.

Coiro, J. (2009a). Instructional strategies for critically evaluating online information. Retrieved from *www.lite.iwarp.com/CoiroCritEval.html*.

Coiro, J. (2009b). Rethinking reading assessment in a digital age: How is reading comprehension different and where do we turn now? *Educational Leadership, 66*, 59–63.

Fidel, R., Davies, R., Douglass, M., Holder, J., Hopkins, C., Kushner, E., et al. (1999). A visit to the information mall: Web searching behavior of the high school students. *Journal of the American Society for Information Science, 50*(1), 24–37.

Frechette, A. (2002). *Developing media literacy in cyberspace: Pedagogy and critical learning for the twenty-first-century classroom*. Westport, CT: Praeger.

Graham, L., & Metaxas, P. T. (2003). Of course it's true, I saw it on the Internet: Critical thinking in the Internet era. *Communications of the ACM, 46*(5), 71–75.

Harris, F. J. (2008). Challenges to teaching credibility assessment in contemporary schooling. In M. J. Metzger & A. J. Flanagin (Eds.), *Digital Media, Youth, and Credibility* (pp. 155–179). Cambridge, MA: MIT Press.

Hirsh, S. G. (1999). Children's relevance criteria and information seeking on electronic resources. *Journal of the American Society for Information Science, 50*, 1265–1283.

Hoffman, J., Wu, H. K., Krajcik, J. S., & Soloway, E. (2003). The nature of middle school learners' science content understandings with the use of online resources. *Journal of Research in Science Teaching, 40*(3), 343–367.

Iding, M. K., Crosby, M., Auernheimer, B., & Klemm, E. B. (2002). Critical evaluation skills for Web-based information: "Lies, damned lies" and Web-based information. In P. Barker & S. Rebelsky (Eds.), *Proceedings of World Conference on Educational Multimedia, Hypermedia and Telecommunications 2002* (pp. 369–370). Chesapeake, VA: Association for the Advancement of Computing in Education.

IRA/NCTE (International Reading Association & National Council of Teachers of English). (2010). Standards for the assessment of reading and writing (rev. ed.). Newark, DE and Urbana, IL: Authors. Retrieved from *reading.org/General/CurrentResearch/Standards/AssessmentStandards.aspx*.

Johnson, D., & Johnson, R. (1999). Making cooperative learning work. *Theory into Practice, 38*, 67–73.

Jonassen, D. H. (1996). *Computers in the classroom: Mindtools for critical thinking*. Englewood Cliffs, NJ: Prentice-Hall.

Kafai, Y., & Bates, M. J. (1997). Internet Web-searching instruction in the elementary classroom: Building a foundation for information literacy. *School Media Quarterly, 25*(2), 103–111.

Kucan, L., & Beck, I. L. (1997). Thinking aloud and reading comprehension research: Inquiry, instruction, and social interactions. *Review of Educational Research, 67,* 271–299.

Kuiper, E., & Volman, M. (2008). The Web as a source of information for students in K–12 education. In J. Coiro, M. Knobel, C. Lankshear, & D. J. Leu (Eds.), *Handbook of research on new literacies* (pp. 241–266). Mahwah, NJ: Erlbaum.

Lapp, D., Fisher, D., & Wolsey, T. D. (2009). *Literacy growth for every child: Differentiated small-group instruction K–6.* New York: Guilford Press.

Large, A., & Beheshti, J. (2000). The Web as a classroom resource: Reactions from the users. *Journal of the American Society for Information Science, 51,* 1069–1080.

Lenhart, A., Madden, M., & Hitlin, P. (2005). Teens and technology. Washington, DC: Pew Internet and American Life Project. Retrieved from *www.pewinternet.org/pdfs/PIP_Teens_Tech_July2005web.pdf.*

Leu, D. J., Jr. (2002). The new literacies: Research on reading instruction with the Internet and other digital technologies. In J. Samuels & A. E. Farstrup (Eds.), *What research has to say about reading instruction* (pp. 310–336). Newark, DE: International Reading Association.

Leu, D. J., Jr., Coiro, J., Castek, J., Hartman, D. K., Henry, L. A., & Reinking, D. (2008). Research on instruction and assessment in the new literacies of online reading comprehension. In C. C. Block & S. R. Parris (Eds.), *Comprehension instruction: Research-based best practices* (2nd ed., pp. 321–346). New York: Guilford Press.

Leu, D. J., Jr., Kinzer, C. K., Coiro, J., & Cammack, D. (2004). Toward a theory of new literacies emerging from the Internet and other information and communication technologies. In R. B. Ruddell & N. Unrau (Eds.), *Theoretical models and processes of reading* (5th ed., pp. 1568–1611). Newark, DE: International Reading Association.

Leu, D. J., Jr., O'Byrne, W. I., Zawilinski, L., McVerry, J. G., & Everett-Cocapardo, H. (2009). Expanding the new literacies conversation. *Educational Researcher, 38,* 264–269.

Lorenzen, M. (2001). The land of confusion?: High school students and their use of the World Wide Web for research. Retrieved from *www.michaellorenzen.net.*

McVerry, J. G., & O'Byrne, W. I. (2011, May). *Publishing as the province of a participatory culture: Evaluating online information.* Paper presented at the annual meeting of the American Education Research Association, New Orleans, LA.

New Literacies Research Team & Internet Reading Research Group. (2007, April). Defining online reading comprehension: Using think-aloud verbal protocols to refine a preliminary model of Internet reading comprehension processes. In D. Alvermann (Chair), *21st century literacy: What is it, how do students get it, and how do we know if they have it?* Symposium presented at American Education Research Association, Chicago.

Palincsar, A. S., & Brown, A. L. (1984). Reciprocal teaching of comprehension-fostering and comprehension-monitoring activities. *Cognition and Instruction, 1,* 117–175.

Putney, L., Green, J., Dixon, C., Durán, R., & Yeager, B. (2000). Consequential progressions: Exploring collective–individual development in a bilingual classroom. In C. Lee & P. Smagorinsky (Eds.), *Constructing meaning through collaborative inquiry: Vygotskian perspectives on literacy research* (pp. 86–126). New York: Cambridge University Press.

Roberts, D. F., Foehr, U. G., & Rideout, V. (2005). *Generation M: Media in the lives of 8–18 year olds.* Menlo Park, CA: Kaiser Family Foundation. Retrieved from *www.kff.org/entmedia/7251.cfm.*

Sanchez, C. A., Wiley, J., & Goldman, S. R. (2006). Teaching students to evaluate source reliability during Internet research tasks. Paper presented at the proceedings of the 7th International Conference on Learning Sciences. Retrieved from *litd.psch.uic.edu/personal/jwiley/Sanchez_ICLS06.pdf.*

Schacter, J., Chung, G. K., & Dorr, A. (1998). Children's Internet searching on complex problems: Performance and process analysis. *Journal of the American Society for Information Science, 49,* 840–849.

Scott, T., & O' Sullivan, M. (2000). The Internet and information literacy: Taking the first step toward technology education in the social studies. *Social Studies, 91*(3), 121–125.

Wallace, R. M., Kupperman, J., Krajcik, J., & Soloway, E. (2000). Science on the Web: Students online in a sixth-grade classroom. *Journal of the Learning Sciences, 9,* 75–104.

CHAPTER 8

If You Think Students Should Be Critically Literate—Show Them How

Peggy Albers

Key Points for This Chapter

- Initiate–respond–evaluate as a discussion strategy does not effectively engage students in critical thinking.
- Reading from a critical literacy perspective supports students as they develop a language of critique, one that examines issues of power, position, and privilege.
- Using a range of multimedia texts (e.g., advertisements, cartoons, photographs) to teach visual methods of analysis encourages students to develop a critical stance.

A BIRD'S-EYE VIEW OF CLASSROOM PRACTICE

Ms. Anderson has worked as a seventh-grade language arts teacher for a number of years, and over the course of the years, she has noticed that her students continue to emphasize their need for "things"—for the newest cell phone, the newest versions of video games, the hottest fashions, and so on. In her attempt to have her students think about advertising and its impact on them, she decides to design several lessons on the role of advertising and consumerism. As part of her practice, Ms. Anderson tries to integrate the arts into her instruction whenever possible. In preparing these lessons on the study of media, and on advertisements in particular, she decides to have students study advertisements, create an advertisement, and then have the opportunity to see their ad in their school newspaper.

To introduce these lessons, Ms. Anderson begins by demonstrating the concept of advertising to students and presents them with a number of advertisements found in magazines/periodicals that her students often like to read. To ensure that her students understand the concepts, she uses I-R-E pattern of questioning (initiate–response–evaluate): She *i*nitiates the discussion with a question, invites students' *r*esponses, and then *e*valuates their responses. She asks them to respond to each advertisement using the following questions:

- "Which ads appealed to you?"
- "Why did they appeal to you?"
- "What 'characters' are the companies trying to create in their ads?"
- "Are they successful? Why or why not?"
- "Are they truthful? How can you tell?"
- "What do you think is the audience for these ads? Give examples to support your answer."

Students respond to her questions, and Ms. Anderson evaluates their responses to see what they noticed in terms of the ads (e.g., colors, the products themselves, the layout, and the people who are in the ads). These questions move Ms. Anderson into the second part of her lesson, which is to teach students to read and study ads in terms of how they are marketed. Marketers design ads around four areas: product, pricing, promotion, and placement. Ms. Anderson presents this information in a PowerPoint presentation that includes a picture of an ad and information about each of the four P's:

1. *Product*: What aspects of the product fits consumers' needs and wants? Does it have a warranty, a guarantee, and support (technical or customer service)? What language is used to describe the product, and how is language used?
2. *Pricing*: Marketers set prices based on what consumers are willing to pay. They consider such things as discounts and including other items (e.g., Does the MP3 player come with an armband?).
3. *Promotion*: What methods are used for promotion and publicity of a product, brand or company (e.g., billboards, magazine, television, radio, and the Internet)?
4. *Placement*: What steps are taken to get the product to the consumer (online, retail stores)? Which geographic area will be most successful

for the product? (For example, John Deere farm equipment is likely to fare better in the Midwest than in New York City).

Once students have learned about the four P's, in small groups they choose an ad from one of the magazines that Ms. Anderson has brought in for this lesson. They study its composition and then share with the rest of the class the four P's they found operating in their chosen ad. Next, integrating the arts as part of this lesson, Ms. Anderson invites students to choose or create a product, and using the available classroom art materials (pencils, pencil colors, magazine images, glue, markers, paper, and crayons), students create an ad using the four P's as their guidelines.

Students share their advertisements with each other and then post them on the wall. Ms. Anderson asks them to fill out an exit slip on what they learned during that lesson. Even though she is comfortable that students learned the four P's, and she knows that she has engaged the students in critical thinking, she wonders what students learned about the world of advertisements and how they act on the consumer. When Ms. Anderson looks at the ads that her students created, she notices that they reproduced similar ads to those that encourage students to become consumers. She wonders if there are ways in which she could include engagements that would help her students take a more critical stance in reading ads, and thereby offer them ways to become conscious consumers of ads rather than passive consumers of products.

DEFINING THE TARGETED PRACTICE

The practice that Ms. Anderson engaged in is called I-R-E, or initiate, respond, and evaluate. This questioning strategy, which continues to prevail in many classrooms, is teacher-centered and -directed. The teacher asks students a question (often a question to which the teacher knows the answer), students respond, and the teacher evaluates the response. If students answer correctly, the teacher often responds with a positive phrase, such as "Good answer" or "Nicely stated."

The I-R-E questioning strategy is troubled in several ways. First, there is a false sense of discussion. That is, the teacher designs, develops, or asks questions to which he or she wants a particular response or answer. In this sense, students do not engage in discussion, but in a guessing game in which they try to figure out "What is in the teacher's mind?"

Second, students are asked to think simply, often with fact-finding at the heart of the answer. For example, here is a short dialogue that Ms. Anderson had with her students about the content of this lesson to demonstrate this point:

TEACHER: Which ads or products appealed to you?

STUDENT: I liked the one with Britney Spears. She's on skates and I'm a skater.

TEACHER: Why did it appeal to you?

STUDENT: The ad says that these skates are made of genuine leather.

STUDENT: Because the wheels are made of titanium.

TEACHER: Good. What aspect of "product" makes this a good ad?

STUDENT: This is a sort of warranty because titanium is a really strong metal.

TEACHER: Yes, good. What else does the ad say?

STUDENT: It says, "Be the best and only the best."

TEACHER: Okay. How does language work here?

STUDENT: It makes us believe that we will be the best if we buy it.

TEACHER: Excellent.

Although Ms. Anderson may think that her students' responses to aspects of the product concept that she taught in the PowerPoint elicited conversation/discussion and deeper thinking, students have merely identified facts within the advertisement. In essence, Ms. Anderson really evaluated the students' ability to identify, not to think about how the language, ad design, and celebrity operate to create desire and encourage consumerism. Thinking about ideas or texts in real ways is crucial, argue Ivey and Fisher (2005): "Students need instruction, but mostly they need opportunities to negotiate real texts for real purposes" (p. 10). Rather than ask students to identify parts of an ad that reflect only superficial aspects of ad making, educators must consider how these ads operate on readers as consumers.

Third, students rely on the teacher to determine whether they have gotten the answer right. In such questioning, students do not listen to others' responses and engage in conversation about an idea, concept, or issue, but look to the teacher for affirmation. Each time Ms. Anderson responds with "Good," "Okay," or "Excellent," she evaluates students' responses—evaluations that, over time, tell students that this is the way in which classroom conversations happen and the way they will be expected to respond in the future.

WHAT DOES THE RESEARCH SAY ABOUT I-R-E?

As a way to elicit responses and assess understanding, questions have been a source of research across the past century and into this century. Identified by Mehan (1979) as one of the most common discourse patterns in class-rooms, I-R-E, a sequential order of three turns, has had negative response by scholars (Afflerbach, 2007; Cazden, 2001; Lemke, 1990). For Lemke, this pattern of questioning positions the instructor as knower and tester of information; the answer to the question is what the teacher seeks. This type of dialogue favors the instructor's priorities—getting students to answer correctly—rather than offering students opportunities to raise issues, con-cerns, and/or questions. For Bowers and Flinders (1990), I-R-E often elicits factual and explicit details about a text and actively involves only a single student while the others remain passive. Students understand that learn-ing is about receiving information rather than generating complex thinking (Bowers & Flinders, 1990). In a more recent study, Zemel and Koschmann (2010) found that students may reconsider their answers when a teacher does not explicitly correct their responses, but rather adjusts his or her questions to correct their responses. Across this work, I-R-E continues to rest in the design of the teacher, and the ultimate goal is for students to reach a particular answer.

WHAT ARE SOME ALTERNATIVES?

In order to consider alternative approaches to teach students how to engage in critical literacy, let's return to Ms. Anderson's class and consider why she chose to develop the lesson as she did. First, she wanted to engage the students in popular culture using advertisements as the major texts. She believed that by including texts that students encounter daily, or what Janks (2010) calls *everyday texts*, she would incite interest in the course material. Second, she thought that by asking questions about the visual information in these advertisements, she would encourage her students to consider how image informs their reading of a text. Third, by creating their own adver-tisements, students would better understand how design, color, language, and image operate together in the construction of advertisements. And, fourth, and perhaps the most significant, is that Ms. Anderson feels that something is missing, and that she wants to engage her students in more thoughtful discussions, not just ask them about content. She wants her stu-dents to be critical consumers of texts, such as advertisements, and not just identify details that designers take into consideration when they create ads. Each of these reasons suggests that Ms. Anderson is ready to try on differ-ent approaches to teaching texts—critical approaches that will engage her students in thoughtful and meaningful discussions. In essence, she wants to know how to teach from a critical literacy perspective.

Critical Literacy

Since the early 1980s and well into the 2000s, literacy and curriculum researchers have drawn upon the work of critical literacy theorists, post-structuralists, and postmodernists to examine the construction of meaning as the complex intersection of power, written language, and knowledge (Britzman,1995; Edelsky, 2006; Greene, 1995; Janks, 2000, 2010; Luke & Freebody, 1997; Macedo, 1994; Macedo & Bartolome, 2000; Shannon, 1993; Vasquez, Harste, & Albers, 2010). Critical literacy draws upon Paulo Freire's (1970) idea that in order to transform the larger political issues that determine whose interests are being served, a person needs to read and write functionally in the language of those in power. Drawing from this work, critical literacy scholars (Albers, 1996; Albers, Vasquez, & Harste, 2011; Comber, 2001; Edelsky; 2006; Harste, 2003; Lewison, Leland, & Harste, 2008; Janks, 2000, 2010; Luke & Freebody, 1997; Shannon, 1993; Vasquez, 2004) situate literacy within the larger issues of society and argue that teachers must prepare students not only to read and write, but to develop literacy practices that engage them in (1) critically examining their world and its assumptions about learning, (2) interrogating the relationship between language and power, and (3) engaging in social action to promote social justice (Lewison et al., 2008). Teachers who operate within a critical literacy perspective set up classroom engagements to support a language of critique—one that examines issues of power, position, and privilege (Comber, 2001)—and to teach students to talk back to texts (Britzman, 1995), or speak to and against constructions of identity in texts, and identify locations of power and privilege in whose voice in the text is most visible (Janks, 2000).

Critical literacy requires a reading of cultures around, behind, underneath, alongside, after, and within the text (Luke, O'Brien, & Comber, 2001). Luke and Freebody's (1997) model of reading as social practice explains reading as a non-neutral form of cultural practice that positions readers and obscures as much as it illuminates. Readers for the 21st century, they argue, need to be able to interrogate the assumptions that are embedded in text as well as the assumptions that they, as culturally indoctrinated beings, bring to the text. There are no right ways or right methods to teach reading and writing; rather, Luke (1998) states, the question is "how and to what ends can we shape students' reading and writing practices" (p. 306)? Education in the English/language arts is about "knowing and engaging students in the kinds of literate culture they are likely to encounter and working with them on designing and redesigning those cultures and their texts" (Luke, 1998, p. 306). Purcell-Gates (1995) furthers this view and argues that "everyone processes information through a cultural lens" and that "all learning takes place within a social context" (pp. 5–6). Scholars of transaction theory (Rosenblatt, 1983) often agree that readers and texts both contribute to the reading process. However, it is the practice of critical literacy that enables students to become aware of the range of messages—explicit and implicit—that underpin texts (Harste, 2010). In other words, in order to understand students' processes of learning, we must seek to understand the social and political context within which learning takes place. Vivian Vasquez (2004) wrote of her own school context, her immigrant status, and her recollection of how she was positioned as "voiceless, as incapable of action, of making a difference in the lives of others, or indeed, [her] own life" (p. xiv). The curriculum and teaching in her school "tilted in favor of dominant cultural ways of being" (p. xv), which left immigrant children as disadvantaged. Critical literacy seeks to support all students' voices and experiences, not just those who are privileged.

To position all voices and experiences as significant, Britzman (1995) suggests that readers must "talk back to texts." That is, not all texts can be read and interpreted from one standpoint. How texts are read and the meaning one gets from texts depend on one's experiences, background, and language; meaning is not situated within the words or the images that comprise a text but the interaction between the reader and the text (Rosenblatt, 1983). Britzman posits that readers must not merely ask "What does this text mean?" but, more importantly, ask "Who am I becoming through the interpretive claims that I make upon another and upon myself?" Hilary Janks (2010) pointed this out in regard to how people are represented and how, as viewers, we are taught by photographers, designers, artists, writers, and so on, how to decipher who or what someone is. From such teaching, we build a network of characteristics around someone or something that then allows us to say "That's a so-and-so." For example, in my own study of children's literature (Albers, 2008), I found that Native Americans, in the 21st century, continue to be represented in virtually the same way they were when artists began to paint them in the 1800s—atop wide open spaces, on horseback, semi-naked, and almost always wearing feathered garments. As a native of South Dakota, which has a large population of Native Americans, these images did not resonate with me as representative. I saw Native Americans in school, at work, at community events—living in a similar way as many of the white community members. Within a critical literacy perspective, we can talk back to, or challenge, commonplace constructions of representations like those of Native Americans, or Asians, or of jobs such as plumbers, teachers, or librarians; assumptions that position some as better than others. Such talking back to texts offers an opportunity to shake up what we consider to be cultural norms by interrogating the constructs within texts; it provides the tools for noticing, analyzing, and reflecting on text (Browett, 2005).

In the next section, I talk about ways in which teachers can help their students develop and take a critical stance toward texts, more specifically, toward multimedia texts. As teachers learn about critical literacy practices, they can support their students' ability to understand that meaning does not reside solely in the text, but within the background, experiences, and language of the reader. This is critical pedagogy, a set of practices in which teachers (1) bring to the surface and make conscious issues that serve some and not others, (2) examine the ideologies that underlie a text, (3) use texts that provoke discussions and bring in alternative perspectives, and (4) rethink their position on issues of learning.

Approaches to Teaching from a Critical Literacy Perspective

In their book *Creating Critical Classrooms*, Lewison and colleagues (2008) suggest that to teach from a critical perspective means that a teacher must want to engage students in discussions around social issues that are embedded in every text they teach. From posters in their school, to the textbooks from which they teach, authors' and designers' belief systems are evident. The ideas presented below will offer insights into lessons that teachers can develop to help their students understand critical literacy, begin to talk back to texts, and engage in social action, not just within their classrooms but worldwide.

Collecting Everyday Texts

In order to integrate texts that would interest students, Janks (2010) suggests that teachers and students begin a collection of everyday texts. These are texts that are a part of our everyday world. Across the day, week, month, and year, we encounter a large number of different texts daily—from bills, to weekly circulars, to magazines, newspapers, cereal boxes, candy wrappers, books, and so on. These texts can be used as resources for classroom discussion and to help students develop a critical stance.

In order to initiate a critical analysis of everyday texts, Ms. Anderson might consider inviting her students to bring in one everyday text that has to do with being a teen (e.g., a photograph, advertisement, newspaper article, cartoon) and how teens are represented or texts in which teens would be interested. She could divide the class into four groups and ask each group to study these texts for patterns that emerge across the images, composition, language, and/or design, and organize and tape them onto the classroom wall. Janks (2010) suggests that students consider questions that elicit critical analysis:

1. How are teens represented? Is it positive, negative? Are they problems or solutions?
2. What claims are made about teens?
3. Who is represented (cultural groups, languages, city–rural, and so on)? Who is left out or not shown? How are the teens engaged in the activity? Are they enjoying it or not?
4. Where (place/time) are teens in this text?
5. What counts in terms of being a teen?
6. What are the commonplace assumptions about teens?

Each group studies its own everyday texts guided by these questions, and then shares insights with the whole group. All groups then paste their texts onto the classroom wall. As a whole group, Ms. Anderson might ask her students to look across all of the texts and to consider these same questions.

To follow up, Ms. Anderson could type in the word *teens* in the Google search engine, click on the "Images" link, and invite her class to look at how teens are represented in photographs. She can ask her students to consider the concept of *discourse* as involving a set of social practices (Gee, 2005) in which teens are involved. From this, Ms. Anderson could engage her students in the concept of how stereotypes are often developed when strong patterns of particular details emerge, and the importance of considering multiple perspectives when talking back to the commonplace assumptions about teens.

Studying Advertisements

In planning her lesson, Ms. Anderson understood that including advertisements as multimodal texts addressed one of her county language arts standards. Furthermore, she understood that her students were always talking about their purchases or their desires for the newest gadget for downloading music, video, or images; the latest fashion; or for really nice products that would make them more appealing to others. Ms. Anderson noticed that her middle schoolers were a potential and significant consumer market, and she wanted her students to be more thoughtful about how advertisements, as everyday texts, shaped their beliefs and practices. Introducing advertisements seemed a good start.

Popular culture produces texts that are attractive to large numbers of children. Our world is filled with a range of visual texts (advertisements, TV, films, Internet sites, billboards, etc.), argues Carr (2000), and these must be interrogated by even the youngest of children who can examine and identify significant concepts, symbols, and systems of representation. The connection between literacy and popular culture has been investigated by a number of scholars, including Steinberg and Kincheloe (2004) and Beach (2007), who have argued that we have become a culture of consumerism. Corporations, with or without our consent, define and shape through their products the identities they believe children and youth want to become. These scholars advocate for a critique of multimodal texts, such as advertisements, by students, but these texts are often given little space in language arts curricula because they are considered not academically rigorous (Marsh, 2006). However, children, youth, and adults view over 40,000 advertisements each year (Schor, 2004), and advertisers use a range of media, including magazines, to present their goods and services to influence consumers' attention to, and interest in, buying certain products (Calvert, 2008).

According to Kelly and Ellwanger (2008), children ages 6–11 access the Internet frequently to find out more about products they see in advertisements. Furthermore, these analysts found that of the 10.7 million young consumers who reported visiting a company's website after viewing its ad, 26.5% are 6–7 years old, 33.3% are 8–9 years old, and 40.2% are 10–11 years old. More surprisingly, experts estimate that children between the ages of 2 and 14 influence how households spend $500 billion dollars a year (Calvert, 2008). These data suggest that awareness of the power relations and intentions that underpin advertisements is essential, especially in school spaces where learners see advertisements in their classrooms, hallways, on the Internet while researching school projects, and so on. In essence, it is never too early to start helping students critically analyze and develop frames for talking about popular culture (Lewison et al., 2008), which includes advertisements. Attention to analyzing advertisements from a critical literacy perspective offers another tool through which students can talk back to popular culture texts.

Albers, Harste, Vander Zanden, and Felderman (2008) introduced critical analysis of advertisements to teachers and to fourth-grade students. We asked these two groups to study popular ads (Walmart, Burger King, Disney, army ads, Skecher, among others) and let us know which of the ads appealed to them and why. Using questions similar to those suggested by Janks (2010) in the previous section, we invited these two groups to study these ads critically and to articulate who was represented and who was not, what activities were engaged in, and what products were endorsed? How were some people represented as positive and some negative? Both populations found the design, color, celebrity, and lifestyle elements presented in the ads to be enticing and to drive their interest in either living the lifestyle or buying the product featured in the ad.

Ms. Anderson, like us, wanted her students to think critically about ads; she also wanted them to produce an ad. What she wished was that her students would have produced ads that paid critical attention to the consumer rather than invite the consumer to be lured into purchasing a product. She could have asked them to create counter-ads, or ads that talk back to the messages of overt consumerism by means of art, language, and design tactics. Counter-ads have been designed to speak against unhealthy products that are marketed in positive ways. For example, children have responded well to the Joe Camel ad. Websites such as *www.adbusters.org* have designed counter-ads such as Joe Chemo to talk back to corporations who attempt to entice populations to engage in unhealthy habits. In Figure 8.1, Ms. Anderson created a counter-ad to talk back to former President Bush's No Child Left Behind Act. She used Smokey the Bear's message of preventing forest fires and made this analogous to teachers speaking against high-stakes testing to prevent students from becoming statistics on national reports. By doing counter-ads, Ms. Anderson could help her students become savvy consumers, rather than passive consumers enticed by color, design, and product.

ONLY YOU

Make the difference in a child's education

Bush is counting on you to leave no child behind.

1. Teach the test.

2. Review for the test.

3. Practice the test.

4. Take the test.

5. Teach the test.

6. Review for the test.

7. Practice the test. . . .

REMEMBER, ONLY YOU CAN PREVENT FAILURE.

FIGURE 8.1. Counter-ad.

Multimedia Approaches to Build Critical Literacy:
Public Service Announcements

To position students to read moving images critically, I introduced the idea of public service announcements (PSAs) to my middle grades language arts teachers. PSAs are 1-minute engaging multimedia texts that present persuasive or informative messages about social issues. To make sense within a language arts curriculum, I asked teachers to consider social issues within a literary text on which they wanted to focus, such as *Animal Farm* (Orwell, 1945/1996), *Monster* (Myers, 2001), *Maniac Magee* (Spinelli, 1999), and so on, and to create a 30- to 60-second self-running PSA using iMovie or Moviemaker. To help students understand the PSA and to begin to think critically, I started with everyday print-based PSAs in newspapers, magazines, or on billboards. For example, I used a number of print versions of how teens are positioned as drug users, often targeted at the parent audience. One of the most familiar is the two-frame PSA, "This is your brain on drugs." The top frame shows an image of two eggs with the text "This is your brain." The bottom frame shows two eggs frying in a pan with the written text, "This is your brain on drugs." One only need Google the word "drugs" and one can see the many images that position teens as vulnerable to their seduction.

To begin our critical discussion, we talk about commonplace assumptions regarding young teens, their habits and interests, and whether all teens do drugs or whether they want to. How are teens portrayed in movies? In novels? In print-based ads? Billboards? Teachers, parents, and the public are taught that teens engage in dangerous practices. However, this is only one perspective. To take on a critical stance, one must look at multiple perspectives about teens. We move this discussion into the importance of taking multiple perspectives and to see this ad as presenting only one such view about teens and their practices. We then look at several other PSAs on YouTube, including the very graphic methadone ads. Such PSAs (and other media, including commercials, videos, movies) portray teens in deviant practices, and PSAs, such as the "brain-on-drugs" ad, position parents to imagine their own child on drugs and to figure out what must be done to dissuade them from using drugs. Our discussion then leads into the design of the PSA and the elements that a designer uses to incite a particular response. Following this extended discussion, teachers chose a literary text (young adult or classic novel), and designed a PSA based on an issue they wanted to address, developing their idea with multimodal features such as images, text, voice-over narration, and transitions (Albers, Vasquez, & Harste, 2008).

As multimedia texts, PSAs juxtapose the more conventional literature studies talk (Langer, 1995; Pirie, 1997; Scholes, 1986) alongside the newer literacies (arts and technology). Once teachers become familiar with the tools needed to create PSAs, they can engage students of all ages (children to older teens) in the process of designing, developing, and producing these texts. Students respond enthusiastically to this assignment because it, at once, situates discussion of social issues in the literary text within their own lives and brings into play their desire to create multimedia texts, drawing upon their knowledge of technology, image manipulation, special effects, music, and so on. And, importantly, they speak to others of their own age group in significantly different ways—not the hard-hitting in-your-face messages that adults send to young viewers.

As critical literacy engagements, PSAs provide a link between litera-ture and social issues such as mental illness, bullying, neglect, and fight-ing inner demons. As designers of PSAs, students learn how to tell a story through multimedia, how to engage their viewers in this story with music, image, written text, transitions and special effects.

Additional Readings/Lessons

A number of articles has been written about how to work with critical lit-eracy. Vivian Vasquez's (2004) work with negotiating critical literacy with children offers a number of good ideas. Students study posters that fea-ture people in different careers, noting how gender is represented within and across these posters. In her classroom in Canada, her students found that the Royal Mounted Police featured only men in this career. Her stu-dents took social action to write to their government to let them know that women can serve in this profession as well. In your own class, your students could study posters to notice and question the implicit assumptions about teens regarding their social behaviors, their food habits, and their attitudes toward education.

In my book *Finding the Artist Within* (Albers, 2007), I introduce a number of arts-based projects that support critical literacy. Especially in Chapter 7, I discuss how to read student-generated visual texts in terms of their structure, design, object placement, color, space, repetition, and so on. In Figure 8.2, I demonstrate a brief analysis of an autobiographical image that an English learner drew. The text reads left to right and, in my research, often indicates that a narrative is being told—this is a story of the student herself. She is the center of attention (space inside the circle) and to her right is a cityscape. The written text at the top says "Fear of the Unknown." The left side of the image suggests the real or the given information (Kress & van Leeuwen, 2006): She *is* this girl. To the right is the unknown, represented by the cityscape and symbolizing experiences that a city offers and that she fears. Interestingly, the girl who drew this was Asian, with black hair. In terms of critical literacy, young adolescents, and especially English learners, want to envision themselves as someone

FIGURE 8.2. Student's visual text. From Albers (2007). Copyright 2007 by the International Reading Association. *www.reading.org.* Reprinted by permission.

else, someone better. In this instance, this young Asian girl wanted to see herself as a young American blond teenager, the epitome of those who are fun and engaging. From a critical literacy perspective, this young Asian girl had relinquished her identity in favor of another—a problematic state of being for her. From a critical teaching practice, analysis of the art elements and organization of students' visual texts can offer teachers and peers ways to interrogate the "ideal" image of an American teen. When students have this knowledge, they are better able to decipher the tactics used by designers, artists, photographers, and so on, to influence their beliefs about which lifestyles should be valued more than others.

In her work with English learners, Carger (2004) supported her students' language learning by having them study classical artwork, respond to it, and then create artwork of their own. Not only did students develop confidence in their writing and reading, but in their art making as well. By integrating the arts with critical literacy practices into instruction, students who are often marginalized because they do not speak English well can participate freely and actively in the discussion of paintings and then move on to written texts.

In another approach, called *cultural heritage project*, I worked with students to create multimodal texts relating to their own heritage (Figure 8.3), in which their lives are central to the reading of literature (Albers, 2006). After reading a classic or contemporary adolescent novel, students make connections to the characters' lives, situations, experiences, beliefs, and/or attitudes through a multimodal project that depicts their life in relation to the lives of the characters. These projects take on a range of different formats, from trifold boards to three-dimensional sculptures to poster

FIGURE 8.3. Cultural heritage project. From Albers (2006). Copyright 2006 by the National Council of Teachers of English. Reprinted by permission.

boards and self-running PowerPoints. Students demystify the concept that text is only written, and explore it in musical, visual, photographic, culinary, and so on, formats. These projects are wonderfully received by students as they make personal, academic, and social connections between the lives of the characters in the novel and their own.

In their book *Creating Critical Classrooms*, Lewison and colleagues (2008) offer a large number of engagements that can support critical literacy practices in the language arts classroom. In one particular engagement, called "Poignant Passages," students read a text (literary, expository, poetic, or other) and find a passage or set of sentences that strikes them because it reflects their particular values and assumptions. As an example, these educators use the picture book *The Carpet Boy's Gift* (Deitz Shea, 2006) and ask students to respond to the phrase "the children need to use a pen." The central character in this book stood up for his rights and eventually died as a result of his social action against child labor. Children discuss the various ways in which they, as children, can take action—writing, speaking, demonstrating, among others. Another engagement, "Happy Holidays for Whom?", helps students to consider how holiday ads position both the consumer and the recipient in particular ways. Students bring junk-mail fliers from home, especially around a holiday, and study the images with these questions in mind: What is being sold? Who is featured? Who is the intended consumer? How has the designer of the ad used art elements to entice the buyer? Are there any stereotypes being perpetuated?

CONCLUSION

Like Ms. Anderson, I too emphasize the importance of teaching students not only to think critically or metacognitively about texts, but to think from a critical stance, in which they discuss social issues that matter; disrupt commonplace assumptions about people, culture, representations, concepts, and so on; and engage in social action to bring to the surface issues of inequity. So, although we, as English language arts teachers, need to develop skills that enable students to interpret text, I argue that we also must help them recognize how texts shape viewers' interpretations. To be fully literate is to engage in thinking from a critical stance and to possess the tools with which to interpret a range of messages, explicit and implicit, embedded in all texts.

ADDITIONAL LESSON EXAMPLES

The following lesson examples from the International Reading Association's Read-WriteThink support critical literacy and offer additional alternatives to I-R-E.

www.readwritethink.org/professional-development/professional-library/critical-literacies-graphic-novels-20922.html
This lesson supports critical literacy and multimodal approaches to teaching *Maus* to high school English learners.

www.readwritethink.org/classroom-resources/lesson-plans/talk-about-stories-shared-57.html
This lesson for elementary students focuses on literature discussions around *Amazing Grace*, a picturebook that elicits discussions of social justice.

www.readwritethink.org/classroom-resources/lesson-plans/exploring-consumerism-where-intersect-1114.html
This lesson focuses on issues of consumerism and how to support students' critical readings of advertisements.

www.readwritethink.org/classroom-resources/lesson-plans/critical-media-literacy-commercial-97.html
This lesson supports students' critical readings of mass media, especially advertising.

TRADE BOOKS CITED IN TEXT

Deitz Shea, P. (2006). *The carpet boy's gift.* Gardiner, ME: Tilbury House.
Myers, W. D. (2001). *Monster.* New York: Amistad.
Orwell, G. (1996). *Animal farm.* New York: Signet Classics. (Original work published 1945)
Spinelli, J. (1999). *Maniac Magee.* New York: Little, Brown Books for Young Readers.

REFERENCES

Afflerbach, P. (2007). *Understanding and using reading assessment, K–12.* Newark, DE: International Reading Association.
Albers, P. (1996). Issues of representation: Caldecott winners 1984–1995. *New Advocate, 9*(4), 267–286.
Albers, P. (2006). Imagining the possibilities in multimodal curriculum design. *English Education, 38*(2), 75–101.
Albers, P. (2007). *Finding the artist within: Creating and reading visual texts in English language arts classrooms.* Newark, DE: International Reading Association.
Albers, P. (2008). Theorizing visual representation in children's literature. *Journal of Literacy Research, 40*(2), 163–200.
Albers, P., Harste, J. C., Vander Zanden, S., & Felderman, C. (2008). Using popular culture to promote critical literacy practices. In Y. Kim (Ed.), *57th Yearbook of the National Reading Conference* (pp. 70–83). Oak Creek, WI: National Reading Conference.
Albers, P., Vasquez, V., & Harste, J. C. (2008). A classroom with a view. *Talking Points, 19*(2), 3–13.
Albers, P., Vasquez, V., & Harste, J. C. (2011). Visual literacy made critical. In D. Lapp & D. Fisher (Eds.), *The handbook of research on teaching the English language arts* (3rd ed., pp. 195–201). Mahwah, NJ: Erlbaum.
Beach, R. (2007, November). *Creating critical classrooms: Double standards and bringing consumerism home.* Paper presented at the annual conference of the National Council of Teachers of English, New York.
Bowers, C. A., & Flinders, D. J. (1990). *Responsive teaching: An ecological approach to classroom patterns of language, culture, and thought.* New York: Teachers College Press.
Britzman, D. P. (1995). Is there a queer pedagogy?: Or, stop reading straight. *Educational Theory, 45*(2), 151–165.
Browett, J. (2005). Critical literacy and visual texts: Windows on culture. Available at *www.education.tas.gov.au/curriculum/standards/english/english/teachers/discussion/browett.*
Calvert, S. L. (2008). Children as consumers: Advertising and marketing. *Future of Children, 18*(1), 205–234.
Carger, C. L. (2004). Art and literacy with bilingual children. *Language Arts, 81*(4), 283–292.

Carr, J. (2000). From "sympathetic" to "dialogic" imagination: Cultural study in the foreign language classroom. In A. Lo Bianco, A. J. Liddicoat, & C. Crozet (Eds.), *Striving for the third place: Intercultural competence through language education* (pp. 103–110). Melbourne: Language Australia.

Cazden, W. (2001). *Classroom discourse: The language of teaching and learning.* Portsmouth, NH: Heinemann.

Comber, B. (2001). Classroom explorations in critical literacy. In H. Fehring & P. Green (Eds.), *Critical literacy: A collection of articles from the Australian Literacy Educators' Association* (pp. 90–111). Newark, DE: International Reading Association.

Edelsky, C. (2006). *With literacy and justice for all: Rethinking the social in language and education.* Mahwah, NJ: Erlbaum.

Freire, P. (1970). *Pedagogy of the oppressed.* London: Penguin.

Gee, J. (2005). *An introduction to discourse analysis: Theory and method* (2nd ed.). Abingdon, UK: Routledge.

Greene, M. (1995). *Releasing the imagination: Essays on education, the arts, and social change.* San Francisco: Jossey-Bass.

Harste, J. C. (2003). What do we mean by literacy now? *Voices from the Middle, 10*(3), 8–12.

Harste, J. C. (2010). Multimodality. In P. Albers & J. Sanders (Eds.), *Literacies, the arts and multimodality* (pp. 27–43). Urbana, IL: National Council of Teachers of English.

Ivey, G., & Fisher, D. (2005). Learning from what doesn't work. *Educational Leadership, 63*(2), 8–14.

Janks, H. (2000). Domination, access, diversity, and design: A synthesis for critical literacy education. *Education Review, 52*(2), 175–186.

Janks, H. (2010). *Literacy and power.* New York: Routledge.

Kelly, A., & Ellwanger, S. (2008). Nearly one-half of kids report being drawn to websites by TV or print advertisements. Retrieved December 11, 2010, from *www.gfkmri.com/PDF/MRIPR_121608_KidsStudy.pdf.*

Kress, G., & van Leeuwen, T. (2006). *Reading images: The grammar of visual design* (2nd ed.). New York: Routledge.

Langer, J. A. (1995). *Envisioning literature: Literary understanding and literature instruction.* New York: Teachers College Press.

Lemke, J. L. (1990). *Talking science: Language, learning, and values.* Norwood, NJ: Ablex.

Lewison, M., Leland, C., & Harste, J. C. (2008). *Creating critical classrooms: K–8 reading and writing with an edge.* Mahwah, NJ: Erlbaum.

Luke, A. (1998). Getting over method: Literacy teaching as work in a "new time." *Language Arts, 75*(1), 305–313.

Luke, A., & Freebody, P. (1997). Shaping the social practices of reading. In S. Muspratt, A. Luke, & P. Freebody (Eds.), *Constructing critical literacies* (pp. 185–225). Cresskill, NJ: Hampton Press.

Luke, A., O'Brien, J., & Comber, B. (2001). Making community texts objects of study. In H. Fehring & P. Green (Eds.), *Critical literacy: A collection of articles from the Australian Literacy Educators' Association* (pp. 112–123). Newark, DE: International Reading Association.

Macedo, D. (1994). *Literacies of power: What Americans are not allowed to know.* Boulder, CO: Westview Press.

Macedo, D., & Bartolome, L. I. (2000). *Dancing with bigotry: Beyond the politics of tolerance.* New York: Palgrave.

Marsh, J. (2006). Popular culture and literacy: A Bourdieuan analysis. *Reading Research Quarterly, 46*(2), 160–74.

Mehan, H. (1979). "What time is it, Denise?": Asking known questions in classroom discourse. *Theory into Practice, 18*(4), 285–294.

Pirie, B. (1997). *Reshaping high school English.* Urbana, IL: National Council of Teachers of English.

Purcell-Gates, V. (1995). *Other people's words: The cycle of low literacy.* Cambridge, MA: Harvard University Press.

Rosenblatt, L. (1983). *Literature as exploration.* New York: Modern Language Association of America.

Scholes, R. E. (1986). *Textual power: Literary theory and the teaching of English.* New Haven, CT: Yale University Press.

Schor, J. B. (2004). *Born to buy: The commercialized child and the new consumer culture.* New York: Scribner.

Shannon, P. (1993). Developing democratic voices. *The Reading Teacher, 47*(2), 86–95.

Steinberg, S. R., & Kincheloe, J. L. (2004). Introduction: No more secrets—kinderculture, information saturation, and the postmodern childhood. In S. R. Steinberg & J. L. Kincheloe (Eds.), *Kinderculture: The corporate construction of childhood* (pp. 1–30). Boulder, CO: Westview Press.

Vasquez, V. (2004). *Negotiating critical literacies with young children.* Mahwah, NJ: Erlbaum.

Vasquez, V., Harste, J. C., & Albers, P. (2010). From the personal to the Worldwide Web: Moving teachers into positions of critical interrogation. In E. A. Baker (Ed.), *The new literacies: Multiple perspectives on research and practice* (pp. 265–284). New York: Guilford Press.

Zemel, A., & Koschmann, T. (2010). Pursuing a question: Reinitiating IRE sequences as a method of instruction. *Journal of Pragmatics, 43*, 475–488.

PART
II

Developing Spoken
and Written Language

CHAPTER 9

If You Want to Take the Ho-Hum Out of History—
Teach Writing That's Right for New Times

Dana L. Grisham
Thomas DeVere Wolsey

Key Points for This Chapter

- Reading and writing in social science require knowledge of text structures that social scientists use in their writing.
- Teachers can effectively scaffold students' writing in the disciplines by teaching both content reading and writing.
- Use of appropriate Web 2.0 technologies can assist teachers and engage students in disciplinary learning.
- Collaboration among disciplinary teachers strengthens and extends students' disciplinary learning.

A BIRD'S-EYE VIEW OF CLASSROOM PRACTICE

Last week, Ms. Capson attempted to get her seventh-grade social studies students to write about the technological changes in transportation that occurred in Europe between 1400 and 1789 C.E. and how these innovations influenced the development of the Western Hemisphere. Students had completed the textbook chapter through round-robin reading because Ms. Capson believes that oral reading may provide access to content knowledge for all her learners, including her struggling readers and English learners.

Then Ms. Capson led the students in the construction of a detailed timeline of that development that extends across two walls of the classroom, so that all the students could see the pertinent dates of important innovations. Next, the students were directed to write a five-paragraph essay (Seo, 2007) about the importance of one of the technological innovations in transportation. "You will need to write a thesis statement," said Ms. Capson. "Then you will support your thesis statement with four paragraphs that provide the reader with information about the changes and document the innovation's importance to development in the Western Hemisphere. Finish with a summary statement that ties all your points together. You may begin." As Ms. Capson walked around the room, she realized that very few of the students were writing. The students were frowning and looking frustrated as they raised their hands to ask Ms. Capson what they should do. It wasn't long before Ms. Capson had to call the writing period to a halt.

When Ms. Capson deconstructed her failed lesson plan with her English teacher colleague, Mr. Whettre, he was sympathetic, but he told her that he had much the same problem. Together, they resolved to do some investigation into writing instruction practices for their middle school students.

DEFINING THE TARGETED PRACTICE

Ms. Capson and Mr. Whettre conducted what they termed a "writing workshop" in their seventh-grade English and social studies classrooms, where they expect students to write on demand in a specific genre to demonstrate their learning in English and history/social science. Both teachers expected their students to be able to write essays with thesis statements and supporting paragraphs, once they had read the content of the textbook (Johnson, Thompson, Smagorinsky, & Fry, 2003).

WHAT DOES THE RESEARCH SAY ABOUT WRITING IN THE DISCIPLINES?

Ms. Capson and Mr. Whettre learned that teaching children to write is a complex construct that requires both art and skill from teachers (Grisham & Wolsey, in press; Wolsey, 2010). To teach writing effectively to middle grade students means that each content-area teacher needs to be familiar with instruction in the type of writing most common in that discipline (Farnan & Fearn, 2008). Writing in science, for example, is not the same as writing in social studies or writing in mathematics. Thus, writing across the content areas means learning how to write in a number of different text structures or genres that most commonly appear in a particular content area (cf. Fang, Schleppegrell, & Cox, 2006).

There is also a distinction between writing across the curriculum (WAC) and writing in the disciplines (WID). Monroe (2003, p. 4) states, "While WAC emphasizes the commonality, portability, and communicability of writing practices, WID emphasizes disciplinary differences, diversity, and heterogeneity." In other words, we need both, but we need to be aware that there are differences in writing in varying content areas.

In their meta-analysis Graham and Hebert (2010) found that writing can improve reading. In their report for the Carnegie Foundation, they addressed the social costs of poor literacy skills in an age of globalization. Graham and Hebert were able to document several ways for educators to address this need for literacy skills in their meta-analysis, suggesting that writing can enhance reading in at least three ways. First, as a functional activity, writing can be combined with reading to learn new ideas from text or to enhance learning in the disciplines. Second, reading and writing are connected in that both draw upon the individual's knowledge and cognitive processes—thus improving writing should improve reading. Finally, reading and writing are essential communication activities—thus writers may learn about reading as they create their own texts (p. 4).

Novice writers, such as those in the middle school classroom, often use a "retrieve-and-tell" approach to writing tasks (Berninger & Richards, 2002). This is qualitatively different from the "knowledge-transforming model" that more expert writers use. The novice's focus is on generating content, whereas the expert also considers goals, plans, and problems inherent in the composing process. When we teach our students to write in a particular genre, we must scaffold such instruction through several such experiences before we can expect more than novice outcomes. Recently, Klein and Rose (2010) reported on research conducted to find out how students at the high school level learn to write explanations. They recommend the following:

- Frequent writing in the content area (shorter pieces three times per week)
- A conception of writing as learning (interpretation of experiences)
- Education in analytic genres (and reading to experience each genre)
- Strategic approach to genre education (a strategy for each genre)
- Strategies for constructive use of sources
- Evaluation and revision for learning
- Assessment designed to support self-evaluation
- Building intrinsic motivation (interesting projects)
- Remediation of mechanics (p. 437)

Klein and Rose (2010) report that high school students who partici-pated in their study design program made gains on the measures used when they taught the nonfiction genre of explanation in this manner. We would argue that the same strategies apply when addressing the needs of middle school students.

Farnan and Fearn (2008) also state: "The concept of writing across the curriculum is not new in education, but it's important to know exactly what it means" (p. 404). They explain that it means using writing as a tool for thinking and learning in discipline-specific ways. Learning to read in the content areas is essential for middle school students, but we would also argue that writing in a given genre is a function not only of analysis of reading but also of instruction targeted at task analysis of the genre. Shana-han and Shanahan (2008) argue that "disciplinary literacy" must be taught differently in each content, because content experts read and write differ-ently in different contents; therefore, explicit teaching of these "advanced literacy skills" is needed in our middle and high schools.

When talking about elementary-age students, Dorfman and Cappelli (2007) suggest that they must have "mentor texts" for writing purposes. We believe that this idea is even more important to middle school students in different disciplines. Having read a selection with knowledge of text structure, the student is better prepared for a supported writing task using the same text structures for the same discipline. When students pay atten-tion to their topic, they construct their own knowledge of the discipline. When they write about this knowledge in the discipline, they learn to write. In this sense, we write to learn. A student who is expert at writing narra-tives may indeed be a novice at writing an essay on technology innovations in transportation over a 500-year period in history (Young & Leinhardt, 1998).

In another study, Montelongo, Berber-Jiménez, Hernández, and Hosk-ing (2006) found that a combination of writing and reading instruction is necessary for students to gain awareness of informational text structures. They suggest that students first be given instruction on writing paragraphs in expository formats; then students may use the writing they have done to help them understand the different text structures they encounter in read-ing.

Teachers often feel least well prepared to teach writing (Grisham & Wolsey, 2005; in press); indeed, there may be little or only fragmented writing instruction in teacher preparation programs (Johnson et al., 2003). There may be writing assignments, such as the one Ms. Capson initiated, but little instruction in the genre or in how to connect writing to reading may occur. However, teachers who seek additional professional develop-ment in writing can make a difference. Graham and Perin (2007) found that professional development was correlated with improved writing by students when the writing workshop model was used. They also found that the study of models resulted in small improvements in writing quality, but that the study of text structures was inconclusive. The problem continues into postsecondary education. For instance, Jonathan Monroe (2003) writes of college freshmen: "The first message any writing requirement should convey to first-year students is that successful writing and communication . . . depend on the development of multiple literacies and a capacity for discursive mobility" (p. 5).

WHAT ARE SOME ALTERNATIVES?

How Ms. Capson and Mr. Whettre Changed Their Teaching

Several weeks later, after investigating and talking about writing instruction in English and social studies with Mr. Whettre, Ms. Capson is again working on getting her students to write about what they have read in class. Ms. Capson is collaborating with Mr. Whettre, who has his students doing book clubs in English class (Daniels, 2002; Wolsey & Grisham with Provost, Chapter 15, this volume), with books such as *Muhammad* (Demi, 2003) and *Islam* (Thomson, 2004), as well as excerpts from *The Genius of Islam: How Muslims Made the Modern World* (Barnard, 2011). Together, they have planned a unit of study that will assist students to better understand narratives and nonfiction works about ancient and modern Islam in order to support students' learning about the history of Islam for social studies.

This time, in her history classroom, Ms. Capson had the students work with partners to read the textbook selection on the history of Islam. Partner reading or peer-assisted learning (Fuchs, Fuchs, Mathes, & Simmons, 1997) helps students to get more "air time" in reading and also pairs readers at different levels so that they can support each other when comprehension breaks down. As they read, Ms. Capson indicated stopping points in the text, where students were to ask each other questions about the text and fill out a graphic organizer (see Figure 9.1) that provided them with a structure for writing.

Ms. Capson and Mr. Whettre also developed a short webquest (Dodge & March, 1995; *webquest.org/index.php*) for students to go online in small groups to learn about Islam. A webquest provides detailed lesson plans for collaborative searching on specified Internet sites. The teachers carefully reviewed potential Internet sites chosen for suitability for seventh graders. Ms. Capson divided her class into six groups of students. Each group would be responsible for searching the recommended two sites for information on the following topics. First, students explored a website (*www.mnsu.edu/emuseum/cultural/religion/islam/history.html*) and read about and

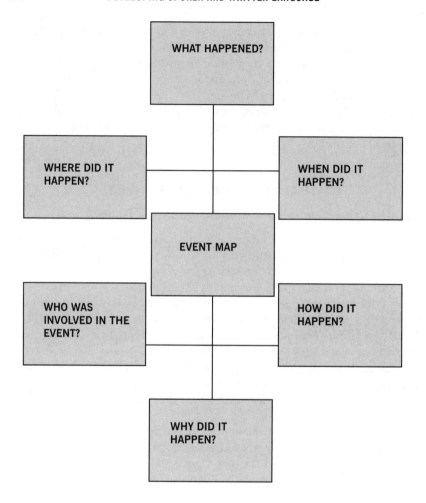

FIGURE 9.1. Sample graphic organizer.

provided a graphic organizer for one of the following areas: history, beliefs, and the prophet Muhammad's life. At a second site, Kidipede (*www.historyforkids.org/learn/islam*), students read about the life of Mohammad and other topics of Islam in history and did a second graphic organizer. In addition, students watched the History of Islam on the History Channel (*www.youtube.com/watch?v=csojgoZvlz8*) in their social studies class and completed a response to the film in their content journals (see Figure 9.2 for an example).

Once the film response entry and the two sets of graphic organizers were finalized, students were asked to review the social studies textbook

> I liked to learn about the profet Mohamad and how he got the word of God while he was in the cave. I learned he did not read or write, but he memoryzed all of it so he could recite it to other people. I did not know that Islan is like being Jewish or Christian. You only believe in one God. I did't know Mohamad was married, but he helped women get more rights. Finally, I was suprised that everything Mohamad said his followers memoryzed and when he died they wrote it all down and check to make sure it had no mistakes.

FIGURE 9.2. Unedited example of a seventh-grade student's response to a History Channel film on Islam.

information, the two online sources of information, the film response, and the texts they read in their English class. In Mr. Whettre's class, students discussed and wrote short responses to literature and information texts on Islam. Ms. Capson and Mr. Whettre are thus working together to build students' knowledge about the history of Islam and to build comprehension and critical thinking in relation to multimedia experiences. Finding positive sources about Islam and having discussions about common misconceptions about Islam turned out to be very thought-provoking content for seventh graders.

As a culminating experience, students were asked to do multimedia reports in PowerPoint with voice and Google images. Figure 9.3 provides the directions for the project and Figure 9.4 is an example of one Power-Point presentation. A few students took Ms. Capson's suggestions to use an alternative to PowerPoint. While there are a number of alternatives, her students chose to try out Prezi (*prezi.com*)

Tools for Writing

What tools did Ms. Capson and Mr. Whettre provide for their seventh-grade English and social studies students? In fact, they incorporated many tools for their students. One important aspect of the unit of study was vocabulary building. In advance of the reading and the webquest, the teachers taught important words such as *polytheism, monotheism, recite* and *recitation, Koran, prophet, conversion, amnesty, authenticate,* and *revelation.* The building of vocabulary assists with creating schema for the new unit. Since words are labels for concepts (Dalton & Grisham, 2011), online word sources—dictionaries and thesauruses—were featured in the unit of study for both the English and the social studies classes. Keeping new vocabulary words and their uses in context in content journals was a useful tool for the students. Ms. Capson made sure that students referred to them often. Yes, Ms. Capson had students do a timeline of the life of

1. Your group has done an investigation of one aspect of Islam.
2. You will create a PowerPoint slide to represent your learning about Islam.
3. You will create only one slide and it will contain:
   a. An image of Islam (you will find this either in your textbook, the websites you have explored, or on Google Image). You must make a screen capture of the image and fit it to size on your PowerPoint slide.
   b. An audio or video file must be chosen and uploaded to your PowerPoint slide. You will have help in finding such a file on the Internet or you may choose to record your voice(s) and include that as an audio file.
4. Your group will present your PowerPoint slide to the class, and the slide will become part of a PowerPoint presentation that we will make to your parents on the school website.
5. Your group will receive a group grade for the slide and the presentation.
6. You will receive an individual grade for your work (response to films, books, and Internet investigation, including completed graphic organizers).

FIGURE 9.3. Directions for creating your PowerPoint multimedia slide.

 # History of Islam

Three Great Monotheistic World Religions: Judaism, Christianity, Islam

Muhammad (or Mohammed) recited from his memory the word of the one God
He was born near Mecca about 570 AD (or CE)
Orphaned young and very poor. He had a wealthy uncle and married well. He became a wealthy merchant.

In 610 CE he began to hear the voice of God (Allah) in a cave. He MEMORIZED every thing because he could not read or write. He RECITED it all to others, who believed it.

In 622 CE he left Mecca because the government was run by people who were pagans (polytheism) and went to Medina. Everyone there converted to Islam.

In 630 CE he took 10,000 soldiers and conquered Mecca. He forgave all the pagans, but he took over the Temple.

In 632 Mohammed died and people began to write down what he had said: Koran. They believe the Koran is a correction of the Torah (Jews) and Bible (Christians).

FIGURE 9.4. Example of a PowerPoint slide on Islam with audio "call to prayer."

Muhammad, but it was brief enough to go in their content journals along with the new vocabulary.

The History Channel films provided an auditory and visual element for these students. They also read, discussed, and wrote briefly about the topics of their investigation, learning through graphic organizers how they might construct their understanding of the content (Islam) and the genre (informational text). The responses written in their content journals focused on the "W" questions (*when, where, why, what, who*) but also provided students with additional information about what seemed most important to them. The content journals were not edited or graded, but they *were* checked by teachers. Students also used the journals to orally share what they had written with reading partners.

The collaboration between Ms. Capson and Mr. Whettre meant that students in their classes could also read and discuss additional texts in various genres about the content, strengthening the literacy and content learning. Finally, the PowerPoint presentation meant reviewing the content again and summarizing it for the slide. In addition, students learned to include visual and auditory (multimedia) elements on the slides, thus honing the technological skills needed in the 21st century.

Once the PowerPoint presentation was put together, students gained an understanding of the genre of writing to explain something. Ms. Capson did, of course, require an "on-demand" essay for students to explain what they had learned about Islam. But Ms. Capson had learned that she first needed to scaffold the students' writing experience, so she modeled the assignment using her own essay. She placed this document on her computer, projected it for students to see, and began to "think aloud" about what she had done. Her essay began with a thesis statement: "Islam is one of the great monotheistic religions of the world." Next, she asked students to suggest other such statements of information, and she wrote them on the chalkboard. She then modeled her first paragraph, which referred to what monotheism means and what other monotheistic religions are prominent (e.g., Judaism, Christianity). The second paragraph discussed prophets who listened to the word of the one God (Moses, Jesus, Mohammed). She modeled a third paragraph that focused on the life of Mohammed, a fourth paragraph on the basic beliefs of Isalm, and a fifth that summed it all up and restated the thesis. Although this approach is still somewhat formulaic in terms of the five-paragraph essay, Ms. Capson definitely provided the support students needed. In addition, she worked with the students by writing on the overhead projector whatever they composed (shared writing). Students then worked in pairs to craft the next paragraph in their own words. Once they had shared their contributions, sorted out the successes, and highlighted them, Ms. Capson asked each student to write the final paragraph that summed up the learning and referred back to the thesis statement. This was the writing that she graded. Then the class looked again at Ms. Capson's ending and their own, discussing how they might improve their own products.

Additional Ideas

Shanahan and Shanahan (2008) suggest that there are different reading strategies for different content areas. For social studies, their content-area groups identified cause and effect as one of the most important genres. A strategy these students liked involved doing the "W" questions for one event, then for another. At that point, students were asked to make connections between events, an activity that mirrors the kind of inferential connections that historians make (p. 56). Klein and Rose (2010) refer to the "explanation" strategy (the content was science), wherein students watch an event, then go through several steps—get informed, include all steps, and tell why each event happened—thereby engaging in content problem solving, while the teachers provided sentence-combining strategies for the support of students' academic writing. When students reconstructed text through writing, both reading and writing were connected and understanding grew significantly deeper for the experimental group. When such inquiry writing is a preferred lesson type, students consult multiple texts, confer with the teacher, and with each other to transform informational text into writing their own texts, exemplifying the process of writing to learn in its most productive guise.

Another strategy that we like for social studies writing is outlined by Sturtevant and Linek (2004), called *progressive writing* (cf. Grisham, 1989). Using the graphic organizer, a general writing prompt is given, such as, "What did you learn from your reading?" (p. 145). Small groups of three or four students begin with a timed writing of perhaps 5 minutes. When time is called, each student "passes the paper" to the student on his or her right, who carefully reads what has been written. In another timed writing, students add to the first student's writing, beginning where the first writer ended. This is continued until the paper, with various students' writing, comes back to the original writer. At this point, students have one additional timed period during which they must read everything, then write a conclusion. After that, completed papers can be passed around and read, or read aloud. A discussion should ensue and one paper from each group is selected by students to be read aloud to the whole class. This process again demonstrates the use of multiple sources (in this case, the students) and the making of multiple models. Students are also engaged in evaluations of the writings.

A multimodal way of having students grapple with new ideas and content is to use podcasting for presentations. Audio podcasts, usually MP3 files, are easiest to implement in your classroom, even if there is only one computer. Figure 9.5 represents the directions whereby students make an audio podcast about Islam (though podcasting can be used for any discipline; e.g., Putman & Kingsley, 2009). Each student writes a script, practices it so that it doesn't sound too stilted, then records the text using a microphone for the computer (Grisham & Wolsey, 2009). Sound effects or background music can be added for interest. Students can record more than once, if necessary, and they can make the podcasts in pairs or small groups. A favorite is the interview technique, wherein one student "interviews" another about a given topic, turning it into a news report, blog post, or radio show. Teachers should try podcasting, as it has beneficial implications for giving directions to students and communicating with parents via the school website.

One last strategy that we like comes from Martha Rapp Ruddell's (2008) text on reading and writing in the content areas. Called *vocabulary self-collection strategy (VSS)*, it involves collaborative student activities after reading a text selection. In partners or small groups, students go back through the text to find and select a word that they think should be on a permanent vocabulary list being compiled by the class. They must select the word, tell where they found it in the text, tell what they think the word

---

Choose a social studies topic. Choose a topic from your textbook. Refer to one other source (such as the websites you used for your webquest or other books, articles, newspaper clippings, etc.) as you compile your "report."

Write a script. Your podcast script should sound much like a radio broadcast when recorded and should include the following components:
- Name(s), the date of your broadcast, and your chosen topic.
- Your rationale for choosing your topic (what interested you).
- The source(s) you consulted to increase your understanding about your topic. (Please identify your sources, authors, dates, and summarize the content.)

Record the podcast. If you work on a Mac, there is an internal microphone to record your podcast. If you work on a PC, you may need an external microphone, usually less than $30 at electronics stores—works with a USB port). Practice so that it doesn't seem like you are merely reading the script you have written. The files will most likely be MP3 files.

Send your podcast and script. E-mail your podcast to the teacher (or better, set up a website at your school where these can be posted*). Post your script and e-mail a link to the teacher.
- Teachers can also post podcasts at Podbean.com (*podcastmachine.com*).

FIGURE 9.5. Sample podcasting directions.

means (in their own words), and tell why it is important for the word to go on the class vocabulary list. One student from each group nominates the selected word, stating the three requirements. The teacher is encouraged to select and nominate one word.

Once all groups have nominated a word, the class moves to select the top five words for the class list. The class discusses each word on this list, eliminating words everyone already knows and words already on the list from prior text readings. When the five have been picked through consensus, the discussion moves to refine the definitions using student knowledge, teacher knowledge, dictionaries, and other reference sources. At that point, all the students copy the words and their definitions into their content journals. The teacher then plans further work with the words (such as placing them on graphic organizers or semantic maps; using them in short writings or other activities for multiple exposures). A great advantage of this strategy is that students refer back to content texts, rereading them to find the vocabulary, noting how the context helps to explain the word/concept, and discussing this process with other students and the teacher. We know from experience how motivating and engaging this strategy is for middle level students.

CONCLUSION

We teachers are often fond of calling ourselves "lifelong learners." As we become more experienced in teaching, we must remember that new ideas, tools, and strategies are emerging every year. Content-area literacy is one such area in rapid transition. As Shanahan and Shanahan (2008) have noted, the gains we have made with our elementary-age students in terms of reading and writing do not automatically translate into more advanced learning at the secondary level. National assessments reflect that such scores are stagnant at best (National Assessment of Educational Progress, 2007).

The lesson is that we must learn to teach reading and writing to our students in more evidence-based ways across the disciplines. Although elementary teachers are responsible for most content areas, at the secondary level (middle and high school), content-area specialists are needed for the increasingly complex and evolving knowledge bases of mathematics, social science, the sciences, world languages, fine arts, and physical education. However, English teachers often bear the brunt of pressure to teach reading and writing to our secondary students. We believe it is important to emphasize that English teachers cannot do it all. Yet, Ms. Capson notwithstanding, we must acknowledge that English teachers are best placed to initiate collaborations with other content-area teachers and to share knowledge about content literacy strategies. Such collaborations are, we believe, essential to making our secondary schools more interesting, useful, and rigorous for our students.

ADDITIONAL RESOURCES

There is a host of graphic organizers on the Internet, but we recommend the CAST website (*www.cast.org/publications/ncac/ncac_go.html*) and ReadWriteThink (*www.readwritethink.org/*) for specific topics and genres. We also recommend Wood, K. D., Lapp, D., Flood, J., & Taylor, D. B. (2008). *Guiding readers through text: Strategy guides for new times* (2nd ed.). Newark, DE: International Reading Association.

TRADE BOOKS CITED IN TEXT

Barnard, B. (2011). *The genius of Islam: How Muslims made the modern world.* New York: Knopf.

Demi. (2003). *Muhammad.* New York: Margaret K. Elderberry Books.

Thomson, J. (2004). *Islam: World religion series.* Vancouver, BC, Canada: Walrus (imprint of Whitecap Books).

REFERENCES

Berninger, V. W., & Richards, T. L. (2002). *Brain literacy for educators and psychologists.* Amsterdam: Academic Press.

Dalton, B., & Grisham, D. L. (2011). eVoc strategies: 10 ways to use technology to build vocabulary. *The Reading Teacher, 64*(5), 306–317.

Daniels, H. (2002). *Literature circles: Voice and choice in book clubs and reading groups* (2nd ed.). York, ME: Stenhouse.

Dodge, B., & March, T. (1995). The webquest page. Retrieved from *webquest.org/index.php*.

Dorfman, L. R., & Cappelli, R. (2007). *Teaching writing through children's literature, K–6.* York, ME: Stenhouse.

Fang, Z., Schleppegrell, M. J., & Cox, B. E. (2006). Understanding the language demands of schooling: Nouns in academic registers. *Journal of Literacy Research, 38,* 247–273.

Farnan, N., & Fearn, L. (2008). Writing in the disciplines: More than writing across the curriculum. In D. Lapp, J. Flood, & N. Farnan (Eds.), *Content area reading and learning: Instructional strategies* (3rd ed., pp. 403–424). New York: Erlbaum.

Fuchs, D., Fuchs, L. S., Mathes, P. G., & Simmons, D. C. (1997). Peer-assisted learning strategies: Making classrooms more responsive to diversity. *American Educational Research Journal, 34*(1), 174–206.

Graham, S., & Hebert, M. A. (2010). *Writing to read: Evidence for how writing can improve reading.* Washington, DC: Alliance for Excellent Education.

Graham, S., & Perin, D. (2007). A meta-analysis of writing instruction for adolescent students. *Educational Psychology, 99*(3), 445–476.

Grisham, D. L. (1989). How I discovered team writing: Its benefits and drawbacks. *California English, 25*(5), 6–9.

Grisham, D. L., & Wolsey, T. D. (2005). Assessing writing: Comparing the responses of 8th graders, preservice teachers, and experienced teachers in a graduate reading program. *Reading and Writing Quarterly, 21*(4), 315–330.

Grisham, D. L., & Wolsey, T. D. (2009, April). *A constructivist view of podcasting: Students create the media.* Paper presented at the annual meeting of the American Educational Research Association, San Diego, CA.

Grisham, D. L., & Wolsey, T. D. (in press). Writing instruction for teacher candidates: Strengthening a weak curricular area. *Journal of Literacy Research and Instruction.*

Johnson, T. S., Thompson, L., Smagorinsky, P., & Fry, P.G. (2003). Learning to teach the five-paragraph essay. *Research in the Teaching of English, 38*(2), 126–176.

Klein, P. D., & Rose, M. A. (2010). Teaching argument and explanation to prepare junior students for writing to learn. *Reading Research Quarterly, 45*(4), 433–461.

Monroe, J. (2003). Writing and the disciplines. *Peer Review.* Retrieved from *www.aacu.org.*

Montelongo, J., Berber-Jiménez, L., Hernández, A. C., & Hosking, D. (2006). Teaching expository text structures. *Science Teacher, 73*(2), 28–31.

National Assessment of Educational Progress. (2007). Nation's report card. Retrieved from *nces.ed.gov/nationsreportcard.*

Putman, S. M., & Kingsley, T. (2009). The Atoms Family: Using podcasts to enhance the development of science vocabulary. *The Reading Teacher, 63*(2), 100–108.

Ruddell, M. R. (2008). *Teaching content area reading and writing* (5th ed.). Hoboken, NJ: Wiley.

Seo, B. (2007). Defending the five-paragraph essay. *English Journal, 97*(2), 15–16.

Shanahan, T., & Shanahan, C. (2008). Teaching disciplinary literacy to adolescents: Rethinking content-area literacy. *Harvard Educational Review, 78*(1), 40–59.

Sturtevant, E. G., & Linek, W. M. (2004). *Content literacy: An inquiry-based case approach.* Columbus, OH: Pearson/Merrill/Prentice Hall.

Wolsey, T. D. (2010). Complexity in student writing: The relationship between the task and vocabulary uptake. *Literacy Research and Instruction, 49*(2), 194–208.

Young, K. M., & Leinhardt, G. (1998). Writing from primary documents: A way of knowing in history. *Written Communication, 15*, 25–68.

CHAPTER 10

If Students Are Unmotivated Writers—
Motivate Them

Jane Hansen
Timothy Shea

Key Points for This Chapter

- A community of writers motivates student writers.
- Reading like writers motivates students.
- Evaluation motivates writers.

TWO BIRD'S-EYE VIEWS OF INEFFECTIVE INSTRUCTION

View 1

Mr. Miller distributes the last of the English textbooks on the first day of school as the dazed teens stack their books one by one in a pile on their desks. The literature anthology, grammar book, and vocabulary workbook will form the backbone of this year's English curriculum. "They will help my students do well on state tests and help them with their writing," he says.

Mr. Miller begins the school year with a review of the parts of speech. Daily, his students will practice identifying the parts of speech and defining them on the worksheets Mr. Miller provides. They also spend regular time each weeks completing exercises in their vocabulary workbooks, and Mr. Miller tests them on these every Friday each week.

For writing, they usually write paragraph responses to workbook exercises and, by the end of the semester, they will also have written a five-paragraph persuasive essay, a book report, and short paragraphs about the literature they read.

When Mr. Miller is asked about the ways he teaches writing, he responds that his students need the structure the grammar book and the prescribed form of the five-paragraph essay provide.

He does not believe that his students should have much choice about what they write. "They know too little at this point in their lives to know what to write about. That is my job—to determine the assignments—and that includes setting the guidelines for what good writing looks like."

View 2

The middle school students in Mrs. Jackson's third-period class huddle over lined notebooks in response to the writing prompt on the screen: *Describe your perfect day.* A few students have their heads on their desks, not even trying to pick up a pencil, while others spend more time staring off into space than writing. Three Vietnamese girls who just moved to the school and who do not speak English very well do not understand the assignment and don't know how to write in complete English sentences, so, afraid to be wrong, they draw pictures and quietly giggle at each other's drawings.

While her students write (or not), Mrs. Jackson stands at the front of the room, watching them, wondering if any of this "new" way of teaching writing is working. After the students write for about 10 minutes, she asks them to put down their pencils and to pass their notebooks to the front of their rows so she can give them feedback.

Mrs. Jackson stacks the notebooks on her desk with a sigh, knowing that, not only does she have these 25 journals to grade that night but also those of the 75 other students in the three periods she will teach later today—and she still hasn't figured out how to assess the pictures the new Asian girls drew.

Her students are writing more than they did in other years, but she finds it hard to keep up with the immense load of responding and wonders if she is giving them the right kind of feedback that will help them improve as writers. She has always wanted to teach English, and especially writing, but now she wonders if this way of teaching writing is beneficial to her students or to her. Surely, there has to be a better way.

DEFINING THE TARGETED PRACTICES

The two teachers have not yet learned about the importance of teaching students the skills they need in the context in which they need them (Lain, 2007). They need to know verbs, for example, in order to write in their strong voices. They need to know vocabulary in order to write clearly. They need to learn about authentic formats for persuasive essays and book reviews by reading and studying exemplars, or mentor texts, as is advocated for today's students as they learn to read like writers (Rief, 2006).

In their study of authors, students realize the significance of writers' commitment to a topic and their decisions about the most effective manner in which to tell their story or state their case. Writers make decisions about what they will write and what formats to use as they explore their ideas. Writing is not, mainly, a school subject. It is a mode of learning used throughout life, and to help students realize that power of writing is a primary goal of writing teachers (Atwell, 2003; Pajaras, Johnson, & Usher, 2007). Students are more likely to experience the significance of writing by writing about what matters to them.

To assign a prompt, to stand guard while students write, and to write responses to 100 students in one evening is not a "new" way to teach writing. It is a misinterpretation of current writing instruction. Yes, students who are writers will write every day in class. And, while they do, their teachers will sometimes write, but most of the time, while the students are writing, teachers will move among them, conferring with them (Kittle, 2008; Moher, 2007) in order to find out what they are writing about and what their intentions are as writers. It is what teachers learn from their students that guides their daily writing instruction. It is teachers' daily instruction that serves as their primary response to students' writing; it is not teachers' written responses to students' journals that serve as primary responses to their writing.

In fact, these teachers mainly read drafts that students periodically choose to revise, to craft, to turn into final drafts (Murray, 2009). Teachers carefully schedule these, so they read only a few each night. Writing teachers know the importance of deadlines, which they stagger across their 100 students.

WHAT DOES RESEARCH SAY ABOUT INSTRUCTION BASED ON AUTHENTIC WRITING PRACTICES?

In order to feel motivated to write, the students in the two classrooms need to be engaged in more appropriate instructional practices: They would benefit from an overall classroom environment in which their knowledge about content, their ideas, and their approaches to learning are notably valued by their teacher and their classmates. In such classrooms, *the community develops a sense of responsibility for the growth of all as writers.*

In doing so, students read as well as write. *Writers read. They often read differently than nonwriters, as they are reading not only for what is on the page, they are studying the writer's craft.* They wonder, "What did this writer do in order to convey the message in a manner than captivates me?"

And, *writers are more likely to thrive when they are in a classroom in which the evaluation system is designed to energize them.* Writing is hard. Writers must be invested in their work. They must know they have something to say that will be valued, and they must know there is someone who will help them say it. Writers who receive criticism they do not appreciate feel deflated. In order to keep writers energized, teachers and classmates carefully provide ongoing occasions for supportive evaluation.

In the sections that follow, the motivational roles of a community of writers, of reading like writers, and of evaluation are explored as alternatives to the instruction provided by the teachers at the beginning of this chapter.

WHAT ARE SOME ALTERNATIVES?

A Community of Writers Motivates Student Writers

A theoretical framework of transformative inquiry underlies the teaching of writing (Sumida & Meyer, 2006). Writers, with their carefully crafted paper voices, take stances that can bind or shatter in our global age, where they speed throughout the Internet second by second. Given the history of exclusion in many cultures and classrooms, where some citizens and students feel alone or neglected, a community of writers can transform alienation into contribution.

The teacher consistently, conscientiously, and intentionally leads students in the creation of a classroom in which all know they are valued. Writing conferences can play a vital role in confirming, for the writers, the value of their contributions. These conversations between the teacher, as a grown-up writer, and the student, who is a more novice writer, can strengthen their personal relationship. The teacher comes to the student to listen, to find out what the student thinks is significant in her writing, what she knows, and what she has done so far as a writer. Then the teacher teaches. He converses with the student about what he thinks is significant, what he sees as the student's knowledge, and what he thinks the student is doing/can do as a writer.

These are genuine and sometimes exhausting events (Atwell, 2003). These conferences occur when teachers look through their students' eyes and ask thoughtful questions in a way that allows the writers to maintain ownership of the information in the draft. Queries such as "How's it going?", "Where would you like this piece to go?", and "What's the one thing you'd like to say?" all help writers think more clearly about their compositions.

Mini-lessons are also times when the adult writer and student writers work together. These lessons are focused, 15-minute segments of direct instruction on a topic the teacher and students know they are seeking to understand as they compose. Many of the students will be able to apply them directly into the drafts they are currently composing. These lessons can be directed to the whole class or to smaller groups, depending on the writers' needs. Whether in mini-lessons or conferences, meetings of writers provide spaces for their voices to be heard—and strengthened.

In contrast, when teachers *tell* students what to do to improve a draft, rather than teaching students to *realize what their options are*—and how to make decisions to improve their work—the students aren't, in actuality, writers. They haven't created, from their internal desire to become public, a paper version of their thoughts, of their knowledge. When their teachers read these students' writing—written to fulfill the teacher's request for specific information in a specific format—they are tempted to listen for the message and/or the format that *they* requested, rather than for the voice of the writer.

When writers know, however, that their words count, they can write with zest as part of a community of other writers who understand and appreciate each others' efforts and contributions.

Students in such classrooms find the highlights of English class to be participation, opportunities to create wonders with words, challenges to think outside the box, and contentment as they feel their writing ebb, flow, and swell to the rhythm of their own internal voice. These students do not put their heads down when it's time to write. Instead, English class recharges and energizes them (Zimmerer, Jia, Ansah, & Whitman, 2010). It is in such classrooms that we find students who are motivated to write— and learn.

Students Engage in Learning Clubs

In the classroom of seventh-grade teacher Sharon Ailine (Casey, 2008– 2009), the students engage in learning clubs that are organically designed to bring all students, and especially the strugglers, into literacy. With a focus more on their processes of learning, rather than the content, the students move from frustration to motivation. The students' decisions influence what they read/learn, their manner of discussion, the forms of their physical products, and the design of their evaluation. Overall, Sharon's students are "motivated by choice and more engaged when directing their learning" (p. 289).

Furthermore, Sharon's interactions with her students create a safe environment in which her learners move forward—as they must, in order to be transformed from hesitators to intentional learners. She says, "Eventually what happens is more and more kids want to share because, no matter what is said, I never say they are wrong" (Casey, 2008–2009, p. 290).

The learning clubs in her classroom, importantly, are not composed of students grouped by ability. Although one-third of her class showed a lack of motivation at the beginning of the year, Sharon resisted the trend to place that third in one group. "The additional problem of grouping by ability, which positions struggling readers with other struggling readers, continues the cycle of frustration" (Casey, 2008–2009, p. 290). Instead, Sharon guides her students' interactions and decisions, and this guidance leads to their eventual engagement.

Student Writers Collaborate

Classrooms such as the above, however, are not a reality for many urban, immigrant youth. In her case study of two Cambodian-American middle school students, McGinnis (2007) found them to be disengaged and unmotivated. Importantly, their test scores were high on the school's standardized tests, but their interest in school was so low, they started to cut classes. In her study of these two students as writers in school and with her in after-school and Saturday programs, she (McGinnis, 2007) documented their engagement out of school and, in rare situations, in school, when they were given a choice of topics, were allowed to collaborate with peers, and were treated as experts on their topics.

Usually, however, McGinnis (2007) reveals a prevailing disconnect between their out-of-school lives and the words their teachers required them to place on paper. Perhaps thankfully, they hardly wrote in their classes. When they did, their writing was not authentic. Totally absent from their school literacy were opportunities to explore "the crucial issues that were important to them, such as their situations as poor, urban, immigrant youth" (p. 34). Instead, they did grammar exercises, wrote sentences, conjugated verbs, copied vocabulary, wrote definitions, wrote short answers to questions, and filled in worksheets. They were not asked to create meaning. These students, who had been engaged learners as elementary students, now preferred to stay home, and one of them concluded that the school did not care.

Sadly, the school "blamed the students' absences on the youth and their parents, and the focus was placed on creating classrooms where the students were controlled, rather than engaged. Discussions about these students never examined if the school was meeting the needs of their immigrant students or brainstormed ways of supporting students' recognition of the relevance of school in their lives" (McGinnis, 2007, p. 36).

English Language Learners Write in Appreciative Classrooms

In general, in their classrooms, the above writers (McGinnis, 2007) did not talk, and that is also the case for many students who are even newer to the English language. They work individually.

English language learners (ELLs), however, especially need to talk with their classmates; they learn English by writing and talking in authentic contexts with students who know English. ELLs need to be "immersed in a rich and meaningful language learning environment, but not drills and learning rules out of context. The only way to learn a language is to use it authentically, thereby forming a language habit through constant trial and error" (Aguilar, Fu, & Jago, 2007, p. 110).

When it comes to academic language, ELLs experience increased difficulty. If they are in classes with other users of their first language, it is helpful for them to talk with each other about material they are struggling to learn. And, before ELLs take part in a classroom conversation about content, it is important for them to write first, so they can form their ideas in their new language. This approach "enables ELLs to engage in meaningful writing from day one" (Fu, 2009, p. 15) with other writers and teachers who write, so everyone works together, in appreciation of all.

Fu (2009) relates the story of one of the students in whom she witnessed this phenomena:

> Zhao, who was from a village in China, started sixth grade in a school in New York City, yet his native language literacy was probably at a first-grade level. His ESL teacher started him with repetitive pattern books in reading and guided him to write by drawing and labeling. He labeled his drawings sometimes with Chinese words and sometimes with English words. Gradually he wrote captions for his drawings in Chinese mixed with English. By the end of the school year, he was more confident writing English pattern books (modeled after the pattern books he read) than writing in Chinese. (pp. 36–37)

Reading Like Writers Motivates Students

"Writing is reading" (Rief, 2006, p. 34). Writers cannot write without reading. When students write, they are engaged in a recursive process of critical thinking. In order to move from word to word, space to space, thought to thought, they constantly read—and they are curious about other writers, so they read the drafts (emergent and final) of the members of their writing community.

Their strong voices keep their community vibrant, alive. In order to provide for these students to develop their ways with words, their teachers provide them with extended, frequent, and regular periods of time in which to explore their ideas, and various members of their writing community provide feedback/evaluation—in response to the writers' requests—while they are in the process of writing/exploring. The response, which usually occurs when writers read their work aloud or others read it, keeps the energy of their collective high.

These busy writers not only read their own drafts and those of their classmates and teacher, they read the writing of professional authors. They read, read, read on their continuous search for new ways with words—and they enjoy the search. "Good writing makes writers want to write" (Kittle, 2008, p. 74).

For these classrooms of readers/writers who are teachers/students, topic choice is one of their major commitments. In order to remain motivated, they need to care about, to be genuinely interested in, what they read and write. Then they are more likely to craft the strongest writing. Writers need to choose their own topics so they can write with "passion and voice" (Rief, 2006, p. 37). "If we want students to become lifelong writers, they must see writing as intrinsically important—not just another school assignment. Students must find writing assignments to be relevant and meaningful" (Gallagher, 2006, p. 11). Students for whom writing resounds within are likely to be engaged and to want their drafts to work—to sound like what they read.

That kind of writing, however, is not easy. Murray (2009) provides sage wisdom regarding students' motivation to pursue the commitment writing requires:

> How do you motivate your student to pass through this process [of writing], perhaps even pass through it again and again on the same piece of writing? First by shutting up. . . . We have to be quiet, to listen, to respond. We are not the initiator or the motivator; we are the reader, the recipient. . . . We must listen carefully for those words that may reveal a truth, that may reveal a voice. We must respect our student for his [or her] potential truth and for his [or her] potential voice. (p. 3)

The potential truth and the potential voice: Teachers read their students' papers to discern potential. Murray (2009) says this when he elaborates about the necessity of teaching writing as a process, not a product. He says that writing is "the process of discovery through language" (p. 2). In middle school teaching, we talk about the ins and outs of teaching the writing process, but sometimes we tend to forget that this process is a process of *discovery*. Our mission is to teach a process by which our students discover how effective, interest-holding reading/writing sounds. What they hear is what they may intentionally seek to create in order to become better writers.

Students Write and Read in a Technological World

Adolescents today are immersed in a world of digital technology that has exploded in the past 5 years and in which they are quite comfortable. Their lives revolve around texts, chats, instant messaging (IMs), blogs, Facebook, Twitter, and hours of screen time. Although many teens, especially boys, do not see themselves as writers/readers, they manage to spend many hours a day doing just that—writing/reading in all sorts of forms and for all kinds of functions. "Today's online technologies have young people reading and writing far more than they were 20 years or even a decade ago. Words are an integral part of today's online world, along with images and sound, and young people read and write thousands of words online each week" (Williams, 2008, p. 682). It is important for writing teachers to explore ways in which these tools can empower their students as writers/readers in various contexts.

Classrooms that allow for technology to be used for adolescent writing witness increased engagement, especially when instructors allow for multi-genre creations such as digital storytelling, wikis, Web design, and student-created videos (Chandler-Olcott & Mahar, 2003b; Kajder & Swenson, 2004). Other technological tools that have been shown to increase student engagement with writing include the use of smartphones, VoiceThread technology, and sites such as Tumblr and Glogster. Each of these tools draws on students' natural inclinations and invites them to use technology in productive and meaningful ways.

Students Write and Read in a Visual World

Not only should teachers use digital tools in writing/reading instruction but also visual texts such as film, graphic novels, and fanfiction. Coencas (2007) supports the use of visual texts to teach reading and writing in engaging ways to students with special learning needs, and Cho (2006) shows the advantages of using visual texts with ELLs. In general, visual texts have been shown in studies, and by practitioners, to yield rich and engaging benefits when used to demonstrate ways to tell stories and to communicate a range of ideas (Carter, 2007; Chandler-Olcott & Maher, 2003a; Golden, 2007). Specifically, learning to view documentaries can strengthen students' persuasive writing, as we show in this scenario, based on our own unpublished research.

It is March and Mrs. Howell is having difficulty getting her lower-level eighth graders to remain motivated, especially as their litany of state tests is looming on the horizon and the weather is getting nicer. She is looking for a way to teach persuasive writing that will help her students understand its usefulness in their lives.

She turns to documentaries as a "text" that may inform her students' reading, writing, and thinking. Together, they examine a range of film clips and analyze the persuasive elements employed in each, such as how they develop a thesis and what they do to create strong supporting arguments. The class studies closeup and wide-angle shots, and discusses why the filmmakers made the decisions they did. The students study faces and talk about why a shot is face-on, profile, angled from below, or angled from above. Ultimately, they talk about what they can learn as writers from these film decisions.

In so doing, the students become engaged in ways Mrs. Howell had not yet witnessed this year. They discuss and argue, and they write with conviction and an awareness of what they are doing and why. Importantly, their writing is stronger than it was when Mrs. Howell did not use documentaries.

Nowadays, middle school students study what successful creators do to capture the attention of young viewers and readers. Adolescent writers enjoy and create a wide range of texts, and their teachers lead them in these explorations. Ranker (2008) studied two, 12-year-old boys "designated as struggling with academic literacy performance in relation to their peers" (p. 411). Wanting the students to be engaged, motivated, and intellectually challenged, the teacher set up his class so the two students worked collaboratively to create a video as part of an inquiry project.

To do so, the boys used the Web, digital video production software, notebooks, and books. They wrote and narrated the audio tracks. Overall, their video captured the potential of multiple modes of communication as they explored the benefits of a wide spectrum of meaning-making possibilities. Evaluation, in the form of revision and editing, were natural parts of their project, as they decided and undecided which parts of their exploration they wanted to include, emphasize, or delete.

Given the discovery process as the forward force, the number one task of writing teachers is to use students' evolving writing, and that of their classmates, teachers, and professionals as the text of a course. Their mentors are the creators who explore possibilities until they find a process and product that convey the message they have in mind. The name of the game is to try new things, and retry—until the words on the page, and the images and sounds emulate the ideas the writers/readers want to convey.

Evaluation Motivates Writers

The motivation paradigm within which many teachers worked for decades was to offer punishment and rewards—external factors—to encourage students to perform well. Research (Daniels, 2010), however, shows that those methods, rather than motivating students, only control students' immediate classroom behavior—if they do that.

We are beginning to understand, instead, what does increase motivation. Importantly, we now focus on *intrinsic* sources of motivation. More specifically, we look at the large picture and create classroom environments in which our students *know* we listen to and hear them.

Evaluation becomes the act of finding value in students' work—and students wanting to offer their work/their writing to readers who can help them hear their thoughts resonate from pages. Their teachers create an environment in which students want to carefully craft their paper voices, and the teachers understand the fragility of the origami of the students' drafts.

This is especially important for ELLs. They are more likely to flourish when their teachers allow them to code-switch in their speaking and writing whenever they feel the need to do so. "We need to learn to read meanings through broken English structures, and not correct every error, or they will produce less and learn less" (Agilar et al., 2007, p. 125). Their motivation will decline—or vanish.

Evaluators Search English ELLs' Essays for Evidence of Possibilities

Carbone and Orellana (2010) provide excellent examples of motivated bilingual youths who use their skills as language brokers for their families to inform their emergent academic voices. The researchers' overall goal was to move the students out of a culture where they are too frequently seen as writers with deficits to overcome. To accomplish this, the two case studies (chosen as exemplars from several students who participated in the project) each wrote a persuasive essay to a person they knew, and then wrote another—on the same topic—to a distant, real audience.

By carefully studying the writers' translations of their own voices into more formal voices, the researchers identified the students' attempts to successfully use academic language—rather than identify the deficits in the students' essays. It is rhetorical moves such as these on the part of motivated students that teachers must value as they help students develop their academic efforts. To look for evidence of possibilities in young writers' essays, rather than searching for evidence of possible failure, is vital.

Writing Conferences Serve as Occasions for Ongoing Evaluation

Writing conferences can be occasions in which students explain their intent and, as such, can be an influential form of evaluation and motivation. Moher (2007), an experienced teacher, writes about the conferences she holds as "journeys into not knowing" (p. 26). They not only enhance her/our ability to teach, they extend beyond the information on the page into the internal motivation of the writer. Conferences are opportunities for teachers to look at adolescent writers face to face, listen to them, and ask questions.

As writing teachers we read students' papers, sometimes before conferences. Moher (2007) reads all her students' papers from one class in about 20 minutes, in preparation for conferences the next day. Reading this way allows her to "enjoy their writing so much more. I'm a far better reader in this mode" (p. 28). She focuses on the potential, the implied, and notices what to watch for the next day. We don't want to "inhibit our writers by judging too soon or correcting or responding in ways that tell them they aren't right or good or important enough" (p. 31). Instead, we encourage their journeys into using writing to learn about their uncertainties about themselves and about what they read.

In my own (Shea) classroom my students do not receive grades on their written work. Rather, I label their papers as *Revision Needed, Accept*, or *Distinction*, and the students and I then examine their writing to determine what they will try to do in order to push their writing forward. In order to pass the class, each of their papers needs to achieve an *Accept* mark, and the students revise their work as much as necessary until they reach that goal. This method of evaluation places the students in situations where they learn, under my guidance, about options to consider in order for their writing to become better. Via decisions they make, they hear the improvements in their papers, and they learn: *I can write*. That, in itself, affects their motivation in a positive manner.

CONCLUSION

On a larger, more influential scale, evaluation influences the tools student- and teacher-writers use—and the tools, taken farther, influence the motivation of middle school students. If tools are worksheets that focus writers' attention on verb tense, a few students may love literacy. If tools are texts that students create on topics of their choice, for purposes of their choice, via multiliteracies, more students may love their work.

When literacy tools are used to enable transformation, the opportunities for engagement can lead students to an enlarged vision of literacy (Beach, Campano, Edmiston, & Borgman, 2010). In no particular order, the following three purposes of literacy can provide students who normally struggle with opportunities to be seen and to see themselves as talented and capable: (1) Students will author an identity that moves them out of the shadows; (2) students will acquire a sense of agency; and (3) students will identify and engage in critical inquiry.

Overall, engaged middle school writers are those who perceive themselves as successful; their self-efficacy is high (Pajaras et al., 2007). At the same time, these beliefs are less likely to be as strong as they were in elementary school and will most likely remain at this lower level during high school. Their years in middle school appear to be vitally important to their motivation as writers.

These stakes raise the bar for middle school teachers. Traditionally, teachers have sought to enhance students' self-perceptions via praise. Self-efficacy theorists, however, emphasize providing writers with actual success in authentic experiences. Then, students' self-evaluations can help them interpret their achievements in ways that can boost their confidence.

Given the robustness of these findings (Pajaras et al., 2007), we must step back and acknowledge the frequency by which they are overlooked. To pay attention to writers' motivations often gives way to lockstep writing instruction. Young writers, however, are more likely to thrive when their teachers focus their instruction and evaluation on students' gradual accomplishments, more so than on what they do *not* do.

This may be especially true when we consider the emotional nature of writing—and of middle school students. Evaluation, when successful in promoting writers' internal motivations, is the act of finding value in self, others, and the work of all. Instruction that carefully fosters positive self-evaluation on the part of writers may be the transformative force behind adolescents' success. Motivated middle school writers can intentionally become better writers.

ADDITIONAL RESOURCES

Books

Fletcher, R. (2010). *Pyrotechnics on the page: Playful craft that sparks writing.* Portland, ME: Stenhouse.

Lesh, B. (2011). *"Why won't you just tell us the answer?" Teaching historical thinking in grades 7–12.* Portland, ME: Stenhouse.

Somoza, D., & Lourie, P. (2010). *Writing to explore: Discovering adventure in the research paper, 3–8.* Portland, ME: Stenhouse.

Websites

All About Adolescent Literacy: Resources for Parents and Educators of Kids in Grades 4–12

www.adlit.org

Resources to help teens become better readers, writers, and thinkers.

Pongo Teen Writing

www.pongoteenwriting.org/pongo-s-group-process.html.

A site dedicated to helping teens become stronger, more confident writers.

Teen Ink

www.teenink.com.

Magazine, website, and books written by teens since 1989.

Teen Online Resources

www.novilibrary.org/teensonline.htm.

A website full of resources to help teens grow as writers.

REFERENCES

Aguilar, C. M., Fu, D., & Jago, C. (2007). English language learners in the classroom. In K. Beers, R. E. Probst, & L. Rief (Eds.), *Adolescent literacy: Turning promise into practice* (pp. 105–125). Portsmouth, NH: Heinemann.

Atwell, N. (2003). Hard trying and these recipes. *Voices from the Middle, 11*(2), 16–19.

Beach, R., Campano, G., Edmiston, B., & Borgman, M. (2010). *Literacy tools in the classroom: Teaching through critical inquiry, grades 5–12.* Berkeley, CA: National Writing Project.

Carbone, P. M., & Orellana, M. F. (2010). Developing academic identities: Persuasive writing as a tool to strengthen emergent academic identities. *Research in the Teaching of English, 44*(3), 292–316.

Carter, J. (2007). Transforming English with graphic novels: Moving toward our "Optimus Prime." *English Journal, 97*(2), 49–53.

Casey, H. K. (2008–2009). Engaging the disengaged: Using learning clubs to motivate struggling adolescent readers and writers. *Journal of Adolescent and Adult Literacy, 52*(4), 284–294.

Chandler-Olcott, K., & Mahar, D. (2003a). Adolescents' anime-inspired "fanfictions": An exploration of multiliteracies. *Journal of Adolescent and Adult Literacy, 46*(7), 556–566.

Chandler-Olcott, K., & Mahar, D. (2003b). "Tech-saviness" meets multiple literacies: Exploring adolescent girls' technology-mediated literacy practices. *Reading Research Quarterly, 38*(3), 356–385.

Cho, K. S. (2006). Read the book, see the movie, acquire more English. *Reading Improvement, 43*(2), 143–147.

Coencas, J. (2007). How movies work for secondary students with special needs. *English Journal, 96*(4), 67–72.

Daniels, E. (2010). Creating motivating learning environments: What we can learn from researchers and students. *English Journal, 100*(1), 25–29.

Fu, D. (2009). *Writing between languages: How English language learners make the transition to fluency.* Portsmouth, NH: Heinemann.

Gallagher, K. (2006). *Teaching adolescent writers.* Portland, ME: Stenhouse.

Golden, J. (2007). Literature into film (and back again): Another look at an old dog. *English Journal, 97*(21), 24–30.

Kajder, S., & Swenson, J. (2004). Digital images in the language arts classroom. *Learning and Leading with Technology, 31*(8), 18–22.

Kittle, P. (2008). *Write beside them: Risk, voice, and clarity in high school writing.* Portsmouth, NH: Heinemann.

Lain, S. (2007). Reaffirming the writing workshop for young adolescents. *Voices from the Middle, 14*(3), 20–28.

McGinnis, T. (2007). Are urban middle schools leaving bright immigrant youth behind? *Voices from the Middle, 14*(4), 32–38.

Moher, T. A. (2007). The writing conference. In T. Newkirk & R. Kent (Eds.), *Teaching the neglected "R": Rethinking writing instruction in secondary classrooms* (pp. 26–38). Portsmouth, NH: Heinemann.

Murray, D. (2009). Teach writing as a process not product. In T. Newkirk & L. Miller (Eds.), *The essential Don Murray: Lessons from America's greatest writing teacher* (pp. 1–5). Portsmouth, NH: Heinemann.

Pajaras, F., Johnson, M. J., & Usher, E. L. (2007). Sources of writing self-efficacy beliefs of elementary, middle, and high school students. *Research in the Teaching of English, 42*(1), 104–120.

Ranker, J. (2008). Making meaning on the screen: Digital video production about the Dominican Republic. *Journal of Adolescent and Adult Literacy, 51*(5), 410–422.

Rief, L. (2006). What's right with writing. *Voices from the Middle, 13*(4), 32–39.

Sumida, A. Y., & Meyer, M. A. (2006). T4 = Teaching to the fourth power: Transformative inquiry and the stirring of cultural waters. *Language Arts, 83*(5), 437–449.

Zimmerer, S., Jia, W., Ansah, P., & Whitman, A. (2010). What makes you want to go to English class? *English Journal, 100*(1), 23–24.

CHAPTER 11

If Students Are Not Succeeding as Writers— Teach Them to Self-Assess Using a Rubric

Judy M. Parr
Rebecca Jesson

Key Points for This Chapter

- Self-assessment is a complex task but important in building a sense of control and autonomy.
- Rubrics that specify, in accessible language, the criteria for quality writing help students see for what they are aiming.
- Annotated writing samples help students apply the criteria to their own and others' writing.

A BIRD'S-EYE VIEW OF CLASSROOM PRACTICE

Ms. Rivers teaches a composite Year 7 and 8 (sixth and seventh grades) class at a small country school. An experienced teacher, Ms. Rivers is committed to providing opportunities for students to participate in their own learning. In her writing program, she involves students in talking to generate ideas, and she uses model texts to provide students with a sense of how authors achieve their communicative purposes. She also includes "sharing sessions" during which peers respond in an evaluative way to one another's work.

To maximize students' participation in their learning, Ms. Rivers takes care to ground their writing in an authentic context by using current and relevant events. Recently her class wrote about the dramatic rescue of three hikers who had been stranded for several days in dense bush in the local area. The whole community had been involved in this event, and the news accounts had provided her class with a ready-made springboard into the "recount writing" that was the current focus in the writing program. She also selects texts to support her writing program, for example, *School Journal*[1] articles recounting events about which they had all read together and discussed. Ms. Rivers draws attention to the fact that these recounts are focused on an event, and she points out the foregrounding of particular aspects of the event.

As they write, the students, who are accustomed to working together, bounce ideas off one another. Later, at a more formal sharing point, students comment on what they particularly like about the piece shared and nominate two things they think would improve the writing (sometimes called "a star and two wishes"); students also record what they are particularly pleased with in their own piece of writing. Sam, for example, wrote: "What I really like about this piece is that I have used a lot of interesting words. . . . " (When asked what sort of word was an interesting one, he thinks for a while and then says that they are words that describe.)

Ms. Rivers thinks that she has clear aims for her writing lessons: namely, that her students understand what they are learning about writing and have a good sense of what they are aiming for—that is, what the desired quality performance looks like. However, if we ask Ms. Rivers's students what they are learning to do, their responses indicate confusion. Her students are not in agreement about what they are meant to be learning about writing, and many give nonspecific answers (e.g., "I'm writing an interesting piece"). When asked what quality performance might look like or what they need to do to improve, students' responses frequently relate to mechanics such as spelling or to length.

Despite the obvious engagement of her students, the quality of the writing produced is disappointing. Ms Rivers is frustrated by not being able to teach the majority of her students in a way that allows them to succeed in writing at the curriculum level required for their grade.

DEFINING THE TARGETED PRACTICE

Because many of her writers are not succeeding in writing, Ms. Rivers has focused on getting them more engaged so that they have opportunities to

---

[1] *School Journal*, begun in 1909, is published quarterly for the New Zealand Ministry of Education (with versions for younger and older primary (elementary) students to around Year 8. The journal is provided in multiple copies free to each school and contains some pieces that are specifically commissioned. Most of New Zealand's foremost children's authors have written for the *School Journal*.

practice the craft in order to learn and develop as writers. For Ms. Rivers, enhancing engagement means increasing students' participation in their own learning. A sense of agency or control over their writing is also a key element in student engagement because it builds self-efficacy as a writer. So Ms. Rivers is aware of the need to develop students' self-regulatory behaviors, such as the ability to monitor and to self-assess. Reflecting on her practice, Ms. Rivers wonders how she can better guide students to provide feedback to one another or to evaluate their own pieces. She realizes that sometimes her feedback does not relate specifically to her learning aims for writing in the lessons or to the criteria she was looking for in the writing, and she thinks this could be confusing for students. For students to learn to self-regulate their writing, they need to understand instructional goals. They need to know specifically what they are learning about writing and the mastery criteria for that particular aspect of learning (what a good _____ would look like; how to tell a quality one). They also need to know how they are doing—how successful they are—in relation to the learning aimed for in writing, the areas that they need to work on in order to achieve the learning goals, and the actions that will achieve this. All of these aspects are involved in building a system within which learners have the knowledge and strategies needed to self-assess their writing.

WHAT DOES THE RESEARCH SAY ABOUT INVOLVING STUDENTS IN THEIR OWN LEARNING THROUGH SELF-ASSESSMENT?

Recently, the emphasis has shifted from the use of assessment evidence to inform teaching to a focus on a learning environment in which such assessment is viewed as a social, collaborative activity (Black & Wiliam, 2009), with the teacher and the students working in partnership to enhance student learning. It is now better understood that students have a significant role in their learning as well as in the assessment of their learning (Hawe, Dixon, & Watson, 2008).

To help students take an active role in the assessment of their own learning and in becoming self-regulating writers, teachers needs to share their "guild knowledge" with them (Sadler, 1989). Guild knowledge is professional or craft knowledge that the teacher has acquired, particularly in terms of what constitutes quality in performance. In writing, this means explaining how qualitative judgments are made about a piece of writing.

Sharing control over the feedback process is also central to student participation in their learning. There is an important difference between viewing students as relatively passive recipients of feedback and establishing a collaboration between student and teacher to evaluate the writing and make decisions on next steps. The teacher plays a vital role in bringing about the transition from a stage of receiving and using feedback to one of self-regulation (see Sadler, 1989). The students of teachers who provide them with the type of feedback on their writing that contains the elements that promote self-regulation make more progress in writing (Parr & Timperley, 2010). Appraising their own work and that of peers is a way for students to develop evaluative and productive knowledge and expertise (Sadler, 1989). It is regarded as more straightforward to evaluate and give feedback on a peer's work than on one's own (Sadler, 1987), so teachers may start with this format.

There is a well-developed rationale for linking self-assessment to higher achievement (see Ross, Rolheiser, & Hogaboam-Gray, 1999). However, there is still quite limited guidance from research regarding the forms and consequences of self-assessment. What we do know is that practices that promote self-regulation of writing through either peer or self-assessment are not widely employed. A study of methods used by teachers in writing classrooms of 13- to 16-year-olds suggests that peer evaluation and similar tasks that give over control to students are not a common occurrence (Hunter, Mayenga, & Gambell, 2006)—and sometimes attempts made to engage students in self-assessment are problematic. First, self-assessment is not necessarily used to inform and support learning. Much of the self-assessment discussed in the literature involves selection of work (mostly by older students) for portfolios or a written reflection on the completed piece or selection. Ms. Rivers has a similar task for her students, wherein they comment about what they particularly like in the piece they have produced. Such acts occur at the end of a process—too late to have a maximum effect on learning. Second, if self-assessment is used in classrooms without appropriate support, it may benefit only some writers because the more effective writers are likely to be the most capable self-evaluators (Perl, 1979).

WHAT ARE SOME ALTERNATIVES?

We know that developing students' understanding of assessment criteria improves learning (Rust, Price, & Donovan, 2003). Ways of incorporating student self-assessment into the classroom include explicitly articulating the criteria that describe the work required to reach a particular level or grade, and using written or oral dialogues in which student and teacher evaluate writing together.

A way to develop this understanding of assessment criteria for writing is through students' use of a scoring rubric. One effective strategy involves students in the construction of the rubric, and then focuses feedback on how well they have applied the criteria (Ross et al., 1999). A second strategy is the use of annotated examples of writing, alongside the associated scoring rubric, so that students and teachers can work together to evaluate the writing (Sadler, 1987). Annotated samples are often employed to train teachers in the scoring of writing. For self-assessment purposes, these can be modified and used to help learners to acquire the knowledge needed to self-assess. There is evidence that annotated samples help. In a small-scale study involving the provision of scripts annotated according to criteria specific to a writing task, participants assessed their own writing and that of a peer. The samples, annotated according to criteria, helped students gain a sense of perspective regarding the quality of their written work and helped them both to self- and to peer-assess appropriately (Brown, 2005).

An Example of Using a Rubric and an Annotated Example to Support Self-Assessment

The following description shows how Ms. Rivers might go about achieving the goal of teaching student self-assessment. (This description is drawn from the classrooms of a number of effective writing teachers whose practice we have been privileged to share.)

Identify the Assessment Criteria and the Relevant Scoring Rubric

First, Ms. Rivers needs to determine the performance criteria for writing at the level of the students she teaches. She can seek out criteria that are appropriate in her school to assess writing. In the school where Ms. Rivers teaches they use a diagnostic assessment measure for writing called Assessment Tools for Teaching and Learning: Writing (known as *asTTle Writing*).[2] Ms. Rivers is fortunate that this resource offers scoring rubrics for seven different writing functions. (As an example, Appendix 11.1 contains the scoring rubric for the deep features of the writing purpose "to persuade" for six levels of the curriculum, from Year 1 to around Year 12, or age 16 or 17.) However, many teaching resources offer scoring rubrics for writing, and Ms. Rivers needs to choose the resource that best fits the curriculum and the goals of her school or district.

Create a Student-Friendly Rubric

Ms. Rivers is likely to use the scoring rubrics first for her own professional learning, for example, as a basis for discussion with colleagues about

---

[2] This tool provides detailed assessment for curriculum objectives in reading, writing, and mathematics for Years 4–12 (a full description of this project, along with technical reports and publications, is available at *www.tki.org.nz/r/asttle*). It is a CD-ROM-based/Web-based assessment suite that gives New Zealand teachers a choice in the design and timing of assessments and access to a range of reporting formats, including comparisons to national norms.

moderating student writing samples (Parr, Glasswell, & Aikman, 2007). But, for student self-assessment, she certainly cannot expect students to work with the rubrics in their current form. So, Ms. Rivers needs to transform the criteria into "student-speak"—into language that her students are likely to understand. However, ultimately, her aim is for her students to use the shared metalanguage that teachers use in the assessment of writing. (This is the language that forms part of teachers' guild knowledge, and one of the "secrets" that teachers need to share with students.) Table 11.1 has an example of the "language resources" part of an asTTle scoring rubric for "to persuade" that has been rewritten for a particular group of students. Ms. Rivers may well need to alter her draft rubric as a result of how the students respond when trying to apply it to their own writing or to that of their peers.

Focus on Key Dimensions of Student Need

Ms. Rivers begins by focusing on one or perhaps two dimensions at a time, according to the needs of her class or groups in her class. A whole rubric is likely to be overwhelming for students. She may group her students according to common teaching needs, based on her scoring of students' writing, using the rubric. If the assessment tool did not supply individual information, Ms. Rivers may need to use her classroom assessments to build a profile about her students' levels, strengths, and learning areas that need assistance. Based on this information, Ms. Rivers can work with her students to develop individual learning goals in writing. To support students, the student-friendly part of the rubric that shows criteria for that goal (Table 11.1) can be pasted into their workbook/folder/journal next to the goal.

So, ways to scaffold student use of a very complex tool (a rubric) are to rewrite it in language that is more accessible to the students you teach and to focus on aspects most relevant to student need first. In addition, students will need support in applying the rubric to a piece of writing, which leads to our next topic.

Use Annotated Examples

To help students apply the criteria in the rubric, it is useful to have examples of student writing that have comments attached about the marking criteria. Ms. Rivers is able to use examples from the asTTle Writing tool that have been annotated. Although these were published for teachers to help them understand more clearly the criteria in each dimension of the scoring rubric, Ms. Rivers can use them with her students as examples of work at each level. Other assessment tools offer similar annotated examples for teachers. Figure 11.1 is an example of a piece written to persuade that has been scored and the scoring annotated. (The writing has been scored

TABLE 11.1. The Criteria for the Dimension Language Resources (for the Purpose "To Persuade") in Student-Speak

Dimension	Level 2	Level 3	Level 4	Level 5	Level 6
Language resources and choices (How the way I use language or choose words has helped my argument)	My writing has statements about my personal point of view. I have used words that are related to the topic. My point of view is not made that clear by my choice of language. I have used some pronouns (*it, he,* etc.) in my writing, but I am unsure if I am using them properly. I have used simple sentences, and they are mostly complete. I have one or two sentences with more detail and ideas.	My writing has special vocabulary that helps it persuade the reader. I am beginning to use language to create an effect and to influence the reader. I have used adverbs and adjectives. I have used words such as *can, might, should,* and *may* to persuade the reader. I have repeated myself to stress important bits. I have used both complete and complex sentences.	I have used appropriate vocabulary. I have used language appropriately to show my point of view and to help persuade the reader. I have used pronouns correctly (it is clear to what they refer). I have used complete sentences and complex sentences.	I have used persuasive language to good effect and have involved the reader. I have used appropriate vocabulary for the topic throughout my writing. I have used language to strengthen my argument. I have used complex sentences where it was appropriate.	I have used appropriate vocabulary for the purpose and the audience. My language choices have been made to manipulate and influence the reader. The tone of my writing is "just right" to strengthen my argument.

Audience Awareness and Purpose 5P The writer directs her argument to the audience by presenting a clearly stated, consistent position. She attempts to persuade the reader using two devices: that of appealing directly to the reader (". . . so play a particular sport"; "think about") and by referring to some scientific evidence ("studies show that . . . ").	START WRITING HERE *School fitness is a very good idea. Fitness essential to being a healthy strong person and should therefore be part of the daily school routine. Not only are the students guaranteed to get exercise on a regular basis it will also help to prevent future disasters such as heart disease.* *Studies show that to keep a healthy body and cholestral level you would need about 20-30 minutes of exercise per day. It doesn't have to be extreme things like lifting weights till you can't feel your arms. it could be simple things like walking your dog to a local park. Exercise should be enjoyable too so play a particular sport that you enjoy or go jogging with a friend.*
Content/Ideas 5B All elements of an argument are evident in this writing. There is a clearly stated position statement, several main points supported by evidence, and the writer concludes with a restatement of the position taken.	*people who get in the habit of not exercising usually end up with high cholestral levels, blood pressure and can't move around as easily as people who exercise. Some people might end up having a heart attack and die, because they can't be bothered doing alittle bit of exercise per day.*
Structure/Organization 5A Key points are identified and the content is managed effectively through grouping and paragraphing. The writer uses linking devices across paragraphs (*although*) and topic sentences to organize within each paragraph. Ideas are linked effectively (through the use of a range of conjunctions).	*Although laziness is one reason why some people don't get into the habit, it is not the only reason. Think about kids who don't have enough time to do everything they have to do. most will be busy with school and then homework, some will have part-time jobs. Who can honestly say that you have ENOUGH time to exercise?* *If everybody did fitness at school every day we would have less people having heart attacks. Our generation would turn to become a bunch of healthy, strong people!*

Language Resources 5P The writer shows knowledge of language choice to influence a reader (powerful adjectives/nouns such as *extreme, disasters, simple, should, guaranteed*). She also uses direct appeals to the reader by the use of the pronoun *you*, which draws the reader into the text. The use of passive structures to report information that supports the position objectifies and adds weight to the argument and amplifies its persuasive power. Conjunction use shows some sophistication (*therefore, although, and, so, because*).	**Grammar 5P** Extensive control of complex sentences evident.	**Punctuation 5P** Sentence punctuation is correct. Basic punctuation is correct. Some evidence of ability to use more complex punctuation (commas to separate clauses).
	Spelling 6B Evidence of ability to spell multisyllabic, irregular, and technical words (single error).	

FIGURE 11.1. An annotated writing sample ("to persuade"). From *e-asttle.tki.org.nz/resources/Teacher-resources#r5*. Copyright 2010 by the New Zealand Ministry of Education. Reprinted by permission. 5, fifth-grade level; B, basic; P, proficient.

according to seven dimensions. For each there is a score for curriculum level and a quality rating of basic (B), proficient (P), or advanced (A) within that level.)

Moving student involvement a step further, Ms. Rivers could choose samples of writing appropriate to the learning needs of her teaching groups to jointly evaluate with her students, using the criteria from the rubric. Together, Ms. Rivers and each group could annotate the writing samples and then display them on the wall or paste them into a workbook or folder, so that students can refer to them when assessing their own, or peers', writing.

Monitor Your Own Progress in Enabling Self-Evaluation of Students

Having worked with students on using rubrics and annotated samples to self-assess, Ms. Rivers needs to monitor whether she has been successful in her goal of encouraging student participation in their own learning. For students to self-assess, they need to have developed the skills and strategies to do so, and Ms. Rivers can check this with her students by asking questions such as the following:

> "What are you learning to do as a writer?"
> "What would that [goal] look like?"
> "What steps are you taking to achieve this?"

Such evidence would help Ms. Rivers find out whether she is providing the type of knowledge the students need to engage in self-assessment. Ms. Rivers can self-evaluate her own performance using the rubric in Table 11.2. The descriptors (like the criteria in a rubric) represent a continuum from less to more expert practice on the part of a teacher in enabling student self-assessment. Ms. Rivers can use it to evaluate her practice as she engages in the process of involving students in their own learning through self-assessing using a rubric and annotated examples.

CONCLUSION

Ms. Rivers was a teacher who worked hard to involve students in their own learning, reasoning that this was important to help them succeed. She felt that her students knew their results from various assessments in writing; that she discussed results with students and that they had occasional opportunities to "mark" or comment on their own work and on the work of peers. Yet there were students whom Ms. Rivers had not managed to teach or reach so that they succeeded in writing.

TABLE 11.2. A Continuum of Progress in Enabling Student Self-Evaluation

	Basic	Mixed	Integrated
Students' understanding of goals and of their learning	Learning goals presented (and success criteria); students supposedly understand what they are learning and what it will look like if achieved.	Students understand reasons for specific learning; are able to work out some of own learning goals; have nonspecific understanding of what to do to reach more immediate goals.	Students able to accurately evaluate own performance; understand where they are in relation to desired quality performance and what specifically is needed in order to reach it.
Students' engagement in self-assessment	Students read over or check their own work; read/hear work of others and comment or give a mark.	Students have checklist-like criteria to use in self- or peer-assessment. Identify where can be improved. Little checking of accuracy of self-/peer-assessment.	Students regularly self- and peer-assess using clear, operationalized criteria/exemplars; identify performance level and where and how can be improved. They are given feedback on the extent to which they do this accurately.

Note From Parr (2010). Copyright 2010 by the New Zealand Council for Educational Research. Reprinted by permission.

As we have seen, it is important in building self-regulation that students have the opportunity to review their own work systematically. They need to evaluate their learning and receive feedback on how they are doing in such evaluation. To inquire into their own learning in writing, students need support. They need to understand the criteria that are required and against which they should measure their learning. They need help in applying these criteria to locate their positions as learners; where they need to go and what they need to do to move forward. To support her students in this, Ms. Rivers can use two main strategies: the use of a rubric and of annotated samples. She can work with students to develop and use the rubrics and annotated samples, and she can provide ongoing feedback to support them in this learning. Finally, Ms. Rivers can inquire into the effectiveness of her own teaching by checking with students about their self-assessment knowledge and strategies, and she can use this evidence also to self-assess.

ADDITIONAL RESOURCES

Droga, L., & Humphrey, S. (2003). *Grammar and meaning: An introduction for primary teachers.* Berry, NSW, Australia: Target Texts Southwood Press.

Knapp, P., & Watkins, M. (2005). *Genre, text, grammar: Technologies for teaching and assessing writing.* Sydney, Australia: University of NSW Press.

Project asTTle (Assessment Tools for Teaching and Learning): *www.tki.org.nz/r/asttle.* Rubrics and exemplars within asTTle can be found at: *e-asttle.tki.org.nz/resources/Teacher-resources.*

Timperley, H. S., & Parr, J. M. (2009). What is this lesson about?: Instructional processes and student understandings in writing classrooms. *Curriculum Journal, 20*(1), 43–60.

Wing Jan, L. (2001). *Write ways: Modelling writing forms.* Melbourne, Australia: Oxford University Press.

REFERENCES

Black, P., & Wiliam, D. (2009). Developing the theory of formative assessment. *Educational Assessment, Evaluation and Accountability, 21,* 5–31.

Brown, A. (2005). Self-assessment of writing in independent language learning programs: The value of annotated samples. *Assessing Writing, 10,* 174–191.

Hawe, E., Dixon, H., & Watson, E. (2008). Oral feedback in the context of written language. *Australian Journal of Language and Literacy, 31,* 43–58.

Hunter, D., Mayenga, C., & Gambell, T. (2006). Classroom assessment tools and uses: Canadian English teachers' practices for writing. *Assessing Writing, 11,* 42–65.

Parr, J. M. (2010). Inquiry into classroom practice for improvement. In H. Timperley & J. M. Parr (Eds.), *Weaving evidence, inquiry and standards to build better schools* (pp. 115–133). Wellington, NZ: NZCER Press.

Parr, J. M., Glasswell, K., & Aikman, M. (2007). Supporting teacher learning and informed practice in writing through assessment tools for teaching and learning. *Asia-Pacific Journal of Teacher Education, 35,* 69–87.

Parr, J. M., & Timperley, H. (2010). Feedback to writing, assessment for teaching and learning and student progress. *Assessing Writing, 15,* 68–85.

Perl, S. (1979). The composing processes of unskilled college writers. *Research in the Teaching of English, 13,* 317–336.

Ross, J. A., Rolheiser, C., & Hogaboam-Gray, A. (1999). Effects of self-evaluation training on narrative writing. *Assessing Writing, 6,* 107–132.

Rust, C., Price, M., & Donovan, B. (2003). Improving students' learning by developing their understanding of assessment criteria and processes. *Assessment and Evaluation, 28,* 147–164.

Sadler, D. R. (1987). Specifying and promulgating achievement standards. *Oxford Review of Education, 13,* 191–209.

Sadler, D. R. (1989). Formative assessment and the design of instructional systems. *Instructional Science, 18,* 119–144.

APPENDIX 11.1. Example of Deep Features Criteria in the e-asTTle Writing Scoring Rubric: "To Persuade"

	Level 1 (Proficient)	Level 2 (Proficient)	Level 3 (Proficient)	Level 4 (Proficient)	Level 5 (Proficient)	Level 6 (Proficient)
Audience awareness and purpose	Writer writes primarily for self. States own opinion with little attempt to persuade. States opinions from a personal perspective and assumes shared knowledge with the audience.	Writer recognizes he or she is writing for an audience other than self. May attempt to persuade audience. States opinions from a personal perspective and may assume shared knowledge with the audience.	Shows some awareness of purpose and audience through choice of content, language, and writing style. Attempts to persuade the audience by stating position in opening. Knows that audience may hold a different point of view but tends to assume there is only one generalized points of view.	Writer shows awareness of purpose and audience through choice of content, language, and writing style. Clearly states a consistent position to persuade the audience. Shows some awareness of intended audience, particularly at beginning and end of text.	Writer shows awareness of purpose and audience though deliberate choice of content, language, and writing style. Identifies and relates to a concrete/specific audience. Shows awareness of intended audience and acknowledges others' points of view.	Writer consistently persuades intended audience. Shows implicit awareness that audience may hold a range of points of view. Uses tone for impact or to manipulate the intended audience toward author's point of view. May effect change.

(cont.)

APPENDIX 11.1. (cont.)

	Level 1 (Proficient)	Level 2 (Proficient)	Level 3 (Proficient)	Level 4 (Proficient)	Level 5 (Proficient)	Level 6 (Proficient)
Content/ ideas	Writing includes one or more domains appropriate to purpose, usually a position statement that conveys a simple idea or a response from a personal perspective. May repeat some ideas. May include information unrelated to the topic and/or task.	Writing includes some domains appropriate to purpose (e.g., a position statement in which the writer identifies a position and makes two or more simple related opinions or statements). May include a conclusion. May present ideas as a list. May include some statements unrelated to the topic and/or task.	Includes **most** domain elements for argument (e.g., main points, some supporting evidence or illustration, a restatement of position). May include a conclusion that makes a **recommendation.** **Relates** almost all material to the given task.	Includes and **begins to develop** identifiable domain elements for argument (e.g., a position statement, support for main points, reinstatement). Restates and **strengthens** position. Provides **relevant** support for ideas.	Develops **mainly consistent** domain elements for argument (e.g., a plausible position statement, support for main points, restatement). Uses conclusion to reflect points made, and may **expand** the argument. Strongly links **supporting reasons** to argument.	Selects content to add. Makes considered, relevant, and elaborate points. Chooses examples to support purpose. Uses conclusion to **integrate** the themes of the argument, rather than simply repeating or summarizing the points made. **Gives consistent support** to main points.
Structure	Some semblance of organization (based around a single idea) may be evident at sentence level. May attempt simple	**Semblance** of organization (e.g., some grouping of ideas generally at sentence level is evident). May make opinion statements as	**Attempts** overall structuring of content by grouping ideas within and across sentences. Uses simple connectives and	**Groups content logically** at the level of main idea by using topic sentences to guide the reader's understanding. **Consistently**	Uses structure to **add** to the intended impact of argument (e.g., by developing a logical, consistently flowing argument).	Uses an **explicit, logical** structure to enhance the argument. Uses **complex** linkages (e.g., varied linking words and

186

(cont.)

	conjunctions (e.g., *and, because,* etc.).	discrete elements. Attempts simple conjunctions to link ideas within sentences (e.g., *and, because,* etc.).	linkages within **and** across sentences (e.g., *since, though,* etc.). Attempts paragraphing.	**uses** a variety of connectives and linkages within sentences and between paragraphs (e.g., *on the one hand, however,* etc.). Uses paragraphing, linking main ideas and supporting details.	Uses **complex** linkages within and between paragraphs (e.g., varied linking words and phrases, conjunctions, and text connectives). Uses paragraphs with main ideas and supporting details. Links sentences thematically to topic of paragraph or section.	phrases, conjunctions, and text connectives). Uses **logically arranged and reasoned ideas** in well-crafted paragraphs and strong topic sentences to guide the reader's understanding of the argument.
Language resources	Uses simple opinion statements from a personal perspective (e.g., "I like," etc.). Uses some topic-specific language to express an opinion. Uses mainly high-frequency words.	Uses **simple** persuasive statements form a personal perspective (e.g., "I think," etc.). Uses topic of content-specific language but language choices convey little	Uses **some** features of persuasive language (e.g., rhetorical questions, imperatives, passive voice, data). **Begins to select** language to create a particular effect	Uses features of persuasive language (e.g., rhetorical questions, imperatives, passive voice, data). Uses language to **identify** a particular viewpoint and	Deliberately uses **a range** of features of persuasive language for effect in order to involve and persuade the intended audience. Uses passive structures and modal auxiliaries to **strengthen** argument.	Uses language features **for effect** to involve and persuade the intended audience. **Considers and selects** language features for effect with the intention of manipulating and/or influencing the audience.

	Level 1 (Proficient)	Level 2 (Proficient)	Level 3 (Proficient)	Level 4 (Proficient)	Level 5 (Proficient)	Level 6 (Proficient)
Language resources *(cont.)*	Shows **some** understanding of pronoun use. May express opinions from a personal perspective. Mainly uses simple sentences, with some variation in beginnings. May attempt compound and complex sentences.	opinion (e.g., mainly neutral nouns, basic descriptors, and limited verbs and adverbials). Shows **some** understanding of pronoun use. Uses some language appropriate to purpose and audience. Uses simple and compound sentences with some variation in beginning. May attempt complex sentences.	to influence the audience (e.g., "point of view" nouns, viewpoint adverbials, and opinion adjectives to add detail and weight to opinion statements and evidence). May use some modal auxiliary verbs. Largely **controls** pronoun use. Uses language that is **generally** appropriate to purpose and audience. Uses a **variety** of sentence structures, beginnings, and lengths.	persuade the audience. Uses language **appropriate** to purpose and audience. Uses a variety of sentence structures, beginnings, and lengths **for effect.**	Uses a variety of sentence structures, beginnings, and lengths for effect **and impact.**	Uses tone (e.g., sarcastic, threatening, humorous, emotive, etc.) to underpin selective language features and strengthen argument. Uses complex, appropriate, varied sentence construction.

Note From *e-asttle.tki.org.nz/resources/Teacher-resources#r5.* Copyright 2010 by the New Zealand Ministry of Education. Reprinted by permission.

CHAPTER 12

If You Want Students to Learn Academic English—Teach It to Them

Dianna Townsend

Key Points for This Chapter

- Adolescents need targeted scaffolding in order to understand and use the academic language of the content areas.
- Word walls, concept maps, and jigsaw are effective strategies for helping students build academic vocabulary knowledge.
- Think-alouds, sentence/paragraph puzzles, and digital media can all support students' comprehension of academic texts.

A BIRD'S-EYE VIEW OF CLASSROOM PRACTICE

Ms. Hayden, an eighth-grade science teacher, is starting a new unit in her life science classes. Her students are motivated and attentive, and their parents are supportive and active in the school community. Many of the students come from homes in which English is not the first language, and few of their parents have formal educational experiences beyond high school. Ms. Hayden knows that most of her students have difficulty reading the textbooks provided by the district, and she struggles with how to help them with the technical and abstract nature of the writing typical of science textbooks. She gives the students a chance to read the first part of the chapter

189

on a new unit on cells and then asks if they have questions. As is often the case, the students stare back at her a little blankly. Most of them were able to read the chapter fluently, but they could not comprehend the reading, so they are not sure what questions to ask. Ms. Hayden moves forward with her two default strategies. First, because she knows vocabulary is important for comprehension, she gives students a list of words and asks them to write out the definitions. Next, she selects central ideas from the chapter and gives students a brief lecture on those ideas. Because she needs to move forward and cover a great deal of content in the new unit, Ms. Hayden does not go back to the textbook with her students. Later in the week, her students take a matching test on the vocabulary words they memorized and the central ideas on which Ms. Hayden lectured.

A teacher of 5 years, Ms. Hayden is doing her very best to help her students meet the content standards for middle school science. She gets to know her students personally, offers extra help sessions at lunch and after school, and communicates often with parents. Her instructional goals are right on track; she wants her students to build the scientific knowledge they need to know to pass the state standards tests and to succeed in future science classes. She also knows that the science textbook she is required to use is above the reading level of most of her students. Indeed, some 70% of ninth graders read below the proficient level (Biancarosa & Snow, 2004). Therefore, rather than build their frustration by asking them to read, reread, and reread again, she tries to make the content accessible and to help students learn the most important pieces of information from the reading. As a result, she often leaves the textbook, and opportunities for her students to understand academic science texts, behind.

DEFINING THE TARGETED APPROACH

Ms. Hayden's two default approaches are best described as *traditional vocabulary instruction* and *reading academic texts without scaffolds*. With respect to *traditional vocabulary instruction*, Ms. Hayden wants her students to understand the life science concepts presented in the chapter, and she knows that students need to understand the related key vocabulary. Therefore, she has students write out definitions for that vocabulary. However, students often cannot understand the technical definitions of science terminology, so writing definitions becomes simply an exercise in memorization rather than an exercise in building scientific language and knowledge. With respect to *reading academic texts without scaffolds*, Ms. Hayden wants her students to understand the chapter, but she has had no professional development in supporting students' comprehension of science texts. As Snow (2010) explains: "Science teachers are not generally well prepared to help their students penetrate the linguistic puzzles that science texts present" (p. 452). Therefore, Ms. Hayden often ends up resorting to reteaching the material in a simplified manner. Students do build some rudimentary understanding of the science concepts, but they never learn to access the scientific language, which will only get more difficult as they progress through the grades. Ms. Hayden's approaches are not necessarily specific strategies that should be avoided. Rather, they are representative of the lack of academic language support that is typical of many middle school content-area classrooms.

WHAT DOES THE RESEARCH SAY ABOUT THE LACK OF ACADEMIC ENGLISH SUPPORT TYPICAL OF CONTENT-AREA CLASSROOMS?

What Is Academic Language?

Despite the widespread attention and agreement given to the notion that we need to do a better job at helping secondary students gain academic language proficiency (Bailey, 2007; Carnegie Council on Advancing Adolescent Literacy, 2009; Schleppegrell, 2004; Short & Fitzsimmins, 2007; Zwiers, 2008), the body of research on the topic has not pinned down a short, accurate definition of academic language. This is partly due to the fact that academic language looks and acts differently in different content areas (Fang & Schleppegrell, 2008), even though there are some elements of academic language that appear in most academic contexts (i.e., cross-discipline academic vocabulary words; Coxhead, 2000). Also, academic language is often construed as being at one end of a language continuum with casual, social language being at the other (Snow & Uccelli, 2009), and there is not a specific point on that continuum where social, conversational language automatically becomes academic. However, despite the lack of a concise definition of academic language, we can identify some general characteristics of school language that make accessing academic texts difficult. In particular, academic language is often dense; clauses and sentences are packed with meaning in order to express abstract and technical ideas as concisely as possible. For example, consider the following definition of Pangaea: "A supercontinent which began to break apart into the modern continents about 260 million years ago, causing the isolation (and separate evolution) of various groups of organisms from each other" (*www.pbs. org, 2011*). To comprehend this definition, students have to be comfortable with technical and abstract vocabulary words (*supercontinent, isolation, evolution, organisms*), and also with interpreting how the clauses in the definition relate to each other (i.e., understanding that the phrase *causing the isolation* refers back to *a supercontinent that began to break apart*. If students do not receive support in unpacking this type of dense text, they are unlikely to access the meaning of such texts.

Thus, academic language is generally characterized as being dense, abstract, and often technical. Furthermore, there is little debate that adolescents need more support with academic language than they have traditionally received in the secondary content areas. Beyond these general statements (which serve as a call to action without being particularly helpful for teachers), we need to crystallize a precise set of characteristics and features of academic English within individual content areas. It is by examining the academic language demands of the individual content areas that we can zero in on what is hard for students and what will work best to support them. Zwiers (2008) contrasts the language of the content areas, explaining that science language expresses technical observations of the natural world, whereas the language of history and language arts expresses social experiences. In more detail, Fang and Schleppegrell (2008) define science language as

> simultaneously technical, abstract, dense, and tightly knit—features that contrast sharply with the more interactive and interpersonal language of everyday spontaneous speech and of reading materials for beginning readers. This language plays a central role in the construction and representation of scientific knowledge, processes, and worldviews. It enables scientists to define, describe, explain, theorize, classify, catalogue, and analyze natural phenomena, as well as to reason, critique, and argue for/against a particular hypothesis, theory, or view-point. (p. 20)

Clearly, science language is charged with a great many functions, and the vocabulary and grammar of science language are in place to serve those functions. Teachers need to help students identify phrases and sentences that, for example, serve a "defining" function versus a "theorizing" or "classifying" function. In addition to these many functions that science language must express, Lemke (2002) notes that science texts are made up of much more than traditional, verbal text: "Science textbooks contain not just words in sentences and paragraphs, but tables, charts, diagrams, graphs, maps, drawings, photographs, and a host of specialized visual representations from acoustical sonograms to chromatography strips and gene maps" (p. 24). Therefore, students will need help with simultaneously navigating traditional verbal text along with multiple types of graphic displays of information.

Why Do Students Need to Build Science Academic Language?

It may be tempting to take Ms. Hayden's approach and bypass the textbook to just lecture on what students need to know using simplified language. However, the precise, technical, and often abstract nature of scientific language is necessary for accurate and thorough understanding and expression of scientific concepts. As Brown, Ryoo, and Rodriguez (2010) note: "In many ways, students' ability to describe a phenomenon is constrained by the science language at their disposal" (p. 1465). For example, a rich understanding of the process of *mitosis* must be accompanied by an understanding of cell types and cell components, including eukaryotic cells, chromosomes, cell nuclei, cytoplasm, organelles, and cell membranes. Students need to understand these terms and how they relate to the process of mitosis. Everyday language, as Vygotsky (1978) theorized, does not have the precision or technical vocabulary to explain scientific concepts such as mitosis; scientific language is needed. Many topics in content areas also have a high level of abstraction. For example, imagine providing an accurate explanation of *communism* without understanding systems of social organization. Everyday language often cannot carry that abstraction, and as a result, complexities and nuances become lost in translation.

Challenges in Learning Academic Language

Like Ms. Hayden, teachers often do a good job of breaking down concepts from the disciplines into bite-sized pieces for our students, but the language of those bite-sized pieces is still academic language. As educators all the way from primary through tertiary education, we need to scaffold on two fronts: content and language. Because content and language are inextricably connected, the goal is not to teach them separately. Rather, while teaching content, we need to attend to the abstract, dense, and technical nature of the language explaining the content, and help students understand how the language is effectively conveying complex information. Importantly, we need to help students build both receptive and productive knowledge of academic language. Honig (2010) notes that classroom instruction often focuses on students' receptive knowledge of science language (what students can understand) versus their expressive knowledge (what students can communicate/produce through discussion and writing). It follows, then, that for students to develop a degree of proficiency in science academic language, they need to be able to both comprehend and *use* academic language. Ms. Hayden's matching tests evaluate only students' receptive knowledge; she'll need to include a writing or discussion element to her assessments to determine what students really understand about the central ideas and vocabulary she is helping them learn.

WHAT ARE SOME ALTERNATIVES?

Again, Ms. Hayden's approaches are not particularly inappropriate. However, if she does not integrate specific scaffolding for academic language into her lessons, her students will continue to have difficulty accessing the textbook content and the overall content of her life science class. Following are alternative approaches that will help Ms. Hayden meet her instructional goals.

With respect to academic vocabulary instruction, a number of principles and strategies has been shown to be effective in intervention studies (Lesaux, Kieffer, Faller, & Kelley, 2010; Snow, Lawrence, & White, 2009; Townsend & Collins, 2009). Perhaps what is most important in relation to academic vocabulary instruction is that academic words be taught in the context of authentic academic texts. In other words, presenting students with a random list of words to learn is not nearly as effective as identifying key terms in texts and helping students understand word meanings as well as how those word meanings relate to each other within the texts. Students also need opportunities to practice and personalize word meanings in multiple contexts (Blachowicz & Fisher, 2000; Stahl & Nagy, 2006). Finally, students need support in building generative word knowledge, or independent word-learning strategies, which includes knowledge of morphology (i.e., word parts) and the ability to use context clues to determine word meanings (Stahl & Nagy, 2006). Teachers can provide opportunities in all these areas by using two specific strategies: word walls, concept maps, and vocabulary jigsaws.

Teaching Academic Vocabulary: Word Walls, Concept Maps, Vocabulary Jigsaws

Consider the following explanation of mitosis (*mitosis*, 2002):

> *Mitosis* is the process by which the nucleus divides in eukaryotic organisms, producing two new nuclei that are genetically identical to the nucleus of the parent cell. It occurs in cell division carried on by human somatic cells—the cells used for the maintenance and growth of the body. These cells have two paired sets of 23 chromosomes, or 46 chromosomes in total. (Cells with two sets of chromosomes are called *diploid*.) Before cell division occurs, the genetic material in each chromosome is duplicated as part of the normal functioning of the cell. Each chromosome then consists of two chromatids, identical strands of DNA. When a cell undergoes mitosis, the chromosomes condense into 46 compact bodies. The chromatids then separate, and one chromatid from each of the 46 chromosomes moves to each side of the cell as it prepares to divide. The chromatids form the chromosomes of the daughter cells, so that each new cell has 46 chromosomes (two complete sets of 23) just like the parent cell. ◊ While both *mitosis* and *meiosis* refer properly to types of nuclear division, they are often used as shorthand to refer to the entire processes of cell division themselves. When mitosis and meiosis are used

to refer specifically to nuclear division, they are often contrasted with *cytokinesis*, the division of the cytoplasm.

First, Ms. Hayden will want to ensure that she is choosing vocabulary words that are essential to understanding the text and/or meeting the objective of the lesson. When choosing words, she should consider both general academic words and science academic words. General academic words (Coxhead, 2000) are words that are used across content areas, and they are often neglected instructionally because teachers focus on the key content words for any particular unit. General academic words can be challenging for two main reasons. First, they often have abstract definitions that make little sense to students without multiple concrete examples. Second, they are used across content areas, but they operate differently in different content areas. Coxhead's (2000) work estimated that general academic words account for 10% of the words in academic texts. Thus, these words can pose real comprehension stumbling blocks for students. The other type of academic words, content-specific academic words, are primarily used in just one content area. Both types of academic words are important if students are going to make sense of science academic language. Examples of general academic words Ms. Hayden might want to target in the above passage are *produces, occurs, maintenance,* and *duplication.* Examples of science words Ms. Hayden might want to target are *eukaryotic, nucleus, chromosome,* and *DNA.*

Once Ms. Hayden has chosen the words she deems most relevant to her objectives, it's time to bring them alive in the classroom. Word walls are a practical strategy for making words visible to students, and activities done with word walls can meet all major principles of academic vocabulary instruction. Ms. Hayden can post all the relevant vocabulary for the mitosis unit on the word wall. As students read the above explanation of mitosis, Ms. Hayden can pause to draw students' attention to the most important vocabulary words and help them practice pronouncing them, which will build students' phonological and orthographic knowledge of the words (research suggests that just seeing the spelling of a word can help students better remember the meaning of the word; Ehri & Rosenthal, 2007). Next, she can organize students into teams, each of which will create a concept map (Stahl & Nagy, 2006) for one of the general academic words and for one of the science academic words. On these concept maps, students can write the formal definition, include descriptive information, and create a personal connection or analogy to the word. Diagrams and sketches can also be important components of concept maps. See Figure 12.1 for a blank concept map and the type of information that may be included in each bubble. Also, see Figure 12.2 for a sample concept map for the term *eukaryotic cell,* one of the science academic words, and Figure 12.3 for a

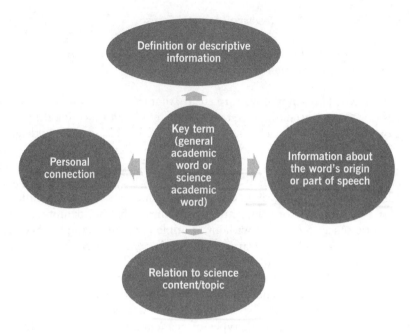

FIGURE 12.1. Sample concept map.

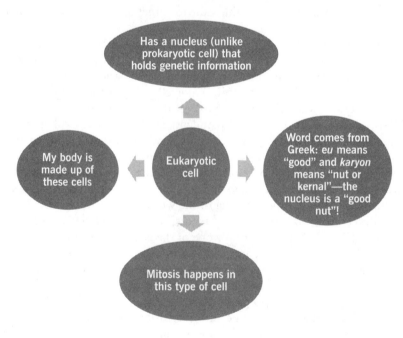

FIGURE 12.2. Sample concept map of a science academic word.

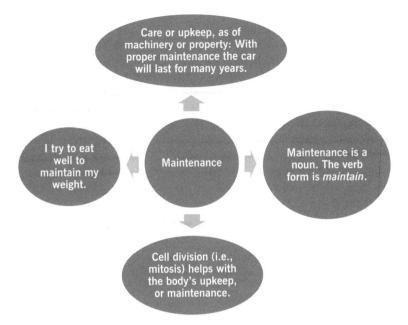

FIGURE 12.3. Sample concept map of a general academic word.

sample concept map for the term *maintenance*, one of the general academic words.

As the groups work, Ms. Hayden will circulate to address any misconceptions and to check the work. When all groups have completed their concept maps, Ms. Hayden can use the jigsaw strategy (Aronson & Patnoe, 1997; see *www.jigsaw.org* for an overview and many examples) so that students can teach each other what they learned about the new vocabulary. With the jigsaw strategy, Ms. Hayden will create "jigsaw groups" of students in which each group member comes from a different "home" group. The home groups were the original groups in which students created two concept maps, one on a general academic word and one on a science academic word. Each of the jigsaw groups consists of "experts," one each from all of the original groups, who then teaches the jigsaw group about the two words for which their home groups created their concept maps. The jigsaw strategy was developed by Aronson (Aronson & Patnoe, 1997) as means of promoting cooperation and collaboration in classrooms rife with racial tension, but it serves multiple purposes. With respect to academic language, this strategy allows students to develop *expressive* knowledge of the new terms. Because each student becomes an "expert" on the terms for which his or her original group created concept maps, each student is responsible for teaching peers in the jigsaw group about those concepts. Students thereby develop their expressive knowledge of the concepts and, in part, the scientific language used to explain it. Concept maps can then be posted on the word wall with the key terms so that students can revisit them, and add to them, whenever necessary. Adding to concept maps during later lessons is an important part of the process; word learning is an incremental process (Nagy & Scott, 2000), and students' concept maps can be a graphic representation of how the richness of their word knowledge develops over time.

Academic Reading Scaffolding Strategies

Think-Alouds

Once Ms. Hayden's students have practiced and personalized the meanings of the key vocabulary, they will still need help unpacking the connected texts in which those words occur. One strategy that Ms. Hayden can start with, as a means of inviting students into the challenging texts, is a think-aloud. Using this strategy, Ms. Hayden will begin reading the text aloud and, either at the clause level or at the sentence level, explain how she makes meaning from, and comes to understand, the text. She is essentially making visible to her students the process of unpacking, clarifying, and restating the dense and technical science writing used to explain a concept. See Figure 12.4 for a sample think-aloud that shows how Ms. Hayden might break down the first sentence in the above explanation of mitosis. Importantly, in this think-aloud example, the final summary statement is nearly twice as long as the original sentence. Ms. Hayden can capitalize on this to help her students understand what is meant by *density* of academic language. Academic language packs a great deal of meaning into clauses and sentences. Just imagine how long textbooks, research articles, and scientific policy reports would be if the language was *not* dense!

Given the realities of the science curriculum Ms. Hayden is charged with teaching, she certainly will not have the time to do this type of think-aloud with every piece of text she assigns to her students. However, consistent and accessible think-alouds used with short pieces of texts every day can expose students to the functions and meanings of scientific language. Over time, Ms. Hayden can help the students identify the types of language typical of scientific texts—the language that signals, as Fang and Schleppe-grell (2008) note, the defining, describing, explaining, theorizing, classifying, cataloging, and analyzing of natural phenomena that are characteristic of science writing. Think-alouds, as strategies, are related to the notion of a cognitive apprenticeship (Collins, Brown, & Newman, 1987), in which the tacit comprehension processes of an expert of academic science language become visible to students.

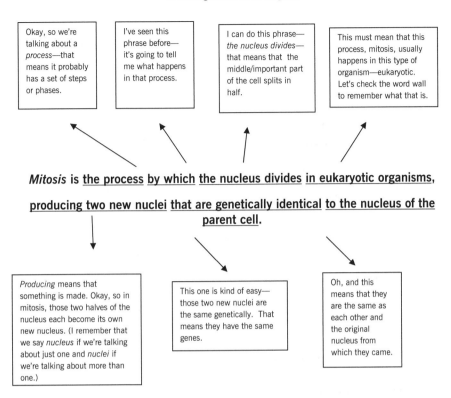

Okay, so we're talking about a *process*—that means it probably has a set of steps or phases.

I've seen this phrase before—it's going to tell me what happens in that process.

I can do this phrase—*the nucleus divides*—that means that the middle/important part of the cell splits in half.

This must mean that this process, mitosis, usually happens in this type of organism—eukaryotic. Let's check the word wall to remember what that is.

Mitosis is <u>the process</u> <u>by which</u> <u>the nucleus divides</u> <u>in eukaryotic organisms,</u> <u>producing two new nuclei</u> <u>that are genetically identical</u> <u>to the nucleus of the parent cell.</u>

Producing means that something is made. Okay, so in mitosis, those two halves of the nucleus each become its own new nucleus. (I remember that we say *nucleus* if we're talking about just one and *nuclei* if we're talking about more than one.)

This one is kind of easy—those two new nuclei are the same genetically. That means they have the same genes.

Oh, and this means that they are the same as each other and the original nucleus from which they came.

Summary, in my own words: All right, so putting all this together, I would say that mitosis happens in eukaryotic organisms, and it involves a set of steps or phases. The nucleus in the first cell breaks in half to create two new nuclei that are the same as each other and as the original cell.

FIGURE 12.4. Sample think-aloud.

Sentence/Paragraph Puzzles

Regular exposure to Ms. Hayden's think-alouds will certainly help her students start to build some meaningful experiences with academic language, but note that this strategy is a receptive one for students. In other words, they may be developing their comprehension of science language, but they still need to develop their expressive knowledge of the language. However, moving from listening to a think-aloud to independent use of dense and technical academic language will be a bridge too far for most students. A better follow-up activity to think-alouds is the sentence or paragraph puzzle, in which students receive the clauses of a sentence (or whole sentences that make up a paragraph) on pieces of paper, which they then need to piece back together to make (express) a cohesive scientific text. See Figure 12.5 for an example of a paragraph puzzle.

Listening to a teacher's think-aloud and then practicing linking those same clauses and scientific ideas support students' receptive *and* expressive science language development. A sentence or paragraph puzzle is a particularly good scaffold for Ms. Hayden's students, because they can read the language fluently but comprehend little of it. The sentence puzzle becomes the middle steppingstone in the process of first comprehending the ideas, to

---

Note: The sentences below would be given to students on individual slips of paper.

Directions: The following sentences make up an explanation of mitosis, but they are out of order. Using what you know about mitosis, put them back in order.

Before cell division occurs, the genetic material in each chromosome is duplicated as part of the normal functioning of the cell.

It occurs in cell division carried on by human somatic cells—the cells used for the maintenance and growth of the body.

The chromatids form the chromosomes of the daughter cells, so that each new cell has 46 chromosomes (two complete sets of 23) just like the parent cell.

Mitosis is the process by which the nucleus divides in eukaryotic organisms, producing two new nuclei that are genetically identical to the nucleus of the parent cell.

Each chromosome then consists of two chromatids, identical strands of DNA.

vWhen a cell undergoes mitosis, the chromosomes condense into 46 compact bodies.

These cells have two paired sets of 23 chromosomes, or 46 chromosomes in total. (Cells with two sets of chromosomes are called *diploid*.)

The chromatids then separate, and one chromatid from each of the 46 chromosomes moves to each side of the cell as it prepares to divide.

When mitosis and meiosis are used to refer specifically to nuclear division, they are often contrasted with *cytokinesis*, the division of the cytoplasm.

While both mitosis and meiosis refer properly to types of nuclear division, they are often used as shorthand to refer to the entire processes of cell division themselves.

FIGURE 12.5. Sample paragraph puzzle. Sentences are taken from the *American Heritage Science Dictionary* definition.

then determining how the language should be ordered to best express those ideas, to finally producing their own scientific explanations of the ideas. The final component in this process, as with the vocabulary instruction, is to give students opportunities to write and discuss what they know about the science content so that they move beyond just receptive knowledge to the in-depth knowledge of science content and language associated with expressing their own understanding. Ms. Hayden can revise her matching tests for measures that better assess students' receptive *and* expressive knowledge of science concepts and the academic language that best explains those concepts.

The Potential (and Potential Pitfall) of Scaffolding Academic Language Development with Digital Media

The power of multimedia to support comprehension, particularly in science in which the texts already include so many semiotic sign systems (Lemke, 2002), should not be underestimated. Such resources should be integrated with the strategies already presented to help students build the concept knowledge that will, in turn, scaffold their understanding of academic language. Indeed, Brown and colleagues (2010) have taken this approach in recent empirical studies, during which they first helped students build understanding of scientific concepts using accessible language, and then used those burgeoning conceptual understandings to scaffold science language comprehension. Multiple video resources are available online to provide students with visual representations of the process of mitosis (for an example of a video, see *www.teachersdomain.org/resource/tdc02.sci.life. stru.dnadivide*, and for an example of a graphic, see *www.suite101.com/ view_image.cfm/404356*). However, such digital media are not a panacea for students' difficulty with science texts. If these videos and graphics are used as stand-alone teaching resources, they may be more engaging than text, but they may not help students who cannot access the language of such digital media. Digital media provide powerful visual support for science concepts, but they still include the challenging academic language that conveys those concepts. Therefore, the activities to support vocabulary development and academic science language can scaffold students' comprehension of digital media resources, and vice versa. The strategies and the digital media must be used *in conjunction* with each other, otherwise students may end up observing digital media that they cannot comprehend. Also, videos and other types of visual support are often passive, or receptive, activities. Students need to do activities similar to the ones explained above in order to build their expressive knowledge of science language and science concepts.

CONCLUSION

There is little disagreement around the importance of supporting students' academic language development. In short, building academic language knowledge is essential for building content-area knowledge. Because the abstract and technical concepts of each content area are most thoroughly and accurately expressed using the academic language of that content area, we must help students build a command of the language used to express the concepts they are learning. However, the scholarship in this area, and the development of materials to help teachers develop their own linguistic understanding and repertoire of strategies, are just gaining momentum.

Traditional instruction in the content areas is characterized by a focus on content and a general neglect of the challenges of academic language. Let us be quick to acknowledge that this is an acknowledgment of a gap in teacher education, not a criticism of teachers. However, this traditional approach to content-area instruction has two serious implications. First, as educators, we are missing many opportunities to develop the content-area knowledge we are teaching, simply because students cannot access the language used to present the content. This leads to the second implication, which is related to the fact that textbooks and content-area concepts only get more challenging. As educators, we need to help students develop the skills and knowledge they need to be ready for the challenges of the next level within our content areas. Supporting students' academic language proficiency in the content areas provides them with the advanced literacy skills they need *and* increases their comprehension of abstract and technical ideas in the content areas. The strategies explained above help teachers provide explicit instruction on academic language as well as opportunities to practice and personalize academic language. In addition, these strategies support acquisition of both receptive and expressive knowledge of language and content.

ADDITIONAL RESOURCES

The following additional readings offer many strategies for scaffolding academic language development in various content areas.

Fang, Z., & Schleppegrell, M. J. (2008). *Reading in secondary content areas: A language-based pedagogy.* Ann Arbor: University of Michigan Press.

Honig, S. (2010). A framework for supporting scientific language in primary grades. *The Reading Teacher, 64,* 23–32

Kieffer, M., & Lesaux, N. (2007). Breaking down words to build meaning: Morphology, vocabulary, and reading comprehension in the urban classroom. *The Reading Teacher, 61,* 134–144.

Marzano, R. J. (2004). *Building background knowledge for academic achievement*. Alexandria, VA: Association for Supervision and Curriculum Development.

Townsend, D. (2009). Building academic vocabulary in after-school settings: Games for growth with middle school English learners. *Journal of Adolescent and Adult Literacy, 53*, 242–251.

Zwiers, J. (2008). *Building academic language: Essential practices for content classrooms*. San Francisco: Jossey-Bass.

TRADE MATERIAL CITED IN TEXT

Mitosis. (2002). Retrieved January 26, 2011, from *dictionary.reference.com/browse/mitosis*.

www.pbs.org. (2011). Evolution. Retrieved January 26, 2011, from *www.pbs.org/wgbh/evolution/extinction/dinosaurs*.

REFERENCES

Aronson, E., & Patnoe, S. (1997). *The jigsaw classroom: Building cooperation in the classroom*. New York: Longman.

Bailey, A. L. (Ed.). (2007). *The language demands of school: Putting academic English to the test*. New Haven, CT: Yale University Press.

Biancarosa, G., & Snow, C. (2004). *Reading next: A vision for action and research in middle and high school literacy*. New York: Carnegie Corporation of New York.

Blachowicz, C. L. Z., & Fisher, P. (2000). Vocabulary instruction. In M. L. Kamil, P. B. Mosenthal, P. D. Pearson, & R. Barr (Eds.), *Handbook of reading research* (Vol. 3, pp. 503–523). Mahwah, NJ: Erlbaum.

Brown, B. A., Ryoo, K., & Rodriguez, J. (2010). Pathway towards fluency: Using "disaggregate instruction" to promote science literacy. *International Journal of Science Education, 32*, 1465–1493.

Carnegie Council on Advancing Adolescent Literacy. (2010). *Time to act: An agenda for advancing adolescent literacy for college and career success*. New York: Carnegie Corporation of New York.

Collins, A., Brown, J. S., & Newman, S. E. (1987). *Cognitive apprenticeship: Teaching the craft of reading, writing and mathematics* (Technical Report No. 403). Cambridge, MA: BBN Laboratories.

Coxhead, A. (2000). A new academic word list. *TESOL Quarterly, 34*, 213–238.

Ehri, L. C., & Rosenthal, J. (2007). Spellings of words: A neglected facilitator of vocabulary learning. *Journal of Literacy Research, 39*, 389–409.

Fang, Z., & Schleppegrell, M. J. (2008). *Reading in secondary content areas: A language-based pedagogy*. Ann Arbor: University of Michigan Press.

Honig, S. (2010). A framework for supporting scientific language in primary grades. *The Reading Teacher, 64*, 23–32.

Lemke, J. (2002). Multimedia semiotics: Genres for science education and scientific literacy. In M. J. Schleppegrell & M. C. Colombi (Eds.), *Developing advanced literacy in first and second languages: Meaning with power* (pp. 21–44). Mahwah, NJ: Erlbaum.

Lesaux, N., Kieffer, M., Faller, S. E., & Kelley, J. G. (2010). The effectiveness and ease of implementation of an academic vocabulary intervention for linguistically diverse students in urban middle schools. *Reading Research Quarterly, 45,* 196–228.

Nagy, W., & Scott, J. A. (2000). Vocabulary processes. In M. L. Kamil, P. B. Mosenthal, P. D. Pearson, & R. Barr (Eds.), *Handbook of reading research* (Vol. 3, pp. 269–284). Mahwah, NJ: Erlbaum.

Schleppegrell, M. J. (2004). Challenges of the science register for ESL students: Errors and meaning-making. In M. J. Schleppegrell & M. C. Colombi (Eds.), *Developing advanced literacy in first and second languages* (pp. 119–142). Mahwah, NJ: Erlbaum.

Short, D. J., & Fitzsimmins, S. (2007). *Double the work: Challenges and solutions to acquiring language and academic literacy for adolescent English language learners.* Washington, DC: Alliance for Excellent Education.

Snow, C. (2010). Academic language and the challenge of reading for learning about science. *Science, 328,* 450–452.

Snow, C., Lawrence, J., & White, C. (2009). Generating knowledge of academic language among urban middle school students. *Journal of Research on Educational Effectiveness, 2,* 325–344.

Snow, C., & Uccelli, P. (2009). The challenge of academic language. In D. Olson & N. Torrance (Eds.), *The Cambridge handbook of literacy* (pp. 112–133). New York: Cambridge University Press.

Stahl, S., & Nagy, W. (2006). *Teaching word meanings.* Mahwah, NJ: Erlbaum.

Townsend, D., & Collins, P. (2009). Academic vocabulary and middle school English learners: An intervention study. *Reading and Writing: An Interdisciplinary Journal, 22,* 993–1019.

Vygotsky, L. S. (1978). *Mind in society: The development of higher psychological processes.* Cambridge, MA: Cambridge University Press.

Zwiers, J. (2008). *Building academic language: Essential practices for content classrooms.* San Francisco: Jossey-Bass.

CHAPTER 13

If You Want Students to Learn Vocabulary— Move Beyond Copying Words

Kathy Ganske

Key Points for This Chapter

- Students need to engage in developing deep understandings of word meanings, not in surface-level memorization.
- When selecting words to teach, consider what each word represents (concept or label), how often and in what contexts it occurs, whether it can be understood without being taught, what knowledge students might have of the word, and what type of word it is—vocabulary of mature language users, academic vocabulary.
- Semantic maps and webs, semantic feature analyses, four square, and morphology are strategies that can support vocabulary development.

A BIRD'S-EYE VIEW OF CLASSROOM PRACTICE

It's Monday morning, first period in Ms. Gardner's seventh-grade English/language arts class, and true to every Monday's routine, Ms. Gardner begins the 48-minute period by handing out a copy of the week's vocabulary words—a list of 30 words deemed important for middle school students to know. As she walks around distributing the list, Ms. Gardner reminds the students that by Wednesday they should have copied each word into their notebooks, along with a definition and a relevant sentence, so that they're ready to talk about the words and their meanings in preparation for Friday's random 15-word quiz. Groans and "*30* this time?" are heard from a few students, though they say nothing further, and most begin copying the words into their notebooks.

Ms. Gardner realizes that vocabulary knowledge is important for her students; she believes knowing more words will make it easier for them to understand what they read and enable them to write with more sophisticated and descriptive language. This knowledge will benefit the students when it comes time for state tests and, she hopes, eventually Scholastic Aptitude Tests (SATs) or American College Tests (ACTs). Furthermore she thinks it's important to consider what the research says, and research supports the value of vocabulary development; in fact, because of recent research, her district has put an increased emphasis on vocabulary knowledge in hopes of raising student achievement. Most of her students have very limited vocabularies as evidenced by the most recent state testing results (over 85% of the students did not pass the literacy portion of the test) and by the word confusions that pop up almost daily during classroom discussions. Ms. Gardner selects words each week from a book provided by her district that is designed for middle and high school students. She feels pressure to increase students' vocabulary knowledge and acknowledges stepping up the number of words this week from 25 to 30 because of the pressure.

So what approach does Ms. Gardner use to teach vocabulary? She admits she's uncertain of how best to teach the words, and adds that the way she's teaching her students is the way in which she was taught and the way the teacher she worked with when she was preparing to become a teacher taught her students. "It's also the way most of my colleagues teach their students." Ms. Gardner then falls silent for a moment and says, "I've never really thought about *how* to teach the words until very recently, with the district's push for more emphasis on vocabulary; I guess I've just had my routine, and the kids haven't really complained. I have wondered, though, just *how many* words I should give the students, especially now with the district push." She expresses concern about having to devote even more time now on Wednesdays to going over the extra words. She already spends considerable time clarifying confusions, and by the end of the week most students perform "fairly well" on the random word quiz, though their retention in the long term is seldom evident in their reading and writing.

When pressed further about her approach to instruction, Ms. Gardner recalls her own experiences as a student: "I put a lot of time into looking up the words, copying down the definitions, and studying for the quiz each week, and I generally did quite well, but to be honest, I can't say I really remember that many of the words; they didn't really become a part of me. But just last week I made an interesting observation: *Amiable* was one of our words and seeing it made me recall when I was in middle school and had been given that word to learn. The experience was memorable, because that same week we also had the word *amicable* on our list, and I was struck back then by how much alike the two words were, both visually and in meaning. It seemed so odd because there was usually no connection between the words we were assigned, other than they were considered important to know. Unlike 95% of the other words, I've never forgotten those two." She pauses and reflects: "I probably should have put *amicable* on my students' list, too. I thought about it, wondered if the two words might also be memorable for them. I wish I knew some other things to try."

Despite Ms. Gardner's recognition that her current approach of assigning dictionary defining and memorization is not a highly effective one for her students, she continues the practice because she needs to do something to try to foster vocabulary knowledge, has limited time to do so, and quite frankly doesn't really know what other approaches might be better.

DEFINING THE TARGETED PRACTICE

The vocabulary practice Ms. Gardner is using is often referred to as the *traditional* or *standard* approach, or the *word list* or *dictionary* approach. In any case, it is a method, with slight variations, whereby students are typically asked to copy words, look up their definitions or a synonym, perhaps generate a sentence using the word, and take a quiz over some or all of the words at week's end. The method relies on rote memorization of words that may be related in no other way than perhaps that they are deemed important for a college-bound young person to know. In some instances the lists are simply levied as assignments without benefit of the type of discussion that Ms. Gardner has each week with her students. The lists used with this approach vary in length; I have seen some as short as 10 or 15 words and heard stories of others as long as 75! It is the approach that many of us experienced in our schooling—or perhaps I should say *endured* in our schooling.

WHAT DOES THE RESEARCH SAY
ABOUT THE TRADITIONAL APPROACH OF COPYING
AND LOOKING UP VOCABULARY WORDS?

A definition is the enclosing of a wilderness of idea within a wall of words.
—Samuel Butler (1912)

Despite general consensus in the academic community about the ineffectiveness of the traditional approach to vocabulary instruction, the actual research on this practice is surprisingly sparse and dates primarily from decades ago. We find explanation for the name *traditional* in the review of vocabulary instruction by Petty, Herald, and Stoll (1967), who begin their discussion of the methods they examined with the *word list* approach, "because it is the oldest of the direct methods" for teaching vocabulary (p. 17). This practice, widely used for decades and still used today in many middle school classrooms, has long been recognized as one that causes students much difficulty (Deese, 1967; Nist & Olejnik, 1995), so much so, in fact, that some researchers have raised serious questions about the value of the definitional approach for vocabulary learning (e.g., Beck, McKeown, & Kucan, 2002; Miller & Gildea, 1987; Nagy, 1988). Others, such as Petty and colleagues, take a slightly less absolute, though by no means encouraging, perspective, concluding that "any attention to vocabulary development is better than none" (p. 85).

What issues have led scholars to hold such negative views about this age-old approach to vocabulary instruction? Numerous concerns stem from teachers' misuse of the dictionary to teach vocabulary rather than for its intended use as a resource for students to understand unfamiliar words they encounter during reading. As a tool for traditional vocabulary instruction the dictionary falls short. Nagy (1988) and Anderson and Nagy (1992) highlight several of the inadequacies, not the least of which is that assigning students to copy dictionary definitions and write sentences results in a large number of strange sentences (e.g., *the tide* regurgitates *to the ocean*) generated by students who often misconstrue the language of the definitions, such as "to flow back" in the case of *regurgitate*. Because dictionary definitions must necessarily be concise, lexicographers (those who write dictionaries) frequently have to rely on vocabulary that is more sophisticated than the targeted word itself in order to try to fully express the concept in the space of a line or two of text; such is the case with *mirror*, below. (Note: the definitions that follow are from the *American Heritage College Dictionary*, 2004, but could easily be from other dictionaries, because the same tendencies hold true across all.)

> *mirror*: a surface capable of reflecting sufficient undiffused light to form an image of the object placed in front of it

To understand the definition of *mirror*, an inquirer would basically have to already know the word and several more sophisticated terms, such as *undiffused*. *Reflection* presents a similar prior knowledge issue because it is defined with words that are related to it—"The act of *reflecting* or the state of being *reflected*." If you don't know what *reflect* means, you're in trouble and will have to search out the meaning of this word in order to understand *reflection*.

Nagy (1988) discusses additional language-related issues, such as definitions that are sometimes inaccurate, at least when the reader's prior knowledge is considered. Although readers may be familiar with all of the words used in a definition, they may not be familiar with *all* of the meanings of all of the words, and application of an incorrect meaning can soon lead to misunderstanding, as with *stewed* in the definition below:

conserve: A jam made of fruits stewed in sugar.

Knowing *stew* as a food dish made with meat, vegetables, and a broth may leave readers turning up their noses and wondering as they envision *conserve* as a jam made with fruit, meat, and vegetables! Even when simpler definitions are substituted for the standard ones, students still have difficulty generating sentences that accurately capture the meanings of half the words (McKeown, 1993). To fully appreciate the challenge of using the dictionary definitions of unfamiliar words to write sentences that express word meanings, you might try the practice, using the following set of four words (not 25!) and their *American Heritage College Dictionary* meanings:

folderol: a trifle; gewgaw

lixiviate: to wash or percolate the soluble matter from

retral: situated or located close to, or directed toward the back

verisimilitude: the quality of appearing to be real or true

As a tool for understanding unfamiliar words encountered during reading, I find the dictionary unparalleled. Students need to be taught how to efficiently and effectively use dictionaries and learn to appreciate what they have to offer as a resource. When misused, the end result may well be a turn-off and avoidance.

Because a key aim of vocabulary learning is to improve reading comprehension, it is important to consider that looking up and writing down dictionary definitions and sentences does not necessarily improve reading comprehension either (Baumann & Kame'enui, 1991), because comprehension depends on in-depth conceptual knowledge of a word, which cannot be consolidated into a dictionary definition (Nagy, 1988). Other studies that have reached similar findings have demonstrated an increase in comprehension when a combined approach of definition and context is used (Stahl & Fairbanks, 1986). Absence of a context for how the word is being used, which could provide insights into word meaning, compounds the problems of dictionary definitions. Knowledge of a single definition can't possibly capture the nuances of the concept being expressed, as, for example, with a word such as *commotion*. Is the commotion merely a *fuss* or a *ruckus*, or is it a *hullabaloo* or *mayhem* or *pandemonium*, or perhaps utter *chaos*? Each of these words is a potential synonym for *commotion*, but their meanings are quite different. Students need instruction on how to choose the most appropriate meaning, and this necessitates an understanding of the context of the sentence and the nuances of word meanings. In addition, students need to be taught how to use context to gain clues to word meaning. It is not enough to simply remind students to "use the context clues"; some students do not know how to approach this. One way to go about teaching them is to use a series of cloze passages that requires students to consider what makes sense for the missing words. A variation of the technique encourages students to balance context clues with letter/sound clues (Ganske, 2006; Strickland, Ganske, & Monroe, 2004).

Despite the importance of context clues for understanding vocabulary and ultimately for improving reading comprehension, the most effective vocabulary instruction goes well beyond combining context with definitions. Research suggests that rather than relying on the superficiality of rote memorization, vocabulary instruction should be focused on developing deep understandings of words (Stahl, Brozo, & Simpson, 1987). This sentiment is echoed by those who argue further for instructional purposes that actively engage students in learning words (Anderson & Nagy, 1992; Nagy, 1988). Drawing on surveys of existing research, Nagy identified three critical ingredients for vocabulary instruction aimed at improving reading comprehension: *integration, repetition,* and *meaningful use.* The *Report of the National Reading Panel: Teaching Children to Read* (National Institute of Child Health and Human Development, 2000), in addition to suggesting these characteristics—which are the categories of *learning in rich contexts, repetition,* and *multiple exposures*—also recommended that vocabulary instruction include:

- Both explicit and implicit teaching
- Incidental learning
- Use of computer-assisted technology
- Active engagement
- Restructuring of tasks, as necessary
- Multiple methods to optimize learning

In the next section we delve into effective research-based strategies for developing the vocabulary knowledge of middle school learners, including determining which words to teach.

WHAT ARE SOME ALTERNATIVES?

In order to develop students' vocabulary knowledge, Ms. Gardner might have chosen words judiciously and used strategies that would develop deep knowledge of the targeted words, so that students would transfer vocabulary knowledge to reading and writing. Transferring word knowledge would enable students to generalize their understandings to more words than just those targeted, such as through the use of morphology, so that word learning could be more efficient. In the following section, we explore alternatives to Ms. Gardner's copy-it-down-look-it-up-memorize approach.

Determining Which Words to Teach

Ms. Gardner expressed concern about choosing words to teach. Nagy and Anderson (1984) estimated that by the time students reach high school, they will have been exposed to about 88,500 different word families—*word family* being defined as a group of words that share a common root, as *democratic, democracy, demographics, demography,* and so on—so the actual number of words is far greater. Given the sheer number of vocabulary words that students must navigate, it is essential that word learning be efficient. So, which words should be taught?

Researchers sometimes have categorized words by type for word learning. Beck and colleagues (2002) describe a three-tier model: Tier I words generally do not have to be taught (e.g., *tired, happy, hungry*); Tier II words are the vocabulary of mature language users (e.g., *fatigued, ecstatic, ravenous*), the concepts of which learners probably already know (*tired, happy, hungry*), and which Beck and her colleagues believe should be the focus of instruction; and specialized, low-frequency, domain-specific Tier III vocabulary (e.g., *longitude, photosynthesis, trapezoid, proletariat*), which the authors of the tiered approach suggest should be taught as needed and within specific contexts.

Another category of words is *academic vocabulary*, the language of schools and schooling: for example, *isosceles triangle, literary criticism, genre, possessive, steppe, sequential, circuit,* and so on. Different scholars define academic vocabulary in different ways (e.g., Baumann & Graves, 2010; Coxhead, 2000; Fisher & Frey, 2008; Hiebert & Lubliner, 2008; Marzano & Pickering, 2005; Snow, 2010; Townsend, 2009). The variation in definition stems in part from the fact that there isn't an exact point at which a word is considered to be academic language; rather, academic language "falls toward one end of a continuum (defined by formality of tone, complexity of content, and degree of impersonality of stance), with informal, casual, conversational language at the other extreme" (Snow, 2010, p. 450). Despite the differences in definition, there is general agreement that academic vocabulary, as well as Tier II and III types of words, are critical for students to know if they are to be successful middle school learners. With so many possibilities to choose from, how does a teacher such as Ms. Gardner determine which words to explicitly teach?

When considering the matter, keep in mind that a common expectation is that readers need to be able to grasp at least 90% of the words in a text in order to comprehend it; however, some research suggests that understanding may be possible when as few as 85% of the words are known (Freebody & Anderson, 1983). Therefore, be selective in your choices for explicit instruction. For narrative text, Hiebert and Ceruetti (2011) recommend choosing synonyms and semantically related words across texts that cluster around character traits, attitudes/emotions, actions, and so on (e.g., *irritated, heroic, suspended, smacked*) because an uncommon word may appear just once or twice within a given story, but it may well be represented across stories by various similar vocabulary (e.g., *worried, fretting, anxious, concerned, fearful, uneasy*). Frey and Fisher (2006) suggest that teachers consider the following characteristics as they deliberate about which words to use:

1. *Representativeness*: Is this a word that stands for a concept and thus has broader utility, or is it just a label (e.g., *photosynthesis* and *justice* vs. *stamen* and *attorney*)?

2. *Repeatability*: Is the word going to appear again and again in reading or conversation and is therefore worth learning?

3. *Transportability*: Is this a word that will facilitate further understanding of other words?
   a. Is the word going to appear in various contexts (*positive/negative* numbers in math, spaces in art, poles in electricity)?
   b. Does the word have a word part—prefix, suffix, word root—that appears in numerous words that can aid understanding of other words (e.g., *disapprove*, *autocratic*)?

4. *Contextual analysis*: Are there context clues that can be used to uncover the meaning? If so, there is no need to teach it (but, as previously mentioned, there is a need to teach the use of context clues).

5. *Structural analysis*: Words with prefixes, suffixes, or roots that can be analyzed don't need to be taught (but here, too, students need to be taught how to use morphology to analyze words for meaning).

6. *Cognitive load*: Just how many words should be targeted for students' learning at any one time is debated. It may be that the old expression of "less is more" applies. In a recent study, as a means of accommodating different learning styles and abilities while attempting to develop deep understandings, one researcher (Faulkner, 2010) focused attention on just three words a week; the words were chosen for their applicability to the weekly writing focus in junior English—the persuasive essay. Considering the need to develop deep meaning in rich contexts, 8–12 words may work well, depending on the words and the learning situation.

Nagy and Hiebert (2011) recommend consideration of similar factors as well as taking into account students' prior knowledge of the word or concept when thinking about cognitive load, noting that some familiarity can increase the likelihood of the word being learned. Flanigan and Greenwood (2007), building on the work of Beck and colleagues (2002) but with a focus on Tier III content-area words, suggest that timing should be a consideration. Their four-level model includes (1) *before words* that are critical and require in-depth understanding at the onset of reading (e.g., *continental drift, impeach*); (2) *foot-in-the-door words* that are essential for understanding but only at the surface level, such as a label for a concept (e.g., *stamen, mercenary*); (3) *after words* that are not essential for the gist of the passage and therefore may be dealt with after the reading (e.g., *infuriated*); and (4) *words not to teach* because they are already known, can be understood from the text, or do not match the instructional goal.

Knowing a Word

Something Ms. Gardner didn't consider is this: What does it mean to know a word? Though she was aware of students' performance on the weekly quiz and of her own lack of long-term retention of vocabulary from her school days, she does not seem to realize that it's not just a simple matter of either knowing a word or *not* knowing it. As early as 1942 Cronbach identified five dimensions to describe a person's knowledge of a word and how the knowledge can be used (see Table 13.1). Different situations require different levels of word knowledge but, clearly, having sufficiently deep understanding of words to be able to use them in discussions, writing, and thinking is a desirable outcome of vocabulary learning. Whether a word is difficult or easy for students to learn will depend to a great extent on how easy it is for them to connect the word to what they already know (Nagy & Hiebert, 2011). For instance, learning a new word for a known concept is easier than either learning a new meaning for a known word or a new word for a new concept (Graves, 2000).

Knowledge Rating

Dale (1965) also considered what it means to know a word and described a progression that encompasses four stages: (1) never saw it, (2) heard it but don't know what it means, (3) recognize it when I see it and know it has something to do with . . . , and (4) could define and/or use it. Various adaptations of Dale's work have been used to help students self-survey their understanding of specific vocabulary and to aid teachers in assessing students' prior understandings so they know which vocabulary words they will need to teach (Allen, 1999; Blachowicz, 1986; Ganske, 2008). Ms. Gardner could

TABLE 13.1. Cronbach's Five Dimensions of What It Means to Know a Word

Dimension	Demonstrated trait	Example of knowledge use
Generalization	Define the word.	"*Tattoo*: a permanent mark on the skin made by pricking or scarring."
Application	Use the word correctly or define its correct usage.	"The sailor had an anchor *tattoo* on his right arm."
Breadth	Know multiple meanings for a word.	"Two other meanings for *tattoo* are a drum or bugle signal that calls soldiers and sailors back to camp, and to beat or tap rhythmically."
Precision	Know when, and when not, to use a word.	"My brother's nervous tapping on the table was like a *tattoo*, but you probably wouldn't say the siren wailed like a *tattoo*, because it's constant."
Availability	Apply the word in discussions and thinking.	"We could plan to include a *tattoo* when the band gets to the cemetery on Memorial Day."

build students' motivation for learning words and increase her understanding of which words need to be taught using the knowledge rating activity (Blachowicz, 1986). Knowledge ratings can also be used to examine students' understandings after vocabulary teaching. Try out the knowledge rating in Figure 13.1 by placing an X in the appropriate cell for each strategy.

List–Group–Label

Ms. Gardner could also have fostered motivation for learning about concepts and at the same time activated (or built) students' background knowledge for a concept about to be studied by using this brainstorming activity. List–group–label (Taba, 1967) encourages students to explore relationships among words. Students can complete the activity collaboratively or independently, though I prefer the former approach because it provides support for those with limited knowledge of the topic. Distribute a set of 8–12 note cards to each group or individual. Demonstrate and explain the following process before asking students to get started:

1. Brainstorm all the words you can think of that relate to the topic/ concept; record each word on a separate card.
2. Examine the brainstormed words for possible categories; group the words accordingly. (*Note*: It can be helpful to suggest that students use a miscellaneous category to place words that don't seem to fit existing groups.)

	Knowledge rating			
	Never saw it	Heard it, but don't know what it means	Recognize it when I see it and know it has something to do with . . .	Could define and/or use it
List–group–label				
Knowledge rating				
Morphology				
Semantic feature analysis				

FIGURE 13.1. Knowledge rating.

3. When satisfied with the groupings and all of the words have been placed, determine a label for each group. Record the labels on separate cards and place at the top of their respective categories.
4. Discuss and refine the results. If the brainstorming was carried out independently, students might first convene in small groups to pool their words and to revise their categories.

The brainstorming, listening, and sharing involved in this activity not only activate and build students' prior knowledge, but they also develop students' interest in the topic and provide teachers with a quick diagnostic of their misconceptions and known terminology.

Semantic Maps and Webs

Ms. Gardner remarked that the two words she definitely recalled from her learning of assigned vocabulary lists were related. She, and her students, would have benefited from examining connections across words. Semantic maps and webs are graphic organizers that are used to depict relationships among words associated with a particular concept, such as *civilization* or *community*. The key term is recorded in the center, with lines radiating out, each ending in a word. Additional terms may emanate from these words. For instance, a semantic map for *community* might include rays for *services, government, schools, recreation, businesses, population,* and so on. The prong for *schools* might include the additional labels of *public, private, preschool, elementary, middle,* and *secondary.* Figure 13.2 shows a semantic map for *civilization* and characteristics that might be taken into account when thinking about a civilization. The map could become a template for exploring particular civilizations in greater detail, such as the Roman, Greek, Egyptian, or Aztec civilization, or even *Weslandia,* a fictional civilization created by noted children's author Paul Fleischman (1999). Bear in

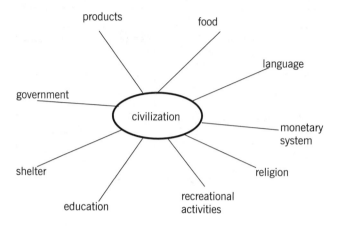

FIGURE 13.2. Semantic web of *civilization*.

mind that though webs and maps can effectively aid vocabulary learning (Heimlich & Pittleman, 1986), an essential element is discussion about the web and its components (Stahl & Vancil, 1986).

Webs or maps can also be used to explore specific relationships among words, such as synonyms and antonyms. This is a particularly useful activity for words that have multiple meanings or words with numerous synonyms whose nuances vary (Paul & O'Rourke, 1988). As with list–group–label and many other activities, categorizing plays a role in helping learners conceptualize the overarching idea. Consider *commotion*, a word used in Patricia Polacco's picture book *Pink and Say* (1994), the story of a friendship that develops between two young men from opposite sides of the Civil War. A brainstorming of *commotion* might result in the synonym web depicted in Figure 13.3, which shows words grouped according to how intense the commotion is: A mild fuss (*disruption*), confusion characterized by lots of noise (*hubbub*), or a confusion that also involves destruction or violence (*mayhem*). An exploration such as this creates an opportunity to highlight the importance of context for determining meaning.

Webbing encourages students to make connections among words and concepts and between new words and words they already know. These relationships can include word parts, such as words that share a common prefix, suffix, or root. Here again, discussion is critical to developing students' understanding. Technology can be used to reinforce these understandings and to increase student engagement. For example, after delving into nuances of a word (such as *condition*) or comparisons of words with opposite meanings (such as *calm* and *commotion*), students might create a Wordle (see *www.wordle.net*) with the two words to show the synonyms and nuances of each, as in Figure 13.4.

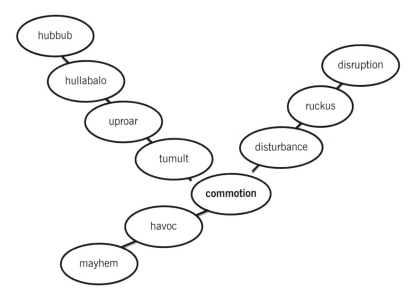

FIGURE 13.3. Synonym web for *commotion*.

FIGURE 13.4. Wordle for *calm* and *commotion*.

Semantic Feature Analysis

Because knowing what a word means lies not only in grasping its character-istics, but also in understanding what are *not* its traits, examining semantic relationships among words and how they compare and contrast is a valu-able part of vocabulary learning. Another graphic organizer that deals with specific relationships among words is the semantic feature analysis (John-son & Pearson, 1984), a tool for exploring the characteristics of closely related words in categories such as *musical instruments, types of trees, 13 colonies*, and so on. The semantic feature analysis has been found to be very effective in helping students develop deep understanding of concepts and vocabulary (Baumann, Kame'enui, & Ash, 2003), and it is another strategy that could benefit Ms. Gardner's students. She would provide them with a table that includes key vocabulary terms listed down the left side and traits or key ideas listed across the top. For each empty cell, students record a symbol to indicate agreement or not. For example, in Figure 13.5 the cell where *trapezoid* and *parallel sides* intersect has been checked to show that a trapezoid figure has at least one set of parallel sides. The table could be completed jointly or discussed after individuals or groups of students filled it out.

Four Square

The four-square strategy builds understanding of a word through multiple associations with it, thereby creating a rich experience of the word and making it memorable—something that would enable Ms. Gardner's stu-dents to recall and use the word. Consider *marauder*, another word from Patricia Polacco's *Pink and Say* (1994). Students not only define the key attribute(s) of the word but also generate an example and a nonexample for

	Equal sides	Parallel sides	Right angles	Equal angles
Isosceles triangle	O	O	O	O
Equilateral triangle	✓	O	O	✓
Trapezoid	O	✓	O	O
Square	✓	✓	✓	✓
Parallelogram	O	✓	O	O
Rectangle	O	✓	✓	✓

FIGURE 13.5. Semantic feature analysis: Geometric figures.

Word	Example
marauder	*a fox that steals the eggs of a chicken*
Definition	Nonexample
a robber	*policeman*

FIGURE 13.6. Four square for *marauder*.

it, thereby exploring the word's meaning through multiple perspectives (see Figure 13.6). The strategy is based on the Frayer model (Frayer, Frederick, & Klausmeier, 1969), a long-used technique recognized for its focus on developing a thorough understanding of the word. Four-square responses can be recorded on note cards that become part of a student's personal vocabulary card file developed over time.

Morphology

As with *amiable* and *amicable*, which stood out in Ms. Gardner's memory, students in her class might be taught to use morphology, which involves the use of meaning units (*morphemes*), to unlock word meanings. There are four types of morphemes. *Prefixes* (e.g., *re, un, pre, dis*) and *suffixes* (e.g., *er, est, ing, ed, ly, ment*) attach to the beginnings and endings of words. *Base words* or *root words* are whole words to which prefixes and suffixes affix (e.g., *view, read*), and *word roots* or *roots* are morphemes that can't stand alone without the addition of one or more prefixes and/or suffixes, as *fer* ("to carry") in *refer, transfer,* and *confer,* or *vis* ("to see") in *television, visor,* and *revise.* Because the meanings of morphemes are quite stable from word to word, students can apply their knowledge of prefixes, suffixes, and roots in one word to an unfamiliar word to try to understand it. The potential of this approach can be seen in the fact that about 60% of the unfamiliar words that readers encounter in grades 3–9 could be analyzed in this way (Nagy & Anderson, 1984). Prefixes are particularly valuable to teach because they are limited in number and are part of lots of words.

The following list of 20 of the most common prefixes occur in some 3,000 words (Graves, 2004); those with asterisks have spelling variations, such as *im, ir,* and *il* for *in.*

> *un, re, in*(not), dis*, en*, non, in* (in/into), over, mis, sub*, pre, inter, fore, de, trans, super, semi, anti, mid, under*

When teaching learners about roots, teachers should keep in mind that (1) the semantic connection is more transparent in some words than in others, as *ped*, meaning "foot," is in *pedal, pedestrian,* and *pedometer* but not so in *expedite*; and (2) spelling and pronunciation can disguise the semantic relationship, as with *persuasion/persuade* and *deprivation/deprive* (Nagy & Hiebert, 2011). Teacher guidance and instruction that begins with the more common prefixes, suffixes, and roots and gradually works toward those of lower frequency are important. Due to the families of words that are studied with this strategy, efficiency of word learning increases, as does the possibility for carryover to reading (Nagy & Hiebert).

What approaches can be used to study morphemes? Explicit instruction with a gradual release-of-responsibility model is one possibility. This approach includes explanation of the purpose and description of the technique, teacher modeling or demonstration, guided practice, collaborative use of the strategy with peers, and finally independent use of the strategy (Fisher & Frey, 2008). Elements of inquiry can be built into the teaching; for example, a web might be used to focus attention on a particular root or suffix, with individuals, groups, or the whole class brainstorming words that include the morpheme. An investigation of the prefix *oct* might result in *octopus, octagon, octave, octogenarian,* and *October,* with students hypothesizing about the meaning of *oct* and about the inclusion of the 10th month in a grouping of words with a prefix meaning "eight." Similarly, an exploration of *ast(e)r* might yield *astronomy, asteroid, astronaut, disaster,* and *asterisk* and lead to a discussion about the meaning of the root ("star") and about the connection between the last two words and *star.* As an alternative, students might be given a set of word cards featuring two to four different roots and be asked to categorize the words, talk about the meaning of each word, and speculate on the meaning of each of the targeted roots (Ganske, 2008).

Category 1	Category 2	Oddball
audience	*television*	*audiovisual*
auditorium	*visible*	
audition	*vista*	
inaudible	*visit*	
	visor	

CONCLUSION

Word studies should be engaging for learners. By setting up vocabulary inquiries and investigations, such as those described in this chapter, for students to learn new words and discover the wonder of our language, teachers ignite a critical aspect of vocabulary study: developing students' word consciousness—that is, their awareness, interest, and appreciation for language that can provide them with not only the impetus for independent learning of vocabulary but also with the ability to flexibly apply vocabulary in their reading and writing. Teachers can promote word consciousness through word plays with puns, idioms, and other figures of speech common to our language and by exploring the etymologies of words and some of the engaging, if not amazing, stories behind words. Doing so helps students to see language and vocabulary as worthy of their notice. For instance, a word such as *bankrupt* takes on new meaning for students when the relationship of *rupt* to "break" is considered. Although transparent in *interrupt* ("break between") and *erupt* ("break out"), the connection is obscured in *bankrupt* (obviously it's not the bank that is broken when someone goes bankrupt!). The story stems from medieval Italian moneylenders who carried out their business on a small bench (*banca*) in the market place; if their business happened to fail, they were forced to break their bench (*banca rupta*), giving us the word *bankrupt* (Ganske, 2008).

Teachers should also promote students' word consciousness by modeling their own interest in words, encouraging students to savor interesting vocabulary, and providing time and opportunity for them to investigate word meanings and apply their knowledge in multiple ways so that deep understandings of words are developed. "Owning" words involves far more than copying them and their definitions; 7–20 meaningful interactions with a word may be needed before it becomes part of a learner's working vocabulary. Meaningful vocabulary instruction, such as described in this chapter, builds habits of mind for a lifetime of vocabulary learning, not just for an end-of-the-week random quiz.

ADDITIONAL EXAMPLES

ABC Bookmaking Builds Vocabulary in the Content Areas

www.readwritethink.org/classroom-resources/lesson-plans/bookmaking-builds-vocabulary-content-276.html

Choosing, Chatting, and Collecting: Vocabulary Self-Collection Strategy

www.readwritethink.org/classroom-resources/lesson-plans/choosing-chatting-collecting-vocabulary-296.html

Flip-a-Chip: Examining Affixes and Roots to Build Vocabulary

www.readwritethink.org/classroom-resources/lesson-plans/flip-chip-examining-affixes-253.html

Solving Word Meanings: Engaging Strategies for Vocabulary Development

www.readwritethink.org/classroom-resources/lesson-plans/solving-word-meanings-engaging-1089.html?tab=1#tabs

Student Interactive: Flip-a-Chip

www.readwritethink.org/classroom-resources/student-interactives/flip-chip-30031.html

Various Other Strategies

Savino, J. A. (2011). The Shakespeare in all of us: A monumental, multitudinous, premeditated approach to vocabulary instruction. *Journal of Adolescent and Adult Literacy, 54*(6), 445–453.

TRADE MATERIAL CITED IN TEXT

Fleischman, P. (1999). *Weslandia*. New York: Scholastic.
Polacco, P. (1994). *Pink and say*. New York: Scholastic.

REFERENCES

Allen, J. (1999). *Words, words, words: Teaching vocabulary in grades 4–12.* York, ME: Stenhouse.
American Heritage College Dictionary (4th ed.). (2004). Boston: Houghton Mifflin.
Anderson, R. C., & Nagy, W. E. (1992). The vocabulary conundrum. *American Educator, 16*, 14–18, 44–47.
Baumann, J. F., & Graves, M. F. (2010). What is academic vocabulary? *Journal of Adolescent and Adult Literacy, 54*(1), 4–12.
Baumann, J. F., & Kame'enui, E. J. (1991). Research on vocabulary instruction: Ode to Voltaire. In J. Flood, J. M. Jensen, D. Lapp, & J. R. Squire (Eds.), *Handbook on teaching the English language arts* (pp. 604–632). Mahwah, NJ: Erlbaum.
Baumann, J. F., Kame'enui, E. J., & Ash, G. W. (2003). Research on vocabulary instruction: Voltaire redux. In J. Flood, D. Lapp, J. Squire, & J. Jensen (Eds.), *Handbook on teaching the English language arts* (2nd ed., pp. 782–785). Mahwah, NJ: Erlbaum.
Beck, I. L., McKeown, M. G., & Kucan, L. (2002). *Bringing words to life: Robust vocabulary instruction.* New York: Guilford Press.
Blachowicz, C. L. Z. (1986). Making connections: Alternatives to the vocabulary notebook. *Journal of Reading, 29*, 643–649.

Butler, S. (1912). *The notebooks of Samuel Butler.* Transcribed by D. Price (2002) from the 1912 A. C. Fifield edition, from Volume 14, "Higgledy-Piggledy— Definitions." Retrieved March 19, 2011, from *www.blackmask.com.*

Coxhead, A. (2000). A new academic word list. *TESOL Quarterly, 34*(2), 213–238.

Cronbach, L. J. (1942). An analysis of techniques for diagnostic vocabulary testing. *Journal of Educational Research, 36,* 206–217.

Dale, E. (1965). Vocabulary measurement: Techniques and major findings. *Elementary English, 42,* 82–88.

Deese, J. (1967). Meaning and change of meaning. *American Psychologist, 22,* 641–651.

Faulkner, J. (2010). Innovative writing instruction: Reducing vocabulary to increase vocabulary: Student-centered vocabulary instruction for writing that makes a difference. *English Journal, 100*(1), 113–116.

Fisher, D., & Frey, N. (2008). *Word wise and content rich: Five essential steps to teaching academic vocabulary.* Portsmouth, NH: Heinemann.

Flanigan, K., & Greenwood, S. C. (2007). Effective content vocabulary instruction in the middle: Matching students, purposes, words, and strategies. *Journal of Adolescent and Adult Literacy, 51*(3), 226–238.

Frayer, D. A., Frederick, W. C., & Klausmeier, H. J. (1969). *A schema for testing the level of concept mastery* (Working Paper No. 16). Madison, WI: Wisconsin Research and Development Center for Cognitive Learning.

Freebody, P., & Anderson, R. C. (1983). Effects of vocabulary difficulty, text cohesion, and schema availability on reading comprehension. *Reading Research Quarterly, 18,* 277–294.

Frey, N., & Fisher, D. B. (2006). *Language arts workshop: Purposeful reading and writing instruction.* Upper Saddle River, NJ: Pearson.

Ganske, K. (2006). *Word sorts and more: Sound, pattern, and meaning explorations K–3.* New York: Guilford Press.

Ganske, K. (2008). *Mindful of words: Spelling and vocabulary explorations 4–8.* New York: Guilford Press.

Graves, M. F. (2000). A vocabulary program to complement and bolster a middle-grade comprehension program. In B. M. Taylor, M. F. Graves, & P. van den Broek (Eds.), *Reading for meaning: Fostering comprehension in the middle grades* (pp. 116–135). New York: Teachers College Press.

Graves, M. F. (2004). Teaching prefixes: As good as it gets? In J. F. Baumann & E. J. Kame'enui (Eds.), *Vocabulary instruction: Research to practice* (pp. 81–99). New York: Guilford Press.

Heimlich, J. E., & Pittleman, S. D. (1986). *Semantic mapping: Classroom applications.* Newark, DE: International Reading Association.

Hiebert, E. H., & Ceruetti, G. N. (2011). *What differences in narrative and informational texts mean for the learning and instruction of vocabulary* (Reading Research Report 11.01). Santa Cruz, CA: TextProject.

Hiebert, E. H., & Lubliner, S. (2008). The nature, learning, and instruction of general academic vocabulary. In A. E. Farstrup & S. J. Samuels (Eds.), *What research has to say about vocabulary instruction* (pp. 106–129). Newark, DE: International Reading Association.

Johnson, D., & Pearson, P. D. (1984). *Teaching reading vocabulary* (2nd ed.). New York: Holt, Rinehart, & Winston.

Marzano, R. J., & Pickering, D. J. (2005). *Building academic vocabulary: Teacher's manual*. Alexandria, VA: Association for Supervision and Curriculum Development.

McKeown, M. (1993). Creating definitions for young word learners. *Reading Research Quarterly, 28,* 16–33.

Miller, G. A., & Gildea, P. (1987). How children learn words. *Scientific American, 257*(3), 94–99.

Nagy, W. E. (1988). *Teaching vocabulary to improve reading comprehension.* Urbana, IL: Eric Clearing House on Reading Comprehension.

Nagy, W. E., Anderson, R. C. (1984). How many words are there in printed English? *Reading Research Quarterly, 19*(3), 304–330.

Nagy, W. E., & Hiebert, E. H. (2011). Toward a theory of word selection. In M. L. Kamil, P. D. Pearson, E. B. Moje, & P. P. Afflerbach (Eds.), *Handbook of reading research* (Vol. IV, pp. 388–404). New York: Routledge.

National Institute of Child Health and Human Development. (2000). *Report of the National Reading Panel: Teaching children to read.* Washington, DC: Author.

Nist, S., & Olejnik, S. (1995). The role of context and dictionary definitions on varying levels of word knowledge. *Reading Research Quarterly, 30,* 172–193.

Paul, P. V., & O'Rourke, J. P. (1988). Multimeaning words and reading comprehension: Implications for special education students. *Remedial and Special Education, 9*(3), 42–52.

Petty, W., Herald, C., & Stoll, E. (1967). *The state of knowledge about the teaching of vocabulary.* Urbana, IL: National Council of Teachers of English.

Snow, C. E. (2010). Academic language and the challenge of reading for learning about science. *Science, 328,* 450–452.

Stahl, N. A., Brozo, W. G., & Simpson, M. I. (1987). Developing college vocabulary: A content analysis of instructional materials. *Reading, Research, and Instruction, 26,* 201–221.

Stahl, S. A., & Fairbanks, M. M. (1986). The effects of vocabulary instruction: A model-based meta-analysis. *Review of Educational Research, 56*(1), 72–110.

Stahl, S. A., & Vancil, S. (1986). Discussion is what makes semantic maps work in vocabulary instruction. *Reading Teacher, 40,* 62–69.

Strickland, D. S., Ganske, K., & Monroe, J. K. (2004). *Supporting struggling readers and writers: Strategies for classroom intervention 3–6.* Portsmouth, ME: Stenhouse.

Taba, H. (1967). *Teacher's handbook for elementary school social studies.* Reading, MA: Little, Brown.

Townsend, D. (2009). Building academic vocabulary in after-school settings: Games for growth with middle-school English-language learners. *Journal of Adolescent and Adult Literacy, 53*(3), 242–251.

CHAPTER 14

If You Value Student Collaboration—
Hold Students Accountable
for Collaborative Group Work

Heather Casey

Key Points for This Chapter

- Group work often fails in the classroom when there is a mismatch between the group activity and the assessment methods.
- Cooperative learning structures invite teachers to balance individual accountability with group productivity.
- Twenty-first-century literacies invite collaboration in virtual spaces through the use of interactive Web 2.0 technologies.

A BIRD'S-EYE VIEW OF CLASSROOM PRACTICE

Jennifer, a student in Mr. Simms's seventh-grade language arts class, sighs in frustration as she once again tries to get her group back on track. She eyes the assignment board anxiously, noting that the group response to *The Outsiders* is due in 2 days. Each group has been asked to develop a sequence of events organized by chapter, a critical analysis of how one or more characters contributed to the conclusion, as well as to author an expanded final chapter. The rest of Jennifer's group does not seem to share her anxiety, as they flip through their notebook in an attempt to appear busy. Mr. Simms reminds them to get back on track, but Justin, one of the members, mumbles to Kristine, "Why? We know Jennifer is just going to do it all anyway."

Next door Ms. Tyler, a sixth-grade math teacher, is watching her students work independently on a series of algebraic equations that they were asked to complete as a team. Ms. Tyler keeps reminding the students to confer with a partner, which the kids do superficially for a few moments, and then turn back to their own work. Later, when Ms. Tyler asks Matthew why he chose not to work with Marla, his partner, he responds, "It would have wasted time. Marla didn't really get it, and I knew my sheet was due at the end, and I didn't want to lose time explaining how to do it."

DEFINING THE TARGETED PRACTICE

In the scenarios above, both teachers have attempted to incorporate group work into their classrooms and have become frustrated when it failed. This is a common scenario played out in many middle school classrooms. Students are invited to participate in a group activity and they either work superficially on the task, one member shoulders the work for many, or the conversations dissolve into socializing. It is for this reason that many middle school teachers are quick to abandon collaborative activities in the classroom (Johnson & Johnson, 1999; Stevens & Slavin, 1995; Webb, Farivar, & Mastergeorge, 2002). Let us consider the classrooms above a bit further, however. Although Mr. Simms and Ms. Tyler have both made the decision to invite students to collaborate around learning activities, there is a clear mismatch between the processes in which these students are asked to engage and the products for which they are held accountable at the completion. What would happen if, in each classroom, the students were held accountable not just for themselves but for each other?

WHAT DOES THE RESEARCH SAY
ABOUT COLLABORATIVE LEARNING?

Cultural-historical-activity theory (CHAT) offers a theoretical paradigm for understanding why collaborative learning is important within classrooms. Vygotsky (1934/1978) described the learning process as socially situated and mediated by participants' prior experiences, learning capacity, and the setting where the learning occurs. Vygotsky's paradigm demonstrates how collaboration across ability levels supports both the novice and the expert as the act of translating information cements understanding for one (the expert) while introducing new information to the other (the novice).

CHAT offers a framework for mapping this sociocultural approach to learning in classrooms (Gutiérrez, 2008). It describes learning as a collaborative process that is influenced by students' histories, their relationships to one another and the teacher, as well as the classroom and larger community where all are situated (Engeström & Miettinen, 1999; Lave & Wenger, 1991; Wells & Claxton, 2002). According to this view, the process of learning is mediated by the past histories and present experiences of the students and teachers and is uniquely situated within the particular contexts in which all are positioned together. It is for this reason that teachers often describe their approaches to curricular topics of study as shifting in response to the unique needs of individual students as well as the relationships among the students in the class. CHAT describes the individual's learning process as socially dependent; students come to "own" knowledge when they have the opportunity to process understanding with others (Lave & Wenger, 1991; Leont'ev, 1978).

Consider this possibility. The eighth grade at River Middle School is studying immigration. In Ms. Gomes's class, the students select different texts (books, articles, and Web sources) to study on this topic and are asked to submit a written reflection at the conclusion of their reading. Next door, in Ms. Murphy's class, the students have the same set of resources from which to select. Ms. Murphy decides to build in one additional step, however. While the students are reading, they are organized into groups focused on topics of interest, such as immigration policy and personal stories, among others. Ms. Murphy sets aside 15 minutes of each class for these groups to meet and discuss what they are learning. The members of each group do not always share the same texts, but they share a particular interest in the selected topic. At the conclusion of each meeting, each student writes a reflection about what he or she learned from the others. Ms. Murphy's students submit the same required individual reflection that Ms. Taylor's students complete at the conclusion of the unit of study. When Ms. Murphy and her colleague Ms. Taylor meet to grade the responses, Ms. Taylor is impressed by the depth and breadth of her colleague's students' work. Ms. Murphy believes that learning is socially mediated, and she attributes her students' success to the opportunity to process the new information they are learning with their peers. Research supports Ms. Murphy's assertion (Casey, 2008–2009; Draper, 2010; Rowsell & Casey, 2009).

Inviting adolescents to collaborate around learning goals is often cited as necessary for motivating and engaging adolescents across content areas (Draper, 2010; Meece, 2003; Ross & Frey, 2009). Teachers often report feeling frustrated, however, when students appear off task during their time together and report that the workload is not always shared equitably among group members (Brophy, 1998; Webb, Nember, Chizhik, & Sugrue, 1998). This complaint leads many to abandon the practice altogether or to invite students to collaborate only for controlled, brief interactions (Johnson & Johnson, 1999; Slavin, 1999; Stevens & Slavin, 1995).

Recently, a seventh-grade math teacher gave voice to this difficulty when he said the following: "Yes, my students collaborate. We do a think–pair–share at the beginning of every period for the problem of the day. I put up a problem, students work on it individually, check with a partner, and then are invited to share with our class." Although the think–pair–share structure works well to engage students for focused goals, there are additional layers to collaborating effectively that can support students' learning. Teachers such as Mr. Simms and Ms. Tyler often abandon the more involved collaborative activities, however, because they find that "students can't handle it." A closer consideration of the group dynamic, however, suggests another scenario. Things often fall apart when students are either not held accountable for their group work or when the assessment methods do not reflect the group processes (Slavin, 1999; Webb et al., 1998).

Collaborating Multimodally in the 21st Century

The accessibility of virtual environments has made collaboration part of the social fabric of many middle school students' lives (Lanksher & Knobel, 2008; Lewis & Fabos, 2005; Pahl & Rowsell, 2006). Virtual platforms have students connecting and collaborating with others across contexts outside (and sometimes inside) the school space. Social networking sites, interactive blogs and wikis, and using video game consoles to link gaming experiences with people from other communities are just a few examples of how 21st-century adolescents have opportunities to collaborate with others in unique ways (Nevgi, Virtanen, & Niemi, 2006; Williams, 2005). Although many classroom teachers embrace this technology and have found ways to integrate these tools into classroom learning, as a profession we are only beginning to tap into its potential (Boling, 2008; Gee, 2003; Lanksher & Knobel, 2008; Pahl & Rowsell, 2006).

Social network sites allow adolescents to make use of varied forms of communication to represent their own identities and to form social relationships with others, some of whom they may never meet in person. Between these meeting "places" and "spaces" is the use of e-mail, instant messages, and text messages as a fluid source of written communication that, for many adolescents, has evolved into its own language to suit the needs of the participants (Lenhard, Purcell, Smith, & Zickukr, 2010). Participating in video games and becoming part of virtual gaming communities have also extended how adolescents shift across communication modes to engage in social acts. Recent research has suggested that these activities can enhance learning (Coiro & Dobler, 2007; Gee, 2003; Nevgi et al., 2006).

Although adolescents are engaging in these events with frequency, many educators and adolescents fail to see any connection to learning. For example, 85% of teens report engaging in some type of online written communication at least occasionally, yet only 60% describes this activity as writing (Lenhard, Arafeh, Smith, & Macgill, 2008). In fact, what counts as "text" for adolescents outside the school space may not be reflected in their learning during the school day (Lenhard et al., 2008; Lewis & Fabos, 2005; Williams, 2005). It is this mismatch that may explain why some adolescents become disinterested in school-based learning activities. Seventy-eight percent of teens believe that they would be more engaged in school if there were more collaborative multimodal tools available (Lenhard et al., 2008). Research points to rich opportunities to capitalize on these forms of communication to help support adolescents' successful participation in the 21st century (Casey, 2011; Pahl & Rowsell, 2006; Rowsell & Casey, 2009; Wells & Claxton, 2002).

Although collaboration is cited in the research literature as a key component to successful middle school classrooms across contexts, the application in individual classes varies widely. If collaboration is going to be an effective tool for learning in middle school classrooms, we need to move beyond simply putting kids near one another when working individually or assigning a project and simply saying "Work on it with your group" (Brophy, 1998; Casey, 2009; Johnson & Johnson, 1999).

WHAT ARE SOME ALTERNATIVES?

Understanding Collaboration

The *Literacy Dictionary* (Harris & Hodges, 1995) defines collaborative learning as "learning by working together in small groups, as to understand new information or to create a common product" (p. 35). It is an umbrella term that describes the social interaction of individuals for academic purposes. Collaborative learning may range from a brief verbal exchange between lab partners to brainstorm a potential hypothesis for a problem a science teacher has posted, to a large-scale group project in a social studies classroom, and the advent of new literacies offers the possibility for synchronous and asynchronous interactions across virtual spaces in different settings as well (Casey, 2011; Gulbahar, Madran, & Kalelioglu, 2010; Prestidge & Glaser, 2000). Collaboration can be an important step in the learning process because it invites students to explore new knowledge and practice using the academic language and processes necessary for understanding in a peer-supported environment (Ross & Frey, 2009; Vygotsky, 1934/1978).

Central to successful collaborations in the classroom are clearly aligned goals for individual participants and group contributions as well as assessments designed to match those goals. This sounds simple, but too often adolescents are invited to "work together" with little understanding of what that means, what that should look like, and how that influences teachers' abilities to assess student learning. After all, if we value collaboration in the classroom, we must hold students, and ourselves, accountable for the processes in which they engage and the products they are asked to produce. There are several alternative practices, explored here, that Mr. Simms and Ms. Tyler might implement to motivate more effective student collaborations in their classrooms.

Cooperative Learning Structures

Cooperative learning is a carefully structured group activity that allows students to accomplish both shared and individual learning goals (Johnson & Johnson, 1999; Slavin, 1999). Cooperative learning structures are highly organized paradigms that clearly articulate the roles of each individual member as well as members' responsibilities to one another. Central to this paradigm are clearly defined assessments that reflect the purpose of the structure as well as the learning goals (Slavin, 1999; Webb, 1997). If Mr. Simms and Ms. Tyler incorporate cooperative learning structures into the assigned group work, there may be less off-task behaviors, and the students may exhibit more investment in one another's success. Multiple structures are explored elsewhere in this volume. A few are highlighted here as examples of coordinating the individual and group roles with the overall tools for assessment (Slavin, 1999).

Think–Pair–Share–Square

Think–pair–share–square is an extension of the popular classroom strategy think–pair–share. The teacher begins by asking students to work on a task independently for a prescribed amount of time. Students then discuss their work with an identified partner and then that partnership works with another partnership (now a group of four) to discuss their work and problem solve together. Ms. Tyler could have used this approach to ensure that students balanced their independent work with their collaboration with others. She might have begun by having students work independently on the assigned math task and then move through this process, culminating with the completion of a group sheet that describes members' answers as well as the processes they used to arrive at shared decisions. The difference in this scenario for students such as Matthew, who does not want to "waste time" explaining to another, is that his understanding and the measures of accountability are dependent both on his individual work as well as his ability to synthesize his ideas with others. It is a clearly articulated classroom vision of what that process involves.

Jigsaw

The jigsaw structure also balances individual accountability with shared group decision making. The structure can be used in various ways and involves moving across multiple groups for different purposes. Students begin in "home" or "expert" groups where they work together on a specific task. This may include discussing a common reading or topic or sharing results from a task completed individually. The students rely on the collaborative discussions in the home group to further understanding of a new topic or to review work. Once the expert groups have come to consensus, the teacher then forms new groups, which now include one expert from each group to teach the other members about his or her topic. This is used by teachers to both introduce new material as well as to review topics of study. Coordinated assessments include the observations and work completed during the group processes as well as the individual completion of assignments and related tasks.

In Mr. Simms's classroom he might have used this structure to help students move through the process of developing a timeline, a character analysis, as well as authoring an expanded ending. Once the class concluded reading *The Outsiders*, students could be invited to create an individual timeline of events. Then expert groups might be organized by chapter or character, and the students would bring these timelines to ground their individual contributions to the group conversations. Using their individual timelines as a platform for conversation, these groups could discuss the events in the chapter and/or how "their" character contributes to the series of events at the conclusion. Mr. Simms could then form new groups with representatives for each of the characters and/or chapters, wherein students would share what they discovered in their expert groups and make decisions about the ways in which they believe the characters in the text contribute to the concluding events as a whole. Mr. Simms may then choose to have students author their expanded conclusions individually. The group process in this scenario is likely to facilitate deeper comprehension and analysis, and the individual task at the conclusion may allow students to internalize understanding for themselves. Throughout, the students are held accountable, and Mr. Simms can use the accountability measures for assessment purposes.

These are just two examples of cooperative learning structures that teachers can adopt and adapt as necessary. The key distinction for teachers to note are that cooperative learning structures are highly organized tasks that invite collaboration for specific purposes and goals and that balance group decision making with individual accountability. When both the processes and products are clearly articulated and carefully aligned, the group work is more successful and the students' learning is more defined.

Learning Clubs

Academic success in the content-area classroom requires that students are able to adopt the literate behaviors of the discipline (Draper, 2010). For example, in social studies students may need to be able to comprehend and construct maps as well as expository text, while in mathematics students may need to be able to comprehend and construct equations and word problems. Learning clubs are collaborative grouping structures that teachers can implement to motivate students to use appropriate academic literacies to build knowledge (Casey, 2011). The learning clubs structure is modeled after the research-supported strategies of book clubs/literature circles (Daniels, 2002) that are often part of language arts classrooms. Book clubs motivate and engage adolescents in texts through the power of choice, and they deepen comprehension and understanding through the opportunity for peer conversation and collaboration (Casey, 2008–2009; Daniels, 2002; Slavin, Cheung, Groff, & Lake, 2008). Groups are formed in learning clubs based on topics instead of texts. This format is based on research that illustrates how content learning occurs when students have the opportunity to share the academic process with others (Guthrie, 2004).

For example, Ms. Tyler might post a series of topics the students have surveyed in math and link them with examples of real-world applications for the concepts studied. Students then select the area in which they are most interested to study further. Groups are formed based on a shared interest, and resources that include physical texts and artifacts as well as those available via the Internet (when possible) are made available for students to use in their investigation. Ms. Tyler determines a defined number of meeting times and organizes the nature of the work so that there is a balance between individual and group accountability. The value in the learning clubs framework is the ability to be flexible and responsive to the unique learning contexts and contents. A potential framework for club meetings may include:

- A focused "mini-lesson" to help adolescents collaborate effectively and use literacy strategically for the content task.
- A "club time" during which adolescents locate information and talk with their groups about what they are discovering.
- A "scribing time" during which adolescents individually record through words, pictures, and/or diagrams what they are learning.

- A "sharing time" during which adolescents meet back with their groups to discuss findings.
- A "planning time" during which groups make decisions about areas to investigate for the next session.

The learning club culminates with a sharing session that invites others in the class to understand each group's topic. For example, if one of Ms. Tyler's groups is studying the use of algebra in architectural design, that group might design multiple diagrams and/or a virtual environment that demonstrates members' learning and opens it up to others.

While formal presentation is a possibility, the most successful transfer of knowledge occurs when groups create products that invite others to investigate (Casey, 2011). For example, another group in Ms. Tyler's class, studying how algebra is used in engineering, could offer examples of how structuring equations assists with the design of a car or a mirror, which other students could "try out" and "try on," making the learning more meaningful for all (Casey, 2008–2009, 2011).

Asking students to create individual activities that are dependent on their group experiences as well as balancing individual investigation and discovery with the collaborative process, as outlined above, helps ensure that the work is shared equitably and that teachers are able to discern individual students' comprehension and application. This structure lends itself well to multimodal tools for individual inquiry and group collaboration (Casey & Gespass, 2009). A complete link to this description is included in the resource section of this chapter.

Multimodal Tools for Collaboration

The interactive possibilities of Web 2.0 technologies invite multiple platforms for collaboration that are exciting, engaging, and relevant to adolescents (Hazari & North, 2009; Lanksher & Knobel, 2008; Zawalinski, 2009). In addition, many of these tools offer teachers mechanisms for following students' individual contributions as well as the group processes and products, increasing the accountability systems available. Many of our adolescents are engaged in social networking sites that allow for synchronous and asynchronous sharing of information and ideas outside of their classroom work. A large percentage of middle school adolescents make use of social networking sites such as Facebook and Twitter and communication formats such as e- mail, text messaging, and video journaling (Lenhard et al., 2010). These practices are often seen as controversial, particularly in the middle school grades, where the questions of "When?", "How often?", and "How do I monitor?" are voiced by many teachers and parents.

Conversations about cyberbullying and issues of identity when working in virtual spaces are growing topics of study inside classrooms and schools, as educators attempt to "catch up" and "keep up" with technology's influences on group dynamics and student learning. In response to this need, "safe sites" such as *www.itsmylocker.com* have evolved that mirror the platform of Facebook but are designed with middle school "tweens" (and their parents and teachers) in mind. These expanding virtual collaborations as well as the new literacies that accompany them are becoming increasingly more accessible at younger ages. Although adolescents may already have the capability to access these platforms, educators can offer the requisite academic skills to help students become informed users of these virtual spaces. Bridging these opportunities with academic learning in the middle grades can serve to motivate and engage adolescents while supporting their academic development (Hazari & North, 2009; Prestidge & Glaser, 2000).

Teachers can access multiple applications on the Internet to build group networks for academic purposes. Many of these platforms are available free of charge to K–12 educators. The rapidly evolving nature of these applications makes what is being offered in this chapter as current examples rapidly dated. What is important is that, as teachers, we adopt ways of understanding this technology so that we can transfer multimodal pedagogy to multiple platforms—even those that have yet to be invented—and so that we can help our students do the same. The Web 2.0 applications continue to offer new and innovative ways to collaborate virtually through shared text and images. That opportunity brings with it tremendous responsibility, which is why positioning it in schools, where students' ability to access technology can be coupled with learning to critically understand its utility, is important (Casey, 2011). Students have the opportunity to collaborate multimodally in virtual environments to support their learning.

Blog and Wiki Applications

The use of blogs and wikis in the classroom invite opportunities for collaboration inside and outside of the school space in both synchronous and asynchronous forums (Boling, 2008; Hazari & North, 2009; Zawalinski, 2009). Blogs invite students to author individual responses to shared experiences and widen their audience. Teachers can create secure blogs for multiple purposes by building a virtual platform in which a classroom of students can respond to one another outside of the school day or within individual groups. The value of these virtual platforms is that they invite the incorporation of multiple modes of communication, including fixed and moving images, links to other resources, as well as printed text. The capacity to create and construct information through these multiple modes is a critical skill for students to develop (Gee, 2003; Lanksher & Knobel, 2008). For example, a social studies teacher could post a series of video clips of election speeches and invite students to respond to particular prompts and to each other. The text and images students post are automatically linked to the student author, creating instant accountability. For example, Mr. Simms could have each group develop a blog to share its project with the expectation that each group member would author a section. This would minimize the inequity of one student completing the entire task, and it would open up meeting times and spaces outside of the classroom.

Whereas the blogs invite the creation of a virtual community for a shared purpose, wikis offer a more sustained collaboration around multiple text types (Hazari & North, 2009). A wiki space allows participants to author together, in an asynchronous or synchronous setting, while automatically tracking individual participation. These wiki spaces allow students to author pages that can include images, links to other sites, and space to upload documents, pictures, and presentations. There is a lot of potential to using wikis within content-area classrooms.

I am currently conducting a research study of a sixth-grade health teacher who has linked learning clubs to these multimodal tools. The students in Mr. C.'s class have each selected a body system to study and have used multiple sources, including books, articles, websites, and Internet video clips, to learn about the functions of the chosen system. As the students are learning, they are documenting their work on a wiki both together and independently (because they have access from home). These group wikis will be used by their peers in the class to learn about all of the body systems and include artifacts such as PowerPoints, student-authored video demonstrations and photographs, links to resources, and student-authored text that has been both uploaded as documents as well as written directly onto the wiki pages. The teacher always has access to prior versions of everything posted, and each posting is clearly linked to the unique user name of each student.

This automatic tracking of individual accountability, coupled with the natural collaboration these Web 2.0 tools offer students, make these a worthwhile tool for supporting student learning in the classroom. When asked about this approach as opposed to the more traditional poster and essay they had done in the past, one sixth-grade student responded: "It's better because more people see it and because you can use all sorts of ways of teaching other people and learning about the nervous system not just writing. Plus our group could meet differently because we could always see each other's stuff." This multimodal "stuff" engages and enriches learning while relying on the natural collaborations Web 2.0 tools invite.

There are multiple ways in which both Mr. Simms and Ms. Tyler can incorporate wikis into their classrooms. Each teacher can build a class wiki where each student has a page to record individual work as well as make use of the group discussion platform to support the collaborative process of learning. The teachers can also have small groups build wiki pages for particular tasks or projects. The two spaces do not have to exist independent of one another, as multiple wiki spaces can be linked together. The nature of these spaces requires individual participation in a collaborative setting creating the natural balance needed to deepen academic learning.

A valid concern among educators is the safety of utilizing these virtual platforms. The examples described above offer multiple tools for securing the sites, and teachers and students together can decide how accessible to make their blogs and wikis. For example, some can be made available to any public user of the Internet, whereas others may choose to allow access only to class members and/or group members. These are decisions teachers and students make together based on the content of the work and the audiences these platforms are intended to reach.

Widening the Classroom Walls: Bringing in the Community

When considering the nature of collaboration, it is helpful to look outside the classroom space as well. The use of new literacies in the classroom opens that possibility in virtual spaces, and there is the same opportunity to link the school community as well as the particular contexts in which all are positioned. Effective collaborations are dependent on the relationships between the individual participants. These are the intangibles of collaboration that are not easily quantified but are central to all effective group activities (Lave & Wenger, 1991). Teachers support this development through the classroom community they foster and mentor as well as the clearly articulated goals and tasks individual students and their collective groups are responsible for completing (Meece, 2003; Webb et al., 1998). One place for teachers to begin this collaboration is with the students themselves. A simple strategy to implement is to build class rubrics and assessment systems together. Coconstructing these assessment systems models the collaborative principles and ensures that all participants are invested in both the processes and the products of learning (Casey, 2008–2009; Prestidge & Glaser, 2000). As teachers and students reach out to their students, to other classrooms, and to the larger community to support specific learning goals, adolescents come to understand their learning as one that is shared with others and is linked to larger purposes.

For example, Mr. Simms might consider inviting students to share their group projects with younger students, as the act of mentoring others has long been supported as a strategy for internalizing new knowledge (Herring, 2005; Vygotsky, 1934/1978). The advent of new literacies has widened the potential audiences as well. Ms. Tyler may choose to have students invite members of the community who use algebra in their work to discuss how the material that students are learning in their algebra class is implemented in the daily tasks of these adult community members. As part of this task development, the students and teachers together can construct a rubric that will be used for assessment. Involving students in this participatory environment (1) allows both students and teachers to carefully examine the task, (2) motivates the alignment of the processes and products, and (3) clearly articulates the vision for implementation and learning.

CONCLUSION

Effective collaborations require so much more than simply putting kids together for an assigned task. Internalizing new knowledge is an individual and social process. Inviting adolescents to engage with others around academic topics is motivating and engaging because it reflects their developmental need to collaborate with others in social settings while offering the necessary space to practice academic language and processes with others (Draper, 2010; Ross & Frey, 2009). This process of individual internalization begins via shared conversations with peers.

In order for this effort to be effective, however, the individual and group tasks must be clearly defined for students, and the methods of assessment must be coordinated with these tasks. In the alternatives described in this chapter the assessment systems are intertwined with the activities students complete, allowing teachers to have an authentic understanding of student learning while making the purpose of the collaborations clear and worthwhile for students. The increasing use of new literacies to support these goals offers additional opportunities and ideas for teachers and students and further supports the need for collaborations inside and outside the classroom space.

We return where we began, in Mr. Simms's and Ms. Tyler's classrooms. Imagine, however, instead of simply putting kids' desks together and assigning tasks, two classrooms wherein students are comfortable using a class wiki to share ideas and it is not unusual to have community members offering examples of how the academic knowledge students are studying is realized in real-world spaces. Integrated into all of these tasks are the shared decisions the students and teachers make to assess learning. The success of any of these initiatives is dependent on the individual responsibilities of the teachers and students designing the activities as well as on the shared decision making of small groups and the larger classroom community. The careful balance of the individual and the collective allows for productive collaborations to occur—collaborations that ultimately deepen the learning process for students and helps us realize our goals as educators.

ADDITIONAL RESOURCES

These are potential resources to support students' learning using online tools.

Blog Sites
www.blogspot.com

Learning Clubs plan
www.readwritethink.org/classroom-resources/lesson-plans/learning-clubs-motivating-middle-1168.html

Middle School Social Networking Site
www.itsmylocker.com

Wiki Spaces
www.wikispaces.com/content/for/teachers

REFERENCES

Boling, E. (2008). Learning from teachers' conceptions of technology integration: What do blogs, instant messages, and 3D chat rooms have to do with it? *Research in the Teaching of English, 43,* 73–98.

Brophy, J. (1998). Classroom management as socializing students into clearly articulated roles. *Journal of Classroom Interaction, 33,* 41–50.

Casey, H. (2009). Intersections and interactions: A case study of a seventh grade teacher's practices with struggling readers and writers. *Journal of School Connections, 2,* 23–47.

Casey, H. (2011). Virtual constructions: Developing a teacher voice in the 21st century. In S. Abrams & J. Rowsell (Eds.), Rethinking identity and literacy education in the 21st century. *National Society for the Study of Education Yearbook, 110*(1), 173–199.

Casey, H., & Gespass, S. (2009). Learning clubs: Blogging to learn. Available at *readwritethink.org.*

Casey, H. K. (2008–2009). Engaging the disengaged: Using learning clubs to motivate struggling adolescent readers and writers. *Journal of Adolescent and Adult Literacy, 52,* 284–294.

Coiro, J., & Dobler, E. (2007). Exploring the online reading comprehension strategies used by sixth-grade skilled readers to search for and locate information on the Internet. *Reading Research Quarterly, 42,* 214–257.

Daniels, H. (2002). *Book clubs: Voice and choice in book clubs and reading groups.* Markham, ON, Canada: Stenhouse.

Draper, R. (2010). *(Re)Imagining content-area literacy instruction.* New York: Teachers College Press.

Engeström, Y., & Miettinen, R. (1999). Introduction. In Y. Engeström, R. Miettinen,

& R. L. Punamaki (Eds.), *Perspectives on activity theory* (pp. 1–18). Cambridge, MA: Cambridge University Press.

Gee, J. P. (2003). *What video games have to teach us about learning and literacy.* London: Routledge.

Gulbahar, Y., Madran, O., & Kalelioglu, F. (2010). Development and evaluation of an interactive WebQuest environment: "Web Macerasi." *Educational Technology and Society, 13,* 139–150.

Guthrie, J. T. (2004). Teaching for literacy engagement. *Journal of Literacy Research, 36,* 1–30.

Gutiérrez, K. D. (2008). Developing a sociocritical literacy in the third space. *Reading Research Quarterly, 43*(2), 148–164.

Harris, T. L., & Hodges, R. E. (1995). *The literacy dictionary.* Newark, DE: International Reading Association.

Hazari, S., & North, A. (2009). Investigating pedagogical value of wiki technology. *Journal of Information Systems Education, 20,* 187–198.

Herring, A. (2005). Pilots and copilots for better reading. *Phi Delta Kappan, 86,* 411–413.

Johnson, D., & Johnson, R. (1999). Making cooperative learning work. *Theory into Practice, 38,* 67–73.

Lanksher, C., & Knobel, M. (2008). *Digital literacies: Concepts, policies, and practices.* New York: Peter Lang.

Lave, J., & Wenger, E. (1991). *Situated learning: Legitimate peripheral participation.* Cambridge, UK: Cambridge University Press.

Lenhard, A., Arafeh, S., Smith, A., & Macgill, A. R. (2008). Pew Internet and American Life Project: Writing, technology and teens. Retrieved November 10, 2010, from *www.pewinternet.org/Reports/2008/Writing-Technology-and-Teens/aspx.*

Lenhard, A., Purcell, K., Smith, A., &Zickukr, K. (2010). Pew Internet and American Life Project: Social media and mobile Internet use among teens and adults. Retrieved November 10, 2010, from *www.pewinternet.org/Reports/2010/Social-Media-and-Young-Adults.aspx.*

Leont'ev, A. N. (1978). *Activity, consciousness, and personality* (M. Hall, Trans.). Englewood Cliffs, NJ: Prentice-Hall.

Lewis, C., & Fabos, B. (2005). Instant messaging, literacies, and social identities. *Reading Research Quarterly, 40,* 470–501.

Meece, J. (2003). Applying learner-centered principles to middle school education. *Theory into Practice, 42,* 109–116.

Nevgi, A., Virtanen, P., & Niemi, H. (2006). Supporting students to develop collaborative learning skills in technology-based environments. *British Journal of Educational Technology, 37,* 937–947.

Pahl, K., & Rowsell, J. (2006). *Literacy and education: Understanding the new literacy studies in the classroom.* Thousand Oaks, CA: Sage.

Prestidge, L., & Glaser, C. M. (2000). Authentic assessment: Employing appropriate tools for evaluating students' work in 21st-century classrooms. *Intervention in School and Clinic, 35,* 178–182.

Ross, D., & Frey, N. (2009). Learners need purposeful and systematic instruction. *Journal of Adolescent and Adult Literacy, 53,* 75–78.

Rowsell, J., & Casey, H. (2009). Shifting frames: Inside the pathways and obstacles of two teachers' literacy instruction. *Linguistics and Education, 20,* 311–327.

Slavin, R. (1999). Comprehensive approaches to cooperative learning. *Theory into Practice, 38,* 74–79.

Slavin, R., Cheung, A., Groff, C., & Lake, C. (2008). Effective reading programs for middle and high schools: A best-evidence synthesis. *Reading Research Quarterly, 43,* 290–322.

Stevens, R., & Slavin, R. (1995). The cooperative elementary school: Effects on students' achievements, attitudes, and social relations. *American Educational Research Journal, 32,* 321–351.

Vygotsky, L. (1978). *Mind in society* (M. Cole, V. John-Steiner, S. Scribner, & E. Souberman, Eds.). Cambridge, MA: Harvard University Press. (Original work published 1934)

Webb, N. (1997). Assessing students in small collaborative groups. *Theory into Practice, 36,* 205–213.

Webb, N., Farivar, S., & Mastergeorge, A. (2002). Productive helping in cooperative groups. *Theory into Practice, 41,* 13–20.

Webb, N., Nember, K., Chizhik, A. S., & Sugrue, B. (1998). Equity issues in collaborative group assessment, group composition and performance. *American Educational Research Journal, 35,* 607–651.

Wells, G., & Claxton, G. (Eds.). (2002). *Learning for life in the 21st century.* Malden, MA: Blackwell.

Williams, B. T. (2005). Leading double lives: Literacy and technology in and out of school. *Journal of Adolescent and Adult Literacy, 48,* 702–706.

Zawalinski, L. (2009). HOT blogging: A framework for blogging to promote higher order thinking. *The Reading Teacher, 62,* 650–661.

PART
III

Establishing Effective
Learning Routines

CHAPTER 15

If You Think Book Clubs Matter— Set Some Up Online

Thomas DeVere Wolsey
Dana L. Grisham
with Melissa Provost

Key Points for This Chapter

- A single text does not support rigorous learning and understanding.
- Engagement with content and reading improves as students use multiple sources and discuss their ideas with others.
- Online discussions promote higher-level thinking.

A BIRD'S-EYE VIEW OF CLASSROOM PRACTICE

In the corner, Rachel and Alida whispered hurriedly. The bell was about to ring signaling the start of first period; then the conversation would have to stop. Alida kept her eyes on the clock, but asked, "Did you see my Tweet about *Countdown* (Wiles, 2010)? I just started reading it, and it's really cool. I don't know why we can't read books like this. The textbook Mr. Hernandez wants us to read is so big and so boring."

"Yeah," Rachel said. "That looks like a cool book. The librarian had it on a display rack on her desk. I was thinking it would be good because . . ." But the bell rang, and that was the end of the conversation.

At the front of the room, Mr. Hernandez took attendance, then he addressed the class. "Did you all finish reading the chapter in the book last night? The Civil War era was such an interesting time. What did you think of the section about Gettysburg?" No hands went up, so Mr. Hernandez kept prodding. "General Lee's men loved him and did anything he asked of them. What do you think of General Meade's leadership of the Union troops at the beginning of the battle?" Again, no hands. The students' eyes told him that they were interested, but the reading just did not tell the story of Gettysburg in a way that invited them to read and find out more. It did not raise questions or seem connected to anything else. Mr. Hernandez was frustrated because he knew history was fascinating and that his students really would be interested if they could once get hooked on it. Rachel and Alida were frustrated, too; they were just discussing an important event they had been reading about, but they'd had to stop conversing. After all, the bell had rung and it was time to start learning.

For Mr. Hernandez, it was even more troubling to hear the students in the class next door. He had been teaching next to Ms. Anderson for many years, and they shared a passion for the history of the United States. They often shared websites, talked about visits to national parks on their vacations, and traded books. But, where Mr. Hernandez's students only grudgingly talked about history, Ms. Anderson's students were always talking about it. They read all the time and carried around e-books, newspapers, and paperbacks on historical topics. In the hall, they always talked about something they had seen on the news channel or had read on the website of the *Los Angeles Times*. Often, the students would say something like, "I read your post about Andrew Jackson." Once, Mr. Hernandez saw Richard, a student, lugging a huge atlas down the hall. Richard called down the hall, "Ms. Anderson, Ms. Anderson! I begged the librarian to let me borrow this for the class period. There is something I figured out, and I have to show you." The student hauled the book into the room as the door closed behind him. Mr. Hernandez wondered why Ms. Anderson's student would tote a huge atlas and be excited about it while his own students would not even take their textbooks home to read the homework assignment.

The Secret

In this chapter, we share two secrets about getting middle schoolers to talk about history and other content areas, while reading about these topics. The first secret is that middle school students like big ideas, expansive notions of how the world works, and complex concepts that challenge them intellectually. Wiggins and McTighe (2005) suggest that "essential questions" are one way to grab students' interest because such questions are open-ended and invite inquiry (cf. Wolsey, Lapp, & Fisher, 2010). This type of inquiry asks students to read to understand such that they want to read more rather than feel compelled by the curriculum to do so. Down the hall from Mr. Hernandez, an English language arts teacher used an approach called *Shared Inquiry*™ (Great Books Foundation, n.d.) in which students use reading and discussion as a way to make sense of complex works of literature. Taken together, Mr. Hernandez believed that complex questions to which there may be multiple answers, coupled with teacher-selected *and* student-chosen texts, would result in the type of engagement he sought for his students.

Concepts that are intriguing tend to engage the students' minds in part because challenges help young adolescents learn more about themselves. To understand an expansive idea, young adolescents begin to situate themselves as thinkers and contributors in the world. Erikson (1968) explained this stage of growth as one that requires both leeway and guidance. These two competing ideas, leeway and guidance, can hinder or help students grapple with big ideas as they construct identities as literate members of the school community.

Reflection about teaching practices probably led you to read this book, and if so, the secret that middle schoolers like a challenge is not really a very well-kept one. Every day, teachers reflect on experiences that engaged their students and try to understand what can be done to promote that kind of engagement again. What may be a better-kept secret is that technology can help students wrestle a big idea into something comprehensible and provide a jumping off point for learning more by working together.

DEFINING THE TARGETED PRACTICE: WHY SINGLE-SOURCE CURRICULUMS DON'T ENGAGE STUDENTS

There is a variety of reasons why relying on a single printed text for content learning works against the goals of the curriculum. Single-source textbooks may be too easy, too difficult, or too one-sided for diverse student populations. Allington (2002) argues eloquently for texts that students can actually read, and Rose and Meyer (2002) propose that students make meaning from their encounters in the classroom when there are many sources or representations of key concepts, many routes for expressing understanding and acting on that understanding, and multiple means of engagement. This last feature means that students have choices that lead them toward standards and curricular outcomes while inviting engagement with the texts, concepts, and with other students.

WHAT DOES THE RESEARCH SAY ABOUT USING ONE TEXTBOOK?

Beyond the argument for readable texts, there are other reasons why a curriculum based on a single textbook is not ideal. First, textbooks often reduce complex issues to relatively simple constructs that do not invite students to grapple with them; thus, there is little for students to discuss, debate, or consider expansively. Even when a single text does examine contrasting points of view, the conclusions are drawn for students rather than asking students to construct sound arguments for themselves. Second, single-source curriculums provide no basis for students to apply critical thinking skills relative to the source of the texts, the information selected or left out, the perspective of the author, and so on.

If students are to read in service of robust learning in the disciplines, an important question arises as to when that reading should take place. Although a common practice is for teachers to assign reading as homework, this practice may be rooted in a belief that teaching means a teacher in front of a classroom or students working at their desks with pen and paper. Excluded from this view is the notion that reading is learning that requires guidance from peers and teacher alike. Tasks worth doing, including read-ing, are worth time spent in class. Congruently, Fisher and Frey (2008) propose that students are more likely to be engaged in homework when they have been adequately prepared for the homework task, and they are permitted to assume responsibility for their learning as opposed to simply being given responsibility for tasks others have assigned to them. Students want time to read at school, and providing time to read may make content-area texts more accessible to students (Ivey & Broaddus, 2001), while invit-ing engagement with texts at the same time. Fortunately, the book club model makes room for both reading in class and reading at home.

WHAT ARE SOME ALTERNATIVES?

The language students use demonstrates the development and organization of their thinking (Berry, 1985; Lee, 2005; Lyle, 1993) and provides the means to acquire, construct, and share ideas (Lee, 2006; Lemke, 1989). In this sense, discussion is a time-honored tradition in classrooms since the time of Socrates. Small-group discussions are more likely to serve as an instructional tool that include students' cultural norms as a means of constructing curricular understanding and making discussion in class more participatory in character (Tharp & Gallimore, 1989), as well as encourag-ing participation and discouraging the competition to speak that is often found in whole-class discussions (Wolsey & Lapp, 2009). Digital technol-ogies can build on these traditions as students explore texts, respond to them, and construct understanding of those texts with their classmates.

When students use threaded discussions (an online discussion forum), blogs, or other interactive Web tools, additional benefits accrue (Boling, Castek, Zawilinski, Barton, & Nierlich, 2008; English, 2007; Grisham &

Wolsey, 2006; Wolsey, 2004). For teachers, some practical benefits include the ability to monitor all conversations, something that is hard to do when eight or more groups are conversing in class face to face. Whether on a blog, threaded discussion forum, or any of a number of new technologies, electronic discussion also builds in opportunities to construct ideas. Students can revisit the ideas of others by simply rereading what their peers had posted. In a face-to-face discussion, constraints of time require students to compose their thoughts almost as they speak and within the allotted time for discussion. However, in cyberspace, students can take their time to compose their thoughts before posting them, and they can post those thoughts during class, after school, at home, or even from a cell phone on the school bus.

There is some evidence that threaded discussion increases students' motivation and engagement with academics. Eighth-grade boys (Wolsey & Grisham, 2007) thought of themselves as better writers, in part because of their interaction with threaded discussions during the school year. Students felt more connected to the classroom community (Grisham & Wolsey, 2006) and the texts with which they engaged, as well.

The Online History Book Club Project

Mr. Hernandez and Ms. Anderson talked about their mutual interest in history all the time. Because he was frustrated with his students' engagement with the Civil War unit, he decided to buy Ms. Anderson coffee at the local mega-coffee retailer and ask her why Richard could not wait to share the library's atlas with her. Just what was it that made her students' history clocks tick? Mr. Hernandez thought about why Ms. Anderson's students talked about history all the time, whereas his students seemed barely able to remember the difference between the Revolutionary War and the Civil War. Both Mr. Hernandez and Ms. Anderson knew the subject matter and cared about their students. The difference, Mr. Hernandez came to understand, could be captured in one word: *opportunity*.

A student once asked Mr. Hernandez if there was anything about U.S. history that he did not know. Students respected his knowledge of the discipline. What puzzled him was why the students did not catch his passion for it from lectures and the textbook. While visiting with Ms. Anderson, he thought about how he came to his own passion for history, and he remembered: opportunity, again. His professors in college suggested books for him to read if he wanted to do so, and he took them up on it. There was always time in class for reading interesting texts, and there was always time for discussing them. The professors and teachers gave interesting lectures, and he lived for those, but there were always opportunities for him to shape his understanding by choosing other sources of information and talking about them with other students. Opportunity for intellectual engagement was what Ms. Anderson's students had. On Monday, that would change for his students, too.

Book Clubs Meet 21st-Century Technology

One approach that Ms. Anderson used that Mr. Hernandez wanted to implement in his classroom was the text set (Short & Harste, with Burke, 1996). Text sets take some planning and some resources to find enough books for students to read. Nevertheless, they formed the foundation for Mr. Hernandez's new approach to teaching social studies. In a text set, the teacher assembles a collection of "five to ten conceptually related books" (p. 158). He decided to expand on the original idea of the text set by combining those with shared texts that students would discuss using the literature circle approach (Daniels, 2002). In literature circles, students work in small groups to read the same book and discuss it as they read. A new idea emerged as he planned the remainder of the Civil War unit, too. What would students do who read more quickly than others? What if one group's book was longer than another? This, Mr. Hernandez realized, was no problem—it was an opportunity for students to read more about the Civil War. He could combine shared literature for literature circles with text sets featuring a wide range of books from which students could choose on a given topic.

Mr. Hernandez thought the idea of students reading and discussing important texts about history topics could be very powerful. But there were some problems that he could not resolve then. First, he noticed that students stuck pretty much to their assigned roles. Questions were often perfunctory, and students rarely explored the topics in any depth; instead, they defined vocabulary, asked surface-level questions, and engaged in discussion as a task rather than an exploration. Second, some speedy readers finished their books far ahead of their peers, and then became either a distraction or just disengaged from the group.

Mr. Hernandez decided to jot down some guiding principles for his new approach on a napkin. He called this new approach "Opportunity to Read History":

- Students need access to lots of texts about U.S. history.
- The reward for finishing reading before others is that students get to choose something else to read.
- When students have something else to read, the exploration continues, and everyone in the group has something to share.
- When students have something to share, they become increasingly engaged in the topic, and their understanding is more robust.

Opportunity to read history would work only if students had time to think about and form their thoughts. Often, face-to-face discussions created fantastic interactions, he knew, because Ms. Anderson described the small-group discussions in her room. She often brought a series of articles from different newspapers or a set of primary sources that students could read in small groups and discuss. However, Mr. Hernandez wanted to add another dimension to the discussions, and he decided that this is where technology could be particularly helpful.

Students, Mr. Hernandez knew, needed time and opportunity to think. Covering the curriculum is always a problem for the social studies teacher. How does one cover 300 years of U.S. history or 4,000-plus years of ancient civilizations and do them justice? But, at the same time, *covering* history is not the same thing as *teaching* it, nor is it the same as *learning* it. The quick tour of the last three centuries is not likely to make for rigorous learning. Another thought was forming in Mr. Hernandez's plan. Online discussions would be the opportunity his students needed to think deeply and make connections to content, between texts, and with their own lives. Because they were online, additional resources were also available, and students did not have to respond immediately. Photos from the Civil War, communications from Confederate generals to battalion commanders, battle maps, and copies of letters President Lincoln wrote are all available online in addition to the books students would be reading about the war.

Putting It Together: Opportunity to Read History

To get started by Monday, Mr. Hernandez had to get to work. First, he gathered up the books he already had about the Civil War. He visited the library and checked out several titles, and then he asked his principal to buy some more books. His principal decided that the experiment in reading was worthwhile, and Mr. Hernandez headed right to the local bookstore to buy several copies of six different titles. When he explained what he was doing, the manager gave him a pretty substantial discount on the books. He put the books in plastic bins and labeled them as Civil War shared reading and text sets. The text set included the books he gathered from his own collection and the library. There were one or two copies of several different books. The shared readings included five copies each of seven different books (see Figure 15.1).

Next, he checked with the school's instructional technology coordinator to ensure that the threaded discussion groups he set up would not be blocked by the Internet filter. The coordinator told him that they were installing Moodle, an open-source (free) course management system with threaded discussion capability next year. For now, he would need to use either Ning or Nicenet, discussion forums available online. He decided not

---

Text-Set Books for Student Individual Choices

Burgan, M. (2006). *Battle of the ironclads* (*We the people: Civil War era series*). Mankato, MN: Compass Point Books.

King, D. C. (2001). *The triangle histories of the Civil War: Battles—battle of Gettysburg*. Farmington Hills, MI: Blackbirch Press.

Shared Books for Literature Circles

Fritz, J. (1997). *Stonewall*. New York: Putnam Juvenile

Murphy, J. (1990). *The boys' war: Confederate and Union soldiers talk about the Civil War*. New York: Houghton Mifflin.

Marrin, A. (1994). *Unconditional surrender: U. S. Grant and the Civil War*. New York: Atheneum.

Paulsen, G. (1998). *Soldier's heart*. New York: Delacorte Press.

Ray, D. (1996). *Behind the blue and gray: The soldier's life in the Civil War*. New York: Puffin.

Reit, S. (1998). *Behind rebel lines: The incredible story of Emma Edmonds, Civil War spy*. Orlando, FL: Harcourt.

Stone, T. L. (2005). *Abraham Lincoln*. New York: DK Publishing.

FIGURE 15.1. Text-set books and shared reading books.

to use a blog for this project because blogs privilege the owner of the blog over those who might comment on it, and blogs are a little more difficult to manage for the classroom teacher. Each group would have a forum of its own. Then he developed some protocols for participation in the online forum and a rubric he could use for scoring (see Figure 15.2). He wanted to promote inquiry about the subject area as well as feature the participatory aspects of the discussion.

First Day

On Monday, Mr. Hernandez's students filed into first period. Rachel Tweeted one last message to her followers about class starting in a minute. "Snorefest #justsayin." Mr. Hernandez did not know about Rachel's Tweet, but he was ready to change *snorefest* to something more interesting. From behind his desk, he pulled out three large plastic boxes. One was light blue and the other two were clear. From the clear box, he took out a stack of paperback books and passed them out to groups he had planned over the weekend. In the cover of each book he had placed a sticky note with a letter on it. He told students not to worry about the books or sticky notes for now. He introduced each book, honoring it (e.g., Gambrell, 1996), describing the content in a few sentences, and reading a paragraph from each.

Discussion Board Rubric for Social Studies

Remember your responsibilities outlined in the acceptable use agreement you and your parents signed at the beginning of the school year. These responsibilities include courteous interactions with colleagues and visiting only websites the teacher has approved.

	Discussion expert	Discussion specialist	Discussion participant
Participation	Posts early and often with more than the required minimum number of posts on at least 4 days. Recognizes and responds to the contributions of group members and the teacher. Also encourages group members with new sources of information, praise for their well-done posts, or thoughtful and respectful questions about their posts.	Posts early and often with more than the required minimum number of posts on at least 3 days. Recognizes and responds to the contributions of group members and the teacher.	Responds to the questions and posts at least three responses in 10 school days.
Referring to texts	Makes specific references to the books or articles the group is reading. Synthesizes or puts together ideas from other sources as well as the book or article the group is reading. In addition, finds other books, articles, or webpages and refers to them to add depth to the posting. Makes connections to other books in the text set. Cites additional sources by author name, copyright date, and book or article title.	Makes specific references to the books or articles the group is reading. In addition, finds other books, articles, or webpages and refers to them to add depth to the posting. Cites additional sources by author name, copyright date, and book or article title.	Refers in general ways to the books or articles being read.

(cont.)

FIGURE 15.2. Rubric for discussion boards.

	Discussion expert	Discussion specialist	Discussion participant
Your own ideas	Evaluates the book or article by comparing it to other books, discussing the accuracy or point of view, or noticing similarities to your own life. In addition, you may notice connections to current events, contrast ideas in this book or article with those found in other books, and propose an idea about something the article or book does not address.	Evaluates the book or article by comparing it to other books, discussing the accuracy or point of view, or noticing similarities to your own life.	Shares thoughts about the book or article with group members.

FIGURE 15.2. *(cont.)*

Then he told students they should find the other members of their groups. Once the members identified their groups, they could negotiate with the other groups to switch titles as long as all members of the group ended up with the same book.

What the students did not know was that over the weekend, Mr. Hernandez had estimated the readability of the books and made sure that students who really struggled with reading tasks had another group member who would be supportive and a book that each could read. When Alida protested that her book was too easy, Mr. Hernandez just smiled. He had a plan for that, too, and he told Alida he would explain that in a minute or two. First, students needed to work in their groups and decide how much they would read each day. Mr. Hernandez decided that 10 days would be enough time to read the books he had selected. Students would then have about 15 minutes per day to read in class, but they could read at home if they wanted to do so. Logan raised his hand, not sure he had heard correctly. "Mr. Hernandez, we don't have to read for homework?"

"Nope, not unless you want to, Logan," Mr. Hernandez said. Logan grinned, for he knew that none of his friends would read a book at home unless it was required.

Next, Mr. Hernandez projected the Nicenet discussion board website using his data projector. Students wanted to know what it was and what they would have to do. "Your job," Mr. Hernandez told them, "is to write messages to the other group members about their books. Just like Facebook in many ways," he explained. He arranged to have five laptops from the portable computer lab available in the classroom every day, and he had to talk fast to convince the computer coordinator to split up the lab. He felt that not all work on the computer needed to be done with the whole class at once. This project was a perfect opportunity to try out his idea that regular access to technology at the point of learning, the classroom, might work better than having a complete lab that had to be used by the whole class and be signed up weeks in advance (Zandvliet, 2006). Alida volunteered to pick up the computers from the cart each day and put them back on the charging station at the end of each class period. She was intrigued with the idea of posting messages about the books she read online.

Everyone Reads

By Tuesday, Mr. Hernandez's first period class was ready to try their new social studies book club. Alida brought in the computers, turned them on, and set them up on a table on the side of the room. She took charge, not even waiting for Mr. Hernandez. Students, she explained, should try to post something three times each week. "When you are ready, just take a sticky note, put your name on it, then leave it on the computer case. After Mr. Hernandez says we can start reading, the first person can take the computer, log on, and make a post. Then take it to the next person whose name is on the sticky note. This way, everyone gets a chance to post and use the computers."

Mr. Hernandez reminded students about the acceptable use agreement (AUP; see *nces.ed.gov/pubs2005/tech_suite/app_a.asp*) each had signed at the beginning of the year that showed they knew and agreed to use the computers and Internet connection appropriately. Some students rolled their eyes, but they knew what the rules were. For this online book club, only the Nicenet and Civil War sites Mr. Hernandez posted on the class wiki were to be visited. Students worked in small groups to review the rubric Mr. Hernandez had developed. Finally, Mr. Hernandez told his students to get out the books they chose yesterday and start reading.

Rodrigo normally did not read for homework and did not participate in class discussions voluntarily. But on Wednesday, when Mr. Hernandez greeted him at the door, Rodrigo apologized to Mr. Hernandez for a mistake he thought he had made. His book had some interesting "stuff about army camp life" during the Civil War, so he went online and posted what he thought was interesting about it. Life in a Civil War encampment was not exactly the same as the campouts with his dad. Mr. Hernandez smiled again as he told Rodrigo that if he wanted to post something interesting at home, he would not have to wait until class the next day.

Already, students were more interested in the Civil War, but Alida was afraid she would be in trouble for reading ahead. She did not tell Mr. Hernandez that she had actually read more than half the book last night.

However, Mr. Hernandez noticed how far into the book Alida was as she read in class, and that was when he pushed the green plastic bin to the front of the room. He told students that as long as they read the group's book and kept up, they could choose another book from what he called the "text set" in the blue box. Makena leaned over and asked Peter, "Do you think he means we can read two books at once if we want?" Peter thought so, but Mr. Hernandez overheard and clarified that reading two books was fine. If they wanted to, students could also read ahead as long as they did not give away endings or what was in the next chapter to students who had not read ahead. No teacher had ever told students they could actually read ahead; usually, they had to stay with the group. Maybe Mr. Hernandez was breaking some unwritten rule about reading in school.

By Thursday, most of the students had posted their first impressions online. Some had even responded to other students, adding new ideas or asking for clarifications. Mr. Hernandez read their posts and sometimes added comments to fill in information or suggest other resources when students had questions. The discussions were really shaping up, and he was pleased with the interaction (compare Figures 15.3 and 15.4).

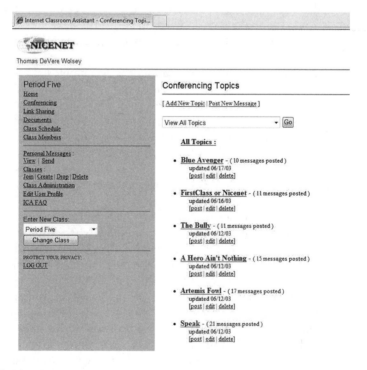

FIGURE 15.3. Nicenet discussion forum for English language arts (literature discussion).

The topic is the heroic cycle as students discuss *The Call of the Wild*

FROM: Dr. Wolsey (01/28/11 3:52 PM PST)
SUBJECT: The Hero Archetype

Archetypes are universal themes that recur in the cultures of people who are widely separated. They are universal symbols that effect most people in a similar way. One such archetype is the hero. The story of Jason and Argonauts and the Odyssey from ancient Greece to the story of Luke Skywalker from modern Hollywood share the archetype of the hero with many other cultures. Often a hero goes on a journey, sometimes reluctantly.

~~~

Henry responded by comparing *Call of the Wild* (London, 1903) with other novels he had read (notice that Henry is posting in the evening from home):

~~~

FROM: Henry (1/30/11 8:38 PM PST]
SUBJECT: What I think
[Edit | Delete]

Hey everyone, I think that the old man and the sea and the outsiders are examples of heroic journeys because in *The Old Man and the Sea* [Hemingway, 1952], the old man is on a quest to catch A fish, that's all he has left, his life depends on catching a fish. When he finally catches the fish, it is a big victory. The old man might not like going out every day but he is forced to by his inner calling for victory, therefore he is a hero.

In *The Outsiders* [Hinton, 1967] Johnny becomes a hero for rescuing kids in the church. When he finally comes home his family is happy to see him. Johnny has to flee because he just got jumped and he is hiding from the cops and his feelings. He goes on a personal journey away from himself. He's not sure why he is who he is.

FIGURE 15.4. Nicenet discussion prompt with a sample student reply.

The Teacher's Role and Discussion Groups

Discussion of complex topics and integrating one's own thoughts into those of others is a skill that develops over time, and students need guidance from the teacher. Mr. Hernandez found that his students needed him to participate in the discussion with them. His responses prompted students to respond in a variety of different ways (e.g., Alvermann, Dillon, O'Brien, & Smith, 1985). Sometimes he asked students to check the accuracy of facts they cited or to find supporting evidence from reliable sources. Other times, he provided a reference to a webpage or an image in the textbook as a way to promote alternative thinking about the topic. At times, students strayed too far from the topic and needed to be gently refocused, and on occasion he found that students appreciated his summation or paraphrase of their discussion.

It was not long before students in one group started comparing information and ideas with students in another group reading a different book. Because students had the opportunity to read additional books from the text sets that they chose, their interest in the Civil War and its implications increased. One result of this inundation of books on Civil War topics (cf. Fader, 1976) was that students soon begged Mr. Hernandez to create an online book club any student could join to discuss the Civil War books. They created their own topics and joined the conversations that interested them. These included discussions of the Underground Railroad, the military and political leaders of the Civil War era, technologies of the Civil War, and Reconstruction.

Additional Alternatives:
Using Other Online Media—VoiceThread[1]

On the best of days, my seventh-grade language arts classroom is a sea of waving hands, rich and thought-provoking discussion, and my students' unyielding desire to share and be heard. My words launch the discussions; in the end, though, they learn from each other. These active-thinking sessions and associated moments when a student grasps the meaning hidden within a novel are no longer lost when class time is over; enlisting tools such as VoiceThread, my students participate in interactive, asynchronous discussions. Each discussion builds on itself through visuals, voice, or text entries, and even on-screen drawings. Participating in VoiceThread affords students the chance to listen, comment, enjoy thinking time, review, and share. For those not necessarily inclined to venture into an energetic class discussion, VoiceThread allows them a platform for taking a risk and putting their thoughts into the mix. While reading and studying Ben Mikaelsen's novel *Red Midnight* (2002), I integrated VoiceThread assignments to encourage reflection and critical text analysis; this thread serves a dual purpose as both an interactive discussion and assessment of learning (see Figure 15.5).

Each student, equipped with his or her own login, accessed the *Red Midnight* (Mikaelsen, 2002) thread once or twice per week. Each week I updated the thread with at least three new questions or discussion topics relating to the novel. The slides sometimes contained an image, such as a Google Earth map detailing the protagonist's journey, text, or both; the weekly additions progressed in complexity according to Bloom's taxonomy (1956), so every student had a comfortable access point into the discussion.

---

[1] This section was written by Melissa Provost.

FIGURE 15.5. VoiceThread. Each icon on either side of the prompt represents a student's comment via voice, webcam, or typed message.

When logged in, students contribute their remarks to the slide via a text input box, voice recording, and/or using the doodle application to draw on the screen (e.g., *"Circle a point on the map and describe how it relates to Santiago's journey"*). As the complexity built, so did the requirements; students must listen to all other posted comments and do their best to add original thinking. Students compared, contrasted, and worked to extend the thinking of their peers while enjoying the time to thoughtfully consider their responses. In the end, the online thread contained a synthesis of our class discussions (retaining and constructing understanding!), new comments and additions (thinking on their own!), and a few hidden surprises (hail the risk takers!). VoiceThread's blend of visuals and voice personify those "best of days" when words generate thoughts and comments generate creative chaos, all while capturing collaborative learning outside the walls of the classroom.

CONCLUSION

The interactive tools available on today's Internet have the potential to open new channels for thoughtful and rigorous discussion. Middle school students, like those in Mr. Hernandez's class, benefit from opportunities to read from many different texts, explore big ideas with their teachers and classmates, and consider how these ideas fit into their own growing concepts of themselves as intellectual beings, citizens in the world, and as contributors to the classroom community.

ADDITIONAL RESOURCES

Online Discussion Forum Hosting

www.ning.com
nicenet.org
groups.google.com

Course management systems, such as eCollege and Moodle, include a virtual space for thread discussions and blogs, as well.

Links to Sample Lessons from ReadWriteThink

www.readwritethink.org/lessons/lesson_view.asp?id=1064
www.readwritethink.org/lessons/lesson_view.asp?id=1163

TRADE BOOKS CITED IN TEXT

Hemingway, E. (1952). *The old man and the sea*. London: Jonathan Cape.
Hinton, S. E. (1967). *The outsiders*. New York: Dell.
London, J. (1903). *Call of the wild*. New York: Aladdin
Mikaelsen, B. (2002). *Red midnight*. New York: HarperCollins.
Wiles, D. (2010). *Countdown*. New York: Scholastic Press.

REFERENCES

Allington, R. L. (2002). You can't learn much from books you can't read [Electronic version]. *Educational Leadership, 60*(3), 16–19.

Alvermann, D. E., Dillon, D. R., O'Brien, D. G., & Smith, L. C. (1985). The role of the textbook in discussion. *Journal of Reading, 29*(1), 50–57.

Berry, K. S. (1985). Talking to learn subject matter/learning subject matter talk. *Language Arts, 62*(1), 34–42.

Bloom B. S. (1956). *Taxonomy of educational objectives, handbook I: The cognitive domain*. New York: David McKay.

Boling, E., Castek, J., Zawilinski, L., Barton, K., & Nierlich, T. (2008). Collaborative literacy: Blogs and Internet projects. *The Reading Teacher, 61*(6), 504–506.

Daniels, H. (2002). *Literature circles: Voice and choice in book clubs and reading groups* (2nd ed.). York, ME: Stenhouse.

English, C. (2007). Finding a voice in a threaded discussion group: Talking about literature online. *English Journal, 97*(1), 56–61.

Erikson, E. H. (1968). *Identity: Youth and crisis*. New York: Norton.

Fader, D. (1976). *The new hooked on books: How to learn and how to teach reading and writing with pleasure*. New York: Berkley Books.

Fisher, D., & Frey, N. (2008). Homework and the gradual release of responsibility: Making "responsibility" possible. *English Journal, 98*(2), 40–45.

Gambrell, L. (1996). Creating classroom cultures that foster reading motivation. *Reading Teacher, 50*(1), 14–25.

Great Books Foundation. (n.d.). What is shared inquiry? Retrieved from *www.greatbooks.org/programs-for-all-ages/pd/what-is-shared-inquiry.html*.

Grisham, D. L., & Wolsey, T. D. (2006). Recentering the middle school classroom as a vibrant learning community: Students, literacy and technology intersect. *Journal of Adolescent and Adult Literacy, 49*, 648–660.

Ivey, G., & Broaddus, K. (2001). "Just plain reading": A survey of what makes students want to read in middle school classrooms. *Reading Research Quarterly, 36*, 350–377.

Lee, C. D. (2005). Double-voiced discourse: African American vernacular English as resource in cultural modeling classrooms. In A. Ball & S. W. Freedman (Eds.), *New literacies for new times: Bakhtinian perspectives on language, literacy, and learning for the 21st century* (pp. 129–147). New York: Cambridge University Press.

Lee, C. D. (2006). Every good-bye ain't gone: Analyzing the cultural underpinnings of classroom talk. *International Journal of Qualitative Studies in Education, 19*(3), 305–327.

Lemke, J. L. (1989). Making text talk. *Theory into Practice, 28*(2), 136–141.

Lyle, S. (1993). An investigation into ways in which children talk themselves into meaning. *Language and Education, 7*(3), 181–187.

Rose, D., & Meyer, A. (2002). Teaching every student in the digital age: Universal design for learning. Alexandria, VA: Association for Supervision and Curriculum Development. Retrieved from *www.cast.org/teachingeverystudent/ideas/tes/index.cfm*.

Short, K. G., & Harste, J. C. (with Burke, C.). (1996). *Creating classrooms for authors and inquirers* (2nd ed.). Portsmouth, NH: Heinemann.

Tharp, R. G., & Gallimore, R. (1989). Rousing schools to life. *American Educator, 13*(2), 20–25, 46–52.

Wiggins, G., & McTighe, J. (2005). *Understanding by design* (2nd ed.). Alexandria, VA: Association for Supervision and Curriculum Development.

Wolsey, T. D. (2004, January/February). Literature discussion in cyberspace: Young adolescents using threaded discussion groups to talk about books. *Reading Online, 7*(4). Available at *www.readingonline.org/articles/art_index.asp?HREF=wolsey/index.html*.

Wolsey, T. D., & Grisham, D. L. (2007). Adolescents and the new literacies: Writing engagement. *Action in Teacher Education, 29*(2), 29–38.

Wolsey, T. D., & Lapp, D. (2009). Discussion-based instruction in the middle and secondary school classroom. In K. D. Wood & W. E. Blanton (Eds.), *Literacy instruction for adolescents: Research-based practice* (pp. 368–391). New York: Guilford Press.

Wolsey, T. D., Lapp, D., & Fisher, D. (2010). Innovations in secondary literacy: Creating a culture of literacy. In A. Honigsfeld & A. Cohan (Eds.), *Breaking the mold of school instruction and organization: Innovative and successful practices for the 21st century* (pp. 9–15). Lanham, MD: Rowman & Littlefield.

Zandvliet, D. B. (2006). *Education is not rocket science: The case for deconstructing computer labs in schools*. Rotterdam, The Netherlands: Sense Publishers.

CHAPTER 16

If You Want Students to Read Widely and Well— Eliminate Round-Robin Reading

Kelly Johnson
Diane Lapp

Key Points for This Chapter

- Round-robin reading does not support fluency or comprehension.
- Reading fluency can be enhanced as readers engage in echo reading, repeated readings, Readers' Theatre, and neurological impress.
- Reciprocal teaching, collaborative conversations, and RAFT are strategies that support comprehension.

A BIRD'S-EYE VIEW OF CLASSROOM PRACTICE

Because Mr. Lambert has many students who, for a myriad of reasons, have difficulty reading the seventh-grade social studies text, he often asks them to take turns reading a chapter aloud as a whole class. When reflecting on this practice, he shared, "It's hard to keep students focused when I have them take turns with one after another reading." Noting his students' lack of engagement, he said, "The proficient readers just figure out when it will be their turn, mark the paragraphs, and then read ahead; they really aren't with us." When he added, "Those at grade level are often so bored that they lose their place, and those below are sometimes too embarrassed to read because the text is too hard for them," it was obvious that this practice was not working well for anyone.

Realizing that there was a problem with this practice, Mr. Lambert confided that he tries to make variations. He sometimes calls on each student, and other times he asks the student who has just finished reading to call on the next reader. Mr. Lambert thinks that by having his students take turns reading out loud, from the same text, they are building their reading fluency and comprehension. Even though he's not completely comfortable with this practice, he believes that it allows him the opportunity to "fill in" the unknown words or concepts that seem to be interfering with each student's comprehension. He feels it also makes most of the students "pay attention" because they don't know when they will be called upon to read.

DEFINING THE TARGETED PRACTICE

The instructional practices that Mr. Lambert is questioning are called round-robin and popcorn reading. Round-robin reading is defined in *The Literacy Dictionary* as "the outmoded practice of calling on students to read orally one after the other" (Harris & Hodges, 1995, p. 222). Popcorn reading is similar, except that students call on one another to read.

WHAT DOES THE RESEARCH SAY
ABOUT ROUND-ROBIN AND POPCORN READING?

The research is quite negative regarding round-robin reading as a positive instructional practice. In fact, Opitz and Rasinski (1998) suggested that it may even cause students to subvocalize while reading along with the student who is doing the oral reading. The result of subvocalizing is that instead of supporting fluency it may have just the opposite effect of causing readers to slow down their silent reading in order to keep pace with the oral reader who is reading at a markedly slower pace. In addition to slowing down the silent reader, this practice suggests to students that how reading sounds—how they pronounce the words—is more important than grasping the meaning being conveyed by the text (Kelly, 1995). Hoping to sound proficient to their classmates, the oral reader who is often nervous, anxious, and embarrassed (Sloan & Lotham, 1981) focuses more on word-by-word reading, which only impedes fluency and comprehension (Daneman, 1991).

Many educators agree that reading is comprehending, and, if not comprehending the student is merely word calling. Being a proficient reader involves one's ability to construct meaning by using prior knowledge of the topic and language to interact with the message shared by the author (Flood, Lapp, Mraz, & Wood, 2006; Pressley, 2000). Popcorn and round-robin reading do not support comprehension; in fact, round-robin reading was found to hinder comprehension because of its overemphasis on decoding and word accuracy (Gill, 2002). This is not to suggest that oral reading does not have a significant place in instruction. Indeed, findings from the National Reading Panel (NRP; National Institute of Child Health and Human Development, 2000) suggest that teachers should provide opportunities for students to read aloud while receiving feedback and guidance.

Rasinski and Hoffman (2003) suggest that oral reading, found to enhance fluency (i.e., the ability to decode and pronounce words automatically), does have a positive effect on comprehension, especially for beginning readers who through oral reading and listening to an expert reader, are able to see the connections between spoken and written texts (Graves, 1983). Oral reading is also an appropriate practice for struggling readers (Swartz & Klein, 1997) and older readers (Rasinski & Padak, 2005), as teachers listen and assess the next steps in their instruction. The key to facilitating positive effects for all students from reading aloud is that it occurs voluntarily, in a low-anxiety environment (McCauley & McCauley, 1992), while being paired with a proficient reader (Osborn & Lehr, 2004) who can serve as a model of fluent reading. Our intent here is to offer instructional alternatives that support the benefits of oral reading while eliminating the negative consequences of round-robin and popcorn reading.

WHAT ARE SOME ALTERNATIVES?

To begin identifying alternatives, let's consider the reasons Mr. Lambert uses round-robin and popcorn reading as instructional practices. His first reason was that he believes these develop reading fluency. As you think about this, do you see the fallacy? How is it possible to develop fluency when the text is not at the independent reading level for many of the students? Second, fluency involves mimicking a fluent reader. Most of the students in this class are not serving as a model of fluency because they cannot read the text either fluently or accurately. Finally, Mr. Lambert is not modeling for his students how a proficient reader sounds or interacts with a text; instead, he is interrupting their reading to offer explanations, correct pronunciations, offer word definitions, call attention to punctuation problems, and clarify comprehension confusions. His well-intended interruptions deter any possibility for fluent reading.

Mr. Lambert's second reason for using round-robin reading is that he thinks that as he hears the students reading aloud, he is able to eradicate any comprehension problems. Since there is no conversation occurring among the students and him about the information being read, it's unlikely that Mr. Lambert is really able to assess any of the students' comprehension strengths or needs. Also, he is only hearing them read a couple of times for a very limited amount of time. What he is really observing is that the text may be at the frustrational or instructional levels for many of the students, and therefore round-robin or popcorn reading is an inappropriate strategy to support comprehension development.

Finally, Mr. Lambert said that round-robin or popcorn reading causes students to attend to the text because of fear of embarrassment. While trying to anticipate when it might be their turn, students are not concentrating on the text or what their peer is reading. Instead they may be reading ahead to gain familiarity with the text so that they will not be surprised by unknown words when it is their turn. Nervous anticipation is certainly *not* motivating. Popcorn reading also encourages students to catch their peers who are not attending and subsequently embarrass them.

Since Mr. Lambert's purpose for using popcorn and round-robin reading to motivate instruction that supports students' reading fluency and comprehension was not being met, let's consider other, more efficient instructional practices that he might implement.

Fluency

To begin to develop fluency, students must be reading a text at their independent reading levels. This supports their being able to decode efficiently and thus allows them to place their focus on comprehending what they are reading. Additionally, students need to hear a model of fluent reading (Shaywitz, 2003). This can occur through listening to:

1. *Repeated reading*, which involves repeating a reading modeled first by the teacher or another proficient reader.
2. *Choral reading*, which means reading together with others who are proficient readers.
3. *Echo reading*, or the student echoing or repeating what the proficient reader has just read.
4. *Readers' Theatre* involves a dramatic reading of a text or script by the students.
5. *Neurological impress*, which involves the student and teacher reading together while tracking words.

Let's look inside other middle school classrooms for examples of how teachers are using instruction other than popcorn or round robin reading to develop students' reading fluency which means their ability to read efficiently, rapidly, and precisely.

Repeated Readings

Rather than use round-robin or popcorn reading, Mr. Lambert could have used repeated readings to improve his students' fluency. Repeated readings (Samuels, 1979, p. 404) is the process of "rereading a short, meaningful passage several times until a satisfactory level of fluency is reached." Research findings (Kuhn & Stahl, 2000; O'Shea, McQuiston, & McCollin, 2009; Valleley & Shriver, 2003) identified repeated readings as an instructional practice that supported the fluency development of students in both elementary and advanced grade levels.

To use the strategy of repeated readings, Mr. Lambert could first have directed his students' attention to the social studies passage they were studying. After setting the purpose, he could have asked his students to silently read the passage. Next, *paired with a partner*, one student could have taken a turn reading the paragraph while the other listened. The two could have then repeated this process, with the listener becoming the reader. To be sure that the students were also comprehending, Mr. Lambert could have set a timer for 10 seconds during which the paired students could have shared a retell. As the students read, listened, and engaged in retelling, Mr. Lambert could have circulated among them listening in to assess their fluency and comprehension. He could also have had them write their retelling, which he could also have quickly read. If he had detected that they were having difficulty with reading fluently or comprehending, he could have modeled both the reading and retelling processes for them.

The repeated reading process continues as students pair with *different partners* to again take a turn reading or listening to the text and then summarizing it. If Mr. Lambert had assessed that the students needed to reread the passage yet again in order to gain fluency for comprehension, he could have asked students to read the same paragraph again *silently* or through *whisper reading*. This process would have given students an opportunity to read a selected paragraph multiple times; each time the student heard and read the paragraph read aloud, fluency was improved.

Choral Reading

Another research-supported strategy (Cox & Shrigley, 1980; Dowhower, 1987; Gamby, 1987) Mr. Lambert could have used with his students is choral reading, also referred to as *unison reading*. Found to support the development of students' abilities to sound out words, read fluently, and comprehend (Homan, Klesius, & Hite, 1993; Mefferd & Pettegrew, 1997), choral reading involves the teacher and students looking at the same text and reading in unison as much as possible. Sometimes students will read slightly behind the teacher's voice because they are not as familiar with the text. Because the paragraphs in the social studies text were several sentences long, Mr. Lambert could have chosen headings, subheadings, repeated phrases, and/or captions to choral read with his students. Reading entire paragraphs together can be difficult and often results in some students reading ahead and some falling behind. Reading parts of a text together as a whole group is also an effective engagement strategy since all voices are heard in unison. Ideally, there is little room for side conversations or off-task behavior if the entire class is reading all together.

Echo Reading

In echo reading the teacher and students have the same text; the teacher reads one part alone and the students immediately reread aloud that same part of text. This can include a word, sentence, caption, heading, and so on. Mr. Lambert could have used echo reading to model for students how fluent readers sound. This is also an excellent engagement strategy because the "sea of voices" often keeps students attending to the text. Teachers should chunk the text carefully. If too much of a text is read first by the teacher at one time, the students can get lost and/or forget how that chunk should sound. Echo reading been found to support the development of both fluency and comprehension fluency (Dowhower, 1994) and to be an effective oral reading intervention (Stahl & Heubach, 2005).

Readers' Theatre

Readers' Theatre is another highly motivating instructional strategy with a sound research base (Worthy & Prater, 2002; Young & Rasinski, 2009) that Mr. Lambert could have used to improve his students' fluency and engagement. Readers' Theatre is a way to involve students in reading aloud as they "perform" by reading scripts created from narrative and non-narrative text. These performances are usually done while students hold their scripts in their hands; no memorization of lines, costumes, or props are needed. Mr. Lambert could have taken the chapter from the text his students were reading and created a script. Creating Readers' Theatre scripts is a great way to differentiate instruction because more fluent students can take on the parts that have a lot of lines and struggling readers could take on a role in the script that has fewer lines. For tips on writing and performing Readers' Theatre in your classroom and a variety of downloadable scripts, visit *www.aaronshep.com/rt/RTE.html.*

Just like actors on stage, Mr. Lambert's students could have improved their fluency and comprehension of the text because the script would have been read several times prior to "performing" in front of the class. Readers'

Theatre groups should also provide a retelling and a summary of their script so that comprehension can be assessed.

Each of these instructional practices would have allowed students to listen to a fluent reader and then to practice what they were hearing multiple times, in a nonthreatening manner. Throughout each oral reading event they would have been able to practice reading the way they had heard an expert reader reading. Together they and Mr. Lambert could have noted pace, tone, phrasing, and expression. While reading, Mr. Lambert could also have identified new content and academic vocabulary and invited students to repeat these. Through these oral reading activities, these students would have been supported to move their attention from word-level decoding to fluency and comprehension (Hoffman, 1987). After modeling his reading with his students, Mr. Lambert could have listened to see if they were also becoming more fluent. Additionally, he could have had a conversation with them about his reading, and what they thought they needed to do in order to also be more fluent readers. This approach would have supported their metacognitve development as they reflected on themselves as readers who have the goal to become fluent readers. This level of engagement would have ensured that students were focused participants because they would have had to be attending to the task at all times.

Neurological Impress Method

If, after modeling and practicing fluent oral reading with a whole class or groups within the class, a teacher assesses that an individual student still needs additional practice, he or she can use the neurological impress method (NIM) to support the student's fluency development. This method, which was developed by Heckelman (1969), has been found to be a very effective practice for developing reading fluency while not sacrificing comprehension (Flood, Lapp, & Fisher, 2005; Klauda & Guthrie, 2008; Miller & Schwanenflugel, 2008). NIM involves the teacher and student reader together, tracking words as they read. Here's how the NIM works:

1. Identify the text segment that you and the student will be reading. The identified material should be read by having the student place his or her finger on yours as you track the words together. For older students, you may want to track together using a pencil or some other type of pointer.
2. Begin by inviting the student to sit slightly in front of you so that you can point to the text the student is reading and also so that you can read directly into the student's ear. If the student is right-handed, read into his or her left ear. Do the opposite for a left-

handed student. To ensure success, begin with easy reading materials. As the student's confidence and fluency develop, the difficulty level can be increased.

3. Before beginning to read, explain that you are going to take the lead in reading the material and that the student is to read along with you as you point to the words. Start reading at a slightly slower pace than normal for you. While reading, be sure to point to each word. Do not vary the procedure even if the student complains that you are going too quickly. You want the student to practice reading fluently while hearing a proficient reader (you) do so.

4. Use NIM with the student for 5–15 minutes two to four times per day. As you begin to notice that the student's fluency is improving, increase your rate until you reach your normal reading rate.

NIM is a multisensory approach of hearing, seeing, reading, and saying the word, and, like the other practices we have identified, it supports reading fluency. These are practices that Mr. Lambert could effectively use with individuals, groups, and his whole class to accomplish his goal of supporting the reading fluency of his students.

Comprehension

Mr. Lambert was also intent on supporting each student's comprehension. To do so a teacher must first understand each student's reading strengths and needs in relationship to the text and topic being studied. Although this may be a difficult task for teachers who teach six periods of 35 students each day, it must be realized that if the instruction is too easy or too difficult for most of the class, then only a few are really receiving any instruction.

Mr. Lambert probably was using round-robin reading because it is easy to implement and also because his teachers had used it. Even though he had been taught more efficient instructional practices, he, like many teachers, returns to the ways he was taught (Ash, Kuhn, & Walpole, 2009; Hill, 1983) even when he knows it is not having a positive impact on his students (Beach, 1993). Teachers take this route because of their familiarity and ease with a practice and, in the case of round-robin reading, because they can hear the strategies the student is using to decode an unfamiliar word (Eldredge, Reutzel, & Hollingsworth, 1996). However, they cannot decide anything about the student's comprehension because there is no conversation after the student finishes orally reading his or her segment of the text.

While it is very important for teachers to accurately assess a student's performance during reading, this information can be more efficiently gained by listening to the student read individually or in a small-group reading setting that does not submit the adolescent reader to embarrassment if he or she stumbles while reading. This smaller format also gives the teacher an opportunity to gain insights about the student's comprehension by interacting with the reader at the completion of reading.

Reciprocal Teaching

In order to improve his students' comprehension, Mr. Lambert could have used reciprocal teaching with them. Reciprocal teaching, which has a sound research base (Hashey & Connors, 2003; Palinscar & Brown, 1984; Slater & Horstman, 2002), places students in groups of four with each taking on the role of (1) predictor, (2) questioner, (3) clarifier, or (4) summarizer. As students read the targeted text in groups of four, they stop periodically to "teach" the information to each other by predicting upcoming information, asking questions, clarifying confusing information, and summarizing as a means of self-review. As students are working in these reciprocal teaching groups, Mr. Lambert would be free to visit each group and listen in on the conversations the participants are having. This practice provides a better picture of how well students understand the text and if reteaching is necessary.

Let's look inside another social studies class and listen in to a group of students who are using reciprocal teaching as a way to engage in a conversation about medieval Europe.

PREDICTOR: I think this section of the chapter will talk about how the people in the towns worked in different jobs. The picture on this page shows one person baking and one person making shoes.

QUESTIONER: I wonder how much they got paid in those days.

SUMMARIZER: Let's read and see what it says and if we're correct. (*Students read the section on Medieval Europe and the towns.*)

QUESTIONER: I was right. It does say that people worked as bakers and made shoes. The shoes were made out of leather.

SUMMARIZER: Yes, this section was about how people in the Middle Ages worked in many jobs. One other job was farming, and the methods they used for farming weren't efficient.

QUESTIONER: What's that mean? *Efficient?*

CLARIFIER: Doesn't it mean that the ways they used to farm weren't that good?

SUMMARIZER AND PREDICTOR: YES!

SUMMARIZER: So many people worked as farmers until the farming methods became efficient. Then they didn't need so many farmers, so some of the people became bakers, shoemakers, and weavers.

CLARIFIER: So the townspeople weren't farmers for a very long time . . . just until the land got better. Then many more jobs were available for these people.

PREDICTOR: I bet the next section of this chapter will tell about how people traded the things they made.

As these students interacted, it was obvious that they were comprehending the material as they asked questions, clarified issues, summarized information, and made predictions about the content in the next sections of the text. Unlike popcorn reading, reciprocal teaching gave these students an authentic reason to engage with the text and each other.

Collaborative Groups

There is considerable research suggesting that students learn best when they are actively involved in the learning process (Johnson, Johnson, St. Anne, & Garibaldi, 1990). Such engagement occurs as students work in small groups because they are focused, participate more, and therefore tend to learn and retain more of the information being taught (Frey, Fisher, & Allen, 2009; Garmston & Wellman, 2009; Gillies, 2008).

As they studied the topic of the Renaissance period in Mr. Lambert's seventh-grade social studies class, he could have invited his students to form heterogeneous collaborative groups as a way to study the topic of, for example, reopening the ancient "Silk Road" between Europe and China. The purpose of reading such a text would be to study Marco Polo's travels and the location of his routes.

Since not all students could read the text equally well, Mr. Lambert either could have assigned one student as the reader, or he could have secured several texts on the topic that were at varying degrees of difficulty. Texts to meet the reading levels of all students could include (1) a passage from the Internet titled Marco Polo and his Travels (*www.silk-road.com/artl/marcopolo.shtml*) and Cath Senker's *Marco Polo's Travels on Asia's Silk Road* (2007; *Great Journeys Across Earth* series). Some examples of tasks that collaborative groups could have completed to evidence their understanding of the assigned text they were reading together include the following:

- *Group 1*: Write a rap/song about Marco Polo's birth and growing up.
- *Group 2*: Using construction paper, make a travel brochure. Students could include information about China, Mongolia, and the long and difficult journey to Cathay.
- *Group 3*: Create and act out a skit or dramatic representation about

Marco Polo's journey home to Venice after traveling for 17 years. Students could act out this sea journey chronicling many of the theories of how 600 passengers died. They could then perform this on Photo Booth as a way to share with their classmates. Photo Booth is a video and recording application designed by Apple for the Mac computer. Students can use Photo Booth to create a video essay.

- *Group 4*: Students could research and create an iMovie about Marco Polo's captivity and time spent in prison in 1295.

Within each group, roles could be assigned to ensure equal distribution of tasks. Each group could be assessed using the rubric in Figure 16.1. With different texts each student could have silently read the text and then shared the information. This approach would have ensured that all students were reading, which is one of the reasons that Mr. Lambert had initially been using popcorn reading.

The important point to remember when encouraging students to work cooperatively in groups is to design tasks where *all* students have a role, and no one student dominates the discussion or completes all the work (Lapp, Fisher, & Wolsey, 2009). This also allows the teacher to assess both the participation of individuals as well as the group. In order to maximize

	Emerging	Developing	Proficient
Content	Student's project contains *few* facts about the Silk Road.	Students project contains *several* facts about the Silk Road.	Students project contains *at least five* facts about the Silk Road.
Organization	Student's project is *difficult* to understand and unorganized.	Student's project is *somewhat easy* to understand, and it is organized in a coherent manner.	Student's project is *easy* to understand, and it is organized in a coherent manner.
Collaboration	Student groups *seldom* work cooperatively and productively.	Student groups work cooperatively and productively *most* of the time.	Student groups work cooperatively and productively *all* of the time.
Presentation	While presenting projects, students *seldom* spoke clearly or loudly.	While presenting projects, students spoke clearly, loudly, and answered questions accurately *most of the time*.	While presenting projects, students spoke clearly, loudly, and answered questions accurately *all* of the time.

FIGURE 16.1. Differentiated tasks within a collaborative group.

student productivity, limit collaborative groups to three or four students. One efficient way to ensure that each group member makes a contribution to the project is to ask each to use a different-colored marker or pen and then to sign his or her name on the product in the same color as his or her contribution.

Jigsaw

Another effective strategy that supports collaboration and that Mr. Lambert could have used to ensure his students' comprehension is described as a jigsaw activity (Aronson & Patnoe, 1997; Bridgeman, 1981; Hampton, Wallace, Keele, & Lee, 2009). To use jigsaw grouping, Mr. Lambert first could have divided the social studies reading passage into four or five sections. Next he could have divided the class into groups of four or five students. Each group called an "expert" group is given one part of the text to read and learn. The purpose of these expert groups is to enable students to read, discuss, and help each other study the material in their section. Then they are redivided into "home" groups. Each home group consists of representatives from each of the expert groups. Each member of the newly formed home group teaches and shares his or her part of the text with the others (see Figure 16.2). The time given to the sharing phase depends on the difficulty and length of the material.

Jigsaw is an effective grouping strategy that ensures student participation because each member of the group is dependent on the others for part of the information, which supports their attending to the text and also the work of their peers.

RAFT

To ensure and assess his students' comprehension, Mr. Lambert could have assigned each group of students to write a RAFT (Santa & Havens, 1995) which would have provided a scaffold to support their writing while also

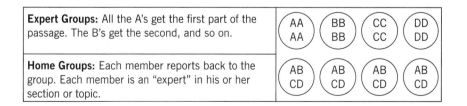

FIGURE 16.2. Jigsaw groups.

ensuring the perspective that when doing real writing, there is an audience. RAFT is an acronym that stands for:

R = role of the writer
A = audience
F = format
T = topic

Each group in Mr. Lambert's class could take on a different RAFT writing assignment, which could then have been shared with the whole class. To develop these assignments, the students could each have silently read a segment of the text which they then discussed or they could have chorally read the text together. How they read the text could have been based on how fluent the group was as readers. This production would have evidenced their comprehension of the material they were sharing in their group. Some of these assignments could include the following:

R = Marco Polo
A = Italians
F = Letter
T = 24-year journey to Asia

R = Christopher Columbus
A = Marco Polo
F = List
T = Ways Columbus inspired Polo

R = Marco Polo
A = Marco's family
F = Will
T = How Marco's assets will be divided

CONCLUSION

Like Mr. Lambert, we and others (LaBerge & Samuels, 1974) believe that as we observe the oral reading proficiency of students, we are able to assess their fluency at automatically attaching sounds to letters, synthesizing these sounds into words, and connecting the words to phrases and then to larger chunks of discourse. In order to also assess comprehension, we believe that students must be invited to retell and to share and extend their thinking through productive collaborative talk (Lyle, 2008). As they do so, we are able view their cognitive processing of the targeted information, which in turn provides the data needed to plan subsequent instruction. The instructional practices we've shared engage students in productive reading and collaboration—two activities that Langer noted support "student achievement in reading, writing and English" during their middle and high school years (2001, p. 838).

ADDITIONAL LESSON EXAMPLES

The following lesson examples from ReadWriteThink support oral reading, fluency, and comprehension development and offer additional alternatives to popcorn and round-robin reading.

Audio Broadcasts and Podcasts: Oral Storytelling and Dramatization

www.readwritethink.org/classroom-resources/lesson-plans/audio-broadcasts-podcasts-oral-901.html

Investigating the Holocaust: A Collaborative Inquiry Project

www.readwritethink.org/classroom-resources/lesson-plans/investigating-holocaust-collaborative-inquiry-416.html

The Reading Performance: Understanding Fluency through Oral Interpretation

www.readwritethink.org/classroom-resources/lesson-plans/reading-performance-understanding-fluency-28.html

Standard Lessons

www.readwritethink.org/classroom-resources/lesson-plans/poet-shoes-performing-poetry-78.htm

TRADE BOOK CITED IN TEXT

Senker, C. (2007). *Marco Polo's Travels on Asia's Silk Road*. Portsmouth, NH: Heinemann.

REFERENCES

Aronson, E., & Patnoe, S. (1997). *The jigsaw classroom: Building cooperation in the classroom*. New York: Longman.

Ash, G. W., Kuhn, M. R., & Walpole, S. (2009). Analyzing "inconsistencies" in practice: Teachers continued use of round robin reading. *Reading and Writing Quarterly, 25*, 87–103.

Beach, S. A. (1993). Research into practice, oral reading instruction: Retiring the bird in the round. *Reading Psychology, 14*, 333–338.

Bridgeman, D. (1981). Enhanced role-taking through cooperative interdependence: A field study. *Child Development, 52*, 1231–1238.

Cox, R. M., & Shrigley, R. I. (1980). Comparing three methods of practicing reading to reduce errors in oral reading. *Reading Improvement, 17*(4), 106–310.

Daneman, M. (1991). Individual differences in reading skills. In R. Barr, M. Kamill, P. Mosenthal, & P. D. Pearson (Eds.), *Handbook of reading research* (Vol. 2). White Plains, NY: Longman.

Dowhower, S. L. (1987). Effects of repeated readings on second grade transitional readers' fluency and comprehension. *Reading Research Quarterly, 22*(4), 389–406.

Dowhower, S. L. (1994). Repeated reading revisited: Research into practice. *Reading and Writing Quarterly, 10*(4), 343–358.

Eldredge, L. J., Reutzel, R. D., & Hollingsworth, P. M. (1996). Comparing the effectiveness of two oral reading practices: Round robin reading and the shared book experience. *Journal of Literacy Research, 28*(2), 201–225.

Flood, J., Lapp, D., & Fisher, D. (2005). Neurological impress method plus. *Reading Psychology, 26*(2), 147–160.

Flood, J., Lapp, D., Mraz, M., & Wood, K. (2006). Effective comprehension for the middle school student, Part 1. *Journal of the New England League of Middle Schools, 17*(2), 5–10.

Frey, N., Fisher, D., & Allen, A. (2009). Productive group work in middle and high school classrooms. In S. Parris, D. Fisher, & K. Headley (Eds.), *Adolescent literacy, field tested: Effective strategies for every classroom* (pp. 70–81). Newark, DE: International Reading Association.

Gamby, G. (1987). Talking books and taped books. *The Reading Teacher, 36*, 366–369.

Garmston, R., & Wellman, B. (2009). *The adaptive school: A sourcebook for developing collaborative groups* (2nd ed.). Norwood, MA: Christopher Gordon.

Gill, S. R. (2002). Responding to readers. *The Reading Teacher, 56*(2), 119–121.

Gillies, R. M. (2008). The effects of cooperative learning on junior high school students' behaviours, discourse, and learning during a science-based learning activity. *School Psychology International, 29*(3), 328–347.

Graves, D. (1983). *Writing: Teachers and children at work*. Portsmouth, NH: Heinemann.

Hampton, E., Wallace, M. A., Keele, K., & Lee, W. Y. (2009). Plastics in our environment: A jigsaw learning activity. *Science Scope, 32*(7), 56–61.

Harris, T. L., & Hodges, R. E. (1995). *The literacy dictionary*. Newark, DE: International Reading Association.

Hashey, J. M., & Connors, D. J. (2003). Learn from our journey: Reciprocal teaching action research. *The Reading Teacher, 57*(3), 224–232.

Heckelman, R. G. (1969). A neurological-impress method of remedial-reading instruction. *Academic Therapeutic Quarterly, 4*(4), 277–282.

Hill, C. H. (1983). Round robin reading as a teaching method. *Reading Improvement, 20*(4), 263–266.

Hoffman, J. V. (1987). Rethinking the role of oral reading in basal reading instruction. *Elementary School Journal, 87*(3), 367–373.

Homan, S. P., Klesius, J. P., & Hite, C. (1993). Effects of repeated readings and nonrepetetive strategies on students' fluency and comprehension. *Journal of Educational Research, 87*(2), 94–99.

Johnson, D. W., Johnson, R. T., St. Anne, M., & Garibaldi, A. (1990). Impact of group processing on achievement in cooperative groups. *Journal of Social Psychology, 130,* 507–516.

Kelly, P. R. (1995). Round robin reading: Considering alternative instructional practices that make more sense. *Reading Horizons, 36*(2), 99–115.

Klauda, S. L., & Guthrie, J. T. (2008). Relationships of three components of reading fluency to reading comprehension. *Journal of Educational Psychology, 100*(2), 310–321.

Kuhn, M. R., & Stahl, S. A. (2000). *Fluency: A review of developmental and remedial practices* (CIERA Rep. No. 2-008). Ann Arbor, MI: Center for the Improvement of Early Reading Achievement.

LaBerge, D., & Samuels, S. (1974). Toward a theory of automatic information processing in reading. *Cognitive Psychology, 6,* 293–323.

Langer, J. (2001). Beating the odds: Teaching middle and high school students to read and write well. *American Educational Research Journal, 38*(4), 837–880.

Lapp, D., Fisher, D., & Wolsey, T. D. (2009). *Literacy growth for every child: Differentiated small-group instruction K–6.* New York: Guilford Press.

Lyle, S. (2008). Dialogic teaching: Discussing theoretical contexts and reviewing evidence from classroom practice. *Language and Education, 22*(3), 222–240.

McCauley, J., & McCauley, D. (1992). Using choral reading to promote language learning for ESL students. *The Reading Teacher, 45,* 526–533.

Mefferd, P. E., & Pettegrew, B. S. (1997). Fostering literacy acquisition of students with developmental disabilities: Assisted reading with predictable trade books. *Reading Research and Instruction, 36,* 177–190.

Miller, J., & Schwanenflugel, P. J. (2008). A longitudinal study of the development of reading prosody as a dimension of oral reading fluency in early elementary school children. *Reading Research Quarterly, 43*(4), 336–354.

National Institute of Child Health and Human Development. (2000). *Report of the National Reading Panel: Teaching children to read—an evidence-based assessment of the scientific research literature on reading and its implications for reading instruction* (NIH Publication No. 00-4769). Washington, DC: U.S. Government Printing Office.

Opitz, M. F., & Rasinski, T. (1998). *Good-bye round robin: 25 effective oral reading strategies.* Portsmouth, NH: Heinemann.

Osborn, J., & Lehr, F. (2004). *A focus on fluency.* Honolulu: Pacific Resources for Education and Learning.

O'Shea, D. J., McQuiston, K., & McCollin, M. (2009). Improving fluency skills of secondary-level students from diverse backgrounds. *Preventing School Failure, 54*(1), 77–80.

Palinscar, A., & Brown, A. (1984). Reciprocal teaching of comprehension-fostering and comprehension-monitoring activities. *Cognition and Instruction, 1*(2), 117–175.

Pressley, M. (2000). What should comprehension instruction be the instruction of? In M. L. Kamil, P. B. Mosenthal, P. D. Pearson, & R. Barr (Eds.), *Handbook of reading research* (Vol. III, pp. 545–561). Mahwah, NJ: Erlbaum.

Rasinski, T. V., & Hoffman, J. V. (2003). Oral reading in school literacy curriculum. *Reading Research Quarterly, 38*(4), 510–521.

Rasinski, T. V., & Padak, N. D. (2005). Fluency beyond the primary grades: Helping adolescent struggling readers. *Voices from the Middle, 13*(1), 34–41.

Samuels, S. J. (1979). The method of repeated readings. *The Reading Teacher, 32,* 403–408.

Santa, C., & Havens, L. (1995). *Creating independence through student-owned strategies: Project CRISS.* Dubuque, IA: Kendall-Hunt.

Shaywitz, S. (2003). *Overcoming dyslexia: A new and complete science-based program for reading problems at any level.* New York: Alfred A. Knopf.

Slater, W. H., & Horstman, F. R. (2002). Teaching reading and writing to struggling middle school and high school students: The case for reciprocal teaching. *Preventing School Failure, 46*(4), 163–166.

Slavin, R. E. (1983). When does cooperative learning increase student achievement? *Psychological Bulletin, 94*(3), 429–445.

Slavin, R. F. (1980). Cooperative learning. *Review of Educational Research, 50*(2), 315–342.

Sloan, P., & Lotham, R. (1981). *Teaching reading is . . .* Melbourne: Thomas Nelson.

Stahl, S. A., & Heubach, K. (2005). Fluency-oriented reading instruction. *Journal of Literacy Research, 37*(1), 25–60.

Swartz, S., & Klein, A. (1997). *Research in reading recovery.* Portsmouth, NH: Heinemann.

Valleley, R. J., & Shriver, M. D. (2003). An examination of the effects of repeated readings with secondary students. *Journal of Behavioral Education, 12*(1), 55–76.

Whitman, N. A. (1988). *Peer teaching: To teach is to learn twice* (ASHE-ERIC Higher Education Report No. 4). Washington, DC: Association for the Study of Higher Education.

Worthy, J., & Prater, K. (2002). "I thought about it all night": Readers' Theatre for reading fluency and motivation. *The Reading Teacher, 56*(3), 294–7.

Young, C., & Rasinski, T. (2009). Implementing Readers' Theatre as an approach to classroom fluency instruction. *The Reading Teacher, 63*(1), 4–13.

CHAPTER 17

If You Want to Eliminate Misconceptions and Errors—Support Learning with Questions, Prompts, Cues, and Explanations

Douglas Fisher
Nancy Frey

Key Points for This Chapter

- Teachers questioning habits can reveal student misconceptions and errors.
- Teachers can transfer cognitive work to students through prompts and cues.
- Teachers can guide students to greater understanding through systematic implementation of guided instruction.

A BIRD'S-EYE VIEW OF CLASSROOM PRACTICE

Mr. Alvarez works hard in his eighth-grade science class to keep his students paying attention. One of the chief ways he does this is by asking lots of questions. "What's the meaning of the term *polymers?*" he quizzes his students. "What do you call the particle that orbits an atom?" he asks. Over the course of a 55-minute period, he asks 42 questions. Some students respond often. In fact, six students in his class of 33 answer the majority of his questions. When they answer correctly, he poses another. When he gets an incorrect response, he often responds by saying "Not quite" or "Can someone help him?" He had learned in his teacher credential program that is was important to address incorrect answers gently. He knows all of these facts about his questioning habits because the instructional coach who works with the department tallied the data for him. "I've got to work on my questioning techniques," he said. "I ask lots of questions but don't see much in the way of results. I've been reading about questioning in my graduate program and I'm determined to get better at this aspect of my teaching."

DEFINING THE TARGETED PRACTICE

As Mr. Alvarez is discovering, questioning is not just about the number posed. A blizzard of questions will not increase student understanding. As the instructional coach noted in the conversation following the observation, the majority of the teacher's questions were at the level of recall and recognition tasks. This pattern is corroborated in the research of Tienken, Goldberg, and DiRocco (2009), who found that 85% of the questions asked by novice teachers (defined in the study as those with less than 4 years of experience) were reproductive in nature. Experienced teachers didn't fare much better—68% of their questions asked students to reproduce information.

Why so many low-level questions? An underlying cause for this trend is the intent of the question. If the purpose is to interrogate student knowledge, then literal questions will do the trick. Unfortunately, this is a widely held assumption in many middle school classrooms. But consider how the types of questions would change if the purpose changed. In an instructional framework that focuses on guided instruction, rather than interrogation, questions become robust in nature. Robust questions represent a broader range of question types and, importantly, are followed by prompts and cues that refine and clarify student understanding.

WHAT DOES THE RESEARCH SAY ABOUT QUESTIONING?

Questioning does not occur in a vacuum. It can't be reduced and isolated so that what occurs before and after the question is disregarded. Instead, researchers often discuss the questioning cycle, in which the student is a participant. The most common type of cycle is called initiate–respond–evaluate, or I-R-E (Cazden, 2001). This is the practice of asking a question (initiate), to which a student answers (respond), and then the teacher makes a judgment (evaluate). The teacher knows the answer already, and is seeking to determine whether the student knows it as well. It is one-sided, as the student is not a full participant in the conversation; it is the teacher who holds all the cards. Consider this exchange that the instructional coach noted in Mr. Alvarez's lesson:

MR. ALVAREZ: Does a proton have a negative charge or a positive charge? (Initiate)

XAVIER: Um, negative, I think. (Respond)

MR. ALVAREZ: No, sorry, it's a positive charge. (Evaluate) Which one has a negative charge? (Initiate)

Determining whether a student understands a basic principle of physical science is necessary, to be sure. But there's no attempt in this exchange to build the Xavier's understanding when he answers incorrectly. Mehan (1979) has an even blunter name for this: pseudo-questioning. It is akin to what a game show host does, rather than a teacher. These "known-answer questions" can be confounding for students whose home culture does not engage in a communication style where adults ask questions of children when clearly they already know the answer (Bransford, Brown, & Cocking, 2000, p. 110). This approach can be disadvantageous even for older students, who do not see the point in answering such questions (Heath, 1983).

Question design has been linked, quite helpfully, to the work of Benjamin Bloom. His taxonomy of learning has been a useful tool in considering how questions can be conceived (Bloom, 1956). Bloom's categorization of levels of knowledge was not meant to be a hierarchy, but rather a means of classification. These levels have often been described as lower-order and higher-order, and are paired with the types of questions designed to explore these levels. Questions that explore the first levels of learning (knowledge, comprehension, and application) are mostly recall and recognition questions, or what Tienkien and colleagues (2009) call *reproductive*. These are primarily factual in nature and are essential first steps to mastering concepts. However, they are not enough. If students are going to deepen their understanding, they must also explore the upper levels: analysis, synthesis, and evaluation.

Upper-level understanding is foundational to inquiry-based science. This approach to learning requires students to do the thinking, while the teacher guides and facilitates their growing understanding. Unfortunately, the inquiry method may conflict with the teacher's perception of what he or she should be doing. In some classrooms, constrained questioning practices such as I-R-E continue to dominate due to fears of loss of control in the class (Lotter, 2004). Even among more experienced middle school science teachers, Furtak (2006) found that it was difficult to maintain this stance when students repeatedly requested that they be told the correct answer, rather than engage in the more challenging cognition of figuring it out. The good news is that professional development and attention to questioning techniques can result in more effective practices (Oliveira, 2010). These effective practices require the use of more open-ended questions that elicit longer student responses and collectively serve to guide student understanding. It is important to note that this does not mean that close-ended questions are excluded altogether, but rather are reduced in order to provide a more balanced discourse (Oliveira, 2010).

WHAT ARE SOME ALTERNATIVES?

Our belief about questioning as a means for guiding learning requires first that the types of questions be identified. This is an essential first step in improving practice. In other words, if you can name it, you can notice it. And if you can notice it, you can teach it. Our study of effective teachers found that they commonly guided learning by asking robust questions to check for understanding. When a student's answer reflected misconception or partial understanding, the teacher prompted the student to use background information or knowledge of a process or procedure. When the prompts did not result in stronger understanding, the teacher cued to shift the learner's attention to salient information. Only when prompts and cues were insufficient did the teacher furnish direct explanation (Frey & Fisher, 2010). A flowchart of this process can be found in Figure 17.1.

Robust Questions to Check for Understanding

Intention is key for effective questioning. Instead of a "guess what's in the teacher's head" line of interrogation, the intent is to determine what stuck (and what didn't stick) during prior instruction. This method of checking for understanding presumes that students (1) need multiple opportunities to reach mastery, and (2) require scaffolds that are intended to guide and facilitate their learning. The questions serve the purpose of initiating and continuing discussion. Close listening to students' responses reveals what they do and do not know at that moment in time. More importantly, student responses provide clues about the types of prompts or cues needed to further their understanding.

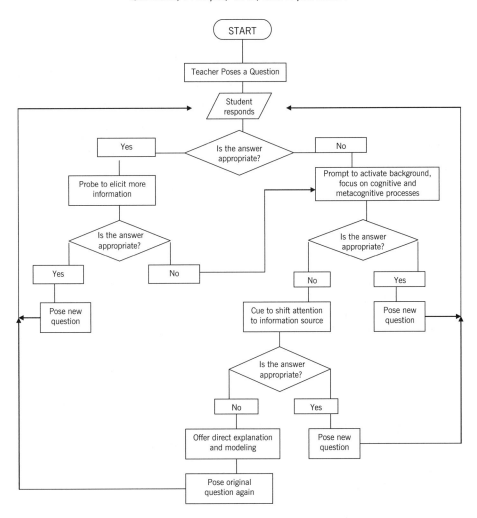

FIGURE 17.1. A flowchart for guiding learning. From Frey and Fisher (2010). Copyright 2010 by the International Reading Association. *www.reading.org.* Reprinted by permission.

Elicitation

Elicitation is a basic type of question that introduces a topic and serves to evoke a response that sheds light on students' present level of understanding. Many elicitation questions draw on factual knowledge, a starting point for deeper conceptual knowledge. Elicitation questions are sometimes described as the "five W's": *who, what, when, where, why,* and of course, *how.* When Mr. Alvarez asks, "What is at the center of an atom?", he is asking an elicitation question. The question itself is of less interest than what occurs next.

Elaboration

Elaboration as a type of question is sometimes called a *probe* because it invites the student to further explore his or her thinking about a topic. Elaboration questions often result in longer and more complex answers, and can further reveal what a student knows at that point in time. Asking a student "Can you tell me more about that?" can motivate him or her to provide more information and in the process illuminate his or her own thinking. Consider this questioning cycle:

> MR. ALVAREZ: What is at the center of an atom? (Elicitation)
>
> BESS: The nucleus.
>
> MR. ALVAREZ: Can you talk some more about that? (Elaboration)
>
> BESS: Well, there's those little particle things.
>
> MR. ALVAREZ: Can you keep going with that? (Elaboration)
>
> BESS: Umm, protons?
>
> MR. ALVAREZ: What else do I need to know about the nucleus? (Elaboration)
>
> BESS: Elec . . . no, wait. *Neutrons!*

Clarification

At times, clarification questions may follow elaboration, whereas at other times that are asked earlier. "I'm not sure I understood. Could you explain that again?" is a clarification question that is posed when the student's response is unclear. More commonly, it is used to further the student's thinking about the concept. The science teacher continues:

> MR. ALVAREZ: It seemed like you were hesitating. What made you change your mind? (Clarification)

BESS: I was thinking about the electrical charge. I know it's just positive in the center, so it couldn't be electrons. Those are negative.

Divergent

The student is increasingly revealing what she knows about the concept of the atom's structure. Sensing that Bess seems to have a grasp of the factual knowledge of the topic, Mr. Alvarez challenges her further by asking her to think more deeply about what she knows regarding atoms by posing a divergent question that requires her to consider other information:

"Now that's an interesting way to remember what's in the nucleus and what isn't. But now I have another question: What holds the nucleus together? Shouldn't all those particles just fly apart?" (Divergent)

Bess now has to consider another knowledge base: what she knows about electromagnetic forces. The expression on her face suggests that this question is causing her to review and reconsider what she knows about these two topics. When Bess indicates after a few moments that she doesn't know, Mr. Alvarez is going to prompt her. We'll leave this exchange for now as we discuss other types of questions.

Inventive

The inventive type of question is posed to stimulate imaginative thought and, for that reason, rarely has a "right" or "wrong" answer. Inventive questions ask students to utilize what they know about a topic to formulate an opinion or position. In this way, they are similar to what Raphael (1986) describes as "on-your-own" questions. In both cases, the student is asked to consider topical knowledge in order to offer an opinion. During a later unit on states of matter, Mr. Alvarez posed this inventive question: "How do you know that gases exist?" After giving students a few minutes to talk to partners, he led the class in a discussion of this question. Students debated with one another, eventually generating a list of examples for evidence of gas:

- Blowing up a balloon
- Smelling natural gas when turning on a stove burner
- Seeing vapors escaping the gas tank of a car at the gas station
- Seeing steam condense on the inside of a hot cup of coffee
- Seeing a neon sign flicker

In each of these cases, students had to draw on what they knew about the properties of a gas and evidence of it in their environment. Their answers couldn't be completely devoid of content knowledge; in this case the challenge was to employ this information to support a claim.

Heuristic

A final type of question is one that causes students to consider their informal problem-solving skills. *Heuristics* can be described as common sense informed by logic, and they tap into both the creative as well as pragmatic aspects of learning. It's helpful to know that the words *heuristic* and *eureka* have a common Greek root, and in both cases refer to an unexpected or highly anticipated find. We can consider the ways in which we solve problems in everyday life—for example, finding a parking space in a crowded event or locating a misplaced set of keys. Most of us have a method for solving such problems, although the method likely varies from person to person. A heuristic question in the classroom also invites students to resolve a problem that could be successfully accomplished in more than one way. When Mr. Alvarez asks, "What information could help the general public understand how a particle accelerator works?", he is posing a heuristic question. In this case, students discussed what information was most important as well as possible formats. Later, they designed brochures and videotaped themselves making public service announcements explaining the technology in understandable terms.

As you may have noticed, the last three types of questions lend themselves to longer discussions, and in some cases, even assignments. Although posed as an initial foray into a topic, the demonstration of understanding becomes increasingly complex. Along the way, students may need additional prompting to further their understanding.

But it's what the teacher does with the response to the question that facilitates student understanding. When students respond incorrectly, inappropriately, or with a misconception, teachers prompt students such that the *students* are doing the thinking, not the teacher. If prompts don't help, the teacher provides cues. If both prompts and cues fail to resolve the error or misconception, the teacher provides a direct explanation. It's through this give-and-take process, in which students think through their responses, that learning really occurs (Fisher, Frey, & Lapp, 2010).

Prompts for Cognitive and Metacognitive Work

Robust questions are posed to reveal partial understandings and misconceptions; prompts are intended to scaffold student understanding. Teachers can use a number of prompts to facilitate students' thinking, including the following.

Background Knowledge

Teachers can remind students about something that they have previously learned or something that they have directly experienced. For example, when Michael was confused about the phases of the moon, his teacher prompted, "Remember the pictures we saw showing the cycle and how they always started on the right?" To this excellent question Michael said, "Oh, it's waxing because that's when you see less that 50% of the right side of the moon." And his teacher added, "For the Northern Hemisphere, right?"

Process or Procedure

In some cases, specific processes or procedures are commonly used to solve problems or complete tasks. A prompt for this type of process relies on standard protocols—such as the first outside, inside last method—for solving problems, the steps in the scientific method, or what to do when you come to an unknown word. When students make mistakes procedurally, these types of prompts are useful in helping them do the cognitive work. For example, in her algebra class, Sabrina hadn't changed the inequality sign when she divided by a negative number. Noticing this, her teacher did not simply tell her the mistake, but instead said, "Take a look at the process chart again and check each step." As Sabrina reviewed her work, she realized that she had forgotten one of the steps. With repeated practice like this, Sabrina and her peers will learn to complete these tasks independently.

Reflective

Sometimes providing students with an opportunity to reflect does the trick of clearing up mistakes. As students reflect, they take some time to think and often identify the error themselves. Reflective prompts are especially helpful when they are based on the established purpose of the class, or the objective the teacher has set for the day. In other cases, reflective prompts can provide students with an opportunity to think about things from their own perspective, not necessarily from their personal experiences, as would be the case in background knowledge prompts. For example, in a discussion about Greek city-states, Brandi's teacher used a reflective prompt to refocus thinking about government, saying, "Why would they want to collect taxes? If you were a government official, why would you need to collect tax money?"

Heuristic

Although not as frequently used, heuristic prompts focus on the informal problem-solving procedures that work for a person but may not be common for other people. For example, that people use a number of writing processes, often dependent on audience, purpose, and format. There isn't just one writing process that works for everyone in every situation. Compare this with a procedure for solving a math problem—it's always parenthesis, exponents, multiply, divide, add, subtract (PEMDAS). Heuristic prompts are especially useful when students are developing their own habits for completing tasks, as was the case when Deon's teacher prompted him by saying, "There are lots of ways to start this problem. There isn't just one right way. How do you want to start?"

Cues to Shift Attention

Prompts will often resolve students' errors and misconceptions and result in significant learning. When teachers do not use prompts, but rather revert to telling students the information they are missing or skipping over the incorrect answer and inviting another student to respond, critical thinking opportunities are lost. However, prompts don't always resolve the situation. When prompts don't work, teachers move to cues. Cues require students to shift their attention to a specific source. As such, they are more direct and explicit than prompts. If at all possible, cues should follow prompts because they involve more teacher control. However, there are times that teachers use a cue rather than a prompt because that's the first thing that comes to mind or it's obviously going to work to resolve the error. There are a number of types of cues, as we discuss below. These are commonly used in initial teaching but are often neglected when students get stuck or make mistakes. As teachers, we need to use cues when the learner needs to do the work of schooling.

Visual Cues

Texts and websites are filled with visual information designed to provide additional or summative information. The range of visual cues include hyperlinks on a website to charts, diagrams, illustrations, and figures on the page. Sometimes refocusing the student's attention to the visual cues resolves the problem. This can as simple as saying, "Take a look at the illustration on page 159. Does your answer still hold?" In addition, there are often graphic organizers that provide a synthesis of information, and students can create graphic organizers to summarize information visually. Cueing students to notice aspects of the graphic organizer, whether they created it or not, can resolve errors. For example, while learning about solar eclipses in their earth science class, the teacher provided a visual cue to a group of students that was stuck, saying, "Take a look at the poster you made to summarize the chapter. See the graphic you created? The first step in the cycle is. . . . "

Verbal Cues

Verbal cues and verbal emphasis cues provide students with hints based on noticing what the teacher does with his or her voice. Verbal cues can be very explicit, such as "This is the important point . . . " or more subtle, as in, "Take a look at this again." Verbal emphasis cues involve the teacher's vocal emphasis, pausing, repetition, or intonation to make a point. For example, by slowing down her rate of speech, the students in Ms. Webster's class noticed that they were missing one of the main points. Mr. Leonard used intonation to stress the words he wanted students to notice (in italics), saying, "I'm thinking that the *serfs* had a hard life. These *serfs* didn't own the land, but had to work it for others."

Physical and Gestural Cues

Teachers can also use their bodies to refocus students. Sometimes we redirect students through direct touch and other times through our gestures. For example, during basketball practice, Coach Artilles regularly stops players to reposition their hands on the ball. Of course, physical cues can also be paired with verbal cues, as is the case when Coach Artilles says, "You gotta keep your hands spaced apart" while physically moving the player's hands. Gestural cues do not involve direct touch, but rather involve all of the nonverbal and movement-related hints teachers provide for students. As we have noted, teachers do this all of the time in their initial teaching. It's important to remember that these cues are also effective when the student is stuck. When Mr. Thibodeaux forms x- and y-axes with his hands, he's cueing students to think about the correct quadrants for their responses.

Environmental Cues

Sometimes the environment that the teacher creates can serve as a cue when students make mistakes. Of course, teachers use environmental cues for other things as well, such as an in-box at the front door to remind students to submit work, or a noise meter on the board to remind students about appropriate volume in the room. Environmental cues can also be used when errors or misconceptions are noted in response to robust questions. In these situations, teachers provide reference to the something in the environment that will help the student think about his or her response. For example, when Ms. Paxton points to a list of words on the wall, she is cueing her students' word choice. Of course, this is both gestural and environmental, as we know that pairing cues is highly effective.

Direct Explanations

When prompts and cues fail to resolve the errors or misconceptions identified during robust questions, teachers move to direct explanations. As Mr. Alvarez noted, it's important that students are not left with incorrect information. However, direct explanations should follow prompts and cues such that students are doing the cognitive work. It's only when prompts and cues fail to resolve errors and misconceptions that direct explanations are used.

Direct explanations provide students with the information they have missed. Importantly, direct explanations should include monitoring such that the student has to present the information back to the teacher, thereby experiencing some level of success. This can be accomplished through a retelling in which the student is asked to explain what the teacher just said in his or her own words or to respond to the original question by incorporating the new information.

As Mr. Alvarez refocused his questioning habits, he realized that he knew more about his students' thinking and could guide them to better understandings. In doing so, he changed his focus from I-R-E to robust questions designed to identify student thinking. As his understanding of student thinking grew, Mr. Alvarez was able to guide his students to greater success through prompts, cues, and direct explanations. Consider the following exchange Mr. Alvarez had with a group of students that was stuck on a problem involving distance, time, and average speed, which read:

> A passenger plane made a trip to Las Vegas and back. On the trip there it flew 432 m.p.h. and on the return trip it went 480 m.p.h. How long did the trip there take if the return trip took 9 hours?

MR. ALVAREZ: Tell me how you started this problem. Tyler?

TYLER: We estimated that it would be more than 9 hours because the plane was slower on the way there.

MR. ALVAREZ: That's some good thinking. And then what, Daisy?

DAISY: Well, we made it a ratio. If the plane went 480 miles in 9 hours, we wanted to know how long it took to go 432 miles. We set it up like this: $432/x = 480/9$. Then we cross multiplied, $432 \cdot 9 = 480x$. We solved that and got 8.1 hours.

ANNALEAH: But that doesn't make sense because it should take longer, not less time.

MR. ALVAREZ: Maybe it's about a formula. Do you remember a formula for these types of problems? Annaleah?

ANNALEAH: The only one I remember is $d = rt$. Is that what you mean?

MR. ALVAREZ: Sure, let's try that one. What does that formula do for us? Daisy?

DAISY: I remember that you can put in any of the information you have and find out the missing information.

MR. ALVAREZ: What would happen if you used that formula? Tyler?

TYLER: So, first, we would have to find out how far the plane went. Oh, wow, we didn't figure out how far the plane went. We mixed up the information. It didn't go 480 miles. It went 480 miles for 9 hours.

DAISY: That's like 4,320 miles. That's far!

ANNALEAH: They must be far away from Las Vegas, not like us.

TYLER: So, then if they went 4,320 miles at 480 miles per hour, it took 9 hours.

DAISY: Then we can use the formula again to find out the time for the way there.

ANNALEAH: 4,320 miles = 432 miles/hour • x hours.

MR. ALVAREZ: I'm liking your thinking here. Is it feeling better?

TYLER: Yeah, we got this: 4,320 divided by 432 is 10. It took them 10 hours to get there.

DAISY: That makes more sense. It should take longer because they went slower on the way there.

MR. ALVAREZ: And there it is. Well done, team! On to the next problem?

Unlike his earlier attempts to correct students based on their responses, when Mr. Alvarez used a guided instruction protocol, his students did most of the work while he provided scaffolds for their learning. As Ms. Alvarez said, "In the old days, I had to keep telling them the same information over and over again. When they work it though in their heads, with my guidance, they really understand it and can do it by themselves later on."

CONCLUSION

Without a system for responding to student errors and misconceptions, middle school teachers are at risk of assuming all of the responsibility for learning and relying on the I-R-E model of questioning and telling students information. When teachers use robust questions and then analyze student responses so that they can guide students to greater understanding, long-term learning occurs. Teachers have a number of scaffolds at their disposal, including prompts and cues, to encourage students to do the cognitive work required of learning.

ADDITIONAL RESOURCES AND LESSON EXAMPLES

Books

Materials useful for developing questions and responding to errors are plentiful and readily available for middle school teachers in all content areas. The following books address the practical elements of constructing and using guided instruction:

Dantonio, M., & Beisenherz, P. C. (2000). *Learning to question, questioning to learn: A guide to developing effective teacher questioning practices.* Boston: Allyn & Bacon.

Fisher, D., & Frey, N. (2008). *Better learning through structured teaching: A framework for the gradual release of responsibility.* Alexandria, VA: Association for Supervision and Curriculum Development.

Fisher, D., & Frey, N. (2010). *Guided instruction: How to develop confident and successful learners.* Alexandria, VA: Association for Supervision and Curriculum Development.

Walsh, J. A., & Sattes, B. D. (2005). *Quality questioning: Research-based practice to engage every learner.* Thousand Oaks, CA: Corwin Press.

Walsh, J. A., & Sattes, B. D. (2010). *Leading through quality questioning: Creating capacity, commitment, and community.* Thousand Oaks, CA: Corwin Press.

Websites

These websites provide useful examples of how questioning and guided instruction are used by teachers.

Effective Questioning Strategies and Effective Feedback

www.prel.org/readingframework/mod6/. . ./Effect_Quest_Strats.doc

How to Develop Questioning Strategies

www.everythingesl.net/inservices/questioning_strategies.php

Questioning: A Comprehension Strategy for Small-Group Guided Reading
www.readwritethink.org/classroom-resources/lesson-plans/questioning-comprehension-strategy-small-408.html

Questioning Strategies
wik.ed.uiuc.edu/index.php/Questioning_Strategies

San Diego County Office of Education, Supporting Differentiated Instruction
kms.sdcoe.net/differ/21-DSY/60-DSY.html

REFERENCES

Bloom, B. S. (Ed.). (1956). *Taxonomy of educational objectives, the classification of educational goals—handbook I: Cognitive domain.* New York: McKay.

Bransford, J. D., Brown, A. L., & Cocking, R. C. (Eds.). (2000). *How people learn: Brain, mind, experience, and school.* Washington, DC: National Academy Press.

Cazden, C. B. (2001). *Classroom discourse: The language of teaching and learning.* Portsmouth, NH: Heinemann.

Fisher, D., Frey, N., & Lapp, D. (2010). Responding when students don't get it. *Journal of Adolescent and Adult Literacy, 54,* 56–60.

Frey, N., & Fisher, D. (2010). Identifying instructional moves during guided learning. *The Reading Teacher, 64*(2), 84–95.

Furtak, E. M. (2006). The problem with answers: An exploration of guided science inquiry teaching. *Science Education, 90,* 453–467.

Heath, S. B. (1983). *Ways with words: Language, life, and work in communities and classrooms.* New York: Cambridge University Press.

Lotter, C. (2004). Preservice science teachers' concerns through classroom observations and student teaching: Special focus on inquiry teaching. *Science Educator, 13*(1), 29–38.

Mehan, H. (1979). *Learning lessons: Social organization in the classroom.* Cambridge, MA: Harvard University Press.

Oliveira, A. W. (2010). Improving teacher questioning in science inquiry discussions through professional development. *Journal of Research in Science Teaching, 47*(4), 422–453.

Raphael, T. E. (1986). Teaching question–answer relationships, revisited. *The Reading Teacher, 39,* 198–205.

Tienken, C. H., Goldberg, S., & DiRocco, D. (2009). Questioning the questions. *Kappa Delta Pi Record, 46*(1), 39–43.

CHAPTER 18

If You Want Students to Take Notes Instead of Copying Them—Teach Them How

Christianna Alger
Barbara Moss

Key Points for This Chapter

- Copying notes does not support retention of lecture content.
- Retention can be enhanced as students engage in skeletal note taking, strategic note taking, and Cornell notes.
- The New American Lecture strategy and interactive notebooks situate note-taking activities within the context of systems of learning that facilitate student comprehension of content.

A BIRD'S-EYE VIEW OF CLASSROOM PRACTICE

John Glenn Middle School is an urban neighborhood school with a commitment to heterogeneous classrooms. During the eighth-grade-level team meeting, Mr. Rappaport, a social studies teacher, tells his colleagues that he cannot understand why his students perform so poorly on the section quizzes and unit tests. He explains that he has developed PowerPoint presentations for each chapter that include many visuals and notes, which he has his students carefully copy down. He reveals to his colleagues, "And for my English language learners who can't read the textbook, and for those students who won't read the textbook, lecturing and note taking seem to be the only way that the students will get the material. Most of my students can't take notes on their own; they can't write fast enough, and some of them have poor listening skills. Copying down the notes should help the students remember better than just reading or hearing the material. I like to have them copy the notes because it keeps them busy and on task during the period. Even so, they are still doing poorly on the tests."

With exasperation in her voice, Mrs. Grim, the science teacher, said, "I have the same problem, except that instead of having my students copy the PowerPoint slides, I prepare graphic organizers, which the students follow as I lecture and we fill in together. If they study the graphic organizer, the students should do well on the quizzes—but they don't."

WHAT DOES THE RESEARCH SAY ABOUT COPYING NOTES?

The ability to take notes is an essential skill for students in the middle grades. In fact, as students reach middle school, teacher reliance on lecture and textbook learning make the ability to take notes even more essential than at earlier grade levels. To successfully negotiate content-area classes, students must be able to take notes from teachers' lectures, as well as from their textbooks. Research has shown that in secondary content classes more than half a student's grade is based on test scores, and lectures represent the main source from which test items are taken (Putnam, Deshler, & Schumaker, 1992). Lectures and note taking continue to comprise a large amount of students' class time (Boyle, 2010); 79% of content-area teachers report that they frequently use lectures in their teaching (Vogler, 2006). With this salience in mind, it becomes obvious that note taking can improve academic achievement in content-area classes. Note taking is generally thought to improve recall, which in turn can improve student performance in learning new content. Most research on note taking has focused on whether note taking aids retention, especially in the context of taking notes from lectures (Brown, 2005). The results of these studies are not clear-cut, however; they have not consistently found that note taking enhances learning (Hidi & Klaiman, 1983; Meyer, 2002).

Students who take lecture notes generally have higher achievement than those who do not (Kiewra, Mayer, Christensen, Kim, & Risch, 1991), and those who review their notes do better than those who do not. Typically, however, students record only about 20–40% of the information provided during a lecture (O'Donnell & Dunsereau, 1993), which obviously impacts their comprehension of the content provided. The more notes recorded the higher the achievement (Kiewra & Benton, 1988). As electronic note taking becomes more popular, however, this circumstance may change.

Note taking is designed to perform two key functions: to record information and to promote reflection (Boch & Piolat, 2005). The function associated with information recording is one that we use every day, whether to write a grocery list or to remember a cell phone number. This "external storage" of information is designed to make it possible for us to retrieve that information at a later time; it provides a means for accessing information that we may not be able to call up from memory at a future time. This external storage function has been found to increase comprehension (Ganske, 1981); students who take notes are actively involved in lectures and demonstrate improved test performance (Peper & Mayer, 1978).

Reflection represents another function of note taking. Reflection involves reviewing notes with the goal of using the information in those notes for more sophisticated cognitive purposes such as solving a problem, making a judgment, or resolving an issue. In this instance, notes become a kind of "rough draft" that can be referred to facilitate the goals of the task (Cary & Carlson, 1999). This reflective process, called *encoding*, helps students assimilate material in order to make it personally comprehensible. When student don't just take notes, for example, but use their notes to review for tests, achievement increases (Armbruster, 2000).

Studies indicate that if encoding occurs during the note-taking process, comprehension increases (Budd & Alexander, 1997). This type of active note taking, rather than passive verbatim recording of notes like that found in Mr. Rappaport's class, demands that students self-question and interact with information. When students actively generate relationships among parts of information and between this new information and their prior knowledge, comprehension is improved (Kiewra, 1985). When students reprocess information in some way, whether through summary writing or self-questioning, long-term memory is improved and material is better recalled (Benton, Kiewra, Whitfill, & Dennison, 1993; Davis & Hult, 1997). According to Boch and Piolat (2005), "The more the information learning process involves understanding and transforming operations, the greater the intensity and effectiveness of the learning process" (p. 104). For this reason, activities such as highlighting notes and writing summaries of notes lead to a deeper understanding than simply reading notes (Kiewra, Benton, Kim, Risch, & Christensen, 1995).

Middle school is a critical point for teaching note taking. In a study of seventh graders' perceptions and note-taking practices (Brown, 2005), students reported that although they did use notes to prepare for tests, they seldom reread notes to monitor for sense, nor did they read material before taking notes. In an analysis of the actual notes taken for a history text, students wrote few notes and had difficulty separating important information from unimportant information—clearly an essential skill if students are to benefit from note taking. As Faber, Morris, and Lieberman (2000) note, "At some point between the seventh and twelfth grades, note taking shifts from the external storage function to an encoding function" (p. 259). Through effective instruction in note taking, teachers can help to facilitate this shift.

Unfortunately, instruction in note taking that actively involves students is sorely lacking. In many classrooms, such as Mr. Rappaport's, students simply copy the PowerPoint notes created by the teacher. These students are not even taking verbatim notes from a lecture; instead they are just copying down notes that someone else has organized. Ms. Grim is on the right track by having her students work with graphic organizers; these tools should help students understand how the new information and concepts relate to one another and connect to students' prior knowledge. However, when Ms. Grim has her students copy the teacher-created organizers, students are not engaged in making meaning. Mr. Rappaport's and Ms. Grim's students are not getting the opportunity to interact with their notes in ways that will help them more deeply understand information and ultimately master course content.

WHAT ARE SOME ALTERNATIVES?

To identify alternatives to having students copy notes, let's consider why Mr. Rappaport has students copy his PowerPoints into their notebooks. He states that many of the students cannot record information on their own because they cannot write quickly enough and have poor listening skills. Although this may be the case, the ability to take their own notes can empower students to take responsibility for their own learning. By providing students with notes to copy, rather than teaching them to create their own, teachers deny students the opportunity to engage cognitively with information in ways that enhance retention of material, and, ultimately, mastery of content. In addition, students need opportunities not to just record the information, but to interact with it in meaningful ways. This requires that teachers take the time to teach students how to take their own notes.

A second reason that Mr. Rappaport gives for having students take notes is that it keeps them busy and on task during the class period. While this practice may support classroom management, asking students to copy notes does not promote real engagement with learning. The mere fact of copying information does not ensure that students will remember or truly understand the information provided. In fact, research has found that the act of copying does not aid recall (Henk & Stahl, 1985). For true learning to occur, students need opportunities to engage in tasks that go beyond just copying As Costa and Kalick (2000) note: "The more senses that are engaged, the greater the learning" (p. 87).

The gradual release of responsibility model provides a framework for helping students develop note-taking skills as well as many other literacy skills. This model includes teacher modeling, guided practice, collaborative practice, and independent practice. The gradual release model of instruction (Fisher & Frey, 2008; Pearson & Gallagher, 1983) is predicated on the view that effective teachers provide scaffolded instruction, during which they "give high support for students practicing new [strategies] and then slowly decrease that support to increase student ownership and self-sufficiency" (Biancarosa & Snow, 2004, p. 14). This model emphasizes instruction that mentors learners into becoming capable thinkers when addressing tasks in which they lack expertise (Buehl, 2005).

In this section we describe a variety of strategies that Mr. Rappaport and Ms. Grim could use to engage students in effective note taking; these strategies promote recall, but more than that, they promote the kind of critical thinking about information that can facilitate deep processing of content. Through this kind of processing, students develop greater recall of information, see relationships between ideas, and are able to draw conclusions about what they have learned. We have arranged these strategies in order of complexity; the first few strategies—skeletal note taking, strategic note taking, Cornell notes, and concept maps—represent individual strategies that can transition students from copying notes to taking notes. The New American Lecture or interactive lecture represents a sophisticated lecture format that combines several strategies, including note taking. This strategy is more complex to implement than the individual strategies, but represents an excellent method for facilitating student recall. Finally, the interactive notebook represents a means for students to personalize and take ownership of most of the learning that goes on in a classroom, from classroom activities, to tests, to homework.

Skeletal Note Taking

One easy way that Mr. Rappaport might help students learn to take, rather than copy, notes would be to use the skeletal note-taking method. Skeletal note taking involves providing students with a partially completed outline of the day's lecture. This outline contains main topics and details from the lecture. Some parts of the outline are completed, whereas others contain blank lines that students are expected to complete themselves.

Students who do skeletal note taking have higher achievement scores than students who take notes without such outlines (Hartley & Davies, 1978; Kiewra, DuBois, Christian, & McShane, 1988). Many students experience information overload when trying to take notes during a lecture. In other words, the cognitive load of the material becomes too much for them, and they are unable to record enough information to make their notes useful for studying (Sweller & Chandler, 1991). Although students are often able to identify superordinate ideas in their notes, they find recording subordinate ideas much more difficult (Kiewra, Benton, & Lewis, 1987). Skeletal outlines provide students with an overview of the organization of a lecture. In addition, they provide students with information that they may not be able to record quickly enough during the actual lecture, and in this way the outlines allow them to focus on understanding. In addition, providing skeletal notes that contain the lecture's main ideas along with space for note taking can help students take more complete notes (Kiewra, 2002). Skeletal notes encourage active learning because the act of doing so shifts students' focus from simply capturing information to reflection on, and questioning of, the material (Wirth, 2003).

As they studied the topic of state and federal powers in his U.S. history class, Mr. Rappaport might have introduced the skeletal outline as a beginning note-taking strategy for his students. Before doing this, however, Mr. Rappaport would model for students the "basics" of note taking. These basics include teaching students to use key words and phrases, symbols and abbreviations, and bullet points, and to paraphrase content. To model these basics, Mr. Rappaport might have completed a short focus lesson designed to show students how to take their own notes. He could begin by having students watch a short, 5-minute video clip about the results of the 2010 California governor's election. He could ask them to listen carefully to the information in the clip. Following this, he could show them the clip again and instruct them to watch how he took notes on the document camera. He might have said:

> "I am going to take notes on the clip as you see it again. As you watch me, I want you to note what I write down and how I write it down. I will write each piece of information on a new line and create a heading for the main idea. Then I will use bullet points to list the details. You will notice that I do not try to write down every word they say; that would be too hard. I do not write in complete sentences when I take notes, and I try to put things in my own words. You will also notice that I try to abbreviate words when I can to save time."

Here is what he wrote:

CA governor's election results
- Brown wins election over Whitman.
- Brown 51% of vote; Whitman 45%.
- Whitman spent $70M.
- Brown's father was governor in the 70s.

After he completed this modeling Mr. Rappaport said, "You will notice that I wrote each note on a new line and used bullet points to show the details under the heading 'CA governor's election results.' Instead of writing complete sentences, I tried to write only the most important words in each sentence and to put them in my own words. Notice that I used abbreviations for *California, million,* and wrote *70s* for 1970s to save time."

Following this modeling, Mr. Rappaport used guided practice to help students take notes. He showed them another video clip about the election results and provided them with a short, partially completed skeletal outline on the document camera. He asked students to listen to the clip and then work to complete those parts of the outline that contained blank lines. He called on students to complete the outline. After this he asked students if there were words that they could abbreviate, paraphrase, and so on. He made these changes on the document camera.

At this point, Mr. Rappaport felt that students were ready for collaborative practice using skeletal note taking. During this collaborative practice, students would have the support of a partner who could help them try out note taking. After activating students' prior knowledge by asking them what the responsibilities of a governor are, he began a short review lecture on PowerPoint that focused on what the Constitution says about the division of powers between state and federal government, focusing on the responsibility of state governors using the skeletal outline in Figure 18.1. He stopped several times at strategic points and let students work with partners to record the notes on the skeletal outline. Students were encouraged to paraphrase, abbreviate, and record only key words. For independent practice, he asked students to take notes on the last part of the lecture individually. Following this, students compared their notes to check on the extent to which they had captured the most important information (a sample completed skeletal outline is found in Figure 18.1).

Strategic Note Taking

Strategic note taking is another method that Mr. Rappaport might use with his students once they have mastered skeletal note taking. Strategic note taking is less structured than skeletal outlining, but still provides students with a framework for recording notes (Boyle & Weishaar, 2001). By providing students with a series of written prompts, strategic note taking guides students in identifying main points, summarizing, and organizing lecture information (Boyle, 1996, 2001; Boyle & Weishaar, 2001). This research-based note-taking system has been successful with high school students with learning disabilities, but can be equally effective with middle-grade learners. Strategic note taking helps students use "metacognitive skills"(i.e., organizing information and combining new information

---

Powers of the Federal Government
Expressed Powers
- Post office
- Coin money
- *Declare war*

Implied Powers
- Regulating airlines

Concurrent Powers (shared with states)
- Taxes
- *Courts*
- *Schools*

Reserved Powers (not directly given to federal government; belong to states)
- Driving age
- Speed limits

CA Governor's Responsibilities
- Make "State of the State" speech to legislature
- *Submit budget*
- Ensure CA laws are enforced
- *Maintain borders*
- Interstate relationships

FIGURE 18.1. Skeletal outline for lecture on state and federal powers.

with prior knowledge) during lectures, thereby increasing their engagement (Boyle, 2001). Boyle (1996, 2001) argued that through using metacognitive skills, students were actively engaged in the learning process, thereby enhancing their understanding of the lecture.

A strategic note-taking guide (see Figure 18.2) is divided into three sections: before the lecture, during the lecture, and after the lecture. The guide requires students to record information before the lecture begins, identify and record information as it is being presented, and summarize the points in the lecture once they have finished recording the information.

Before beginning a lecture, for example, Mr. Rappaport would ask students to record the topic of the lecture, what they already know about it, and some vocabulary terms they expect to hear. In this way students can reflect on their prior knowledge about the topic. During the lecture, students would record three main points with details related to the day's topic. Students then would identify and record new vocabulary terms from the lecture. After the lecture students would write a two-sentence summary of the ideas presented, focusing on their relationships. In addition, they could record new vocabulary terms they heard in the lecture.

BEFORE THE LECTURE

Record today's topic here _____

List three things you know about this topic

1.   2.   3.

List three vocabulary words you think will be in the lecture.

1.   2.   3.

DURING THE LECTURE

Record three main ideas and details from today's lecture here.

Main Idea 1 _____

Details

Main Idea 2 _____

Details

Main Idea 3 _____

Details

AFTER THE LECTURE

Summary: Write a short summary of today's lecture here:

List three new vocabulary terms that you learned today.

_____

_____

_____

FIGURE 18.2. Strategic note-taking guide. Based on Boyle and Weischar (2001).

Cornell Notes

Cornell notes represent another more sophisticated way to record notes during a lecture. Like the strategic note-taking guide, Cornell notes (Pauk, 1974) provide a system in which students record notes. They have an additional dimension, however; Cornell notes require that students not only take notes, but engage with their notes by identifying key ideas and summarizing information.

This note-taking method involves folding a paper lengthwise so that one third of the paper appears on the left. Students draw a line vertically on their paper to make a 2.5-inch column on the left and a column of 6 inches on the right. Then they draw a horizontal line to create a section of approximately 2 inches on the bottom of their page (see Figure 18.3). Students record notes from a lecture or text on the right two-thirds of the page. After this, they reflect on their notes. On the left third of the page they "reduce" the notes by formulating questions and/or main idea statements about the notes on the right. They can then cover the notes on the right and try to answer the questions found in the narrow column on the left. After this, they use the 2-inch section at the bottom of the page, running full width, to write a short summary of their notes.

Cornell notes are extremely popular with middle school and high school teachers, but require instruction if students are to use them successfully. By preceding Cornell notes with skeletal outlines and strategic note-taking guides, students will be more likely to succeed in using Cornell notes.

Lecture Title and Date	
◆ Narrow column On this side of the paper, reduce the notes by creating big questions or main idea statements from the lecture.	◆ Notes column Include details from the lecture, including illustrations, definitions, and examples.

Summary

Create a short summary of the notes above. Use the big questions or main idea statements from the left-hand column to help you create a two- or three-sentence summary of the lecture content.

FIGURE 18.3. Cornell note-taking format.

New American Lecture Strategy

The New American Lecture strategy, sometimes referred to as interactive lectures (Silver & Perini, 2010), combines a traditional lecture format with instructional activities that promote retention of information and in-depth understanding of content. According to Silver and Perini (2010), this strategy meets several important goals: It (1) increases student engagement, (2) helps students take notes, (3) aids in information management, (4) deepens comprehension, and (5) builds background knowledge and habits of mind. The format is focused on improving student memory for content through four types of activities: (1) *connecting* activities that relate new information to the known; (2) *organizing* information in logical ways; (3) *deep processing or dual coding* of content; and (4) *exercise and elaboration* experiences. Lectures begin with connecting activities that involve a hook, or a compelling question or activity, that stimulates student curiosity or wonder. Students think or discuss this question and record their ideas on paper during the "kindling" phase, when students develop their own interest in the topic. Following the sharing of students' thoughts, the teacher creates a bridge between student prior knowledge and the new content.

For example, to introduce the American Revolution to students, teachers might use *connecting activities* to help students begin to think about the topic at hand. For example, teachers might begin by asking students what they think of when they hear the word *revolution*. They might then ask students to listen to the first few stanzas of the John Lennon song, "You Say You Want a Revolution" to further consider the concept of revolution. Students might work in pairs to discuss the following questions: When, if ever, is a revolution necessary? Do revolutions always involve destruction? Why or why not? Do revolutions always change the world? Can there be a peaceful revolution? Why or why not?

Following this discussion, the teacher could explain that the war for American independence, often referred to as the American Revolution, represented a dramatic break from the status quo for the American colonies and the people who lived in the colonies. Their lives were, in many ways, never the same, and the country that became America underwent a seismic shift that affected it for years to come.

In the *organizational* phase of this strategy, teachers present information in chunks. Silver and Perini (2010) recommend presenting information for 3–7 minutes and then asking students questions about the content. In addition, during this phase teachers use visual organizers to give students an overview of the lecture in its entirety and to allow them to record "chunks" of information on specific sections of the visual organizer. For example, following the preparation described earlier, the teacher might begin a lecture to introduce the factors that contributed to the revolution. To give students an overview of the key causes of the revolution that they would learn about during this unit, as well as a format for recording notes, the teacher could provide them with a cause–effect graphic organizer. During this phase the teacher would "chunk" the information, working on a single section of the causes at a time.

During the *deep processing or dual coding* phase, teachers provide students with images, visual aids, or demonstrations to facilitate their learning of one chunk of information. In addition, students might construct their own knowledge by exploring their own examples or reactions to the content. During this phase of our sample lesson, the teacher would assist students in identifying icons that they could use to help them remember the different categories of causes of the revolution. The icons are found on the graphic organizer in Figure 18.4. In addition, the teacher would share primary source documents, such as Paul Revere's engraving of the Boston Massacre, to reinforce their learning and to help them consider the ways in which the colonists used propaganda to further their cause.

The *exercise and elaboration* component of the strategy involves periodically asking students reflective questions as the teacher moves through each chunk of information, as well as once the lecture has ended. At strategic points in the lesson students are asked four different types of review questions that require them to apply information and ideas from all parts of their organizer. These types of questions include the following:

- Mastery questions, to facilitate recall and review.
- Understanding questions, to help students make inferences.
- Self-expressive questions, to stimulate students' imaginations.
- Interpersonal questions, to help students examine their own beliefs.

In our American Revolution example, the teacher would ask questions throughout the lecture to aid student reflection. For example, a mastery question after the first chunk of information about the Enlightenment might ask: What kind of thinking did the Enlightenment create? After presenting information about the British laws, the teacher might ask an understanding question that required students to compare and contrast the different laws presented during that section. Upon completion of the lecture, the teacher might ask students a self-expressive question about whether they think they would have participated in the revolution on the side of the colonists, the crown, or not at all.

After the lecture is completed, the teacher engages students in some type of creative synthesis task. Students might engage in a role-play or Readers' Theatre task where they assume the roles of American colonists, British soldiers, slaves, Southern planters, Northern tradesmen, and colonial women and offer their opinions of the conflict, its effects on their lives, and their perceptions of its merits.

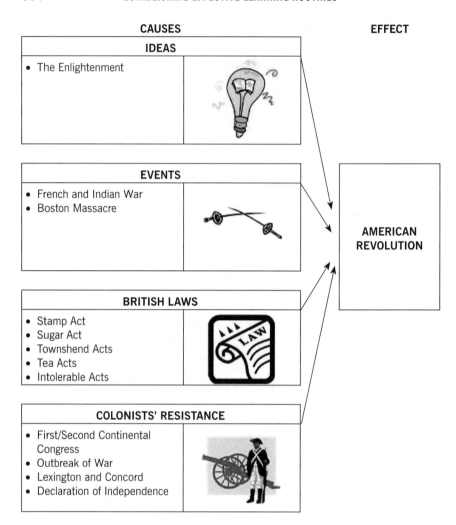

FIGURE 18.4. Cause–effect graphic organizer.

Putting It All Together: Interactive Notebooks

Originally developed by a teacher in the 1970s, the interactive notebook gained popularity in the 1990s when the Teachers Curriculum Institute incorporated this instructional tool in their *History Alive!* middle and high school curriculum (Bower & Lobdell, 1999). Since then the interactive notebook has been successfully adapted to other content areas such as science and math (Waldman & Crippen, 2009). Several studies have documented the effectiveness of the interactive notebook (Ebert, Kent,

Kern, Reichenbach, & Waldman, 2009; Endacott, 2007; McKay, 1996). This tool combines research-based strategies, such as the ones discussed above, but it operates as an organized learning *system* by including not just lecture notes, but also notes from readings, homework assignments, and classroom activities along with opportunities for students to actively engage with their notes. As students build their notebooks, they become a "personal, organized, and documented record of their learning" (Waldman & Crippen, 2009, p. 53). Although this system requires initial teacher planning and class time to train students at the start of the school year, as students become familiar with the format, the interactive notebook becomes an integral part of teaching and learning.

The interactive notebook is particularly appropriate for middle school students, in developmental terms, because it fosters student autonomy in learning and motivation through the mechanisms of choice and personal expression. Teaching students how to create and use the interactive notebook models organization, information management, and effective study habits—all skills that middle school students will need to develop for high school. According to Ebert and colleagues (2009), the interactive notebook provides students with "opportunities to manage their own cognitive, metacognitive, and motivational strategies" (p. 259).

To implement the interactive notebook approach, students will need a spiral-bound notebook, colored pencils or markers, pens and pencils, scissors, and glue sticks. Instruct students to save the first 8–10 pages at the front of the notebook for a cumulative table of contents. Then, starting with a left-hand page, have the students number the remaining pages so that they will begin with some organization.

The remaining structure of the interactive notebook is similar to Cornell notes, but the left side and right side are a full page each (see Figure 18.5). The right side is for teacher-directed input, such as lecture and reading notes, handouts, teacher-made graphic organizers, annotated primary source materials, lab instructions, and diagrams and charts. In some cases, students need to glue handouts onto a right-hand page. The left-hand side is for student-directed output, a place for the students to process and display what they have learned from the notes and activities on the right-hand page. For example, before lecturing on the Bill of Rights, Mr. Rappaport might ask his students to do a quick write on the left-hand page of their opinion about whether or not Americans should have the right to own and carry guns. The purpose of the prompt is to spark students' prior knowledge about rights and to garner interest in the topic to follow. After the lecture, he might give the students a choice to summarize the notes, draw an illustration, or create a concept map on the page to the left of their notes. In each case, Mr. Rappaport is asking his students to translate and manipulate the information in some new way.

Student-directed output	Teacher-directed input
• Student-developed concept maps • Illustrations • Journal entries • Questions • Reflective writing • Quick writes • Storyboards • Other creative ways to better understand information	• Notes from lectures • Notes from reading • Vocabulary words • Sample problems • Lab instructions • Diagrams • Charts • Handouts • Maps • Summary of notes

FIGURE 18.5. Interactive notebook.

Evaluation is a key component of the interactive notebook. It is necessary for the teacher to devise a consistent, clear, and regular plan for evaluation (Endacott, 2007; Waldman & Crippen, 2009) that includes frequent
completion checks. One simple way to accomplish this task is to circulate
around the classroom and place a stamp on the homework assignment that
has been entered on the right side while students complete a journal entry
on the left side. When the notebooks are collected, it is a simple matter of
counting the stamps and entering the points in the grade book. Summative evaluation should occur several times over a semester. Waldman and
Crippen (2009) suggest that notebooks be graded at the end of each unit.
Providing a rubric for grading at the start of the semester will help students
meet expectations for the notebook. Criteria might include: completion of
assignments on the left, organization, evidence of critical thinking, visual
appearance, and more. Endacott (2007) recommends that the teacher periodically allow students to use their notebooks while they are taking a test.
His rationale is that this helps middle school students who have not developed good study skills see the connections between their daily work and
tests. Knowing that they may be able to use this resource also motivates the
students to complete the work assigned in the notebook because they learn
that these can be help them be more successful on tests.

CONCLUSION

Mr. Rappaport and Ms. Grim, along with their students, will benefit
greatly from taking the initial time at the start of the year to teach and
reinforce note-taking skills. Note taking is an essential skill that all middle
school students will need to master before going on to high school and college. As middle school students move through the grades, they will need to

manage more and more information and teachers will expect them to take more responsibility for their learning. Teaching students how to take notes, through gradual release of responsibility, will be key to their success in mastering that skill and increase their potential for learning in the content areas.

ADDITIONAL LESSON EXAMPLES

The following lesson examples from ReadWriteThink support note-taking skill development and offer additional alternatives to asking students to copy notes.

e-Book Reading and Response: Innovative Ways to Engage with Texts

www.readwritethink.org/classroom-resources/lesson-plans/book-reading-response-innovative-30670.html

Exploring Careers Using the Internet

www.readwritethink.org/classroom-resources/lesson-plans/exploring-careers-using-internet-1159.html

Exploring Plagiarism, Copyright, and Paraphrasing

www.readwritethink.org/classroom-resources/lesson-plans/exploring-plagiarism-copyright-paraphrasing-1062.html

REFERENCES

Armbruster, B. B. (2000). Taking notes from lectures. In R. F. Flippo & D. C. Caverly (Eds.), *Handbook of college reading and study strategy research* (pp. 175–200). Mahwah, NJ: Erlbaum.

Benton, S. L., Kiewra, K. A., Whitfill, J. M., & Dennison, R. (1993). Encoding and external-storage effects on writing processes. *Journal of Educational Psychology, 85*(2), 267–280.

Biancarosa, G., & Snow, C. E. (2004). *Reading next—a vision for action and research in middle and high school literacy: A report to Carnegie Corporation of New York*. Washington, DC: Alliance for Excellent Education.

Boch, F., & Piolat, A. (2005). Notetaking and learning: A summary of research. *WAC Journal, 16*, 101–114.

Bower, B., & Lobdell, J. (1999). *History alive: Engaging all learners in the diverse classroom*. Rancho Cordova, CA: Teachers Curriculum Institute.

Boyle, J. (1996). Thinking while note taking: Teaching college students to use strategic note taking during lectures. In B. G. Brown (Ed.), *Innovative learning strategies: Twelfth yearbook* (pp. 9–18). Newark, DE: International Reading Association.

Boyle, J. R. (2001). Enhancing the note taking skills of students with mild disabilities. *Intervention in School and Clinic, 36*, 221–225.

Boyle, J. R. (2010). Strategic note-taking for middle-school students with learning disabilities in science class. *Learning Disability Quarterly, 33*, 93–109.

Boyle, J. R., & Weishaar, M. (2001). The effects of strategic notetaking on the recall and comprehension of lecture information for high school students with learning disabilities. *Learning Disabilities Research and Practice, 16*, 133–141.

Brown, R. (2005). Seventh-graders' self-regulatory note-taking from text: Perceptions, preferences and practices. *Reading Research and Instruction, 44*(4), 1–25.

Budd, K., & Alexander, J. (1997). *Arthurian legends and the medieval period for grade 9 study.* (ERIC Reproduction Service No. ED413599)

Buehl, D. (2005). Scaffolding. *Reading Room.* Retrieved November 25, 2007, from *www.weac.org/News/2005-06/sept05/readingroomoct05.htm.*

Cary, M., & Carlson, R. A. (1999). External support and the development of problem-solving routines. *Journal of Experimental Psychology: Learning, Memory, and Cognition, 25*(4), 1053–1070.

Costa, A. L., & Kalick, B. (2000). *Activating and engaging habits of mind.* Alexandria, VA: Association for Supervision and Curriculum Development.

Davis, M., & Hult, R. E. (1997). Effects of writing summaries as a generative learning activity during note taking. *Teaching of Psychology, 24*(1), 47–49.

Ebert, E., Kent, J., Kern, C., Reichenbach, R., & Waldman, C. (2009). Learning science with inquiry in the Clark County School District. In R. E. Yager (Ed.), *Inquiry: The key to exemplary science* (pp. 253–272). Arlington, VA: National Science Teachers Association Press.

Endacott, J. (2007). Social studies interactive notebooks: Helping to meet the needs of middle school students. *Social Studies Research and Practice, 2*(1), 128–138.

Faber, J. E., Morris, J. D., & Lieberman, M. G. (2000). The effect of note taking on ninth grade students' comprehension. *Reading Psychology, 21*, 257–270.

Fisher, D., & Frey, N. (2008). *Better learning through structured teaching: A framework for the gradual release of responsibility.* Alexandria, VA: Association for Supervision and Curriculum Development.

Ganske, L. (1981). Note-taking: A significant and integral part of learning environments. *Educational Communication and Technology Journal, 29*(3), 155–175.

Hartley, J., & Davies, I. K. (1978). Note taking: A critical review. *Innovations in Education and Teaching International, 13*(2), 58–64.

Henk, W., & Stahl, N. (1985, November). *Meta-analysis of the effect of note taking on learning from lectures* (College Reading and Learning Assistance Technical Report 85-05). Paper presented at the annual meeting of the National Reading Conference, St. Petersburg Beach, FL.

Hidi, S., & Klaiman, R. (1983). Note taking by experts and novices: An attempt to identify teachable strategies. *Curriculum Inquiry, 13*, 377–395.

Kiewra, K. A. (1985). Investigating note taking and review: A depth of processing alternative. *Educational Psychologist, 20*(1), 23–32

Kiewra, K. A. (2002). How classroom teachers can help students learn and teach them how to learn. *Theory into Practice, 41*(2), 71–80.

Kiewra, K. A., & Benton, S. L. (1988). The relationship between information-processing ability and note taking. *Contemporary Educational Psychology, 13*, 33–44.

Kiewra, K. A., Benton, S. L., Kim, S., Risch, N., & Christensen, M. (1995). Effects of note-taking format and study technique on recall and relational performance. *Contemporary Educational Psychology, 20*, 172–187.

Kiewra, K. A., Benton, S. L., & Lewis, L. B. (1987). Qualitative aspects of note taking and their relationship with information processing abilities. *Journal of Instructional Psychology, 14*, 110–117.

Kiewra, K. A, DuBois, N. F., Christian, D., & McShane, A. (1988). Providing study notes: Comparison of three types of notes for review. *Journal of Educational Psychology, 80*(4), 595–597.

Kiewra, K. A., Mayer, R. E., Christensen, M., Kim, S., & Risch, N. (1991). Effects of repetition on recall and note-taking: Strategies for learning from lectures. *Journal of Educational Psychology, 83*, 120–123.

McKay, R. (1996). Journal writing in the social studies classroom. *Canadian Social Studies, 30*, 56–57.

Meyer, J. (2002). Note taking training: A worthwhile proposal. Retrieved September 23, 2010, from *www2.unca.edu/~mcglinn/jaymeyerrevPaper.doc*.

O'Donnell, A., & Dunsereau, D. F. (1993). Learning from lecture: Effects of cooperative review. *Journal of Experimental Education, 61*, 116–125.

Pauk, W. (1974). *How to study in college*. Boston: Houghton Mifflin.

Pearson, P. D., & Gallagher, M. C. (1983). The instruction of reading comprehension. *Contemporary Educational Psychology, 8*(3), 317–344.

Peper, R. J., & Mayer, R. E. (1978). Note taking as a generative activity. *Journal of Educational Psychology, 70*(4), 514–522.

Putnam, L. M., Deshler, D. D., & Schumaker, J. B. (1992). The investigation of setting demands: A missing link in learning strategy instruction. In L. Meltzer (Ed.), *Strategy assessment and instruction for students with learning disabilities: From theory to practice* (pp. 325–351). Austin, TX: Pro-Ed.

Silver, H. F., & Perini, M. J. (2010). *The interactive lecture*. Alexandria, VA: Association for Supervision and Curriculum Development.

Sweller, J., & Chandler, P. (1991). Evidence for cognitive load theory. *Cognition and Instruction, 8*, 351–362.

Vogler, K. (2006). Impact of a high school graduation examination on Tennessee science teachers' instructional practices. *American Secondary Education, 35*, 35–57.

Waldman, C. A., & Crippen, K. J. (2009). Integrating interactive notebooks: A daily learning cycle to empower students for science. *The Science Teacher, 76*, 51–55.

Wirth, M. A. (2003). E-notes: Using electronic lecture notes to support active learning in computer science. *ACM SIGCSE Bulletin, 35*(2), 57–60.

CHAPTER 19

If You Want to Help Students Organize Their Learning—Fold, Think, and Write with Three-Dimensional Graphic Organizers

Nancy Frey
Douglas Fisher

Key Points for This Chapter

- Three-dimensional graphic organizers aid students in acquiring, retaining, and transforming information.
- Visual and hierarchical representations of information enhance verbal representations.
- These graphic organizers are an intermediate step to other literacy practices, such as discussion and writing.

A BIRD'S-EYE VIEW OF CLASSROOM PRACTICE

The students in Ms. Richardson's eighth-grade social studies class know that their teacher likes to use graphic organizers—they just don't know *why*. Each week Ms. Richardson distributes a graphic organizer to be completed by the class. Regardless of the concepts being studied, the graphic organizers are always the same. They rotate through Venn diagrams, cause–effect tables, and semantic webs. As Ms. Richardson dictates what goes into each section, the students dutifully scribe the terms and phrases in boxes. To vary the activity, she sometimes awards extra points for graphic organizers that include color or drawings. After grading them, she returns them to her students so that they can put them in their social studies notebooks. By the end of the semester, the notebooks are bulging with graphic organizers that look virtually the same from student to student.

"What I can't understand is why they don't seem to be doing any better on their quizzes and tests this year than my students last year did," she confided one afternoon. Ms. Richardson had attended a workshop the previous summer on graphic organizers and was convinced that these visual representations of knowledge would help her students master the material. "That doesn't seem to be the case, though," she admitted. "I don't understand why it's not helping. We're doing them every week."

DEFINING THE TARGETED PRACTICE

Visual representations of information do indeed have a reputation for supporting the learning of middle school students (e.g., Irwin-DeVitis & Pease, 1995; Robinson & Kiewra, 1995). Traditional graphic organizers include those previously mentioned, as well as ones that emphasize sequence or chronological order, main ideas and supporting details, and similarities and differences between ideas, events, or phenomena. A subset of graphic organizers, called Foldables™ (Zike, 2009), underscores the most salient feature of graphic organizers—the need to interact with concepts and strengthen associations between and among bits of information.

These three-dimensional graphic organizers are developed by students using one or more sheets of paper, scissors, and glue (Fisher, Zike, & Frey, 2007). Concept headings are introduced by the teacher in advance of the lesson. Students take notes during subsequent instruction. The purpose of grouping concepts together is to encourage schema building through association with related facts and ideas. Although there are benefits to having students create the interactive graphic organizers, what is even more important is what they do with them *after* they have been created. Students should construct these as tools in order to read, write, and speak about the content.

WHAT DOES THE RESEARCH SAY
ABOUT GRAPHIC ORGANIZERS?

The notion of organizing concepts to enhance the learning and understanding of concepts has been around since the mid-20th century, when Ausubel (1960) developed advance organizers. Originally, these were short written statements that summarized both the information to be learned, as well as related concepts that would not be taught directly. For example, an advance organizer for a lesson about the election of the first president of the United States might also contain information about the Constitutional provisions for choosing the president. These statements, which extend beyond the learning reach of the students, can "direct your attention to what is important in the coming material; they highlight relationships among ideas that will be presented; and remind you of relevant information you already have" (Woolfolk, 2001, p. 288).

From Ausubel's early work in the use of advance organizers, others began to apply these theories to visual representations of concepts. Although not completely understood, it appears that information is organized in the brain through networks of associations, rather than via a linear arrangement of facts (Paivio, 1986). This theory of dual coding holds that knowledge is organized both verbally and nonverbally through visual and auditory memory. At a given moment, information is recalled by activating visual and verbal representations of the concepts needed. It is for this reason that best practices in learning require that students receive and process information using a variety of modalities. Establishing and strengthening these pathways enhance retention and retrieval of information.

Many content-area textbooks routinely contain graphic organizers that are designed to be used with specific passages or chapters. A persistent question is whether students should generate their own, or whether it is better to have a graphic organizer selected in advance for them. Although there are conflicting findings on this matter, it appears that learner-developed graphic organizers work best when the purpose is to generate another product, such as a writing assignment. Conversely, if the purpose is to glean information from a written passage, a preassigned graphic organizer may be better (Stull & Mayer, 2007). At issue is the subject of cognitive load, which varies from student to student. There is great benefit to students who create their own graphic organizers, as this task challenges them to put information into a logical form. However, for some students, the additional attention needed to determine exactly what graphic organizer might work best for a particular task may shift their attention away from the material itself. This is especially true when the information is new, extends over many pages, or is written in a manner that doesn't make apparent how the information is organized (e.g., a lack of signal words).

Another factor related to its effectiveness is how the graphic organizer is used. Without established purposes, even the best graphic organizer is reduced to the level of a worksheet. Any graphic organizer, whether two- or three-dimensional, should be an intermediate step to something else. Students need to think, speak, and write using these organizers as a tool. In other words, they need to "transform ideas in their head and on paper" (Fisher, Schell, & Frey, 2004, p. 26). The first phase is during the initial development of the headings for the interactive graphic organizer. This practice provides students with initial schema-building experience, much like setting up a file drawer of information that will come. When students have a basic framework of hierarchical representations by which to order new information, they are more likely to retain and retrieve it (McVee, Dunmore, & Gavelek, 2005). In addition, a partially constructed graphic organizer directs student attention to the most important information. In one study, students who developed graphic organizers that were partially constructed outperformed peers who used skeletal or completed graphic organizers (Robinson, Katayama, Odom, Hsieh, & Vanderveen, 2006).

A clearly established purpose for the graphic organizer further enhances students' learning experience (Fisher & Frey, 2008). When students have an idea of what they will eventually do with the graphic organizer, they are better able to construct it in a manner that better suits the needs of the task. For example, an interactive graphic organizer on the characteristics of the protagonist and antagonist in a novel can be utilized in a literature circle discussion with peers. Other purposes include more formal writing experiences. A layer book on the five pillars of Islam could be used to organize a formal essay on the topic. A graphic organizer can also be used as an aid during productive group tasks, as when students consult their three-dimensional graphic organizer to solve a complex word problem using algebraic computation.

WHAT ARE SOME ALTERNATIVES?

A good solution to the dilemma of cognitive load versus self-generation in the interactive graphic organizer is the Foldable. This category of specialized graphic organizers was first developed by Zike (2009) when she was a middle school student herself. Determined to make sense of the flood of information coming at her as a sixth grader, she began transcribing her notes using folded paper. She found that this technique aided her in recalling information as well as acquiring new learning. As she progressed through high school and college, she began sharing her "paper-based study aids" (p. 8) with classmates. During her career as a teacher, she expanded the types of interactive graphic organizers and where and when they could be applied.

Basic Folds

Most folds are made using an 8½″ × 11″ sheet of notebook paper or printer paper. The simplest folds involve folding the paper in half lengthwise (commonly called a "hot dog" fold, a term first coined by Zike), and then folding again into three, four, or five sections. Once creased, students, cut on the lines they have made to make tabs. Each tab is then labeled with the major concept, and notes are added to the interior of the fold. (For a two-tab interactive graphic organizer, fold the paper widthwise, then crease in half to create the line where it will be cut. This is commonly called a "hamburger fold.")

The key to determining the number of tabs needed is deciding how many concepts should be linked together. For example, the three branches of government (executive, legislative, and judicial) would require a three-tab fold. A four-tab fold would be useful for taking notes about the influences of Washington, Jefferson, Adams, and Madison on the development of the U.S. Constitution. Notes on the five Southern colonies (Maryland, Virginia, South Carolina, North Carolina, and Georgia) would require a five-tab fold.

A Venn diagram can be added to the outside of a three-tab fold to challenge students to compare and contrast concepts. For instance, this type of fold could be used to compare the English settlements of the Jamestown and Roanoke colonies to speculate why the first survived whereas the second may have failed. Each of the outside tabs would contain notes about unique aspects of the colony in question, including its location, size, and year it was first established. The center tab is reserved for concepts held in common between the two. For example, both suffered from the impact of disease, weather, and ill-prepared settlers. As students learn more about each, they add information about each colony's relationship with the Native American people who had lived there for thousands of years, and the differences in economic prosperity. Although this information is typically built over several lessons, the use of an interactive graphic organizer allows students to return to it and add new information. In the meantime, they are continually reminded of the way the two concepts are associated with each other. This dimensionality assists students in disrupting the perception that learning is the ability to memorize a string of unrelated facts.

Still another variation of this basic fold requires students to section a sheet of lined notebook paper into eight tabs, cutting on every third line of the page. This fold is useful for organizing content vocabulary. The target word is written on the outside of each tab, with definitional, contrastive, and contextual information written on the inside and back of the graphic organizer. For instance, a list of terms related to Washington's first term in office would appear on the outside (*president, election, electoral college, inauguration, oath of office, terms of office, Whiskey Rebellion*, and *Fugitive Slave Act of 1793*). On the first inside surface, the student writes a definition of the term in his or her own words ("An election is when people vote for a person or a rule, and the majority wins"). The second inside surface is used for a contrastive meaning ("An appointment is when there is no election and a person is assigned a job"). On the back surface, the student uses the term in a sentence ("Every four years there is an election to vote for a president"). Importantly, these definitions and applications are intended to be used as study aids. Although their creation is an important first step, it is what happens *after* that reinforces vocabulary learning. Please see Chapter 13 for further information about vocabulary acquisition. A diagram of these basic folds can be found in Figure 19.1.

Advanced Folds

Although tab folds are useful for many conceptual associations, other types are better suited for visually representing these relationships. A layered fold requires two or more sheets of paper, and is an excellent choice for grouping a larger number of related concepts together. For example, students in science learn about the five layers of the atmosphere. However, the terms are confusing (they all end with -*sphere*) and keeping the characteristics straight can be a challenge. Students often try to learn these in isolation from one another, which puts them at a disadvantage because they fail to see how the temperature and density progress as the altitude rises. A layered fold makes this progression more apparent. To make a five-layer book, place three sheets of paper on top of one another and stagger the length by about 1 inch each page. Fold the layered paper hamburger-style and glue

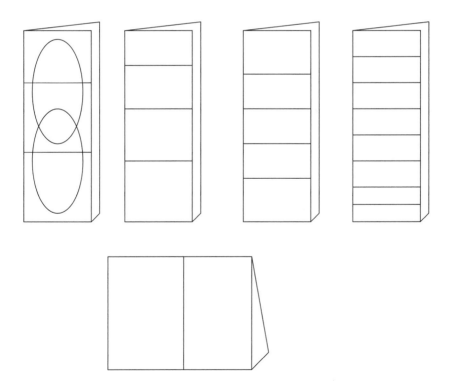

FIGURE 19.1. Basic folds for interactive graphic organizers.

or staple the fold together. (If gluing, run a small bead of glue on the inside of each fold.) Each folded layer is labeled with the levels of the atmosphere, starting with the highest (*exosphere, thermosphere, mesosphere, stratosphere,* and *troposphere*).

Another type of fold that offers students more space and further reinforces physical or temporal associations is the shutter fold. This requires only one sheet of paper but a bit more folding to accomplish. Hold the paper in either a portrait or landscape orientation and locate its midpoint. Don't crease it, but rather just pinch it so that there is a small visible mark. Place the paper on a flat surface and bring each edge to the midpoint so that the paper resembles the closed shutters on a house. Make the same kind of "pinch" mark on both shutters make a horizontal cut on each side. The result is a shutter fold with a total of four tabs. This fold can be used to organize four concepts, of course, but consider the opportunity to highlight sequence and placement. A great example of this is with the Cartesian coordinates used for graphing in mathematics. Make the shutter fold using a 11" × 17" piece of paper. Label each tab with a coordinate type and place a corresponding sheet of graph paper inside (the larger paper will allow for a standard sheet of paper to fit perfectly inside). The graph paper can be labeled with the same portions of a graph, with the x-axis and y-axis falling at the center. The graph underneath then aligns with the coordinate labels on the shutter fold. Please refer to Figure 19.2 for examples of the layer fold and shutter fold.

Following the confidential conversation Ms. Richardson had with her peer coach, she revised her use of graphic organizers for an upcoming unit. Instead of using two-dimensional, flat, photocopied graphic organizers, Ms. Richardson introduced her students to interactive graphic organizers. Unlike her previous attempts to integrate graphic organizers into her instruction, the use of Foldables provided her students with an opportunity to interact with the content and their notes simultaneously.

For example, as they were reading their textbook and learning about Manifest Destiny, students took notes using a layered book. On the top, students wrote *Manifest Destiny* and then previewed the text to find out which places would be discussed. On the tabs of their layered books, students wrote places such as *Oregon Country, Texas, New Mexico, California,* and *Utah.* As they read and discussed the text, they updated their notes. For example, during a discussion about the Oregon Trail, students shared the notes they had taken on their Foldables. An excerpt of one of the group conversations highlights the rigor of students' discourse and the learning that occurred as a result of deeply thinking about the text.

BRANDON: When I first started reading this, I was thinking that they really did get sick. Do you remember when they said *Oregon*

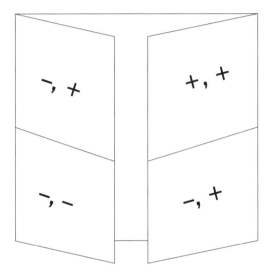

FIGURE 19.2. Advanced folds for interactive graphic organizers.

Fever? I was thinking that it was like that movie about the disease that killed all those people in France.

DEVON: Yeah, I know, that Black Plague, that's what I was thinking, too. But then it says *migration*, which was the word we learned in the beginning.

BRANDON: Yeah, I know it's not really that death, but I thought that first. I think it's cool how people were making plans to survive the trip.

JESSICA: Yeah, I wrote that it was 2,000 miles and they had to go in the covered wagons. Here's the picture that I drew of the wagon. I saw these on a TV show.

DEVON: That's how I pictured it. Can I look again so that I can draw one, too?

BRANDON: I put in my notes all of the places that they had to go though to get to Oregon, like the Great Plains, Platte River, and the Rocky Mountains.

JESSICA: What does it mean, the *Great Plains*? I think I've heard it, but I don't really know what it means.

BRANDON: It's the part in the middle of the United States—see, right here (*pointing to his map*)—because its long and flat.

DEVON: I Googled it, and it says that it's grassland. And it says that's where the buffalo lived, like from the song, "where buffalo roam." You remember that one?

JESSICA: Oh, yeah, "Home, home on the range"—that one. I'm writing that down to remember.

BRANDON: I have in my notes this word: *emigrants*. But I don't know why I have it there. I know that emigrants are people who move into the country. I don't get it. I gotta look again (*referring back to the text*).

JESSICA: But it says that they *left* the United States. Because, remember, that Oregon wasn't in the country yet. So they had to leave to get to Oregon. That's hard to think about because I think of Oregon as one of our states. But it didn't used to be that way. So those people had to *leave* the country to get there.

DEVON: Yeah, it says right here, "They left the United States to go to Oregon." I missed that before, but I bet that's important. That's what *emigrants* means.

BRANDON: But I thought it was about people who moved in, not who moved out.

DEVON: I'll Google it (taking out his smartphone). No, it says that *emigrant* is a person who leaves his or her country. Oh, wait, on Wikipedia, it says that *immigrants* are people who come in, *emigrants* are people who leave. It's those words that sound the same, but have different meanings.

JESSICA: *Homophones*. Cool! I bet we're the only ones with this info!

As her students fold, think, talk, and write, Ms. Richardson meets with groups of students and listens to their conversations. No longer wanting to remain confidential, Ms. Richardson proudly exclaims at a staff meeting a few days later, "My students were working! They took responsibility and asked and answered questions of each other, all because I gave them a tool that encouraged thinking."

CONCLUSION

Without purposes for constructing graphic organizers, such as discussion and writing, even the most well-designed graphic organizers are nothing more than glorified worksheets. The key to the usefulness of any kind of visual representation of information lies in the interactions between the student and the content. This interaction is strengthened with three-dimensional graphic organizers that build associations between concepts. This is a first step in establishing schema so that students can recall and manipulate information. In addition, the active nature of constructing these teaching aids further reinforces new information. Middle school students crave the kinds of learning experiences that allow them to take an active part in the classroom, and these graphic organizers are a way for them to do so.

ADDITIONAL RESOURCES AND LESSON EXAMPLES

Books

The materials useful for developing three-dimensional graphic organizers are plentiful and readily available for middle school teachers in all content areas. The following books address the practical elements of constructing and using them.

Zike, D. (2001). *Big book of science for middle and high school*. San Antonio, TX: Dinah-Mite.

Zike, D. (2003). *Big book of math for middle and high school*. San Antonio, TX: Dinah-Mite.

Zike, D. (2004). *Big book of United States history for middle and high school*. San Antonio, TX: Dinah-Mite.

Zike, D. (2009). *Foldables: Notebook foldables and VKVs for spelling and vocabulary*. San Antonio, TX: Dinah-Mite.

Websites

The following websites provide useful examples of how these graphic organizers are used by teachers.

Dinah Zike's website

www.dinah.com

Foldables wiki for Teachers

foldables.wikispaces.com

Get in the Fold blog

getinthefold.blogspot.com

Articles

Several articles describe ways in which educators use three-dimensional graphic organizers with secondary students.

Fisher, D., Zike, D., & Frey, N. (2007, August). Foldables: Improving learning with 3-D interactive graphic organizers. *Classroom Notes Plus, 25*(1), 1–14.

Hill, R. C. (1994). Concept mapping, graphic organizing and structuring: Visual techniques for functional content-centered reading comprehension. *Education, 115*, 26–30.

Leno, L. C., & Dougherty, L. A. (2007). Using direct instruction to teach content vocabulary. *Science Scope, 31*(1), 63–66.

REFERENCES

Ausubel, D. P. (1960). The use of advance organizers in the learning and retention of meaningful verbal material. *Journal of Educational Psychology, 51*, 267–272.

Fisher, D., & Frey, N. (2008). *Better learning through structured teaching: A framework for the gradual release of responsibility.* Alexandria, VA: Association for Supervision and Curriculum Development.

Fisher, D., Schell, E., & Frey, N. (2004). "In your mind and on the paper": Teaching students to transform (and own) texts. *Social Studies Review, 43*(1), 26–31.

Fisher, D., Zike, D., & Frey, N. (2007, August). Foldables: Improving learning with 3-D interactive graphic organizers. *Classroom Notes Plus, 25*(1), 1–14.

Irwin-DeVitis, L., & Pease, D. (1995). Using graphic organizers and assessment in middle level classrooms. *Middle School Journal, 26*, 57–64.

McVee, M. B., Dunmore, K., & Gavelek, J. R. (2005). Schema theory revisited. *Review of Educational Research, 75*(4), 531–566.

Paivio, A. (1986). *Mental representations.* New York: Oxford University Press.

Robinson, D. H., Katayama, A. D., Odom, A. B. S., Hsieh, Y. P., & Vanderveen, A. (2006). Increasing text comprehension and graphic note taking using a partial graphic organizer. *Journal of Educational Research, 100*(2), 103–111.

Robinson, D. H., & Kiewra, K. A. (1995). Visual argument: Graphic organizers are superior to outlines in improving learning from text. *Journal of Educational Psychology, 87*(3), 455–467.

Stull, A. T., & Mayer, R. E. (2007). Learning by doing versus learning by viewing: Three experimental comparisons of learner-generated versus author-provided graphic organizers. *Journal of Educational Psychology, 99*(4), 808–820.

Woolfolk, A. (2001). *Educational psychology* (8th ed.). Saddle River, NJ: Prentice-Hall.

Zike, D. (2009). *Foldables, notebook foldables, and VKVs for spelling and vocabulary: Test prep, academic vocabulary, and ESL strategies 4th–12th.* San Antonio, TX: Dinah-Mite.

CHAPTER 20

If Homework Really Matters— Assign Some That's Valuable

Cynthia H. Brock
Julie L. Pennington
Jennifer D. Morrison

Key Points for This Chapter

- Research demonstrates that homework is more useful for middle and high school students. Experts suggest 10 minutes of homework per grade level (e.g., 10 minutes for first grade, 60 minutes for sixth grade).

- Children need support to be successful with homework, including access to after-school programs and access to the resources needed to successfully complete homework.

- Homework should be differentiated and meaningful for students; it should build upon skills and concepts already learned in class.

A BIRD'S-EYE VIEW OF HOMEWORK PRACTICE

David and Shakeya are sixth-grade students who attend a math/science magnet school couched within a large inner-city middle school in Dallas, Texas. Approximately 75% of the over 2,000 students in the middle school are African American. Over 90% of the 200+ students in the math/

science magnet school are European American. David and Shakeya have four classes together (i.e., math, science, language arts, and social studies); the focus of this chapter is their homework in these four classes. We begin this chapter by sharing some background information about Shakeya and David and their magnet school. Then we talk about the homework practices in Shakeya's and David's four common classes, beginning with math and social studies.

The math/science magnet school that Shakeya and David attend has a reputation for being one of the most prestigious schools in the district. Admission to the magnet school is determined by a rigorous application process that includes examining students' standardized test scores, overall grades, personal and professional references, and propensity for engaging successfully in math and science. During "Back-to-School Night," parents of Shakeya and David, recent admissions to the magnet school, were told that they are expected to provide nightly homework assistance to their children.

Even though Shakeya and David both show considerable promise in math and science, their lives could not be more different. Shakeya is an only child. Her parents are divorced, and she lives with her mother, who is the director of a prestigious private preschool. Shakeya's father is an engineer who lives in the same city as Shakeya and her mother. Shakeya spends time with her father every week. David is the oldest of four children. He lives with his mother and three siblings in public housing. David's mother works long hours at a minimum-wage job. When David's mother works in the evenings, David babysits for his younger brother and sisters.

So, what do homework assignments in social studies and math typically look like for David and Shakeya as they begin their school year, and how do David and Shakeya typically complete their homework? First, both Shakeya's and David's social studies and math teachers rely heavily on the respective course texts for their class work and their homework assignments. While the school has a policy of no more than 2 hours of homework per night, because many of the teachers do not talk about the homework they are assigning, some teachers—such as Shakeya's and David's math and social studies teachers—often assign 2 hours of homework in their individual classes alone. In social studies, Shakeya and David are learning about world cultures. Most of their social studies class time is spent engaging in round-robin reading from the social studies text. (See Chapters 2 and 5 in this volume for information about using social studies texts in instruction as well as round-robin reading.) Shakeya and David typically have social studies homework on Tuesdays and Thursdays. Each of those nights, the students are expected to finish reading the chapters begun in class that day and answer the questions at the end.

David and Shakeya are assigned math homework every evening that consists primarily of drill and practice; however, their math teacher assigns drill and practice work with a twist. She does not send pages with math problems home for children to complete; rather, she requires her students to access and complete their math homework problems online, arguing that this not only saves paper, but gives students much-needed practice with technology. While their math teacher typically lectures on the types of problems that Shakeya and David are required to do for homework, they are sometimes assigned homework problems they have not covered in class. It is important to note that Shakeya's and David's social studies and math teachers are well intentioned. They each see homework as a means to help children practice and extend what they are learning in class. Moreover, they see homework as an important way to help prepare children for college.

DEFINING THE TARGETED PRACTICE

Homework (i.e., school-related academic tasks completed outside the classroom) has been a mainstay in U.S. schools for over a century (Vatterott, 2009). Interestingly, however, both public attitudes toward homework and actual homework tasks have shifted considerably over the past century (Brock, Lapp, Flood, Fisher, & Han, 2007; Cooper, Lindsay, Nye, & Greathouse, 1998). For example, during the late 1800s and early 1900s, most homework consisted of drill and memorization (Vatterott, 2009). Current homework practices can still include rote memorization and drill, but they can also include activities such as the development of extensive social studies or science projects using technology (Mendicino, Razzaq, & Heffernan, 2009). Just as homework practices have varied across time, so have Americans' attitudes toward homework (Vatterott, 2009). For example, in the early 1900s, progressive educators questioned homework practices and, in particular, the value of rote memorization and drill (Cooper & Valentine, 2001). However, during other eras, such as the 1950s with the Russian launching of the Sputnik satellite, and the current push to improve test scores, public opinion has favored homework, and many Americans have viewed homework as integral to children's academic success (Cooper et al., 1998; Cooper & Valentine, 2001). Although public opinion about homework is an important consideration for teachers, perhaps more important is the current research on homework. By understanding current research, teachers can both inform and educate parents. In the following section, we explore research pertaining to homework. In particular, we examine what research studies have to say about the math and social studies homework practices in which David and Shakeya's teachers engage.

WHAT DOES THE RESEARCH SAY
ABOUT HOMEWORK PRACTICES?

What does research have to say about the homework practices of Shakeya's and David's math and social studies teachers? First, teachers must consider issues of equity when establishing homework practices. Bloom (2009) argues that "homework itself is intrinsically discriminatory" (p. 15) and "one in five homework tasks unfairly benefits middle class pupils" (p. 15) like Shakeya because poorer students do not have access to necessary resources, including books, paper, writing instruments, parental support, and particularly, computers with Internet access. Sallee and Rigler (2008) agree that differences in access need to be taken into account when teachers assign homework because failure to do so can inadvertently widen the achievement gaps most educators are "committed to closing" (p. 49). Although some educators may argue that students without resources, such as computers, could simply go to a library or other public location to use computers, this solution does not account for other factors students in poverty may experience, such as family commitments, jobs, lack of transportation, and lack of quiet spaces in which to work (Bloom, 2009; Milne, 2008). For example, David's mother works most evenings, so she is not available to help David with his homework. His family does not own a computer, nor do they have Internet access. Finally, since David often babysits his younger siblings in the afternoons and evenings while his mother works, it is not possible for him to go to the library to use computers. Clearly, David's home situation puts him at a disadvantage for having the necessary time, resources, and support to complete his homework.

Students have varying resources available to them at home that can make homework experiences vastly different for each individual. As researchers have argued, homework is inherently discriminatory to impoverished children (Wormeli, 2006). It may also be discriminatory to immigrant students, students learning the English language, and students who speak African American Vernacular English as a primary discourse because teachers may grade more for behavior than academic quality (Wormeli, 2006). However, Sallee (2010) reminds us that homework can be inequitable for other students as well. Sallee found that reading speeds among her students ranged from .16 pages per minute to 1.29 pages per minute. For a 20-page assignment, what might take a faster reader 15 minutes to complete could translate into more than 2 hours for a slower reader. What a teacher may intend to take a short period of time may actually become cumbersome and hopeless, especially when such reading is assigned repeatedly over time. Recall that David's and Shakeya's social studies teacher assigns reading from their text and questions to answer at the end of the chapter twice a week. Although David demonstrates tremendous proficiency in math and science, he struggles in reading. The social studies assignment for a student such as Shakeya may take less than an hour to finish; however, that same assignment takes David well over 2 hours to complete.

A final concern with the nature of the social studies and math homework that Shakeya and David are assigned is that it is tedious, irrelevant, purposeless, and daunting. Homework of this nature does little to improve students' academic achievement; on the contrary, it often turns children off to school, in general, and to specific subjects, in particular (Sallee, 2010; Wormeli, 2006). In order for homework to motivate students and benefit them academically, it should be authentic, project-based, inquiry learning generated by students' questions, ideas, and opinions or thematically organized concepts related to specific disciplines (Nelms, 2008). In the following section, we highlight the more effective homework practices in which David's and Shakeya's English and science teachers engage as well as the research that supports these more effective homework practices.

WHAT ARE SOME ALTERNATIVES?

Homework in English and science is very different for Shakeya and David. In science, David and Shakeya have been engaged in a unit on how different kinds of living things have adapted to and survived in their respective environments. One of the students' tasks within the unit, some of which was completed in class and some of which was completed as homework, was to work with a partner, choose a living thing, research its environment and the ways in which the living thing survived in and adapted to its environment, and create a PowerPoint to share their findings with other students and parents at a Back-to-School night event. Throughout the unit, the science teacher, Mrs. Lawson, provided extensive scaffolding to the students on both the science inquiry process and the research process (Douglas, Klentschy, Worth, & Binder, 2006; Worthy, Broaddus, & Ivey, 2001). Additionally, Mrs. Lawson had recently written and received a technology grant. As a part of the grant, she bought 20 laptops that her students could take turns checking out to use during after-school hours.

In English, David and Shakeya had been reading a novel entitled *Maurice Dufault: Vice Principal* (Primeau, 2006). One of the words used in the book is *jackass*. In conjunction with reading, talking about, and writing about the book using a book club instructional framework (e.g., Raphael, Florio-Ruane, & George, 2001), the class studied censorship as well as the genre of persuasive writing (Tompkins, 2008). One homework assignment involved engaging in a prewriting task pertaining to taking a stand about banning books that include controversial language and/or ideas, such as *Vice Principal*. This prewriting task involved completing a graphic organizer that included components in a persuasive argument, and prior to assigning the homework, the teacher modeled how to complete such a graphic organizer in class. After bringing their prewriting homework to class, students then chose an audience (e.g., parents, school board members) and worked in small groups to create persuasive projects (e.g., essays, brief multimedia messages) to present their ideas.

Undoubtedly, the nature of homework in social studies and math is very different from the homework assigned in science and English for Shakeya and David. What are some of the key differences, and what does research have to say about these differences? First, the homework tasks in English and science are high quality and purposeful; additionally, they are authentic, project-based, and inquiry oriented (Nelms, 2008). Finally, the homework tasks in English and science are differentiated. At the heart of differentiation is the idea that people learn differently, have different passions and interests, and are ready to learn material at different times; however, every student and every person has something valuable to contribute. Although standards and expectations are set high for everyone, the paths students take to reach those standards may vary in method and time frame (Tomlinson, 2001, 2003). To be effective, differentiation requires precisely what the homework research calls for: clarity of purpose, high standards, explicit explanation to students, and flexibility in achieving objectives (Tomlinson, 2001).

Research focusing on homework points increasingly to the need to differentiate not just learning that occurs within the classroom, but also assignments students take home (Bang, Suarez-Orozco, Pakes, & O'Connor, 2009; Sallee & Rigler, 2008; Vatterott, 2009; Wormeli, 2006). This differentiation may include providing the following:

- Accommodations to avoid unfairly penalizing students from non-dominant backgrounds, such as well-equipped libraries and after-school homework programs for impoverished, struggling, or immigrant students (Bang et al., 2009; Huang & Cho, 2009)
- Instructional scaffolding such as matrices, graphic organizers, or modified texts (Wormeli, 2006)
- Greater choices or input in homework tasks (Sallee, 2010)
- Increased use of inquiry-based, independent study (Nelms, 2008).

By providing homework tasks differentiated by course content, processes, and products based on students' readiness levels, their individual interests, and their learning modalities, students are more invested in the work and more capable of independently learning in their time away from school (Tomlinson, 2001, 2003; Wormeli, 2006).

Clearly, the different kinds of homework tasks assigned by Shakeya's and David's science and English teachers included many of the kinds of differentiation that scholars (e.g., Bang et al., 2009; Nelms, 2008; Wormeli, 2006) consider important. For example, Mrs. Lawson, Shakeya's and David's science teacher, got a grant so that she could provide laptop computers to students who did not have access to computers at home. The students' English teacher made sure that she provided extensive scaffolding on the use of graphic organizers prior to asking her students to complete them as homework assignments. Both teachers gave inquiry-based homework and made sure students had input and choice with respect to homework content and products.

In addition to differentiating homework in the ways previously mentioned, Vatterott (2009) calls for designing homework tasks that support students' learning in four different ways. (1) Some homework tasks can focus on *prelearning*, which stimulates interest or builds anticipation. (2) Other homework tasks can focus on *checking for understanding*, where teachers determine the extent of student concept mastery. (3) Still other homework tasks can focus on *practice of concepts already understood* and measured through informal assessment within the supported classroom environment. (4) Finally, some homework tasks can focus on *processing*, wherein students reflect upon new learning, apply skills, or synthesize information. She asserts that quality homework tasks must have clear academic purpose, a positive effect on student efficacy, and be personally relevant to students.

The different homework tasks provided by David's and Shakeya's science and English teachers address many of these different ways to support students' learning. For example, their English teacher modeled in class how to use a graphic organizer to construct a persuasive argument. As a homework assignment, the students were asked to create their own graphic organizer, focused on persuading others to "buy" their argument on book banning. When the students brought their own graphic organizers back to class the next day to work in small groups with others, the teacher could see the extent to which individuals understood how to construct a persuasive argument. That is, she could *check their understanding*. Because the students were using ideas from their own graphic organizers to construct an overall argument within their small groups, however, they were not penalized if they did not fully understand the process of using a graphic organizer to construct a persuasive argument. Thus, by working individually on their homework and then working together in small groups the next day, the students could meaningfully *practice the concepts* involved in creating a persuasive argument, which is a complex genre for children to master (Tompkins, 2008).

Finally, the science inquiry project assigned by Mrs. Lawson provides an example of using homework tasks to help students *process their learning*. As the children worked together to create their PowerPoints on living things adapting to their environments, they were reflecting on their learning, including the science content as well as the science inquiry and research processes, synthesizing what they were learning, and applying this newly gained knowledge in the creation of their PowerPoint presentations.

CONCLUSION

So far in this chapter, we have talked about the nature of homework that research suggests we as teachers should, or should not, assign. We have not, however, talked about the relative value of homework across grade levels and how much homework should be assigned. We address these issues briefly now. Although most current research claims that homework in moderation is linked positively to student achievement (cf. Cooper, 1989; Cooper, Robinson, & Patall, 2006; Milne, 2008; Sallee & Rigler, 2008; Zimmerman & Kitsantas, 2005), research also indicates that homework is more beneficial for middle and high school students and less beneficial for elementary students (Cooper, 1989). Most studies recommend a maximum of 1½–2 hours of homework per night for secondary students; less for elementary students (e.g., see Brock, Lapp, & Fisher, in press; Cooper, 1989; Cooper et al., 2006; Dettmers, Trautwein, Ludtke, Kunter, & Baumert, 2010; Nelms, 2008; Tang & Fu, 2008; Vatterott, 2009). As noted previously, Cooper (1989; Cooper et al., 2006), recommends a useful rule of thumb for how much homework to assign: 10 minutes per student's grade level. A first grader would then have a maximum of 10 minutes of homework per night (10 minutes × 1); an eighth grader no more than 80 minutes of homework (10 × 8). Given that most scholars point to the need to assign homework in moderation, it becomes important that we as teachers carefully design the homework tasks we assign so that they optimize student learning by being meaningful, purposeful, and engaging.

As we conclude this chapter, we draw on the work of Bang and colleagues (2009) to provide some key ideas to keep in mind in assigning students homework. Notice that these ideas reflect the more positive homework practices in which David's and Shakeya's science and English teachers engaged:

- Use assigned homework to build upon skills and concepts first learned thoroughly in class.
- Recognize possible homework impediments for students from nondominant backgrounds and provide accommodations to avoid unfairly penalizing them for limited knowledge of the English language, limited knowledge of expectations in U.S. classrooms, or lack of resources.

- Provide after-school programs and resources to support students' ability to do homework.
- Avoid giving good grades to students who are merely compliant with doing homework and not submitting high-quality work or who have not gained mastery of course content. This undesirable practice inadvertently conveys low expectations.
- Communicate criteria for high performance explicitly to all students.
- Distinguish between effort and skill and provide separate feedback in each area.

It is clear that teachers and parents expect students to be responsible for successfully completing their homework (Brock et al., 2007; Cooper et al., 1998; Cooper & Valentine, 2001). However, according to Fisher and Frey (2008), "'responsibility' is a two way street" (p. 45). That is, just as students have responsibilities with respect to homework, so too do teachers. The current research on homework, reviewed in this chapter, emphasizes that it is not just students who must be responsible for out-of-class assignments. Teachers must be thoughtful and purposeful with homework assigned, taking into account degrees of access to required resources, learning challenges that may interfere with students' abilities to successfully complete homework, and ways in which assignments meet both course objectives and individual students' needs.

ADDITIONAL RESOURCES

The following websites provide valuable information about homework and homework practices. For additional information about homework, type the word *homework* into the search engine for each website below.

Discovery Education
www.discoveryeducation.com/students

International Reading Association
www.reading.org

National Council of Teachers of English
www.ncte.org

National Parent Teacher Association
www.pta.org/topic_student_success.asp

TRADE BOOK CITED IN TEXT

Primeau, M. (2006). *Maurice Dufault: Vice principal.* Calgary, Canada: University of Calgary Press.

REFERENCES

Bang, H. J., Suarez-Orozco, C., Pakes, J., & O'Connor, E. (2009). The importance of homework in determining immigrant students' grades in schools in the USA context. *Educational Research, 51*(1), 1–25.

Bloom, A. (2009, July 3). How homework is weighted in favor of middle classes. *Times Educational Supplement*, p. 15.

Brock, C. H., Lapp, D., & Fisher, D. (in press). Homework practices: Myths and realities. *The California Reader.*

Brock, C. H., Lapp, D., Flood, J., Fisher, D., & Han, K. (2007). Does homework matter?: An investigation of teacher perception about homework practices for children from non-dominant background. *Urban Education, 43,* 6.

Cooper, H. (1989). Synthesis of research on homework. *Educational Leadership, 47*(3), 85–91.

Cooper, H., Lindsay, J. J., Nye, B., & Greathouse, S. (1998). Relationships among attitudes about homework, amount of homework assigned and completed, and student achievement. *Journal of Educational Psychology, 90*(1), 70–83.

Cooper, H., Robinson, J. C., & Patall, E. A. (2006). Does homework improve academic achievement?: A synthesis of research, 1987–2003. *Review of Educational Research, 76*(1), 1–62.

Cooper, H., & Valentine, J. C. (2001). Using research to answer practical questions about homework. *Educational Psychologist, 36*(3), 143–153.

Dettmers, S., Trautwein, U., Ludtke, O., Kunter, M., & Baumert, J. (2010). Homework works if homework quality is high: Using multilevel modeling to predict the development of achievement in mathematics. *Journal of Educational Psychology, 102*(2), 467–482.

Douglas, R., Klentschy, M., Worth, K., & Binder, W. (2006). *Linking science and literacy in the K–8 classroom.* Arlington, VA: National Science Teachers Association.

Fisher, D., & Frey, N. (2008). Homework and the gradual release of responsibility: Making "responsibility" possible. *English Journal, 98*(2), 40–45.

Huang, D., & Cho, J. (2009). Academic enrichment in high-functioning homework afterschool programs. *Journal of Research in Childhood Education, 23*(3), 382–392.

Mendicino, M., Razzaq, L., & Heffernan, N. (2009). A comparison of traditional homework to computer-supported homework. *Journal of Research on Technology in Education, 41*(3), 331–359.

Milne, J. (2008, February 1). Homework falls victim to the economic divide. *Times Educational Supplement*, pp. 16–17. Retrieved from *www.tes.co.uk/article. aspx?storycode=2577590.*

Nelms, B. (2008). Homework on homework: Involving students with a controversial issue. *English Journal, 98*(2), 22–29.

Raphael, T. E., Florio-Ruane, S., & George, M. (2001). Book Club Plus: A conceptual framework to organize literacy instruction. *Language Arts, 79*(2), 159–169.

Sallee, B. (2010). The best of times?: A tale of teaching, reading, and homework. *English Journal, 99*(6), 89–92.

Sallee, B., & Rigler, N. (2008). Doing our homework on homework: How does homework help? *English Journal, 98*(2), 46–51.

Tang, L., & Fu, L. (2008). An empirical study of relationship between schoolwork burden and academic achievements. *Front Education China, 3*(4), 504–515.

Tomlinson, C. A. (2001). *How to differentiate instruction in mixed-ability classrooms.* Alexandria, VA: Association for Supervision and Curriculum Development.

Tomlinson, C. A. (2003). *Fulfilling the promise of the differentiated classroom.* Alexandria, VA: Association for Supervision and Curriculum Development.

Tompkins, G. (2008). *Teaching writing: Balancing process and product.* Columbus, OH: Merrill Prentice-Hall.

Vatterott, C. (2009). *Rethinking homework: Best practices that support diverse needs.* Alexandria, VA: Association for Supervision and Curriculum Development.

Wormeli, R. (2006). *Fair isn't always equal: Assessing and grading in the differentiated classroom.* Portland, ME: Stenhouse.

Worthy, J., Broaddus, K., & Ivey, G. (2001). *Pathways to independence: Reading, writing, and learning in grades 3–8.* New York: Guilford Press.

Zimmerman, B. J., & Kitsantas, A. (2005). Homework practices and academic achievement: The mediating role of self-efficacy and perceived responsibility beliefs. *Contemporary Educational Psychology, 30*(4), 397–417.

Index

Page numbers in *italic* indicate a figure or table

Literacy, impact on student self-perception, 170
Literacy education
    hybrid literacy curriculum, 99, 101–102
    new literacies perspective, 92–93. *See also* New literacies

"Managed choice," 76
Mathematics instruction
    context-based approach, 45–48
    direct instruction
        alternatives to, 37–39
        classroom practice, 35–36
        defined, 36
        research about, 36
        resources, 39
    integrated curriculum approach, 37–39, 41–43
    "teaching by telling"
        alternatives to, 41–43
        classroom practice, 39–40
        defined, 40
        research about, 40–41
        resources, 43
    undoing approach to solving algebraic equations
        alternatives to, 45–47
        classroom practice, 44
        defined, 44
        research about, 44–45
        resources, 48
    using social media in, 61–62
    using young adult literature in, 57–58
"Mentor texts," 148
Metacognitive skills, 8–10
Mini-lessons, in writing, 163
Morphemes, 219–220
Motivation. *See* Reading motivation; Writing motivation
"Multiliteracies pedagogy," 91
Multimodal collaborative learning, 228–229, 233–236
Multiple texts, 58–59

"Narrative effect," 58
Neurological impress method, 266–267
New American Lecture strategy, 302–303, *304*
New ethos, 91
New literacies
    classroom practice, 89
    components of, 91–92
    definitions of, 90, 91
    designing comics, 97–99, *100*, 101
    hybrid literacy curriculum, 99, 101–102
    podcasts, 89, 93–95, *96*
    research about, 90–93

resources, 102–103
    VoiceThread, 93, 96–97
Nicenet discussion board website, *252*, *254*, *255*
Note taking
    classroom practice, 292–293
    Cornell notes, 300–301
    functions of, 294
    gradual release model of instruction and, 296
    importance of, 306–307
    interactive notebooks, 304–306
    lesson examples, 307
    New American Lecture strategy, 302–303, *304*
    research about, 293–295
    skeletal note taking, 296–298, *299*
    strategic note taking, 298–299, *300*

Online discussion forums
    benefits of, 246–247
    with a history book club, 249–250, *252–253*, *254*, *255*
    resources, 258
    VoiceThread, 93, 96–97, 256–257
Online history book club project, 247–256
Online inquiry
    benefits of, 107–108
    critical thinking skills involved in, 109
Online inquiry instruction
    creating a customized search engine, 114, *115*
    encouraging peer support for critical evaluation, 117–118
    finding out what students know about critical evaluation, 111–112
    gathering information from a spoof site, 112–114
    importance of, 118
    modeling critical evaluation strategies, 116–117
    rationale for teaching the critical evaluation of online resources, 109–111
    resources, 118–120
    teaching the five W's of website evaluation, 114–115
Online responding, 61, 62
Oral reading
    instructional practices to develop fluency, 263–267
    lesson examples, 273
    round-robin and popcorn reading, 260–262

Partner reading, 149
Peer-assisted learning
    in the history classroom, 149
    through discussion, 24–25